FREEDOM'S BATTLE

J. Alvarez del Vayo

TRANSLATED FROM THE SPANISH
BY EILEEN E. BROOKE

 HILL & WANG   NEW YORK

These scenes, their story not unknown,

Arise and make again your own;

Snatch from the ashes of your sires

The embers of their former fires;

And he who in the strife expires

Will add to theirs a name of fear

That Tyranny shall quake to hear,

And leave his sons a hope, a fame,

They too will rather die than shame:

For Freedom's battle once begun,

Bequeath'd by bleeding sire to son,

Though battled oft is ever won.

—BYRON: *The Giaour*

Contents

Preface to the 1971 Edition

In 1971 *Freedom's Battle*, the title under which this book first appeared more than thirty years ago, may have been won. It has been a long hard fight, rich in drama and courage. Since the official ending of the Spanish Civil War in the spring of 1939, the struggle against the dictatorship of General Francisco Franco has known many ups and downs. Franco profited from the splits in the opposition, from the Cold War, from the support of the United States, and from the panic that seized Spain's upper and middle classes at the thought of a political change that would jeopardize their wealth—much of it dishonestly acquired—and their social status.

The Franco regime came to power thanks to the open support of the fascist nations, Hitler's Germany and Mussolini's Italy; but thanks also to the weakness and cowardice of the Western democracies which, fearful of the *Führer* and the *Duce,* maintained the sham of nonintervention described in the pages below. Many years passed before the foundations of Franco's regime began to crumble.

There were three pillars of the fascist dictatorship in Spain: the Catholic Church, the Falange, and the Army.

The Church was the first to draw away from Franco. Its dissociation from the regime arose from two sources: opportunism on the part of the Church hierarchy, genuine discontent on the part of the lower clergy. The most intelligent group in the hierarchy, aware of the government's growing unpopularity, felt that it could not afford to await the moment of Franco's downfall to register its opposition—at first timid, then more vigorous. It sought thus to prevent an explosion of popular sentiment against the Franco dictatorship from turning against the Church that had initially supported the dictatorship and had collaborated with it for so long a time despite its un-Christian policies of repression and persecution.

Influenced by Pope John XXIII, whose profound humanity had led him on various occasions to express his disapproval of Spanish fascism, and then later by the decisions of the Second Vatican Council, several bishops dared to criticize publicly the lack of social justice and the abuses of authoritarian power in Spain.

Although some of the protesting bishops were guided solely by opportunism in their efforts to save the Church from the people's wrath, others such as Monsignor Cirarda denounced the Franco regime because of their deeply held conviction that one could not be a good Catholic and support Franco.

This feeling was especially strong in the ranks of the lower clergy. In the historic tradition of the *curés* of the French Revolution of 1789 who took the side of the common people against the oppressive feudal lords, Spanish village priests spoke out against social injustices as grave as those that provoked the "bread riots" in late eighteenth-century France. In no other country—not even in Saudi Arabia or the most underdeveloped nations of Latin America—is there so sharp a contrast between an arrogantly wealthy minority and a desperately poor majority as in Franco Spain. Over the years millions of United States tourists have visited Spain, contributing their dollars to Franco's treasury and thus indirectly helping to finance the dictatorship. They have basked in the sun and landscape of Andalusia, yet few have tried to find out how the Andalusian peasants live. In Andalusia a peasant earns a dollar a day when he works. Many of the Spanish peasants have left their native villages and gone to seek work in the industrial regions of northern Spain, or in France, Switzerland, and Germany. Signs have appeared in Andalusia: "This village for sale." Not a house, not a farm— an entire village for sale.

So the village priest who lived close to his destitute flock turned against a regime he held responsible for so much misery. Franco did not forgive the Church its opposition. Bishops, such as Monsignor Cirarda, were attacked in the Franco press. The lower clergy were victims of much harsher measures. At the moment of this writing twenty-seven priests are in Spanish jails. Two others have been involved in the notorious Burgos court martial trial of the Basque Nationalists which, as 1970 drew to a close, marked the turning point of a badly discredited regime.

The entire Church did not turn against the dictatorship. Some bishops remained on Franco's side. But every month their number decreased. When, during the Burgos trial, one of the accused priests described the tortures inflicted on him in an attempt to wrest a confession from him implicating the other defendants, the National Conference of Spanish Bishops found itself forced to condemn the torture publicly. In this way a new conflict between the Church and the Franco government broke out.

The second pillar of Franco's authority was the Falange, the only political party permitted in Spain. Fascist in origin, it was influenced at the outset more by Mussolini than by Hitler—particularly in the case of the party's founder, José Antonio Primo de Rivera.

Known for his ingratitude toward those who serve him best, General Franco thrust the Falange from power in 1969, replacing the Falangists in key cabinet posts with his new favorites, the men of *Opus Dei* ("God's Work"). The latter is a world-wide Catholic movement that is especially powerful in Spain, even though it numbers less than 25,000 members there. But skilled in intrigue, *Opus Dei* gradually gained control of the banks, publishing houses, and some of the newspapers, preparing to take power when Franco passed from the scene. It did not have to wait that long. Because of widespread fears that Franco's demise would result in a popular uprising, *Opus Dei* was entrusted with the task of nipping any democratic movements in the bud. In the government it formulated a two-pronged policy: on the one hand, improved economic conditions for a majority of Spaniards; on the other hand, repression.

Opus Dei promised every Spaniard an average annual income of $1,000, provided the workers would renounce strikes —which in any case are illegal under Franco's laws—and that the rest of the Spanish people would forfeit their civil rights and liberties. It was an attempt to buy the conscience and dignity of a whole people for an average annual income of $1,000.

The cabinet ministers in the *Opus Dei* movement, called by their adversaries "Christ's technocrats," were young and cultured individuals. Many of them, educated in the United States, were enamored of the word "efficiency." But they committed the basic mistake of believing that Spain's fundamental political problems could be solved by simplistic economic measures.

It did not work. Under the *Opus Dei* ministers there were more strikes in Spain than before—and these strikes grew progressively more political, directed more against the authoritarian and repressive practices of the government than for higher wages.

The Falange had remained in office for twenty years before it was unceremoniously tossed out; *Opus Dei,* after only a single year in power, proved to be a failure. Its ministers had to assume responsibility for the "Matesa" affair, characterized in the Falangist press as "the biggest scandal of the century." Costing the Spanish Treasury several hundred million dollars, it revealed the far-reaching corruption that has been one of the features of the Franco regime. The disclosure of the "Matesa" swindle, by which sales and exports were listed as genuine when in fact they existed merely on paper, ended the *Opus Dei* myth. No longer were they looked upon as a team of administrators capable of turning Spain into a model country and of markedly raising the living standards of its people. *Opus Dei* claimed to be above politics and sought to settle Spain's problems by economic and technocratic means. But it was above all in the economic field that it failed. So the country was left in a greater uproar than ever, as shown by the waves of violent strikes and protest demonstrations accompanying the Burgos trial.

Feeling itself betrayed by Franco, the Falange—the second pillar of the regime—followed the Church into opposition. There remained the Army. Of the three pillars on which General Franco had built his dictatorship, only the Army seemed fortified against the disillusionment and loss of faith that had undermined the allegiance of the Church and the Falange. Up to 1970 the Spanish Army, provided with funds from the United States, equipped and modernized by American aid, maintained its monolithic appearance. The Burgos court martial trial brought the first perceptible rifts within the armed forces. While Vice President Admiral Carrero Blanco and General Perez-Viñeta, military commandant of the Catalonian district, demanded that the Burgos court hand down death sentences and that at least one such verdict be carried out as a lesson, General Diez Alegría—Army Chief of Staff—and General García-Rebull favored clemency. The latter is said to have asserted: "The Army doesn't want to dirty its hands." But at the cabinet meeting held on November 27, 1970, General Franco sided with the "hardliners." "The trial," Franco declared, "must take place no matter what. My government cannot appear weak."

If I dwell repeatedly on the Burgos court martial of the Basque Nationalists, it is because for the first time since the Spanish Civil War the protest movement against the dictatorship has brought together all those who want a change in Spain: liberals, socialists, communists, and anarchists. In their ranks has resounded the cry of "Franco the murderer!" Among the anti-Franco moderates, men like Franco's former Ambassador in Washington, Count de Motrico, and the former Spanish Ambassador to the Vatican, Ruiz Jiménez, one hears statements such as: "We are back where we were thirty years ago." And some naive souls have protested: "No, no! We thought all that—the tortures and repression—was over and done with. We thought we had become Europeans."

As the pro-Franco forces split apart, the forces of the opposition united. Within a few months' time the country grew more politically conscious than during the previous twenty years. Spaniards lost their fear of fear. In Pamplona, a traditionally conservative city, workers armed solely with bottles they had snatched from neighborhood bars attacked the Guardia Civil. In Burgos the Basque Nationalist defendants, accused by Franco's military judges of all sorts of crimes, and facing death sentences, rushed with manacled hands toward the judges who drew their swords—turning the courtroom into a veritable battlefield.

During the closing days of 1970, revolutionary fervor rose swiftly in Spain. Forming a united front against Franco, workers, students, artists, intellectuals, and priests fought bravely against the police state. The "hardliners" in the dictatorship, fearing that the people would take to the streets on the day Franco disappeared, sought to create a climate of terror and panic. Inside Spain two theories were current.

One theory assumed that after Franco the situation in Spain would resemble the situation in Portugal when Premier Salazar left the political stage. In other words, nothing would happen; another form of dictatorship would follow on the heels of its predecessor. The other theory, held by the majority, asserted that Spain was not Portugal; that the Spanish people, having fought heroically from 1936 to 1939 only to lose, would this time refuse to be done out of their victory.

In 1971 the workers and students form the backbone of freedom's battle in Spain. Fighting for free and independent trade unions, the Workers' Commissions—*Comisiones Obreras*—play a vital part in preparing for a Socialist Spain. In general the tide in Spain today is running toward socialism, toward a more socially advanced republic than that of the Second Spanish Republic of 1931, against which Franco revolted five years later. Among the various groups of the opposition there is complete agreement as to the urgent need for a more radical and more constructive agrarian reform than the timid agrarian reform program of the 1930's which, despite its moderation, helped provoke the military uprising backed by the big landowners.

As almost everywhere else in the world, the Spanish youth are leftist. In the case of Spain the progressive attitude of the young is especially noteworthy: Many of the young people now fighting against the Franco dictatorship were not even born when the Spanish War of the 1930's took place. They have heard nothing but Franco propaganda against democracy and socialism; they have read no other newspapers except the Franco-controlled press. Nevertheless these Spanish youths—young workers and students—have on their own achieved a political maturity to which I can personally attest as a result of many conversations I have had with them.

Various movements, acting in parallel fashion through strikes and political demonstrations, have emerged in the past few years. Action groups have steadily extended their scope. Among the dozens that might be cited here are such groups as the Spanish Front for National Liberation, the Socialist Vanguard, several student associations, Marxist-Leninist groups, Maoist-oriented groups, leftist Catholic youth, and nationalist movements such as the ETA in the Basque country and similar movements in Catalonia and other regions of Spain.

The majority of the movements I have just mentioned have one trait in common: acceptance of violence. Not because they like violence for its own sake, but in answer to the violence of the Franco regime. The moderate opposition rejects violence, but it has recently come to realize that the so-called "liberalization" policies of the "Europeans" in the *Opus Dei* movement are an utter fraud.

Many ask what will happen the day Franco goes. During the Burgos trial insistent rumors circulated in Madrid that Franco had suffered a stroke that left him partially paralyzed. In theory it is possible that he will be replaced by Prince Juan Carlos, officially designated as his successor. But for one thing the monarchy has no broad popular base in Spain; for another, Juan Carlos as an individual does not inspire either confidence or respect. It may well be that an attempt to restore Juan Carlos to the Spanish throne will unleash a people's uprising in favor of the Republic.

But suppose the most reactionary elements in the Army and other interest groups of the dictatorship seek to impose a "monarchist" solution and thereby provoke a popular uprising in Spain—what then? Bound up with this question is the presence of U.S. armed forces on Spanish territory. This American presence is the result of agreements concerning U.S. military bases in Spain—agreements renewed in 1970 after lengthy negotiations. It is a very serious matter.

As I write this Preface, the question of U.S. bases in Spain is being passionately debated by the Spanish people. Not only are the long-time opponents of the Franco regime against this indirect form of U.S. military occupation. Many who had previously supported Franco have come out openly against the agreements signed in 1970 by the two governments. Despite official denials both in Washington and Madrid, many Spaniards suspect the existence of a secret clause.

Opposition to the U.S. bases did not end with the signing of the new treaties. This opposition arises from two distinctly different motives. First is the fear that the existence of American bases in Spain—such as the key naval base of La Rota in southern Spain, from which U.S. submarines carrying atomic missiles can operate—may involve Spain in a nuclear war in the event of a direct confrontation between the United States and the Soviet Union.

This is no fear born of atomic hysteria. It is based on grim reality. During one of my visits to Moscow over twelve years ago, after the signing of the first Washington–Madrid agreements, I discussed with high Soviet officials the existence of these U.S. bases in Spain. I heard one of them say: "We love the Spanish people. But if a nuclear war breaks out, we have no choice but to aim our first bombs at the American bases in Spain, because they have been installed there against us. No one is going to believe that those bases are directed against Portugal or France."

The second reason why the Spanish people oppose the United States military presence in Spain is the suspicion that U.S. armed forces may be used against the Spanish people in the event of a popular uprising on behalf of a Republic. It is difficult to envisage a graver prospect. Should U.S. troops intervene to guarantee "law and order" in Spain—fascist law and order—Spain will become a second Vietnam, with all the consequences that that entails.

After so long and oppressive a period of dictatorship, the Spanish people will never agree to United States intervention in Spain. Spain is going to be free. Perhaps when this book appears she will already have begun to be free. The victory of the Spanish people will be an event with major repercussions in Europe, Latin America, and elsewhere in the world. The historic cycle that began in 1936 will have come to a momentous end.

Translated from the Spanish by Joseph M. Bernstein

Prologue

THE GREATER PART of this book was already in manuscript when the war with Hitler broke out. I have finished it without making any alteration in what had already been written, or allowing the remaining pages to be coloured by the new situation. History is history, and in this case events have, alas, served to prove the truth of my words.

The first great battle of the present war was fought out in Spain. It was preceded and followed by a series of aggressions —in Manchuria, the Rhineland, Abyssinia, Austria, Czechoslovakia, Albania—but it was in Spain that the battle against totalitarian barbarianism was fought with the greatest intensity, in Spain that there was still a chance to stop the aggressor powers, and in Spain that these powers were, instead, helped to victory and given encouragement for further advances which have since become history.

The defeat of Republican Spain was the starting-point of the present war. Future historians will recognize it as such, but there are already men and women of consequence—even in the most conservative British and French circles—who accept this as axiomatic. If the armed intervention of Germany and Italy in Spain had not been tolerated by the great democracies, Austria would not have been annexed, Czechoslovakia invaded, or Poland attacked, and the present war would have been impossible. If Republican Spain had triumphed, the peace front would have been strengthened, and it is hardly going too far to say that the Russo-German Pact would never have been signed.

The conquest of Poland in the first four weeks of war has thrown new light on the struggle waged by the Spanish people for more than two and a half years. At the worst period of the war, when the lack of arms and munitions had reduced the loyalist army to a state of defencelessness, and famine and despair had ravaged the people, the great offensive in Catalonia launched by the rebels and the foreign armies on December 23, 1938, over a territory one tenth the size of Poland, did not succeed in thrusting the Republican troops into France until February 9, 1939. Madrid withstood more than two years of siege. For over two weeks in 1936 the Republican air force had only one pursuit plane for the whole of loyalist territory. The figures quoted later in this book can give no real idea of the disparity between the war material which the Republic eventually succeeded in acquiring after tremendous efforts, and that used by Germany and Italy throughout the course of the war. Apart from Russia, from whom she was able, for a time, to buy arms, Republican Spain had no great powers at her side to supply her with men and munitions and to promise not to withdraw them until she had fully regained her sovereignty. The only "assistance" received from Paris and London was the Non-Intervention Agreement, which deprived her of her means of self-defence and proved itself a monstrous and deliberate farce. Alone, abandoned to their fate, with no prospect of any immediate change in the international situation, the Spanish people fought for nearly three years against the armed might of the totalitarian states.

It would be both unjust and in bad taste for a Spaniard, in praising the heroism of his own countrymen, to attempt to disparage the resistance of Poland against the tremendous forces of Germany. The defence of Warsaw was a glorious achievement that will be recognized in the annals of world history. The sacrifices made by the Poles betoken a spirit of independence so intense that the resurrection of Poland is not only demanded by justice, but dictated by natural law. A nation whose capital can go down bravely fighting, as Warsaw did in the last days of her death agony, is not destined long to disappear from the map of Europe.

My one desire is to show what it would have meant to the Western democracies to have had in Spain a certain ally ready to defend the liberty and dignity of Europe against all attempts at domination and oppression. If, as I have said, Republican Spain had not been defeated, the present war would never have begun. Just as in September 1938 if the energies used in forcing Prague to capitulate had been directed against Berlin, Czechoslovakia would have been saved, so in the same way a firm attitude toward Spain on the part of Great Britain and France would have checked Hitler once and for all. It was the bloodless victories that encouraged Hitler's Germany to continue her policy of intimidation up to a point where it was difficult for her to turn back. But even if Hitler in his madness had declared war two years—or even one year—ago, he would have had to encounter, besides the Western democracies, the armed forces of two other countries—Spain and Czechoslovakia.

Now that Spain is lost to the peace front, the most to which the Spanish Republicans can aspire is the neutrality of their country. Not a "benevolent neutrality" of double-dealing, such as facilitated the operations of German submarines in the Mediterranean from 1914 to 1918, but a complete and genuine neutrality.

The Spanish Republicans stand firmly for such a policy. In view of our openly expressed position Franco cannot but be aware that if he should maintain a genuine neutrality he could count on our support in respect to this particular question for the duration of the war or for so long as he remained an authentic neutral. In spite of the fact that we consider that our defeat was largely due to Anglo-French policy, we place the victory of the Western democracies above all personal bitterness and disillusionment. To fight against a domination of Europe by Hitlerism is the chief task of the present hour. Against this peril the Spanish people fought for nearly three years, and no consistently-minded Republican can do other than work and hope for the overthrow of Nazism wherever it exists in the world as well as in Germany.

Thousands of Spaniards in French concentration camps would once again have risked their lives for the freedom of Europe if they had been allowed to do so. Instead of this, they were subjected to pressure to return to Spain. Only through the clear-sighted intervention of the French Minister of Munitions, M. Dautry, and the Ministers of Labor and of Agriculture, who did not wish the war and agricultural industries of France to be deprived of Spanish labor, was a mass deportation prevented. Yet the stratagem was obvious. Franco wanted the refugees back for two reasons: First, the very existence of several hundred thousand Spaniards remaining in exile a year after the end of the war is a living condemnation of his régime. Secondly, by demanding of France that she send back the refugees he serves the interests of Hitler by depriving France of an invaluable source of farm and factory labor which might have been used to fill the huge gaps left by French mobilization. Franco knew that the pressure of the forces in France who still wished to appease him could be counted on to override France's own need. With the mobilization of five million Frenchmen and the available Polish and Czech exiles engaged in legions of their own in the French army, this need is clear. Members of the last loyalist Government have not been provided with any documents by the French authorities, and are doomed to the life of outlaws. A

Spanish Republican—that is, an old and trusty friend of France and England—is in a worse position than any other foreigner in France today.

What has been said of the political measures does not affect the gratitude which, in the humanitarian field, the Spanish Republicans owe to France for all that she has done to help the refugees. One may question whether everything in the concentration camps has been managed as well as the French Government surely wished it to be, but on the one hand France had to deal with an influx of refugees numbering nearly half a million whose upkeep, inadequate as it is, has been costing France approximately five million dollars a month, and on the other hand it was natural that, upon the outbreak of the war with Germany, the French authorities should find themselves faced with a many-faceted problem difficult to resolve. It would be equally unjust not to recognize all the efforts personally made by the Minister of the Interior, M. Albert Sarraut, to counteract the pressure of those groups who insisted that the best way to solve the problem of the Spanish refugees was to send them back *en masse* to Franco without taking into consideration the fact that many of the refugees who went back to Spain in good faith, believing in the policy of clemency announced so many times in Madrid, merely exchanged French concentration camps for Spanish prisons—when they were not shot.[1]

Past mistakes revenge themselves. It is possible that under present circumstances the British and French Governments have no choice but to play Franco's game. In our determina-

[1] Answering the deputy Ybarnegaray in the Chamber of Deputies on December 14, 1939, Albert Sarraut, Minister of the Interior, said: "And we note this admirable fact: that the different Departments, and particularly those working for national defence, are competing for the services of these workers [the Minister is referring to the Spanish refugees] and even our allies abroad are asking us for their services. The results obtained have been such that all the reports which I have read from the commanders of the military regions express satisfaction with the work of the Spaniards, in the districts near the front, in the industrial establishments, and in agriculture." (Applause.)
M. Henri Thiballet: "That is true."

tion not to create any difficulties, we have even abstained from giving public expression to our feelings. We do not complain of having been sacrificed to the "great neutral," as one of the most influential London newspapers has described Franco.

But in the very interests of the Allied cause, which certainly would not be served by a concealment of the truth, it is not advisable that we should follow a policy of unlimited confidence in the continued neutrality of the present Spanish Government. The Franco broadcasts and a perusal of the press of Burgos, Madrid, and Barcelona counsel a great reserve.

Our strongest desire is that while the war lasts, Spain's neutrality shall never at any time be placed in question. But the war has only just begun. A great deal depends on the situation of Italy, for Franco will follow in Mussolini's footsteps. Replying on October 9, 1939 to the speech made on the presentation of his credentials by the new Italian Ambassador to Spain, General Gambara, who had commanded the Italian invading forces during the Spanish War, General Franco said that the two countries were bound by indissoluble ties, and "guided by the same ideals of truth and of social and international justice"; he also expressed his conviction that it was the task of Fascist Italy and the new Spain to work together for the restoration of peace. At that time the peace which they were trying to restore was Hitler's peace, proposed by the Führer from the Reichstag tribune three days before, and welcomed by the Franco press in the same terms as those of the *Völkischer Beobachter* and the other Nazi newspapers.

Up to now—the middle of October 1939—Italy has seemed inclined to maintain a neutrality which, without implying any break with Germany, will protect the "specifically Italian" interests to which Signor Virginio Gayda alluded in the *Giornale d'Italia* [1] just before the outbreak of the war. The Pact of Steel signed in Berlin on May 22, 1939, the third article of which laid down that in the event of "one of the con-

[1] August 26, 1939.

tracting parties becoming involved in hostilities with a third power or powers, the other contracting party was to come immediately to its support with all its forces in the air, on sea, and on land," has not been implemented. On September 1 the Council of Ministers in Rome announced that Italy would take "no initiative in military operations," although it is true that this statement coincided with the publication of a telegram from Hitler assuring the Duce that "he would not have need of military aid from Italy." Three weeks later, in his speech of September 23 to the Fascist dignitaries of Bologna, Mussolini took up Hitler's position, in favor of a peace on the basis of the *faits accomplis* and in opposition to a "reconstitution of positions which history and the natural dynamism of peoples have condemned." On the other hand, when the "peace proposals" were drawn up, Hitler did not find in the Duce the mouthpiece which he had expected after Count Ciano's visit to Berlin. But when Mr. Chamberlain replied to Hitler, the Italian press once more began talking of English "intransigence." Thus ever since the beginning of the war Rome has followed the characteristic zigzag of Italian foreign policy.

Up to what point has the change in the eastern European situation—the proximity of Russia to Hungary and Rumania, as a result of the Soviet advance into Poland, and the growth of pro-Slav sentiment in the Balkans to the detriment of Italy —helped to change the Italian position? Have the "specifically Italian" interests of which Signor Gayda spoke already been promoted by the Allies, at least as far as Djibouti and the Suez Canal are concerned? Or is Italy merely waiting, as she did in the last war, to see which way she can jump to her best advantage?

Among the causes for any possible change in the Italian attitude I do not include the blow dealt by Hitler at the Anti-Comintern Pact. As its principal author has just shown, this pact never had the ideological significance attributed to it; it was at no time more than another manifestation of the aggressive policy of the totalitarian states, aimed in the last analysis at Great Britain and France. What Hitler detested in the Soviet Union was not Communism, but the French-Soviet Pact and Russian adherence to the principles of collective security. As soon as there was any possibility of detaching Russia from Great Britain and France, the "Reds" became brown, and Stalin was acclaimed in the Reichstag. This evolution took place with a speed which proved how little convictions and ideas counted. On August 12, 1939, in the presence of the representative of the League of Nations in Danzig, Hitler—according to M. Burckhardt's own report—broke out into a storm of abuse against the Bolsheviks; two days later the first Russo-German agreement was enthusiastically celebrated all over Germany. German diplomacy took advantage of the hesitations of London and Paris to obtain one of the greatest successes of the past twenty-five years. In the French conservative newspaper *L'Époque,* whose connection with the French General Staff is well-known, Henri de Kerillis could write uncensored: "History will show how strange, paradoxical, and doomed to certain failure were the negotiations during the spring and summer of 1939, in which the English and French urged the Russians to fight for a Poland which they abhorred, while by refusing them all other advantages they left it to Hitler to offer Stalin the opportunity to seize Poland without firing a shot, and to take the Baltic States as a kind of make-weight." The Anti-Comintern Pact dissolved like sugar in water. In Franco Spain the shock of finding that their ally in the fight to the death against the "Spanish Bolsheviks" was hand-in-glove with the *real* Bolsheviks was shortlived. While General Franco, in an interview with a Madrid newspaper reporter—reproduced with great satisfaction in Great Britain and France—represented the consolidation of Soviet influence in eastern Europe as a threat to that Western civilization which he and the Germans had so effectively upheld at Durango and Guernica, at the same time the Franco press and radio were gradually reconciling the country to the idea of a powerful Russo-German coalition likely to have serious consequences for the democracies.

As long as Italy's position remains obscure, Franco's neutrality must be accepted with reserve. Great Britain and France must not give him the slightest pretext for taking offence. But at the same time they must keep a discreet watch on his movements.

There are of course many ways of preserving neutrality. Even if Italy should one day decide to take up arms on the side of Germany, it is almost certain that Spain would continue in theory to remain neutral. Whenever in my lecture tour of the United States in the spring of 1939 I was asked if, in the event of a European war, I thought that Franco would join Hitler and Mussolini against the democratic powers or remain neutral, I always replied that the latter course seemed to me the more likely. Since, after all, Italy did not enter the war at the beginning, and since France was not confronted during the initial period of mobilization with a threat to three frontiers at once and the prospect of having her colonial troops intercepted, what benefit can Germany hope to obtain from Spanish military intervention? If Spain were quickly defeated, the Western powers would have gained a victory which could not fail to have repercussions both on their own morale and on that of the enemy. For the rest of the war Spain would be immobilized and her naval and air bases subjected to the control of the Allies. On the other hand, a "benevolent neutrality" towards Germany throughout the war can be of the greatest assistance to that country.

We Republicans hope that Franco will be not a romantic, but a selfish neutral. It is to his immediate interest to know how to take advantage of the favourable circumstances offered by the war. He has been given a heaven-sent opportunity. Spanish economy can be more easily built up by furnishing Great Britain and France with supplies than by the fantastic ten-year plan which was recently announced by the Franco Government, and which is destined to no

happier fate than the Göring four-year plan responsible
for Germany's present catastrophic situation.

So long as he does not look at the situation from the point
of view of a passionate admirer of the Hitler régime, it should
not be difficult for Franco to convince himself that Germany
has already lost the war. The war was lost for Germany from
the moment her peace manœuvres—on the basis of the recognition of her Polish conquest and a truce in the west—failed
through Allied firmness. Hitler's path to *"Lebensraum"* is
blocked by two obstacles impossible to be overcome at the
same time—Russian territorial expansion and the Maginot
Line. As the days pass, the threat implied in his interpretation
of the Russo-German agreements, designed to present Great
Britain and France with the terrifying dilemma of capitulat-
ing or facing a coalition of 250,000,000 Germans and Russians
has begun to lose its force, until it no longer impresses anyone
but commentators in the Franco press. Neither the abandonment of his dream of *"Baltikum,"* under whose star nineteen
years ago, the first Nazi formations were born, nor his constant messages to the Kremlin, have yet obtained for Hitler
the coveted military collaboration of the Soviet. The development of commercial relations between both countries has not
succeeded in counteracting the effects of the blockade. Nor
is it at all certain that the new friendship will flourish in
conditions of ideal harmony. Every movement of the Soviet
Union since the appearance of her troops on Polish territory
gives grounds for anxiety in the strategic sphere. Her interest
in ensuring that the fortresses and harbours of Estonia, Latvia,
and Lithuania shall be placed at her disposal, and in utilizing
the agreement with the last-named country in order to construct a species of Maginot Line between Lithuania and East
Prussia, is significant of her attitude towards Germany.

Over a long term of years Hitler will not find a certain ally
in the Soviet Union. Still less will he be able to do so if
London and Paris diplomacy learns how to avoid a repetition
of former mistakes. In this respect Mr. Winston Churchill's

speech of October 1, 1939 will go down to posterity as a masterpiece of clear vision, self-control, and intelligent realism. The task of bringing back Russia to the Anglo-French front is worthy of the greatest effort and persistence.

In speaking of Russia, it is essential to point out that the foreign policy of the Spanish Republic is in no way affected in retrospect by the Russo-German Non-Aggression Pact. The foreign policy of the Republic was at no time linked with that of the Soviet Union, and the assistance and support which the latter gave during the Spanish War was not aimed at achieving a political solidarity between the two countries, but was born of the Soviet Union's desire to prevent a hostile force, able to render the French-Russian Pact practically valueless as a safeguard for the Soviet Union, from massing on France's third frontier. On the other hand, the Russo-German Pact has destroyed the very foundations of what was supposed to be the rebel foreign policy, the authors of which had unreservedly identified themselves with the Italo-German anti-Communist crusade, declaring their basic aim to be the prevention of Communism in Spain.

Now that the greater part of the German territory occupied by the French army since the beginning of September has been recaptured, Hitler has to decide either to expose his army to a prolonged war of attrition on the western front, or to confine his attacks principally to sea and air—while remaining on the defensive in the west—in the hope that his peace offer (to be renewed if necessary every three months) will be welcomed by a population worn down by the effects of air raids. If the position should develop into a stalemate in the west, the monotony of a campaign without any large-scale military operations to kindle the fighting spirit of the troops might work in his favour. It is not unlikely that a certain discouragement and weariness might set in if every day the list of killed and wounded grew longer without any "real war" to justify the continual sacrifice of lives. We have had this experience in Spain. After two months of inactivity on the fronts, the morale of the civilian population was always lowered. The people would say to themselves: "If we're not going to fight, then let us have peace once and for all." But even though such a situation might encourage defeatist propaganda in the Allied countries, the decision to continue fighting until Hitler's final overthrow would not be seriously affected. People may become impatient, but the nerves of the First Lord of the Admiralty and of the Commander-in-Chief of the Anglo-French forces are not likely to be impaired.

On the other hand, this inactivity would mean for Germany the loss of six months' provisions, while she would be faced next spring with the same military problem, a problem increased by the growth of the British and French armies and the development of the air force, especially now that the raising of the embargo has brought to the Allies the invaluable industrial assistance of the United States.

A third possibility is suggested by the disguised partisans of Hitler, whose name is legion. Now that the German territory occupied by the French during September has been recaptured, Germany should remain on the defensive on the Western front. She should set to work on the construction of two or three lines of defence behind the original Siegfried Line, and take advantage of the winter months to penetrate the Balkans, politically or militarily, in order to obtain the foodstuffs, oil, and raw materials which she so badly needs. This would be a very promising program if the interests of Italy, Russia, and Turkey did not stand in her way. Of course they could also penetrate Scandinavia, but that would mean extending their lines to a war on two fronts.

Whatever happens, Germany is doomed to defeat. It is possible, however, that there may be difficult times ahead for the Allies before they achieve final victory. In preparing for a three years' war Great Britain has not underestimated the strength of the enemy. It will be a hard and bitter struggle. Before giving in, the Nazis will endeavour to despoil or destroy everything within their reach. And one should not rely ·

too much on rumours of internal disorder in Germany. Everything one hears today concerning the low German morale and economic difficulties within the Reich has some foundation in fact. A terrorist régime, however, can ward off its final collapse for a long time. When in 1916 I returned to Berlin after an absence of two years, I was astonished to find how hatred of the war and of the Kaiser had grown, but two more years had to elapse before Imperial Germany was defeated.

At that time the dissident elements possessed certain political machinery to further their ends. In spite of police vigilance, the independent Socialists who—with Karl Liebknecht, Rosa Luxemburg, and Franz Mehring—constituted the nucleus of the opposition had their own deputies, provincial organizations, and cadres. Liebknecht was imprisoned, but from his cell he succeeded in keeping in touch with his comrades. Rosa Luxemburg's celebrated pamphlet under the pseudonym "Junius" was passed round from hand to hand. The Prussian police did not behave with the same ferocity as the Gestapo. The opportunities for enlightenment and for agitation among the people and in the army itself were infinitely greater than they are today. Moreover, the war party did not have a propaganda machine at its disposal like that set up by the Third Reich, a machine which is able to represent the sinking of the *Royal Oak* as the end of British dominion in the North Sea, which can delude the German public with false reports of French and British demoralization, and can present the Führer to the German people as a true apostle of peace.

The prospect of a long war, with alternate successes and setbacks, increases the danger of the neutrals being drawn into the conflict on one side or the other. Hence it is only elementary prudence not to give Franco a free hand until the situation becomes clearer.

If experience proves that our fears are unjustified, our satisfaction will be genuine and complete.

Paris, October 1939

Freedom's Battle

CHAPTER I

The Rebellion

By midnight on the 16th of February 1936 the election results
which were coming in from the provinces were decidedly in
favour of the Popular Front.

The campaign had been a hard one. Many of the best Left-
wing fighters were, for all practical purposes, eliminated
from the struggle, having been in prison or in exile ever since
the repression which followed the anti-dictatorial movement
of 1934. Thus the whole weight of the campaign fell on people
like ourselves who, more by luck than anything else, had
escaped the reprisals made during that first attempt to turn
Spain into a totalitarian state.

This gave me personally the opportunity to tour the country from end to end. There were few days during the election
campaign when I was not speaking in five or six different
places, and the last meetings in my own constituency, Madrid,
were a terrible strain on a throat which, after much hard
usage, finally refused to respond to the inward conviction and
enthusiasm of its owner.

After a period of reaction known as "the two black years"

Spain turned again to a life of freedom with amazing zest. In their attempt to stamp out the democratic régime in Spain, the Government of Gil Robles and Lerroux, against whom the Spanish people had rebelled in 1934, had carried out such far-reaching reprisals that even in our own ranks many doubted the possibility of a rapid revival. Some forty thousand were imprisoned; thousands had had to flee the country. I heard more than one of our leaders say that the Republic was doomed for ten or twenty years. But one of the qualities of the Spanish people is their astonishing vitality, and it is this vitality that enables them to recover from a period of repression in much less time that might be logically expected.

In the rural districts especially, this popular awakening was hailed with a most encouraging enthusiasm. The villages of Spain had always been, at every election, a dead weight on the democratic parties. The Spanish peasants, subjected to a régime of exploitation and usury which had no counterpart in any other European country, were faced with two alternatives: to vote for the candidate nominated by the landlord, or to suffer the economic consequences of defying one who not only was owner of their land, but who considered himself, not without reason, the master of their souls.

At this election every tiny village was a flame fanned by the desire for freedom. "We will vote for our own man, even if we have to starve for it": this was the pledge, afterwards so bravely kept, which ended all the election meetings—meetings held against the picturesque moonlit background of the village square, filled at a late hour of the night by crowds eager to listen to the message of freedom.

The struggle between the Popular Front and the combined forces of Spanish reaction could not have been more one-sided. Our first obstacle was the lack of money. It appealed to the subtle Spanish sense of humour when the reactionary press spoke of Russian gold being handed over in large quantities to the Left-wing parties in order to secure a Stalinist victory. "We could do with as much in copper, if only to pay for the posters," the trade-union treasurers would exclaim, their coffers drained dry after eighteen months of giving assistance to the victims of the October reprisals. In the second place, the Government of Señor Portela Valladares, under whose auspices the elections were held—and in Spain the expression *"hacer elecciones"* (literally "to make elections") has always conveyed the idea of engineering results—followed the time-honoured tradition of employing the whole machinery of State to prevent the triumph of the popular parties. The difficulties with which the Republican and Socialist candidates had to contend in order to carry on their propaganda were so great, and the manner in which they were treated so arbitrary, that one day just before the elections Señor Azaña, who at that time was marked out for Prime Minister in the event of a Popular Front victory, suggested, I remember, that it might be preferable to boycott the elections rather than risk the defeat which he considered inevitable if such methods continued.

The Spanish episcopate, with honourable exceptions, marched in the vanguard of the frenzied campaign against the Popular Front. "It is sinful to vote for the Popular Front. A vote for the conservative candidate is a vote for Christ," publicly declared the Bishop of Barcelona; and from their pulpits the clergy, both high and low, consigned to eternal damnation all those who did not do everything humanly and divinely possible to bring about a victory at the polls for the forces of reaction.

The morning after the elections the Popular Front victory was fully confirmed. At noon Señor Largo Caballero and I, as elected members for Madrid, called on the Prime Minister to protest against the first of the Fascist assaults, which had taken place that very day in the streets of Madrid. (Members of the Phalangist organization had fired on a demonstration, chiefly composed of women, who were marching to the prison to bring the political prisoners the good news of the election.) Señor Portela Valladares received us with courtesy, and said unhesitatingly: "In you I greet today's victors." A year later, during the war, Señor Portela Valladares, when he attended a meeting of the Cortes in Valencia for the express purpose of proclaiming to the world that the Parliament formed after the elections, over which he had presided, was "truly representative of the nation's will," disclosed that our call on the Prime Minister had not been the most important he had received that day. "At four in the morning on the day after the elections"—I quote Señor Portela Valladares—"I was visited by Señor Gil Robles" (leader of the Right-wing coalition), "who proposed that I should assume dictatorial powers, and who offered me the support of all the groups defeated in the elections. At seven that evening the same suggestion was made to me by General Franco himself."

In these words, spoken by the leader of the Government which conducted the elections of February 1936, lies the key to the military rebellion. They give the lie categorically to the mistaken belief, so widely held outside Spain, that the death of Señor Calvo Sotelo—undoubtedly the strongest leader among the Government's adversaries—on July 13, 1936, was the starting-point and principal cause of the revolt, a revolt whose instigators were naturally at great pains to represent to foreign opinion as a natural and legitimate reaction against the Popular Front "terror." In point of fact, Spanish Fascism, encouraged and supported by Italy since 1934 at the very latest (as witness the interview which took place in Rome between Mussolini, Señor Goicoechea, the Spanish Monarchist leader, and the future rebel General Barrera, in March of that year), was ready to impose itself by force. If it won the elections, it would set up a dictatorship with an appearance of legality on the following day; if it lost, it would rise in revolt against the elected Government. From the first moment of the Popular Front victory a *coup d'état* became the one objective of the Fascist forces defeated in the elections, an objective worthy of their every effort. The partisans of dictatorship recognized the new Parliament by taking their seats in it—and among these seats were a good many "doubt-ful" ones handed to them by an excessively benevolent Gov-ernment after examination by the Credentials Committee—and then proceeded to use it as a platform for incitement to rebellion.

In the new Parliament there were 268 Popular Front and 140 Right-wing members (this was slightly changed by the Cuenca and Granada run-offs involving 19 seats), while the remainder were independents or members of Centre parties. The Republicans dominated the Popular Front majority. The Socialists came next in number, while there were only 15 Communists out of a total of 473. The Government was pre-sided over by Señor Azaña, and consisted solely of Republi-cans; 9 of the Ministers belonged to Señor Azaña's Left Re-publican Party and 3 to the Republican Union, a party led by Señor Martinez Barrio, the Speaker of the House; while a non-political General was War Minister. From the Front bench the Prime Minister constantly employed his well-known eloquence to convince the opposition that the triumph of the Popular Front would not bring with it any persecu-tions or reprisals. Señor Azaña's first message to the country, on February 20, 1936, the day after he formed his Cabinet, was addressed "to all Spaniards," and was so imbued with a spirit of reconciliation that many of us feared that the Repub-lic would once again fall into the error of excessive generosity towards its enemies which had characterized Republican policy since the advent of the new régime.

In itself the Popular Front program could not have been more moderate. We Socialists, who were without question the most efficiently organized and disciplined party in the country, had sacrificed many of our oldest and most important claims to the need for forming a wide democratic front unit-ing all anti-Fascist elements. In the new political constellation the Communists were too small a group to exert any decisive influence. With the exception of the amnesty for the victims of the "two black years," which had been the outstanding feature of the Popular Front campaign, the other points in the Government program could be summed up as a desire to re-establish the Republic—a most justifiable desire, seeing that it was the Republicans who had been returned to power. This involved respect for the Constitution; reorganization of the legal system in order to ensure its independence; and a continuation of the Agrarian Reform begun in 1931. This Agrarian Reform by no means implied the nationalization of land; on the contrary, it was governed by the principle of indemnifying the proprietors, whose large uncultivated estates, survival of a mediæval system of agriculture, not only condemned the peasants to a life of misery, but also hindered the normal development of Spanish economy. The only law to be repealed was that under which the estates of those grandees implicated in the Sanjurjo rising of August 10, 1932 had been returned and paid for by the Government of Gil Robles and Lerroux. The other planks in the Popular Front platform were the protection of small industrialists and traders; a vast plan of public works; and the creation of new schools and educational centres. This last was the first concern of a Republic which had inherited from the old régime a state of affairs in which one third of the population could neither read nor write, and in which the universities and other centres of learning had to struggle with the deficiencies of an antiquated and entirely inadequate educational system. For the rest, the Popular Front program embodied the program of the Republic when it first came into being except for the plank on collectivization of large estates originally sponsored by the Socialists. This plank was rejected by the Popular Front, with the acquiescence of the Socialists, although to do so cost them many votes. Any other liberal party in Europe would have been amazed that such a program of State reform should have been necessary in the third decade of the twentieth century. It was a program which offered every guarantee that the inevitable changes in the political and social spheres would take place without endangering the existence of the Spanish bourgeoisie.

The more intelligent members of the bourgeoisie realized this. "The elections which have just taken place in Spain," said *La Vanguardia,* the most moderate of the important Barcelona newspapers, on February 18, 1936, "have two main characteristics; they are a conclusive manifestation of the popular conscience, and they have taken place in conditions of perfect discipline and normality. Faced with a phenomenon of this type, there is nothing to do but yield democratically. National sovereignty resides with the people. The Spanish people have said what they want. They have said it clearly and with extraordinary calm. The only reply which can be made to them is this: 'Let your will be done.'" *El Debate,* however, saw things in a very different light. "The issue," commented the organ of the Clerical-Fascist alliance, "was one of revolution against law and order, with Socialism as the real enemy."

Unfortunately the latter point of view predominated. Instead of respecting the will of the country, Spanish Fascism prepared to obtain by force what it had been refused by popular vote. It was during the debate on the Ministry of Agriculture's bill providing for restitution to the municipalities of their ancient common lands that Señor Calvo Sotelo revealed, with impressive frankness, the die-hard position of the defeated Right wing. "The only hope for agriculture," said Señor Calvo Sotelo, "is not in this Parliament or any other that could be elected, nor in this or any other Popular Front Government, nor in any political party; it lies in the Corporate State. Only by the Fascist revolution can the middle classes defend themselves against proletarianization."

In this way Parliament was used by Señor Calvo Sotelo and his friends merely as an agitator's platform. The debates in the House became more and more heated. Those who had been defeated in the elections talked as though they had been victorious, as though they had the whole country behind them. Responsible for a state of increasing disturbance, they yet held themselves up as the only sponsors of law and order. On May 6 Señor Casares Quiroga, Minister of the Interior, was cheered by his supporters when he counter-attacked Calvo Sotelo. (The latter had replaced Gil Robles, who was considered by the Right wing to be too greatly contaminated with parliamentarism and too mild in his attacks as leader of the opposition.) "Disarm?" exclaimed the Minister; "*we* are disarming; we have rounded up thirteen thousand firearms in Granada, seven thousand in Jaen. But these belonged to the Right. It is the Phalangist gunmen in the motor-cars, and not the working men, who are causing the bloodshed."

The Right wing were not daunted by this partial confiscation of the war material which they had carefully accumulated against an electoral defeat. They relied on the army generals and pinned all their hopes on a military rising. From Berlin and Rome came messages of encouragement, together with good news of the reception given to the various emissaries sent to solicit support from the two great Fascist powers when the signal for attack should be given. Ever since February 4, before the elections, when General Sanjurjo, and José Antonio Primo de Rivera, the Phalangist leader, under the pretext of an innocent winter-sports visit to Partenkirchen, arrived at the Kaiserhof, Berlin (a hotel reserved for guests of the German Government), the bonds between National Socialism and Spanish Fascism had been sealed. As we have seen, the negotiations with Rome dated from 1934, and at no time, least of all during the Gil Robles Government, did the Italian Embassy in Madrid fail to show the greatest interest in the activities of its ideological associates and future brothers-in-arms.

The idea of a *coup d'état* was not a hasty improvisation or conceived in a sudden fit of rage. In 1935 the violent departure of Gil Robles from the War Ministry had upset a vast and elaborate plan for imposing Fascism from above. A meeting held at the time in the house of General Fanjul, who a year later led the Madrid insurrection from the Montaña

Barracks, had to be adjourned because of the unexpected speed with which the Cabinet crisis arose and was overcome. But Señor Gil Robles had lost no time at the War Office. All the generals on whom the honour of the 1936 rebellion was to fall were given key positions in the army. General Franco was appointed Chief of Staff, General Goded Director of Military Aviation, and General Fanjul Under-Secretary for War. General Mola was given command of the army in Morocco. When on one occasion even the lukewarm and condescending President Alcalá Zamora referred to this preference for generals well known for their anti-Republican sentiments, Señor Gil Robles answered that he had chosen the most capable ones. He said nothing, however, of the fact that their chief merit in his eyes was their amazing aptitude for breaking the oath of loyalty by which they swore to obey no other power than the established Constitution and to remain faithful to the Republic.

An army does not serve its purpose, however, merely by maintaining a fine group of generals. It must be well trained, and as the enemy against which Señor Gil Robles was preparing his military machine was the Spanish people themselves, the chief objective of the manœuvres which took place during his period of office as War Minister was to familiarize the men with the territory where the rebels might expect to encounter the greatest resistance. Thus in the summer of 1935 General Aranda, Military Commander of Asturias, had the honour of being warmly congratulated by the War Minister and by General Franco, Chief of Staff, when these gentlemen attended the manœuvres which he had organized in that region. It was here that the Asturian miners had, in the previous October, given proof of so much bravery and strategic ability that Franco was forced to bring over from Africa sufficient Moroccan soldiers to carry out a campaign of extermination. The northern manœuvres, like those which took place in the same year in the Guadarrama Mountains, when the problem of an attack on Madrid was studied in all its aspects, formed part of a plan which had for some time been maturing in the minds of the Spanish Fascist leaders and which took concrete form after their defeat at the elections.

Towards the end of February the Popular Front Government appointed General Franco Military Governor of the Canary Islands. If the Government had no desire to keep him in Madrid, where they considered his presence unduly disturbing, at the same time they could not bring themselves to dispense with his services. Before leaving, General Franco, General Mola, and other military chiefs met in the house of Señor Delgado, a member of Parliament, and agreed upon the general plan of attack. Franco did not leave Madrid without attempting to intimidate the Government, in visits which he made to Señor Alcalá Zamora, the President of the Republic, and to the Prime Minister, Señor Azaña. He represented Spain as about to fall a victim to the worst extremist excesses, and hinted that if his prophecies came true, he could render greater service to his country by remaining in the Peninsula than by going to such a distant post as the Canary Islands. President Alcalá Zamora, to whom he complained of the lack of army equipment and of the difficulties which would be encountered through lack of supplies in the event of a Bolshevik rising, consoled him by recalling how the Asturian movement of 1934 was easily suppressed, thanks chiefly to the valuable co-operation of General Franco himself. After all, he said, the Canaries are not so far away, and one can soon get back in an airplane. Prime Minister Azaña, on his part, replied, with his usual confidence, that he had no fear of a rising on either side. He knew about the Sanjurjo rebellion in the summer of 1932 long before it took place. He could have prevented it, but he preferred to let it take its course in order that it should end, as it did, in disaster and so bring ridicule on its leaders. Franco profited by this lesson and took the necessary precautions to ensure that his projected rebellion should not give Señor Azaña the slightest pretext for indulging his caustic irony at the expense of the army generals.

In the meantime the fiction of a rising of Left-wing radicals (whom Franco was the first to make fun of among his friends) supplied an excellent red herring to draw across the trail.

The U.M.E. (*Unión Militar Española,* Spanish Military Union) now came into action. This was a military organization on trade-union lines, whose members were army officers inclined to conspiracy, and a continuation of the former "Defence Councils," whose activities during the monarchy, and more especially in the reign of Don Alfonso, had constantly endangered the existence of any government tinged with the slightest shade of liberalism. The officers discharged from the army after General Sanjurjo's abortive rising in 1932, or given posts with which they were dissatisfied, found their natural allies in the ten thousand officers who in the first years of the Republic had been pensioned off on full pay by the Government. The reason for this retirement scheme was to put an end to a completely anomalous situation in which there was one general for every 150 soldiers, and to a state of affairs in which the army consumed in peace-time thirty per cent of the national budget. Unfortunately the majority of the officers who profited by that unprecedentedly generous pension scheme were enemies of the Republic and took advantage of a privileged position, in which they were paid for doing nothing, to use their leisure to plot against the Government. All these officers together formed the U.M.E., which had branches throughout the country and was the natural channel through which instructions from above were conveyed.

A Council of Generals was formed to lead the movement. It was originally composed of General Rodríguez Barrio, Inspector-General of the army; General Franco, Military Commander of the Canary Islands; General Saliquet, who held no active command at the time; and General Goded, Military Commander of the Balearic Islands. The need for a central command, however, was responsible for General

Mola's being entrusted with the main organization of the rebellion. While on May 29 General Sanjurjo, by reason of the part he had played as leader of the first revolt against the Republic, was given the principal role and formally appointed leader of the movement, it was in reality General Mola (undoubtedly the most intelligent of them all) who acted as head of the conspiracy in the Peninsula as soon as Franco had left to take up his new post in the Canary Islands.

From the very first day of his arrival in Pamplona, where he had just been appointed Military Commander—so writes his biographer and secretary, Iribarren—General Mola began his work of organizing the insurrection. The local papers, all extremely reactionary, obeyed instructions and mentioned him as little as possible. His appointment as Military Commander was given two lines tucked away in the society columns. General Mola had learned how to work silently, and his term of office as Chief of Police in Madrid during the Primo de Rivera dictatorship had taught him a great deal regarding the boasting and indiscretions in which radical conspirators are so prone to indulge. A few weeks after his arrival in Pamplona he held all the threads of conspiracy in his hands. Through Lieutenant-Colonel Seguí he was in permament contact with the African garrisons (where the year before he had taken advantage of his position to work upon the Moroccan army); he was in touch with the Phalangist organization through the intermediary of an officer who had easy and regular access to the Alicante Prison (where José Antonio Primo de Rivera was in a better position to send orders to his followers than if he had been at liberty); and he was certain, when the time was ripe, of being able to rely on the Carlists, the most influential group in that region, without having to keep them informed of his plans long beforehand.

However great the discretion and cunning of the army officers, reports of their activities were bound to leak out in Republican circles. Towards the middle of May the Government, having received disturbing reports of the feeling in the Pamplona garrison, sent General Gómez Caminero, an army leader whose sincerity and loyalty to the Republic could be relied on, to conduct an inquiry on the spot. His report confirmed the suspicions of the Government, but no one knows for what mysterious reason Mola continued in his command until the day of the rebellion.

The future insurgent generals had an unquestionable talent for dissimulation and deceived the War Minister most deplorably. For them their word was by no means their bond. Because he trusted General Mola's word of honour, General Batet, his immediate superior, was shot by the rebels a few hours after the outbreak of the rebellion. On July 16 General Batet had an interview with Mola, who swore to him that neither he nor the army would consider for one single moment breaking their oath of loyalty to the Constitutional Government. "On your word of honour?" asked General Batet. "On my word of honour," replied Mola. Forty-eight hours later Mola rose against the Government, imprisoned Batet, and gave orders for his execution. Franco acted in the same way. But the man who really surpassed all others in the art of tricking the War Minister was the Military Commander of Saragossa, General Cabanellas. As late as July 19, when Saragossa was in open rebellion against the Government, he replied to the official summons from Madrid with the most fervent protestations of loyalty and the assurance that everything in the city was as calm as a mill-pond.

We ourselves were naturally more sceptical regarding the word of honour of the generals. As Member of Parliament for Madrid, and Vice-President of the local Committee of the Socialist Party, I headed workers' delegations to Señor Azaña, the Prime Minister, on various occasions, to express our great concern at the underhand work of the army leaders. Señor Azaña would smile benevolently. Our tendency to believe these tales of banditry seemed to him a trifle childish. We were not, however, discouraged by this from sending the

Government all available information concerning the growing activity of the enemies of the Republic.

Concurrently with this organization of revolt, the forces defeated at the elections were applying the same terrorist methods as those used by the Nazis in the summer of 1932 on the eve of Hitler's seizure of power in Germany, with the object—in Dr. Goebbels's own words—of creating an atmosphere of continual insecurity and of waging a "war of nerves" against the authorities. On March 11 some Phalangist students made an attempt on the life of Señor Jiménez de Asúa, Deputy Speaker of the Parliament and Professor of Criminal Law at Madrid University. On the 15th of the same month an attempt was made to murder Señor Largo Caballero. On the eve of April 14, the anniversary of the Republic, Don Manuel Pedregal, the magistrate who had presided at the trial of the would-be assassins of Professor Jiménez de Asúa, was killed by the Fascists.

The policy of creating a permanent atmosphere of uneasiness was furthered by certain industrialists of Fascist sympathies, who declared a series of lock-outs in order to force the workmen to counter with the strike weapon. There are people, even in the Socialist Party, who since the war have endeavoured to draw from the Spanish struggle the moral that it is dangerous to press working-class demands too far, and who attribute the rebellion to the large number of strikes which took place in Spain in the months following the general election. Documents found in the Phalangist headquarters after the revolt failed in Madrid prove that in point of fact some of the strikes at that time were the work of *agents provocateurs* in the trade unions. Not that I deny that some of these strikes—such as that of the builders—went on too long, against the advice of those leaders with the greatest experience and political acumen. I well remember the efforts made by the Socialist Committee of Madrid and myself to dissuade the C.N.T. (*Confederación Nacional de Trabajo*, National Confederation of Workers)—a trade-union organization with Anarchist tendencies—from declaring a general strike after the scandalous Phalangist attack of April 16. (This attack was directed against some labourers who were peacefully working in the Castellana Avenue, and resulted in three men being killed and some fifty wounded.) Finally we succeeded in persuading the Anarchists to content themselves with a twenty-four-hour strike, and that impressive demonstration of protest and solidarity passed off without the slightest incident. There is, however, a great difference between recognizing that some of these strikes ought perhaps not to have taken place, and attributing to them a rebellion whose causes and antecedents are well known.

In actual fact, because the Spanish people, with their fine political intuition, were aware of the impending danger, they gave proof, in the months between the elections and the insurrection, of splendid discipline and common sense. Only on one occasion was there any intense popular excitement, and that was when an amnesty was demanded on the two days following the elections. Impatient crowds attacked the prisons to set free the October prisoners, many of whom had been kept for eighteen months without trial, and whose immediate release was one of the principal planks of the Popular Front platform. But not even in those impassioned days of February was there any serious incident. Señor Azaña's Government, before the wave of popular agitation for the release of these thirty thousand political prisoners, very wisely issued an emergency decree, in accordance with the Constitution, which, with a single signature, cut through all the bureaucratic red tape. Apart from this, complete order was maintained, in spite of the fact that those men who had been provincial governors up to the elections, abandoned their posts after the great Popular Front victory without waiting for successors to be appointed.

With the exception of this spontaneous and natural mobilization of the masses to demand an amnesty, nothing happened until the month of July to justify the accusations of anarchy and chaos levelled against the Government, by the Fascist conspirators, the better to cloak their own subversive activities. What did happen was, in fact, largely a concomitant of the preparations for the rebellion which were going on actively from the week following the elections. *Agents provocateurs* abounded. After the rebellion many of them were to boast of their exploits in the spring months in sowing the disorder which the leaders of the rebellion regarded as an essential part of their preparations. Moreover, there was complicity on the part of many men in Governmental agencies, civil governors, Civil Guard commanders, and others who, charged with the sacred duty of keeping order, connived at provoking disorder. One has only to scan the rebel press for the first days of the rebellion to see how many supposed Republicans were in league with the military. Thus, though the Government did everything possible to keep order, its efforts were in part sabotaged by men on whom it had the right to count. But the violence of these months has been greatly exaggerated and repeatedly men like Gil Robles and Calvo Sotelo, engaged in actively preparing the rebellion, stood up in Parliament and read inflated lists of church burnings and other supposed outbreaks as a part of their revolutionary propaganda. An event of such political importance as the impeachment of the President of the Republic, Señor Alcalá Zamora, for having violated the Constitution took place without the slightest disturbance. On May 1, a day on which the temperature of a country can easily be gauged, all the foreign correspondents in Spain reported "perfect order."

Neither could the Right-wing extremists at that time bring any allegations of diabolic influence against the Soviet Embassy, for there was no Soviet ambassador in Spain, nor had there ever been one since the Russian Revolution. When the rebellion broke out, Republican Spain was maintaining normal diplomatic relations with every country except the U.S.S.R. The Republic did not recognize Soviet Russia until

1933. At that time I was Spanish Ambassador in Mexico, and was appointed to the Moscow Embassy. While I was on the way to Russia, however, the Azaña Government fell, and I handed in my resignation; the next Ambassador in Moscow, Dr. Marcelino Pascua, subsequently Ambassador in Paris, was not appointed until I became Foreign Minister in September 1936, two months after the outbreak of the rebellion; and the first Soviet Ambassador did not arrive in Spain until the end of August of that year.

With their weakness for symbolic dates, preferably of a religious character, the insurgent leaders had planned their revolt for the period between St. John's and St. Peter's days, June 24 and 29. It was postponed, however, on instructions from General Mola, who at the same time ordered that as from the 15th of the following month everyone should be at his post and ready for the signal of attack.

On the evening of July 13 Largo Caballero and I were in Paris, on our way back from the International Trades Union Congress in London, when we read in *Le Temps* of the death of Señor Calvo Sotelo. His corpse, with a bullet in the head, had been left at midnight, by persons unknown, in one of the depositories of the Madrid cemetery, and was identified some hours later. The day before, Señor Castillo, the well-known Republican officer of the Assault Guards, had been killed by Fascists while standing arm-in-arm with his wife at the door of their home. The connection between these two events was not difficult to establish.

We took the first train back to Spain. Madrid was charged with electricity. Various Right-wing newspapers had been suspended for the barefaced effrontery with which they accused the Prime Minister of being almost personally responsible for the death of the principal leader of Spanish Fascism. A meeting of the Permanent Committee of the Cortes, which took place two days later, gave an opportunity to opposition members to launch a broadside attack on the Government. Señor Gil Robles made what was undoubtedly the most insolent and aggressive speech of his whole political career. It was interspersed with Biblical phrases, one of which, reproduced the following morning in the reactionary press, was afterwards found to be a warning to the conspirators that the decisive hour was approaching. Over that meeting the threat of violence hung like a heavy cloud.

Government circles, however, remained confident. On Friday the 17th the Socialist members left Madrid as usual to tour the provinces during the week-end and to take part in the various propaganda meetings organized every Sunday by the party to counteract the intensive demagogic campaign of the enemies of the Popular Front. It so happened that, as we had not been expected back from London so soon, no arrangements had been made for me to speak anywhere. Thanks to this, I escaped the fate of many of my colleagues in the Parliamentary Group who found themselves in rebel provinces when the revolt broke out, and were immediately shot by the insurgents. This was the reason why the Socialist benches in Parliament, which before had been the fullest, were, when the Cortes met again during the war, almost half empty.

With the strong conviction that that week-end would be the last that I should enjoy in relative quiet for many months, and having no meeting on the Sunday, I left Madrid for France, where my wife and children were spending the summer in a seaside place near the frontier. Before setting out, however, I obtained official assurance that there was nothing to indicate that it would be unwise to go away until the following Tuesday, when a lively Parliamentary debate was expected. My request for this assurance was looked upon almost as an impertinence, and ironic comments were made on our remarkable capacity for seeing bogies at the corner of every street.

I had scarcely passed the frontier when the *Gazette de Biarritz* published the report of a military rising in Morocco.

Since the proclamation of the Republic all this part of southern France had been the refuge of die-hard Spanish Monarchists. These men, although they had never been persecuted
or interfered with in their own country, showed their hatred
of the new régime by living in voluntary exile, where they
alternated their golf and tennis with the easy sport of playing
at conspiracy from foreign territories, without in the ordinary
way cherishing any great hopes or unduly disturbing their
placid existence. The relish with which that afternoon on the
terrace of the Bar Basque in Biarritz they devoured the news
in the local papers, the noisy merriment with which they
passed remarks from one table to another, and the various
outspoken comments which I overheard in passing, were
eloquent proof that to some at least of those gentlemen of
Spanish Coblenz, the revolt in Africa came as no surprise.

My suspicions were confirmed at once. In order to get in
touch with Madrid as quickly and discreetly as possible, I
went to the Post Office and asked for my own telephone number. The telephone lines were cut. I hailed a taxi and drove
to the first Spanish village on the other side of the frontier. A
large crowd, among which I recognized various old Socialist
and Republican friends, was listening with obvious excitement to the radio at the door of a bar in Behobia. The U.G.T.
(*Unión General de Trabajadores*, General Union of Workers)
was giving orders from the Madrid station to be prepared for
any emergency, and to declare an immediate general strike in
any towns where the local garrisons should attempt to aid
and abet the Morocco rising.

There was no doubt about it. The rebellion had surprised
the Government in the sweetest of slumbers. And, what was
worse, even with the aid of such an ear-piercing alarm clock
it had difficulty in waking. The Civil Governor of San Sebastián, whom I managed to get on the telephone, told me that
the revolt was confined to Africa, that the Government was
confident of being able to suppress it in the course of a few

hours, and that there was perfect order in the rest of Spain. Provincial officialdom was as intoxicated with optimism as the ministers in Madrid.

The truth was that the rising, after four and a half months of preparation, took place in most parts of Spain with only a slight difference in hours. At half past two on the morning of the 18th Franco received in the Canaries a cable from Melilla reporting the first rebel triumphs. He had made plans well in advance to proceed to Morocco and from thence to the Peninsula. On July 11—that is to say, two days before the death of Señor Calvo Sotelo (and here is further conclusive proof that the violent disappearance of the Fascist leader was not, as has so often been said since, the cause of the rebellion) —the British aviator Captain Bebb, under special contract from a Franco agent in London, flew from Croydon to Las Palmas to pick up the rebel leader. Captain Bebb has since described [1] that historic flight with many interesting details, and has recounted how, on July 18, he smuggled Franco through the French customs and took him to a country-house in Casablanca where his liaison officers were awaiting him.

The military rising, planned with the complete agreement, and promise of support, of Germany and Italy, and carefully organized from the moment the Popular Front came to power at the February elections, spread like wildfire. Its leaders were convinced that within a few hours, or at the most a couple of days, they would be masters of the country. Everything had been carefully arranged.

But these generals, who have never been distinguished for their political acumen or knowledge of mass psychology, had overlooked one small detail when they drew up their plans with so much care. They had forgotten the Spanish people.

[1] *News Chronicle*, November 7, 1936.

CHAPTER II

The Response

Wherever the rebel leaders had been unable to seize power instantly, either by surprise tactics or by taking advantage of the weakness of the authorities, the people rose up in defence. From each town and village there flowed a steady stream of recruits; every man who could get hold of a rifle set off for the front. Until the Government made its tardy decision to open the arsenals to the impatient masses, there were more shotguns than rifles. In the meantime, in every town a hundred men or so were posted in the neighbourhood of all barracks where officers were suspect, and were entrusted with the control of the highways. Tree-trunks or lorries were placed in the bends of the roads to obstruct traffic, and bridges which might have been used by the rebels were blown up without compunction. Swift resolutions had to be taken; unquestioning obedience to the men who proved themselves able to lead was demanded. It was a general mobilization without instructions, save those hastily circularized by political parties and trade unions, or dictated to every man by his

23

own conscience. In the twinkling of an eye the liberty front was formed and manned.

There was nothing, even in the war years which followed, more magnificent than those first few days. In Bilbao, on the evening of July 19, the city suddenly emptied on the rumour that Navarrese troops were advancing towards Ochandiano. Lorries, taxis, private cars, everything on four wheels which could be made to go, sallied forth to meet Mola's shadow column; while men, armed and unarmed, women and children, youths and girls, joined in the march, all fired with the same eager enthusiasm, the same passionate longing for freedom. Imprecations mingled with heroic vows, slogans with popular songs. . . . In Madrid, on the following morning, the people marched behind two cannon manned by three Republican officers—for every man with a rifle there were fifty with only a pistol each, and that was not always loaded—to capture, by assault or any other means, the Montaña Barracks, the rebels' most formidable redoubt, well stocked with arms and ammunition. Here the resistance of the professional officers broke down before the onrush of a multitude determined to enter the barracks or to break themselves in pieces against the walls. . . . Barcelona, whose revolutionary tradition and temper were well known, was assigned by the rebels to General Goded, who after Mola was their most able leader. The large garrison, who were fully implicated in the rebellion, were already in the streets when the signal came, but the Catalans, both workers and middle classes, detesting dictatorship and fearing the loss of their regional Statute, went unhesitatingly to the defence of their city and by their success thwarted the insurgents' plans for a wide and triumphant advance. . . . And in every village where treason had not entered in like a thief in the night, there were the same scenes in miniature of devotion to the Republic, the same determination to fight to the death.

Before the mayors of the towns had received instructions from the Ministry of the Interior on July 20 to form, in close collaboration with the workers' organizations, the first bands of shock troops, a handful of combatants had anticipated the Government's call to arms in every loyal corner of Spain. As soon as each local rebellion was put down, every man who had a shotgun or a pistol, or whose hands were itching to hold one, made off to that part of the front where the fight was hardest, if he did not feel that his presence was necessary to prevent any fresh Fascist attempt at home. Five thousand Asturian miners from Sama, Mieres, and Trubia arrived in Madrid on the third day of the rebellion. From Andalusia, Extremadura, Catalonia, and the Levant, messengers kept pouring in with offers of men and requests for arms. Farm labourers, who for nothing else in the world would have left their native soil, were the first to enlist. Artists, students, workmen, schoolmasters, traders, army officers of many years' retirement, lawyers, engineers, musicians, all flocked to the recruiting stations—a human flood in which the various classes of society, ages, and professions mingled freely. So the Republican militia was born, a body of men which, until the formation of the new army, held up an enemy armed from without and within and ten times superior in the purely military sphere.

A belt and a pair of cartridge pouches were fastened over the mechanic's overall, which thus acquired the status of a uniform. The great thing was to get hold of a rifle and as much ammunition as possible, even if it had to be kept in pockets for lack of cartridge belts. Sandals took the place of army boots. The question of food was of secondary importance; a few tins of sardines and a good-sized piece of bread go a long way when the mind is set on higher things.

Every man fought with the weapons at his disposal. In the mountains the shepherds used their slings against the rebels, hurling sticks of dynamite instead of stones. Behind the military columns would march reservists, unarmed, ready to take the place of the men who fell, or hoping that a good haul of prisoners would give them not only something to shoot with,

but also the satisfaction of being able to arm themselves at
the Fascists' expense.

In the rear guard, women did the work of men. Many of
them, however, were not willing to resign themselves to this
relatively passive role, and the more determined among them
—in particular those belonging to Youth organizations—went
off to the front as soon as they could get hold of a mechanic's
overall. Nevertheless they did not forget, in their enthusiasm,
to carry out the instructions of the responsible authorities.
In Madrid the workers' organizations, as soon as the rebel
centres had been destroyed, gave orders to return to work—
to the bakeries in particular—and the city rapidly assumed a
normal appearance. The communiqué exhorting members of
political organizations to be calm and disciplined ended with
the words: "Workers, we have conquered! This is the triumph
of men of courage and goodwill over our country's traitors."
That inspiring summons brought all those who had no soldier's work to do back to their daily tasks.

Lorries of militiamen filed through the main streets of the
towns amid the cheers of the populace; and above the patriotic or political songs, like the final note of a symphony, resounded the cry: "They shall not pass!" Along the road to the
firing-line went the same joyful procession. The peasants in
the fields would break off their work for a moment to wish
them Godspeed, and the children, who had learned untaught
to give the clenched-fist salute of the Popular Front, would
leave their game of "beating the rebels" to gaze after them
until they were lost to sight in the distance.

Every town and village had its heroes. In Madrid they were
the men who led the assault on the Montaña Barracks. In
Barcelona it was commanding officer, Pérez Farras. In Valencia it was Fabra, sergeant in an engineers' regiment, who
turned the tables on the insurgents by imprisoning them in
the barracks and inciting the men to mutiny against the rebel
officers who wanted to send them out into the streets. In Irún,
Lieutenant Ortega. In Valladolid, the thirty workmen who

held up an advancing Fascist column in the street of María de Molina for a whole night. In Huelva, the miners who fought a desperate and heroic struggle against four rebel regiments. And in every part of Spain there were the priests who refused to join the rebellion; the schoolmasters shot for being liberals or Protestants; the Members of Parliament surprised by the rebels on a speaking tour or when trying to organize resistance; the girls of the Young Socialist movements killed when they spoke to the soldiers and begged them not to fire on the people.

The appearance and discipline of the militiamen improved daily. They would complete their equipment with a couple of machine-guns carried off, after much negotiation, from the artillery ground; wherever they could find any steel plating, and the assistance of a metalworker comrade, they would turn their lorries into armoured cars, whose arrival at the front would be hailed with great enthusiasm; they learned not to waste their ammunition, to shoot straighter, and to throw themselves headlong on the ground in an air raid.

These men knew exactly why they were fighting. On July 31, 1936, before the news had come over the wires of the crashing of three Savoia trimotor bombing planes in the neighbourhood of Saida-du-Kiss—the first intimation of Italian military assistance to the rebels—and before the calamitous policy of Non-Intervention had been formulated, French newspaper correspondents were set wondering by the words of some members of the Spanish militia: "We are not only fighting for Spain; we are fighting for the whole world." From the very first moment of the war the Spanish people were filled with this deep conviction, a conviction which all the disillusionment caused during the subsequent two and a half years by the game of international politics could not destroy. Fascism for them was not merely an internal enemy whose victory would mean the destruction of the Republic and the return to a period of reaction incompatible with individual and national dignity. They saw in it, too, the scourge of

Europe and of the whole world, and were proud to be the first to take up its challenge with such strength and determination.

The first battalions were named after the most popular of the Republican leaders. Political parties and trade unions vied with each other to form contingents and to equip them in the best possible way. On the steps of the War Ministry in Madrid there was a continual stream of delegates, who would go in hoping to secure arms for an entire battalion, and come out again each with a long face and an order for some twenty or thirty rifles and a few dozen pistols. The arms depots were emptied during the first days of the fighting. Still, thanks to the foresight of the Chief of Artillery in Madrid and of a few Republican military leaders who, tired of giving vain warnings of the imminence of a rising, had formed as large an arms reserve as possible, the most urgent demands could be met. When there was not a single rifle left at the various centres, the militiamen began to search for Fascist deposits; private gardens and country estates were carefully investigated, sometimes with amazing results.

Military posts of vital importance, which had become vacant through desertion or lack of personnel, were soon filled by the spontaneous initiative of private individuals or trades-union members. Doctors and medical students formed the first ambulance brigades, and from these developed the splendid Military Health Service (*Sanidad Militar*), of which the Republican army was justifiably proud. In the offices of the U.G.T. in Madrid, a permanent Information Bureau was set up, and this for some time was the War Ministry's finest news agency. From every province, from every village where a representative of this organization was installed, the slightest movement of rebel troops was telephoned immediately to the central office, and was in turn communicated by direct line to the General Staff. While its collaboration was highly appreciated at the time, few people realized the tremendous service rendered by the U.G.T., an organization which, under the active leadership of Largo Caballero, was, from the very beginning of the war, one of the strongest and best supports of the forces of resistance.

The Spanish telegraphists, who, not in vain, had set the Republican flag flying over the General Post Office in Madrid on April 14, 1931, four hours before the Republic was proclaimed, co-operated in the formation of a new communication service by listening in day and night to the rebel telephone wires. How often would the local telegraphist stay in a town after the enemy had entered, in order to inform the Government of its capture and so prevent any unwise movement on the part of the loyalist troops! And how often did this desperate determination to send the last alarm cost the man his life!

This popular reaction during the first few weeks was a great setback to the rebels. Until the middle of August they were not able to make any material advance. Their boldest exploits consisted in raids on territory occupied during the first days of the rising, in search of Government supporters of all shades of Red, whose suppression was the first item on their program. Some may think that only Communists and Socialists, workers and peasants, came under this heading. No indeed; a Mason was a Red; a Protestant was a Red; a Basque Nationalist was a Red; those of the same party as Señor Martínez Barrio— Speaker of the House and leader of the most moderate section of Spanish Republicanism—were Reds; Red too were the schoolmasters who believed that education should be in the hands of the State and not of religious bodies; and those suspected of the practice of reading certain foreign newspapers. It is no exaggeration, but the most grotesque and tragic reality, that a man was shot as a Red in the province of Seville because his very modest library included a Spanish translation of Ramsay MacDonald's *Socialism*.

In Andalusia young bloods on their fine thoroughbreds would gallop through villages and farms in the search for Republicans. As the latter were likely neither to have kept

their political party cards, nor to be denounced by their
neighbours, their pursuers would repair to the house of the
local political boss, whose memory of the voting in the last
election was as accurate as any polling register. To have
voted for the Popular Front was enough to condemn a man
to death.

In the midst of this self-created atmosphere of hostility, the
rebels, demoralized by popular opposition, did not dare run
the risk of any large-scale action until sufficient foreign aircraft and Moroccan troops had arrived to add to their military
superiority—a superiority consisting not only of arms but also
of the number of technicians and professional officers, of
which there was a great scarcity in the Republican militia. In
spite of all this, however, their first attempts to advance were
an utter failure.

It was not till the end of August that our situation deteriorated. Foreign assistance to the Rebels began to make itself
felt. Badajoz was captured, thanks partly to the co-operation
of the Portuguese frontier authorities, who, not content with
allowing munitions lorries to be unloaded in Portuguese ports
and to be sent without delay through Portuguese territory to
the rebels, handed over to the insurgents all Republican combatants who attempted to fall back into Portugal. On the
Castilian plains swift and powerful German and Italian airplanes inflicted heavy punishment on the militia and forced
them to retreat in the Talavera sector. In the north, pressure
on Irún increased daily. On the other hand, in the Guadarrama Mountains all rebel attacks were repulsed, and in
Asturias the miners besieged the rebel garrison in Oviedo and
resisted every rebel attempt to break through a circle held
in defiance of the enemy's superior artillery.

Only when the city was devoured by flames did Irún fall.
The defence of Irún was one of the most glorious episodes of
the war, and even correspondents of French newspapers
hostile to the Spanish Republic paid admiring tribute to that

ever lessening group of men who held out within its walls. To the last moment they fought on, always in the hope that some Government ammunition trucks which had been detained near Hendaye by the French authorities would be released and sent to their destination. This was one of the hardest trials which the Non-Intervention policy inflicted on loyalist Spain. While large numbers of machine-guns and munitions from Germany and Italy were being landed in the port of Cádiz, the defenders of Irún could see a mile or so away the very trucks which might have spared them the tragic necessity of yielding up the key to northern Spain. It was this lack of ammunition that brought the *"dinamiteros"*—later to play so important a part in the conquest of Teruel—into action. With a stick of dynamite in their mouths and a box of matches in their hands, they would advance towards the enemy, hurling the explosive with unbelievable skill and spreading panic in the rebel lines. But all these efforts were in vain, and once Irún was captured at the beginning of September, San Sebastian had to be given up for lost.

These partial successes, however, could not compensate the rebels for their early failures, and in the knowledge that time was against them, they did everything possible to hasten the progress of operations. The Republican positions in the Guadarrama Mountains had shown disturbing signs of firmness and strength. Winter snow would only add to the difficulties of a campaign which promised to become more and more rigorous as the militia improved with training, and their early formations became regular units—the first step towards the creation of a real army. The authority of the Government increased daily. As the administrative machinery—damaged by those who had rebelled against the legal Constitution—began to function once again, and as the State regained control of those instruments which are universally employed to enforce the law—primarily an efficient and reliable police force—conditions returned to normal, to the discomfiture of all those who tried to justify their treason by citing the inability of the Republicans to restrain extremists who wished to impose a Soviet régime on Spain. Statements made by the Government and the political parties supporting it—a genuine National Front—showed that loyalist Spain was determined to fight as long as necessity demanded. From every point of view—but especially from the military one—it was essential for the rebels to force a rapid decision before the Republican army became a reality. There was only one way of doing this —to capture Madrid. When, with all the troops and material at their disposal on the Talavera front, the insurgents succeeded in taking Toledo on September 28, victory seemed to them almost as near as it did on July 18, when they had felt certain of gaining it without having to fire a single shot.

On September 29 Franco was appointed Generalissimo and proceeded to Toledo to prepare the great advance on Madrid. All the other objectives—Bilbao, Santander, Oviedo, Málaga— were relegated to the second rank. In the country between Toledo and Madrid there are few natural defences, and the militiamen were forced to fight in the open. There was not a blade of grass in the fields; the harvest had been gathered; not even the wheat remained to give protection against the incessant attacks from enemy bombers, whose mastery of the air grew daily as the Republican air force lost both its planes and its chance of taking the initiative in the increasingly unequal struggle.

After October 6, when General Varela's column entered Santa Cruz de Retamar and wrested from the Republicans a position which, by reason of its link with the Toledo sectors and the mountains of Gredos and Guadarrama, was of high importance, the situation rapidly deteriorated. The next day enemy pilots tried to take psychological advantage of this rebel success by dropping ultimatums on Madrid fixing a time for the evacuation of the civilian population and the surrender of the capital. That same afternoon the rebel radio announced that the insurgents would enter Madrid on October 12, the *"Fiesta de la Raza."* [1]

The Government issued a decree for the incorporation of the militia in that section of the regular army which had remained loyal. Madrid was unaware, however, that the enemy were only fifteen miles from the Puerta del Sol, the main square in the centre of the town. The city still retained its everyday appearance; the cafés were full, and labourers were calmly repairing roads and working on new buildings just as if nothing had happened. It was not until the last two weeks in October that a war-time atmosphere suddenly pervaded the capital. Work on fortifications was intensified; the reservoirs in the Lozoya Canal were enclosed by a strong shell-proof wall; the lines of trenches in the suburbs grew longer every day. An exaggerated optimism gave place to an attitude of healthy realism. In the press, at meetings, in war communiqués, warnings of the imminent peril were given in clear and unmistakable language. The effect was electrifying. Madrid underwent a complete change overnight. The people became aware of the menace hanging over their city and answered the call of the Government to a man.

Meanwhile the rebels were advancing on both wings of the front, closing in on Madrid in the form of a semicircle. The scarcity of material on the loyalist side was so great that when on October 28 (I remember the exact date because it was such an important event) a single armoured car was displayed in the streets of Madrid—a subtle device to raise the spirits of the people—it caused a whirlwind of enthusiasm.

The next day the loyalist command launched an offensive intended to ward off the danger of immediate encirclement. All through the previous week towns and positions had been falling to the enemy with lightning speed. On the night of October 26–7 the rebels reached Móstoles, some seven miles from the outskirts of Madrid. A bold attack by Government troops forced them to retire. "The time has come for the great

---

[1] Anniversary of Columbus's discovery of America on a voyage sponsored by the Spanish Catholic monarchs Ferdinand and Isabella.

and final effort," declared Señor Largo Caballero, Premier and War Minister, in a moving speech in which he announced the introduction of fresh factors into the struggle. Fresh factors there were indeed. In an Order to the Army he said: "Today we have planes and tanks. We can go forward." And that day some Russian armoured tanks did go into action. They had just arrived by ship. And every one, every plane and tank, was put to use the moment the army could lay its hands on them. In the air pilots' quarters the graph on the chart showing their hours of flight rose sharply. Day had scarcely dawned when the troops began to advance in the direction of Seseña.

The result of the first fighting was most encouraging. Various important positions were retaken—Torrejón de la Calzada, Seseña, the most dangerous points to the south and south-east of Madrid. The pressure on Illescas made itself felt all along the front. A considerable length of railway line from Aranjuez was also recaptured. Shades of the Battle of the Marne passed over a city which had begun to suffocate and which was now able to breathe a little more freely.

The civilian population co-operated with the military in the work of fortification. The poster recruiting for the brigade of volunteers who went out every day to dig new trenches was tinged with that Spanish humour which never deserted the great city of Madrid even in its most tragic moments: "Working hours—from sunrise to sunset. Maximum wage—the victory of Madrid." Fresh contingents, however, were needed not only for the fortifications. The casualties of a counter-offensive carried out in such unfavourable conditions called for the formation of new reserves at a few hours' notice. By a Government decree of October 30, all men between the ages of twenty and forty-five were mobilized. But thousands of men and boys who did not come within this age limit went to the recruiting stations and asked to be sent to the front.

The Republican counter-offensive had two days of victory. In some places the enemy was forced to retire to a distance of nine miles. Unfortunately the insurgents' radius of action was already so wide that they were able to advance wherever the breakdown of Government defences made further resistance impossible. While the Republicans, with ever lessening men and material, were attacking on the south, the rebels renewed their offensive on the west. On November 1 they captured Brunete, fifteen miles from the capital, and increased their pressure on Madrid at three different points. The militiamen were routed by Moorish cavalry and, exposed to the continual danger of being cut off from their bases, were forced to retreat, digging anti-tank pits and blowing up bridges as they went.

Air raids on the city were intensified. Rebel planes, aware of the inadequacy of the anti-aircraft batteries on the terrace of the Fine Arts Building, flew over the War Ministry. Leaflets demanding surrender were followed by incendiary bombs. On October 30, 148 deaths were caused in one single bombardment. The sign of the Red Cross was no protection, and the Getafe Hospital, where children from the danger zone had been sent for safety, was brutally destroyed. This barbarity, however, only increased the people's determination to resist the entry into their city of men whose feeling of hatred and desire to kill could be carried to such lengths.

On November 3 Mola, who was in command of all the forces operating in the Madrid sector, called a conference of military and civil authorities at the General Headquarters in Avila. The intention was to draw up their final program for the entry into the capital, now announced for November 7. The new Mayor of Madrid, already appointed by the Generalissimo, informed them of the measures taken to ensure supplies for the populace. Lorries of food—bread and dried vegetables—were concentrated in the outskirts of the town, ready to follow in the rear of the military columns. Lists had been drawn up of non-combatant volunteers who were to leave immediately for Madrid in order to establish normal conditions. Groups of telephone and telegraph technicians,

police, members of municipal departments, were only awaiting the order to proceed. The speech which was to be
addressed to all Spaniards had been prepared; one of its main
paragraphs, abounding in fine logic, was directed to the
"Red" fighters, with the object of convincing them of the
futility of carrying on the struggle, while making vague
promises of a relative clemency if they laid down their arms
at once. Even the place for the victory parade of the troops of
occupation had been chosen. The foreign journalists at army
headquarters had been told that they could not enter Madrid
until General Franco had fixed the day. This was a general
order. Not even combatants from sectors other than the
southern were to be allowed to enter the capital without first
obtaining the necessary permit. Everything was planned
beforehand to the smallest detail, and in that atmosphere of
absolute confidence no one had the impertinence to question
the first item on the program—the capture of the city.

At midday on the 5th the loyalist troops were forced to
evacuate Leganés, Alcorcón, and Getafe, eight and a half
miles from the capital. "All men to the front—to conquer or
die," proclaimed the headlines of the evening papers, faithful
to their resolve not to hide the truth from the people. To have
done so would in any case have been childish and would have
had a damaging effect on morale. The rebels were at the very
gates of Madrid. Dispatch riders from the front, War Commissars asking the General Commissariat for speakers to
harangue the militia, Parliamentary deputies and members
of the Government who had already gone out to encourage
the troops, all reflected in their faces, as they mounted the
steps of the War Ministry, the gravity of the situation. The
sound of enemy cannon could be heard not far from the
centre of the town.

At midnight it was announced that there had been a Government reshuffle, and that four C.N.T. Ministers had entered
the Cabinet. The ranks had to be closed and everybody had
to shoulder responsibility. A wireless communiqué from the

War Ministry ordered the commandeering of all vehicles, the quartering of all militiamen who had not been sent to the front, and the intensifying of fortification work.

The morning of the 6th dawned on a city protected in all its most exposed spots by barricades which had been erected overnight. The whole district of Delicias, where the roads from Toledo and Andalusia meet, was ready for battle. Men, women, and children were working on the construction of new parapets. Government planes flew overhead dropping leaflets with this terse warning: "People of Madrid, you have an air force to defend you. But you too must carry out your duty. Do not yield an inch of ground!" At the front the militiamen were putting up a desperate resistance to the column advancing through Villaviciosa de Odón; finally they had to fall back before the superior fire of the enemy. At other points the retreat began to degenerate into a rout. Remnants of scattered units straggled into Madrid, while War Commissars and political delegates were faced with the tremendous task of reassembling them and leading them back to the front. In the centre of the city the influx of people from the directly threatened suburbs not only blocked up the main streets, but also created a serious billeting problem. The situation could not have been graver. The army command stated that in its opinion the departure of the Government from Madrid, deliberately delayed in order to stave off for as long as possible the disastrous effect which it would have on the people's morale, could not be deferred a moment more. The Government left for Valencia in accordance with the arrangements made that same morning at a meeting of the Cabinet. Madrid remained in the hands of the military authorities.

The recruiting of all able-bodied men went on feverishly throughout that long and tragic night. The best units, reassembled as well as could be expected in the circumstances, were sent to the most dangerous points. In order to turn Madrid into a self-contained fortress, instructions were given to blow up the bridges over the River Manzanares as soon as the rebel troops attempted to enter the city.

On the 7th the rebels began an attack on all fronts, from Pozuelo to Cuatro Caminos. Their main attack was in the Casa de Campo, but their repeated attempts to advance along this route—which threatened the very heart of the city—were a complete failure. On the heights of Carabanchel Alto they were also repulsed. Wherever pressure was greatest the citizens of Madrid stood shoulder to shoulder with the militia. A hastily formed company of barbers fought with amazing heroism and succeeded in holding the bridges of the Manzanares where the Varela column was trying at all costs to cross. Within a few hours scarcely a man remained of that brave little band. The stupefaction of the rebel leaders was unbounded. It was only surpassed by that of the Tercio regiment when they discovered that they were engaged in bayonet fighting with women dressed in the uniform of militiamen.

The Burgos radio station, which in announcing the first details of the offensive that morning had summarized the confident impression of the rebel officers in these arrogant words: "This afternoon we shall have coffee in Madrid," became suddenly silent, and when the broadcasts were resumed a distinctly more cautious tone was noticeable; while from Seville, General Queipo de Llano, with a greater realism, anticipated the impatience of his partisans by warning them that "a capital like Madrid is not taken as easily as a cup of chocolate." Nevertheless, other radio stations in the hands of insurgents or foreign sympathizers announced that the Castejón column were already fighting in the Retiro Park.

While the enemy forces were being held at the entrance of the city, inside Madrid the construction of fortifications and trenches was going on apace. The safest basements were chosen for defence posts in case of need. Machine-guns were installed on the roofs of houses. Everything was being prepared for street fighting. The Fifth Column, with understandable haste, had begun to show its head and could now be seen at close quarters. Mola himself, in his blind assurance, had given the alarm when he declared that, besides the four columns advancing on Madrid, there was a fifth waiting inside the city to cut off the Republican retreat. Embassies and legations, where thousands of insurgents were only awaiting the signal to exchange their role of refugees for that of combatants, were closely guarded.

On the 11th the situation definitely changed in the Republicans' favour. On the Manzanares not a single bridgehead had been lost. In the Casa de Campo the Republican infantry, reviving the glories of the former Tercio, had launched a fierce attack on contingents of Moors and members of the Foreign Legion who had for two days been trapped there, and the park of the former Royal Palace—once the playground of princes—was strewn with the bodies of Moors and Legionaries. The first International Battalion, whose arrival in Madrid had shown the people that they were not alone in this life-and-death struggle, fought successfully against Yagüe's troops, and on other sectors, such as that of Villaverde, the militiamen succeeded in advancing nearly a mile. To gain nearly a mile, and another day of resistance—only those who were there can appreciate what that means!

For a whole week attack followed counter-attack with amazing violence. Once again on November 17 the rebels believed that they had gained the city when the Varela column succeeded in getting a foothold on the left bank of the Manzanares, in advancing towards the Hermitage of San Antonio de la Florida—immortalized by Goya's frescoes—and in climbing up through the West Park to the Model Prison. But it was the illusion of an hour. The loyalist troops drove back the enemy and held them in the University City.

Madrid withstood attacks from aircraft, from artillery, and from rain and snow. There was scarcely a pane of glass left unbroken in the whole city, and the keen air from the Guadarrama Mountains cut like a knife through houses where firewood was even scarcer than meat and bread. But the morale of the people stiffened, conditions returned to normal, and on November 18 General Miaja, President of the Defence Council, was able to announce in his communiqué that "the barrier of defence was insurmountable."

The next day there was a reply to General Miaja's communiqué—though not on the battlefield. On November 18 Germany and Italy, aware of the failure of the rebel offensive against Madrid, recognized Franco's administration. What could not be achieved by force of arms must be obtained by the game of diplomacy. Two days later the General ordered all foreign ships, of whatever nationality, to leave Spanish waters immediately and declared a blockade of Barcelona. These were the reactions of a leader furious in defeat.

For the rest of the month, and throughout December, the rebels continued their unsuccessful attack on Madrid. The Republican authorities took advantage of every quiet interval to evacuate civilians to Valencia. In spite of transport difficulties they succeeded in reducing the population by a third, even though, with the later return of confidence, most of these subsequently came back. Supply services, restricted by the fact that the town was surrounded on three sides, were organized. A hard winter was ahead. But Madrid had conquered, and throughout the rest of the war she became the symbol of heroism and resistance.

CHAPTER III

Non-Intervention

THE FAILURE of the rebel offensive against Madrid might have meant a speedy victory for the Republicans if Germany and Italy had not felt certain that they could carry through their Spanish enterprise with impunity to the very end. Non-Intervention opened up for them the path to total intervention. Convinced that, left to themselves, the rebels had no chance of winning, Hitler and Mussolini decided to carry on the war on their own account. The dispatch to the insurgents of technicians and aviators, airplanes and war material—in increasing numbers, but only by way of subsidiary support—was followed by the shipment of units of the German and Italian regular armies, whose presence in Spain, while it scandalized world opinion, left the London Committee completely unmoved.

Only once did it seem likely that there would be an end to this suicidal tolerance. In September 1937 Great Britain and France formally committed themselves in Geneva to revise their policy of Non-Intervention if "in the near future" the Italian and German troops were not withdrawn from

Spain. This was at a meeting of the Drafting Committee of
the Sixth Committee—the most animated session since the
Italo-Ethiopian conflict had plunged the League of Nations
into a lethargy more demoralizing than would have been its
actual demise. Dr. Negrín had once again confronted the
Assembly with the problem created by an act of aggression
against a state member of the League. The Spanish delegation
could not hope for any very heroic decision on the part of
either Council or Assembly. It knew that they would not dare
to name the aggressor, and that in no event would the measures laid down in the Covenant be applied. It merely wished
to give the British and French Governments an opportunity
of bringing their influence to bear on Berlin and Rome, in
order to enforce the withdrawal of non-Spanish combatants
from Spain.

The Spanish request was sent to the Sixth Committee. On
this committee I had the honour of representing my country.
At the very outset of the meeting of the Drafting Committee
I let it be clearly understood that this time they could not
count on us to sanction one of those stereotyped resolutions
of the Secretariat which mean absolutely nothing and whose
one and only object is to preserve appearances. As soon as
Mr. Elliot, the first British delegate, had finished reading a
draft resolution from which the fundamental problem had
been carefully excluded, I rose to inform the meeting that the
Spanish delegation could not so much as consider it as a basis
for discussion. The first session was over. A further text,
slightly more precise, was drawn up during the night, but
without our participation. I politely declined to assist at one
of those private conferences so dear to the heart of the Secretary General, and responsible for the incessant concessions
and settlements which brought the League of Nations to its
ruin. I was thus free to reject the draft when the committee
met again on the following morning.

Throughout the meeting I could feel the angry gaze of
M. Avenol fixed on me. In the eyes of the Secretariat the

imperilling of a draft resolution was a crime more deserving of sanctions than the rudest act of aggression. The debate flagged. Twice the session broke up. During both intervals attempts were made to convince me that in our situation we ran the risk of the question brought up by the Spanish Government being talked out before it reached the Assembly. Disillusioned by the failure of his own dialectics, M. Delbos, the French Foreign Minister, discreetly commissioned M. Litvinov to make a conciliatory gesture. The Spanish delegation kept strictly to its contention that if no time limit was set for the fresh diplomatic approach which Great Britain and France had declared themselves ready to make to the Italian Government in order to secure the withdrawal of the invading troops from Spain, it could not vote for what in its opinion was nothing more than another platonic resolution, lacking in all meaning and practical value.

I was now faced with the task of resisting pressure not only from friendly delegates, but also from certain members of the Spanish delegation itself who feared that we should be considered responsible if the Sixth Committee was unable to agree upon a resolution to place before the Assembly. I found that the only way of withstanding this pressure was to turn my thoughts to the Spanish Front—where the self-denying Republican army had for months been resisting German and Italian air and artillery bombardments—and to the rear guard, where the people fighting for the independence of their country were condemned to the horrors of a war which, but for the lamentable policy of Non-Intervention, would long since have been over.

I renewed the debate with a statement recounting the sufferings of the Spanish people, victims of an intolerable aggression, and reminded the meeting that for every day lost in re-establishing international law, hundreds of soldiers were dying in Republican trenches and women and children were being murdered by German and Italian airplanes. Turning to the British and French delegates, as representatives of the two powers which had taken the initiative in concerting the Non-Intervention Agreement, I asked them to state their attitude on the problem in its essentials. After a particularly heated, and at times painful, discussion, a formula was reached whereby the British and French Governments promised to revise their policy of Non-Intervention if "in the near future" Germany and Italy had not withdrawn their troops from Spain. "What," I asked before registering our vote, "do the honourable delegates of Great Britain and France mean by 'the near future'?" "Probably an earlier date than the Spanish delegate thinks," replied Mr. Elliot, immediately seconded by M. Delbos. But when eighteen months later, on March 6, 1939, I left Spain with the Negrín Government, the "near future" had still not been converted into the present.

Juridically there was no possible defence for Non-Intervention. To refuse a legitimate Government, with whom the United Kingdom and France were maintaining normal diplomatic relations, their indisputable right to acquire the material necessary to subdue the revolt of a few rebel generals was the very extreme of arbitrary conduct. The case arose where the Spanish Government, which, in accordance with the commercial treaty at that time in force with France, was required to spend some million francs in the purchase of French war material, could not even obtain delivery of the orders placed before the outbreak of the rebellion. From a political viewpoint, this was tantamount to giving Germany and Italy carte blanche to turn Spain into a satellite of the Axis, in opposition to the vital interests of Great Britain and France. It was not difficult to foresee that the totalitarian states, accustomed systematically to break their most solemn international obligations, would ignore the policy of Non-Intervention. And yet it was French diplomacy that revived a formula so aptly defined by Talleyrand a century ago: "Non-Intervention? Between ourselves, it's the same thing as profitable intervention—but profitable only for the other side."

It is therefore understandable that Germany and Italy welcomed enthusiastically the reintroduction in European politics of a formula so useful in the furtherance of their plans, and that they were the first to adhere to it, and the loudest in its praises. While all the time increasing their shipments to the rebels, they indignantly denied every concrete accusation likely to expose their double game of official non-intervention and effective intervention. On August 8, 1936 the German Ambassador in London called at the Foreign Office to give the most definite assurance that "Germany was not assisting the rebel generals, that she had not sent them any war material, and that she did not intend to do so." Italy, on her side, eloquently expressed her resolve not to intervene in the Spanish struggle. On October 9 of the same year the German and Italian representatives on the Non-Intervention Committee replied to the allegations that both Governments had sent war material to General Franco, and to the precise and well-documented charges contained in the Spanish Government's note of September 15 to the signatories to the Non-Intervention Agreement, by stating that "all these assertions were completely fantastic and without the slightest foundation."

This first stage of masked and unacknowledged intervention gave the rebels an excellent opportunity to organize their military expeditions. The "irrefutable proof" of German and Italian intervention, which in September 1936 Messrs. Delbos and Eden amiably but insistently demanded from me, was provided by the German and Italian Governments themselves. The next diplomatic "documents," which in spite of their persuasive power were no better able to rouse the London Committee from its lethargy, were no documents at all, but the actual landing of Italians in Málaga and the Italian offensive at Guadalajara in the month of March.

The Italian divisions were in the vanguard of the attack. The transport of these men to Spanish territory cannot have passed unnoticed by those Governments which, in adopting a policy that, despite its name, was merely one of unilateral intervention directed against Republican Spain, had assumed responsibility for fettering a country fighting for its independence. No one, least of all Berlin and Rome, can seriously believe that the British and French intelligence services could have suffered over a period of weeks from such a bad attack of mental aberration as to have overlooked the dispatch from Italian territory of one hundred thousand fully equipped soldiers—the figure is Italy's own, proclaimed by *Forze Armate* on June 8, 1939 after the war was over—or that the consular agents of both countries in the ports of departure and arrival could have confused troop-ships with Italian tourist vessels calling at Cádiz and Málaga on a pleasure cruise. Italy had measured the ground well. She was convinced that she could intervene in Spain with impunity, and that no one, save the Republican militia, would stand up to her.

The time for dissembling passed. In the London Committee Count Grandi entered on the second stage of openly acknowledged intervention, when at the meeting of March 23, 1937 he stated that "the Italian volunteers will not leave Spanish territory until General Franco has gained a complete and final victory." The London Committee, deeply impressed by the laudable frankness of Italy's distinguished representative, entered this gallant statement, not without a certain pride, in its minutes.

Any doubt which might still have existed on the question of Italian intervention in Spain was dissipated three months later by Mussolini himself on his visit to Berlin, when he declared: "Fascism has fought with words and with weapons. When words are not enough, and if circumstances require it, then it is the weapons that speak. This is what we have done in Spain."

The rough language of weapons does not, however, preclude a soft word if it can serve to quiet the conscience of those who believe that everything is possible in this world if only good manners are preserved. Eight days after the challenge thrown down in the London Committee by Count Grandi, a no less official statement by Signor Alfieri, Minister of Press and Propaganda, on March 31, 1937, renewed the assurances that "the measures taken by the Non-Intervention Committee have been, and always will be, respected by the Italian Government."

Non-Intervention became one of the greatest farces of our time. The long and brilliant repertoire of Italian comedy has no better spectacle to offer than this, where the debatable qualities of Lord Plymouth as stage manager served as a foil to the dexterity and abandon of the actors. The most intelligent review of the comedy was given in *Stampa* on July 20, 1937, in a single phrase—a model of simplicity and of honest and impartial dramatic criticism: "While the diplomats play for time, the legionaries cut the Gordian knot with their swords."

It was only when with the fall of Barcelona they felt assured of certain victory that the totalitarian states gave up all pretence and jeered at the childishness and passivity of the Western democracies. Now began the third stage of intervention, a stage of sarcasm and caustic irony and ridicule directed against the simple souls in London and Paris. A note published in the official *Informazione Diplomatica* stated: "Italy replied to the first call of Franco on July 27, 1936; our first casualties date from this time." All the Italian press echoed the *Popolo d'Italia*: "We have intervened from the first moment to the last."

Germany, on her side, abandoned the relative reserve practised by her up to then. Save for an occasional burst of arrogance such as the speech of Marshal Göring on March 13, 1937, in which he rendered homage to "the heroes who have laid down their lives in Spain to ensure the victory of civilization over the destructive forces of world revolution," the leaders of National Socialism had refrained from calling public attention to their share in the Spanish struggle. The presence of the Germans in Spain had been marked by an obvious desire to pass as unnoticed as possible. While the Italians, with their propensity for military parades and for extending their conquests to the dance-hall (where their behaviour often provoked unpleasant incidents with Spanish officers), could be seen everywhere in rebel territory, the Germans worked quietly and undoubtedly obtained more positive results. More than the glory and the shining laurels they coveted the riches of Spain; they were happier in the offices of some powerful mining combine, for instance, than flaunting their authority in the Spanish streets. The *Kölnische Zeitung* of May 31, 1939 explained this difference of tactics. "In contrast to Italy, which during the war left nobody in doubt as to the part played by her legionaries, Germany awaited a Franco victory and the end of her self-imposed tasks before disclosing all that the German legion, which, under the name of the Condor Legion, enjoyed a high reputation in Spain, had performed."

The fall of Barcelona, however, decided Hitler to break his silence. In his speech of January 30, 1939 he extolled the bravery of "the many National Socialist volunteers" who fought for the victory of Nationalist Spain, and spoke of "Germany's share in Franco's rising." While up to then the slightest allusion in Germany to German intervention was punished by a prolonged stay in a concentration camp, after that time the whole propaganda system was devoted to praising the foresight of the Führer, who from the very first had realized the tremendous importance of bringing Spain into the Axis, and who by helping Franco in his rebellion against the Republic had struck a mortal blow at Great Britain and France.

The dictators have won, and they laugh at everybody and everything. Even the legend of the danger of a Communist Spain, invented by them to win over the American Catholics and British conservatives, is now the object of their frequent sarcasm. They want to leave no doubt as to the aims and motives of their intervention, whose purpose was to consolidate the Axis and to ensure strategic bases of the highest importance in the event of war. It could not, of course, be otherwise. The American Catholics and British conservatives, who during the so-called Spanish conflict ingenuously believed that Germany and Italy were intervening in Spain with the chivalrous desire to free the Spaniards from Bolshevism, could read some months later, during the most critical period of the Anglo-French negotiations in Moscow, the most enthusiastic eulogies of Soviet foreign policy in the Italian press, and could watch Berlin's strenuous efforts to seduce Stalin away from Paris and London in order to sign a pact with Germany.

"We have intervened from the first moment to the last." This is the sober truth. Under the title of "Mussolini's Promise," the rebel General Millán Astray published an article in the *Popolo d'Italia* on May 30, 1938 recalling his interview with the Duce in the Chigi Palace in 1926, at the end of which the Italian dictator had said to him: "Colonel, if the decisive and historic moment should one day arrive for Spain, be sure that Italy will come to her aid."

By 1926 Mussolini had already foreseen the possibility of Primo de Rivera's dictatorship—that fragile Spanish imitation of his own system of government—being consumed by its own weakness, and had pledged his support to those who had decided to transform Spain, when the "critical and historic moment" should arrive, into a totalitarian state at the service of the Imperial interests of Fascist Italy. This "moment" began with the advent of the Republic, and reached its decisive stage for Mussolini with the electoral triumph of the Popular Front, ten years after his promise was made. In March 1934, when General Barrera and the Monarchist leader Señor Goicoechea, two of the future rebel leaders, went to Rome to ask his advice and help, Mussolini renewed this promise in much more precise terms. As proof of his goodwill the Duce offered them 20,000 rifles, 20,000 hand-grenades,

200 machine-guns and 1,500,000 pesetas, to be delivered at any time. He made it quite clear that "such assistance was only of a preliminary nature and would be followed at an opportune moment by greater support, as and when the work justified it or circumstances made it necessary." [1]

Germany, too, intervened "from the first moment to the last." General Sanjurjo brought back from his previously-mentioned visit to Berlin, at the beginning of 1936, the promise of the German authorities to place at the rebels' disposal the airplanes necessary for transporting troops to the Peninsula in the event of the Spanish fleet not giving sufficient collaboration.

Military assistance was preceded by political support. In the many Gestapo agents sent to Spain, as to every country, in order to carry on extensive intrigues and to undermine any government which was not a party to their designs, the Spanish conspirators found their staunchest collaborators. The large number of documents discovered by the Republican authorities in the *Landesgruppe* headquarters of the National Socialist party in Barcelona proves the existence in Spain of a widespread German spy organization, which had succeeded in penetrating every stratum of Spanish life, and which was working for the rebellion with the same zeal as Franco's own generals. During the months following the election the German Embassy and its consulates took advantage of their diplomatic privilege to import into Spain a large quantity of arms and propaganda material, whose source the Spanish police, although they watched the suspected printing-houses of Madrid and Barcelona, were quite unable to discover.

It is the same method as that practised later in Austria, Czechoslovakia, Memel, Danzig. First the selected country as the victim of aggression is represented as having reached

---

[1] The document in which this agreement is recorded, in the handwriting of Señor Goicoechea, was found in his archives after the rebellion, and published in facsimile in May 1937 by the British and French press.

the verge of anarchy. Then, to assist them in their rescue work, the so-called supporters of law and order are given the means to rebel against a situation whose imaginary excesses and dangers are elaborated and dramatized by Fascist propaganda in order to present the *coup d'état* to balanced public opinion as something entirely logical and inevitable. Thus in the weeks before the rebellion the German and Italian press gave more and more space to reports from their "special correspondents," some of whom did not even take the trouble to move from their editorial offices in order to write their stories of "disorders," "Red atrocities," "growing and unrestrainable indignation of the Spanish people at the incompetence of a Government dominated by Communists," and so on. On July 15, 1936, after this intensive period of ideological preparation, the *Völkischer Beobachter*, official organ of the Third Reich, openly prophesied that "it will not be the first time, in the course of these twenty years, that the summer holidays in Spain are interrupted by grave political surprises." It was the official announcement of a rebellion which broke out three days later.

Initial assistance soon grew into a regular invasion. The names of the Italian units operating in Spain are known to all. The Italian press indulged in a continuous panegyric of their feats of arms and gave great prominence to portraits of their leaders. "Littorio," "23rd of March," "Black Flames," "Black, Blue, and Green Arrows," their sonorous and colourful names made them stand out in the popular imagination and ensured that their achievements should not pass unnoticed. With their powerful artillery and armoured-car sections, these divisions, together with the "legionary air arm" and the C.T.V. (Volunteer Corps), constituted the great military organization of Fascist Italy in Spain.

Of these six divisions, four were entirely Italian; the other two were chiefly composed of Spaniards, under the command of Italian officers. Each division was made up of two brigades of two regiments each, some 12,000 men in all, not counting the specialists, artillery-men, tank-drivers, engineers, and instructors. By a simple process of multiplication one arrives at a total of approximately 50,000 or 60,000 Italians fighting on Franco's side. This figure, as we shall afterwards see, is considerably smaller than the real one. Nevertheless in itself it ought to have been sufficiently high for the Non-Intervention Committee, and its chief sponsors, the British and French Governments, to have reached the obvious conclusion that a veritable army of occupation had been sent to Spain and was being maintained there by one of the powers which had subscribed to the agreement not to intervene, and which was taking its place at the committee table.

The presence of these divisions was denounced by the Spanish Government as soon as the documents seized at Guadalajara came into its hands. On April 1, 1937 the Spanish Embassies in London and Paris, in a note based on these documents, drew the attention of the British and French Governments to the following facts:

1. That there existed in Spanish territory complete units of the Italian army, with Italian soldiers, material, communications, and command.
2. That the Italian units behaved in the operating sectors like a genuine army of occupation.
3. That the Italian Government had set up public services for the exclusive use of their military units in Spanish territory.
4. That prominent personages (cf. the famous telegram sent by Mussolini to his Guadalajara troops as he was embarking for Libya) were taking an active interest in the Italian forces, either by encouragement or leadership.
5. That all this was tantamount to an Italian invasion of Spain, causing a serious loss of confidence in solemnly concluded agreements and constituting a grave danger to European security and peace.

A few weeks later the "White Book," a large volume of 319 pages, reproduced one hundred of the two thousand Italian documents which had fallen into the hands of the

Spanish Government after the victory at Guadalajara. Its disclosures, however, although they made a strong impression on all sides, were as systematically ignored by the British and French Governments as were the rest of our allegations, both previous and subsequent. Apparently they still failed to give the "irrefutable proof" which my honourable colleagues, the Foreign Ministers of Great Britain and France, had been demanding, with such great solicitude and insistence, ever since the meeting of the League of Nations in September 1936.

The Italian press, however, continued its noble work of clearing up any doubts which might still have existed as to the consistency of our statements. In April 1938 the Italian troops arrived before Tortosa. In Rome there was unbounded enthusiasm when their soldiers advanced along the coast of the Latin sea. The Italian press published the number of Italian combatants who had taken part in an action whose historic significance gave rise to great hopes for the future. "The number of Italian troops taking part in the Battle of Tortosa," says the *Stampa*, "was 39,000; and all of them fought magnificently." The participation of 39,000 men in a single battle would certainly do honour to any invading army in an enterprise which had been preceded by no declaration of war, and which, as everyone knows, had no official objective except that of helping to save Spain from complete domination by Moscow.

Another detail which the London Committee might have taken into account was the list of Italian casualties, whose regular publication was tantamount to an official recognition of intervention, although the full number of losses suffered by the Italian army were not given. The reason for this understatement is obvious. The Spanish adventure was by no means popular in Italy, least of all, of course, among the workers. On various occasions it had given rise to demonstrations in Milan, Turin, and other places, which, while not reaching the proportions of a revolt, as some Left-wing commentators have alleged, must have served as a warning to Italian leaders to proceed with a certain moderation in the publication of casualty lists. The tendency in consequence was to reduce the official number of casualties by a few thousand.

An official communiqué published in Rome at the end of hostilities gave the number of killed and wounded as 7,000 and 10,000 respectively. The mere fact that the Italian divisions took part in all-important offensive and defensive operations would in itself give sufficient cause for doubting these figures. General Pariani, Italian Under-Secretary for War, took it upon himself, however, to explain this discrepancy when in the Fascist Chamber he confirmed the figure for the army, but admitted that "there was an equal number in the Fascist militia." This would give 34,000 casualties, with 14,000 killed. Even taking these figures as correct, if one adds the 50,000 Italian soldiers (who, according to the Italian reports under review, were in Spain throughout the war), the constant relief forces of the Volunteer Corps, and, above all, the air arm, one reaches the conclusion that Fascist Italy sent Franco an army of considerably more than 100,000 men.

There were fewer Germans in Spain, yet because of the nature and extent of their activity they wielded far greater influence than the Italians. If they succeeded, as we have seen, in passing unnoticed in the outside world, at the same time they were at great pains to make themselves indispensable to the authorities. They became to a certain extent the specialists of Franco's army—and they were certainly his favourite organizers and instructors. They ran the schools for commissioned and non-commissioned officers; and as *Die Wehrmacht*, the official organ of the Reichswehr, has since proudly confirmed, "56,000 Spanish youths" passed through their hands and were instructed not only in military science but also in the superiority and advantages of the totalitarian régime. Their opinion carried weight in moments of difficulty, and whenever a fresh offensive was being prepared they were always entrusted with the task of working out the plans. The Italians in rebel territory were regarded with a slight contempt. The Germans, on the other hand, enjoyed a respect and esteem which allowed them to reap the greatest possible benefits from the war. "I have always considered the Condor Legion," said General Franco in his farewell speech of May 22, 1939, "as one of the institutions of our crusade." In this tribute there was not the slightest rhetorical licence.

The Germans had complete control of the anti-aircraft defences. M. Georges Oudard, one of the most fervent partisans of General Franco, writes from personal experience in his book on the Spanish War: "The anti-aircraft defences are in the hands of the Germans and are so carefully guarded that no Spanish or Italian officer has ever been able to examine one of them at close range." It was the same with the artillery. All the rebel artillery was supplied, operated, and commanded by the Condor Legion. Our own soldiers knew this only too well. When the Germans, in accordance with their military tactics, would concentrate hundreds of shells on one small piece of territory in order to lay everything bare before the infantry came into action, I have often heard our men greet these frightful cannonades with an ironic "*Heil Hitler!*"

The Germans were in charge of the work of fortification. The dense walls of cement erected with such alarming speed by German engineers, which so often broke our soldiers' attack, were a further proof of the tremendous assistance given by Germany to the rebels. The instructors and commanding officers at the air bases were German. So also were the tank instructors. The cartographic headquarters in Vitoria were controlled by them. In the navy they acted as advisers, officers, artillery-men, mine-layers, or anything else that was required. The naval detachment of the Condor Legion was there to provide a varied and expert staff. According to *Die Wehrmacht*, it was composed of a great many officers, a large number of specialists, and a few "Spanish Germans" who acted as interpreters. (I must confess to anxiety in the matter of the "Spanish Germans." If one day Franco should fail the German Führer, or, as is more likely, if the Spanish people should rise against him, Hitler may well discover in Spain the existence of another German minority on whose behalf he will decide to intervene afresh.) "Their chief mission," stated the above-mentioned review, "was mine-laying, coaching candidates for the Naval College, and training Spaniards in the use of the arms and machines acquired in Germany."

Their zeal and ability did not flag when the firing ceased. "Rather than a fighting unit, it was a military and a civil mission"; in these words the Franco telegrams described the Condor Legion at the time of their official departure from Spain. A large group of economists and industrialists formed an integral part of this Legion, and effectively carried out their instructions to penetrate every branch of Spanish economy, in order to secure complete German domination at a later date. Another and even more numerous contingent, consisting of Gestapo agents, initiated the Franco police in the methods employed by the Third Reich in preventing all possible reaction and in rooting out opposition. Concerning the activities of the first group, the London *Times* of January 14, 1938 published the following account by one of its correspondents who had recently returned from rebel territory: "The 10,000 Germans in Spain, apart from those who act as air-pilots, operate the radio and telegraph, mark out the roads, check up on the water supplies, act as engineers on the bridges, direct the railroads, and are represented in almost every department of State administration." As regards the second group, the savage reprisals following Franco's victory are eloquent proof of how efficiently the Gestapo worked in Spain and how fruitful was its tuition. Until quite recently Gestapo agents were entrusted with the task of controlling the services of public order in "liberated" Spain, and of persecuting the "new Reds"—in other words, the Requetés and Monarchists.

The generally admitted figure for German intervention is 20,000. It seems to me a very low one, even if it is taken as referring only to German participation in the Spanish war *at any one time.* But if one accepts this interpretation, the figure of 20,000 still gives no idea of Germany's real contribution, in man-power, to Franco's victory. On this point *Le Temps* was more correct when it wrote on June 1, 1939: "It is now known that the German forces in Spain were frequently relieved. While the number of troops at any given time probably never exceeded 10,000—12,000 fighting men or technicians, by this system of constant reliefs the German army was able to give war-time training to eight or ten times that number of men. In this way the three S.S. regiments composing the Führer's bodyguard were employed in Spain for periods of from three to six months each."

Eight or ten times 10,000—12,000 brings the number of specialists in the German army taking part in the Spanish War nearly up to Italian figures. Let us suppose that the estimate of *Le Temps* is exaggerated (though it comes from a paper which, while interpreting French interests in its own way, certainly never distinguished itself for its sympathies towards loyalist Spain). Let us make a considerable reduction and assume 50,000 German specialists to have served successively in the rebel camp. Can those who have never witnessed the splendid efforts of the Republican army realize the unequal conditions of a struggle in which the enemy could replace its personnel with such facility? Whereas our officers on the General Staff and in the trenches never knew an hour's rest, and while they had to be in two or three places at once because of the scarcity of commanding officers and the deficiencies of those whose enthusiasm and goodwill were greater than their technical abilities, fresh groups of specialists from one of the most powerful armies in Europe were being sent to the rebels every three months or so.

But these men did not come alone. As in the case of the Italians, their arrival was preceded, accompanied, or followed by a vast quantity of war material. Therein lies the key to our defeat. There is no need to distort arguments or to look for causes farther afield. Information regarding this decisive aspect of Italo-German intervention in Spain is scantier, and the figures are not so well known. It is still impossible to state with any precision how many rifles and machine-guns, how many cannon and tanks, how many armoured cars and lorries were received by the rebels from Germany and Italy during the thirty-two months of the war. At all times their superiority in artillery was overwhelming. The Franco authorities admitted it themselves immediately after their victory. A telegram from the Havas Agency in Madrid, dated April 13, 1939, which had passed the censor and which bore all the appearance of an official report, stated that of the 450,000 men estimated to have been killed in the war, only 130,000 were rebels, and explained this disproportion by "the crushing superiority of the Nationalist army in artillery and aviation." The correspondent gave a few details which tally fairly well with our own. "The greatest display of Republican artillery took place in Teruel, where 180 cannon were lined up. On the other side it was in the Ebro counteroffensive that the Nationalists showed their greatest superiority in arms, when General Franco brought up 1,400 cannon to oppose 120 on the enemy front."

The figure of 1,400 pieces of artillery lined up in such a small sector is sufficient to give an idea of the enormous quantity of war material supplied to the rebels by Germany and Italy. Another important detail is the volume of Franco debts.

The totalitarian credits in war material are estimated at about £30,000,000 and £7,000,000 in favour of Italy and Germany respectively. Part of the war debt has already been recovered by despoiling Spain. The war, to Germany and Italy, was a war not only for strategic objectives but also for raw materials. The insistence of the General Staff in the spring of 1937 that the great rebel offensive then in preparation should take place in the north is explained by Germany's desire to gain possession of the vast mineral resources of the Basque country. Bilbao, with its huge smelting works and its abundant iron ore, was a glittering prize. The Germans had their way, against the wishes of General Mola, who wanted to use all his troops in a fresh attack on Madrid. Immediately after the fall of Bilbao, ship after ship began to arrive at the northern Spanish ports, to return later to Hamburg loaded with ore. The country was being looted as a precautionary measure against eventualities.

The Italians, on the other hand, had a greedy eye on Almadén. The object of their repeated attempts to advance in that sector was the quicksilver mines. These mines were the richest in the world and, though only a few miles from the front, had been worked so well by the Republicans that in 1937 they produced 2,500 tons, the highest yield for ten years.

An examination of the graph of so-called exports to Germany and Italy over the past two years will show how the saviours of Spain, in the midst of their ideological preoccupations, took advantage of the splendid opportunity offered them to feed their war industries, in preparation for the extension of their civilizing influence to other nations. In 1938 Germany imported from Spain 1,000,000 tons of iron ore, against 310,000 tons in 1937; 25,563 tons of copper against 7,309 in 1937; 13,167 tons of zinc where none had been imported in the preceding year. Italy also managed to provide herself—although in much smaller proportions—with some of the raw materials (principally wool) which she needed, and she now has free access to the quicksilver which she was unable to obtain by her repeated attacks on Almadén.

A further aspect of Italo-German intervention—that of aviation—remains to be examined. Among the many German and Italian testimonies concerning the activities of the air forces of both countries during the Spanish War, there are two publications which I recommend to all those who still refuse to believe that it was Germany and Italy, and not Franco, who won the war.

Published in Rome during the war, *L'Aviazione Legionaria in Spagna* by Guido Mattioli may be considered an official publication, since it could never have appeared without the approval of the Italian Government. With a remarkable collection of photographs and a short but informative text, it gives a most convincing picture of the manner in which, from the very beginning, Italy assisted the rebels in the air. "On August 4, 1936 General Franco was able to pass in review, in Tetuán, a formation of 9 trimotor Savoia 81's, heavy bombers." On page 34 we find a description of their participation in the attack on Majorca: "At the same time the legionary air force co-operated in the occupation of the largest of the Balearic Islands. A handful of legionaries in civilian attire carried out the coup in Palma, with a patrol of airmen from the Tercio to assist in these spirited adventures from above. In twenty-four hours the situation on the island was changed. Majorca was bound to become, as she became, a formidable base for the legionary air force." On page 40 their action extends to the interior of Spain: "Mérida, Badajoz, Guadiz, Antequera, Córdoba, Málaga, Costa del Río, Oropesa, Toledo, Huelva—in all these towns the powerful legionary trimotors were a frequent sight. All over Spain the Nationalist columns marched with the support and the protection of the legionary air forces." On page 107 there is a just appreciation of the progress of the "Nationalist air force": "Soon General Franco and the Nationalists possessed, as we have seen, a nucleus of bombing planes, a nucleus which grew into the forcible organism which it is today. With the Savoia 81's, the Savoia 79's, and the Breda 20's, products of Italian industry, aided by the German Junkers, the Italian legionaries, and the German volunteers, General Franco quickly succeeded in creating a powerful bombing force, which, even on its formation, as we have seen, rendered most valuable service in the cause of Nationalist Spain." The British Foreign Office, at least, had seen this interesting publication. The Spanish Embassy in London forwarded it with a covering note, which rather naturally received no acknowledgment.

The other publication is the impressive special number of

Die Wehrmacht, published in Berlin in the summer of 1939 with the arrogant title: *Wir Kämpften in Spanien (We Fought in Spain),* the principal collaborators in which were Captain Dr. Ritter von Goss, a member of the Reichswehr High Command, General Sperrle, Colonel Freiherr von Funck, Captain Edler von der Planitz, and other distinguished heroes who took part in the destruction of Spain. Each one describes the part played by his unit in the Spanish War. With great pride in his work, Captain von Goss says that, thanks to the effective co-operation of the Condor Legion, "no longer in the spring of 1937 could one talk merely of the *Spanish* War. It had become a real war," and describes "how German soldiers, carrying out their duties in exemplary fashion, and in most difficult circumstances, performed discreetly but effectively their task of forming the new Spanish army."

As far as aviation was concerned, Franco depended entirely on the generosity of his allies. The powerful air arm of which he was later so proud was ninety-eight per cent Italian and German. Numerically the Italians were the dominating force, but in material and personnel the Germans were throughout the war superior to the Italians. Our enemy in the air was Germany.

The first German machines which made their appearance in Spain—the Junker trimotors and Heinkel pursuit planes—were not of any great importance. They were antiquated and manifestly inferior to the machines which we had bought in Russia. From the moment the Messerschmidt came into action, however, the Germans had at their disposal in Spain a magnificent fleet of bombing planes, a handful of which were worth all the Fiats put together. Our airmen were never very much impressed with the Italian material employed in Spain; the "legionary air force" which, with its headquarters in Majorca, constituted the bulk of the rebel air arm (of which General Kindelán was only the nominal leader) was able to display considerable activity on account of the large number of machines of which it was composed, but not on account of their quality nor of the exceptional ability of their pilots. So far as quantity is concerned, the lion's share was supplied by Rome. This is confirmed not only by a large number of Italian documents, but also by Mussolini's own words in the Italian Senate on March 30, 1938, when, alluding to Abyssinia and Spain, he declared: "Thousands of machines and pilots have been tried out in these two wars."

But the aerial war in Abyssinia, although entirely an Italian affair, was child's play compared with the Italian air war in Spain. During the whole Ethiopian campaign 400 Italian airplanes were used, carrying out 3,979 raids in 35,000 hours of flight, and dropping 1,500 tons of explosives. Let us compare these official figures of the Air Ministry with the no less official ones of the November 1938 number of the review *La Via dell' Aire:* "Better than any specific account of brilliant episodes, the figures speak for themselves: In the Year XVI, and between November 1 (1937) and October 22 (1938), the legionary air force made 26,880 flights, and dropped 7,720 tons of explosives in the course of 3,465 bombing operations."

Finally, according to the official statistics for the whole of the Spanish War—published in the Italian press in June 1939 —there were 86,420 air raids on loyalist Spain, compared with 3,979 during the Ethiopian War; 5,318 bombardments in western Europe compared with 872 in east Africa; 11,584 tons of explosives hurled on the Spanish people, compared with 1,500 tons on the Abyssinian Negroes.

During a considerable period of the war the rebels had some 600 to 650 first-line planes permanently at their disposal. This assumes the dispatch of thousands of machines to Spain from Germany and Italy. On the outbreak of the rebellion Franco could have counted his seaplanes—half of them antiquated and useless—on the fingers of one hand. The numerical inferiority of our air force to that of the enemy was regularly in the proportion of between 1 to 5 and 1 to 6. At times the ratio was even more to our disadvantage. When the Republican army withdrew from the Talavera front, we had only one pursuit machine for the whole of Spain.

Our airmen were thus subjected to a gruelling task. After fighting all day on the Madrid front they would, if fresh operations were to take place in the south, be obliged to set off again at five in the afternoon, snatch a few hours' sleep, and go once more into action. This was possible only thanks to the excellent organization of the land services. In every aerodrome fresh crews awaited the return of the squadrons. The machines had hardly landed before they were ready to go up again. Thus by this multiplication of personnel the Republican air force, which at no time consisted of more than 120 to 130 first-line planes, was able to stand up to an enemy five or six times more powerful.

There was no lack of pilots. The Republican schools turned out all the airmen necessary. Others were sent to French and some to Russian training schools. Six months were enough to train a good pilot. The men were recruited from the fronts and were mostly workmen. Their ability was proved by the mere fact that it was in Spain on the Republican side that, for the first time in the history of aviation, organized night pursuits were carried out—and with excellent results. The invaders never made any attempt to do this.

In the construction of airplanes miracles were performed. At the end of the war we were turning out two a day, including engines, with the exception of certain parts which had still to be imported, but which in a short space of time would also have been manufactured by us.

On the other hand, not only the machines, but also the crews of the rebel air arm were for the most part Italian and German. As is clear from the words of the Duce already quoted, the pressing desire of the two dictators was to obtain the greatest possible number of experienced aviators. The Spanish skies were the training ground *par excellence* for the Axis airmen. In April 1938 the Italian press stated that "from March 10 to April 9 last, the Italian air force, 5,346 men strong, has carried out a total of 10,898 hours' flight." There were, therefore, at a given moment, 5,346 Italian aviators, pilots, and auxiliaries in Spain. If we take a proportionate figure for German airmen, bearing in mind the frequency with which the German command renewed its personnel in Spain, and adding the relief forces, it is no exaggeration to say that Italy and Germany sent to Spain, not merely to dominate the country but also to train men for a future European war, more than 50,000 aviators.

The following details give some idea of the proportion of Italian, German, and Spanish combatants. Over a period of twelve months the number of rebel airmen who were taken prisoner by the Republicans, or whose bodies were discovered and identified, was as follows: 98 Italians, 49 Germans, and 16 Spaniards. It would not be unreasonable to apply that proportion to the whole of that "Nationalist air force" which vented its fury so cruelly on the towns and villages of Spain.

"God sent the best airmen in the world to assist us," exclaimed General Kindelán in his farewell speech to the Italian and German aviators. I do not know whether the British and American Catholics who sympathized with Franco will also see in the massacre of thousands of Spanish women and children the hand of Divine Providence. But these words of General Kindelán at least show some signs of humility and gratitude, and have more respect for reality than his telegram to General Valle, chief of the Italian air force, in which he declared: "Together we have gained the victory; together we will triumph in future enterprises." On the other hand, the political significance of this second message is greater, and if there is anything in the wide world capable of making British and French statesmen see the Spanish question clearly, this should have been enough to open their eyes. Yet even now Great Britain and France toy with the idea of winning the favour and friendship of those who owe their entire victory to Germany and Italy and who are today—as they were throughout the Spanish War—the natural allies of the totalitarian states.

CHAPTER IV

Counter "Non-Intervention"—Russia's Role

In the last week of October Russian war material reached us. On October 29 Russian tanks and artillery made their first appearance on our front. On November 11 the first Russian plane appeared in Spanish skies.

For three months before this, German and Italian material had been coming in, unhindered by the London Committee or by anybody else. For three months our rights had been denied us, and this was not to be the last time in the appeasement chapter that a free republic was to be handed over *by its friends.* Or perhaps it should be said otherwise: for three months our friends, the nations which should have been our friends, scrupulously observed their pledges under the "Non-Intervention" plan and with equal scrupulousness refrained from insisting on a similar observance by the powers that were so openly aiding General Franco.

The powers to which, during the brief history of our Republic, we had become accustomed to look as our friends might have abandoned Non-Intervention when they saw that it was being used to strangle us and to carry Franco to victory.

They might have. And many in those countries recognize ruefully today that they should have. But they did not. Only Russia—after three months—refused to play at the farce of Non-Intervention any longer.

Then from October 29 right on until the end of the war we received Russian aid. We never thought we could win with Russian aid alone. Not a day passed, until almost the end, when we did not have fresh reasons to hope that the Western democracies would come to their senses and restore us our rights to buy from them. And always our hopes proved illusory.

I will tell the story from the beginning.

That the French Government should have been the one officially to take the initiative of proposing, late in July 1936, the conclusion of a Non-Intervention agreement came as a shock to democrats everywhere. For Socialists it was especially disagreeable that it was M. Léon Blum who, as head of the French Government, sponsored the scheme.

Throughout the whole of the Spanish war the conduct of the Second International was to be blighted by this original error. The various sections of the Second International thought it incumbent on them to support a policy that, ostensibly at least, had been fathered by the distinguished leader of the French Socialist Party. There were some praiseworthy exceptions among Socialists in various European countries who from the start saw Non-Intervention for what it was. There was a considerable number of them. I can think now of Emil Vandervelde, former Foreign Minister of Belgium, Senator Louis de Brouckère, Belgian delegate to the League, Pietro Nenni, exiled Italian Socialist leader, Senator Georg Branting of Sweden, Isabel Blume and Camille Huysmans of the Belgian party.

The simple truth is that Non-Intervention was fathered in London. The legal experts of the British Foreign Office must not have been very proud of their brain child; for they made such efforts to attribute its paternity to a person less suspect than they of hostility to democratic principles. In M. Blum and the French Government they found the ideal sponsors for their creation and thus they were able to kill two birds with one stone. On the one hand they were able to avoid what would surely have been a quick and dangerous revulsion from the millions of supporters of the Popular Front in France who would certainly have raged against the plan had it been frankly labelled what it was, the work of a British Tory Government. On the other hand they were able to justify the plan to their own Labour opposition, in Parliament and in the country, by evoking its supposed paternity. And the more ductile British Labour leaders were quick to declare that what was good enough for Blum was good enough for them.

But we Spanish Socialists were never able to understand, much less to defend, the line taken by our French comrades. He among us who exhibited the greatest indignation was Indalecio Prieto. And his expressions of indignation were in the highly temperamental key that Spaniards are so used to from him. He made no secret of his deep disillusionment and of his bitterness, and these sentiments were widely publicized in the foreign press in the early days of Non-Intervention. Neither time nor the explanations which our French friends gave us in confidence were ever able to placate him. Perhaps this bitterness on Prieto's part accounts for his stand in the summer of 1937 when the question of the fusion of Socialist and Communist parties was raised. This was at a meeting of the Executive Committee of the Spanish Socialist Party in Valencia in midsummer. Señor Prieto came out flatly in favour of fusion and of a policy which, he said, should take into account "the fact that the only help we could ever hope for was what we were getting from Russia in view of the defection of the Western democracies." I cannot here give his exact words, for I was not present at the meeting.[1]

[1] At that time I was not, as today, a member of the Executive Committee of the Socialist Party. Thus I was not present. But Señor Prieto's attitude at that time, as I have given it here, was cited, in his hearing, by that old and

68 *Freedom's Battle*

In Paris those who defended Blum's position always said two things: first, that he had had to submit to British pressure; and, second, that he was striving to avoid a European war. That there was British pressure no one can now deny. In the preface to the English edition of that revelatory book by Mr. E. M. Dzelepy: *The Spanish Plot*,[2] Pertinax (André Geraud) tells us how "at the beginning of August M. Léon Blum was informed that the guarantee given by Great Britain to maintain the frontiers of France would not remain valid in the event of independent French action beyond the Pyrenees. This was the origin of the policy of Non-Intervention."

This British warning, as we knew at the time, was conveyed to M. Yvon Delbos, the French Minister of Foreign Affairs, in the course of a visit by Sir George Clerk, British Ambassador to Paris. Sir George is understood to have said that if France should find herself in conflict with Germany as a result of having sold war material to the Spanish Government, England would consider herself released from her obligations under the Locarno Pact and would not come to help.

From that day on, the Quai d'Orsay, in all that referred to Spain, became a branch of the Foreign Office. France lost her independence as to foreign policy. If only there had been a Louis Barthou in charge of French diplomacy! Barthou was a conservative all his life. At the age of seventy he had more imagination and more courage than all the functionaries under him. And not only did he bring to a successful conclusion the French-Soviet pact, but he was magnificent in his mockery of enemies who tried to make him out as prey to a kind of Bolshevism of senility. With a Barthou in the Quai d'Orsay the British bluff would never have been attempted.

respected Socialist Manuel Cordero at a meeting of the Executive Committee of the party in Paris in July 1939. At that meeting I was present, having been elected to membership. Señor Cordero, whose integrity and authority in Spanish Socialist circles have never been questioned, brought up the fact that at the Valencia meeting Prieto had taken the position above referred to. Prieto listened to what Señor Cordero had to say and did not demur.

2 London: P. S. King & Son; 1937.

Of course, with Hitler in power, France needed English support. *But* a good French army was no less indispensable to Great Britain.

The fact remains that while in July 1936 France ostensibly took the initiative in proposing Non-Intervention, for the next three years she was to be denied any initiative whatsoever. Every time I tried to convince our French friends that their Spanish policy was suicidal, I heard from them with sorrow the same evasions. "It is in London that you should exert yourselves," they would say.

Then there were those who held that the Blum Government, in proposing Non-Intervention, was motivated by a determination to avoid war in Europe. According to this view, the French Government was sincere when, on August 8, 1936, in its decree suspending "all exports of war materials destined for Spain," it stated its confident belief that its attitude would facilitate "the quickest possible conclusion" of an agreement "in the interests of international peace." The Blum Government found itself paralysed by the double fear of losing the support of England and of finding itself engaged in a general war. And this paralysis set in during those first weeks of the war when the Republican army, had it been able to count on a mere hundred planes and very little more in the way of artillery, as M. Blum later admitted, would have been able to put down the military rebellion before German and Italian help could have reached Franco to any decisive extent. There were in the French Government a number of ministers who not only sympathized with the Spanish Republic but were justifiably preoccupied by the danger to France; they argued that France could stand by the Non-Intervention agreement and at the same time enable the Republican Government to receive enough in the way of armament to counteract the aid which was being given discreetly to the rebels by the totalitarian states. This was also the view of the most influential sector of the French General Staff.

In French Cabinet councils, there were serious clashes of opposing viewpoints. At one notable meeting of the Cabinet the President of the Republic took the Air Minister, Pierre Cot, most severely to task because of certain charges in the reactionary press in Paris that a French war plane of late model had reached the Republican Government. Pierre Cot took advantage of the President's attack to set forth with exceeding frankness his own views on the Spanish problem. Certain other members of the Cabinet backed him up. But the discussion was brought to an abrupt end when President Lebrun turned on the Minister of Air and, in tones both solemn and sharp, said: "Monsieur, you are asking for war! (*Vous voulez la guerre!*)" Pierre Cot, startled and indignant, turned to his Prime Minister for support. But M. Léon Blum chose to sit in silence.

It would be unjust, however, not to point out that later realization of the mistake committed in these early weeks, which was to bring in its wake such disastrous consequences for France, was to cause the Socialist Premier much anguish. Every time I went through Paris it was my duty to go to him and tell him frankly how things were going; at such meetings I saw his grief and something like despair. That he felt this despair attested to his deep sensitivity but does not absolve Léon Blum from the political responsibility he incurred when he gave his name and that of the French Socialist Party to the farce of Non-Intervention.

Today no one should be able to deny that the collapse of the Spanish Republic was due to Non-Intervention. Today, after the entry of Hitler's troops into Prague, and almost every other development on the international scene have confirmed our contention that appeasement, which reached the supreme limits of folly in the case of Spain, would lead inevitably to war, there are still people who contend that Non-Intervention held off the conflagration.

For Professor Norman J. Padelford of the Fletcher School, Non-Intervention was justified historically for that reason.

He writes: "If the devices have not succeeded altogether in stopping the entrance of supplies and men into Spain: If they have glossed or provided a screen behind which violations of pledged undertakings have occurred; if they have become popular laughing stock and have allowed unfortunate Spain to become a military laboratory for the testing of weapons and strategy, they have, nevertheless, been instrumental, with other things perhaps, in averting an extension of hostilities to other territories." [1]

In his opus the distinguished American scholar leaves nothing to be desired when he treats of the theoretical applications of Non-Intervention in Spain. The months to come will show whether his opinion that by Non-Intervention a European war was avoided will stand up.

Professor Padelford's view is not shared by the realistically minded Herr von Rauschning. In an article in *Foreign Affairs,* Herr Rauschning, his eyes opened by years of association with the Führer, said: "In essence the war was being fought all along. It was stupid then to try to prevent its breaking out."

A week after the Blum Government had issued its invitation to the powers to enter an agreement to Non-Intervene in Spain, the Government of the Soviet Union accepted the French proposal. This was on August 10. As a consequence of this acceptance the foreign trade commissariat in Moscow issued on August 28 a decree forbidding the "export, re-export, or transit to Spain of all kinds of arms, munitions, war material, airplanes, and warships."

In Geneva at the Assembly of the League of Nations on September 25, where I publicly denounced "the legal monstrosity of the formula of 'Non-Intervention,'" M. Litvinov, the Soviet Foreign Minister, explained why his Government had given its approval to a plan which contravened the most widely accepted principles of international law.

"The Soviet Government," declared M. Litvinov, "ad-

[1] *International Law and Diplomacy in the Spanish Civil Strife* (New York: The Macmillan Company; 1937).

hered to the agreement of non-interference in the affairs of Spain only because a friendly country feared the possibility otherwise of an international conflict. We acted thus in spite of the fact that we considered the principle of neutrality inapplicable to war levied by rebels against their lawful government, and, on the contrary, to be a breach of the principles of international law—on which point we are in full agreement with the views of the Spanish Minister for Foreign Affairs."

But the definitive reply from Berlin and Rome to the invitation to adhere to the Non-Intervention plan was held up many weeks, during which period the rebels continued to receive war material, as they had received it from the very first days of the movement from German and Italian ports, and naturally this was the reason for the delay in the Italo-German reply. In these critical weeks, while quibbling notes were being exchanged between Berlin and Paris, and Rome and Paris, the Germans and Italians thought to send enough in the way of airplanes, artillery, and munitions to secure the victory of their puppet rebel. But, as at many other times during the course of the war, the calculations of Franco's foreign backers turned out to be wrong. Republican resistance proved stronger than the very metal of the cannons, tanks, and planes which had been considered sufficient to carry the rebel advance to Madrid. Then no sooner had Germany and Italy reluctantly accepted the French invitation—with so many conditions and reservations as to render their acceptance quite valueless—than General Franco had to appeal for more war material, with the result that while Paris and London were celebrating the conclusion of the Non-Intervention agreement, it was already being violated.

On my desk on the very first day that I took over the Ministry of State I found a whole series of reports on such violations. The Non-Intervention agreement was then hardly two weeks old. My first task was to examine these reports, and on September 15 I sent to the Governments of Germany,

Italy, Portugal, and the other signatories of the agreement a note proving these violations and underlining the fact that they were in flagrant contradiction in the cases of Italy and Portugal not only of the Non-Intervention agreement but also of the Covenant of the League. This was the first in a long series of protests that were to be ignored in the Non-Intervention Committee and by the French and British Governments, which were responsible for the very fact of Non-Intervention and were thus morally obligated to Spain, to their own peoples, and to the world to exact its strict observance.

The fact has been established that on July 15, 1936, two days before the rebellion broke out in Morocco, Italian pilots received orders to prepare war planes of Italian army aviation units for flight to Spain. It was on July 30, 1936 that Colonel Yagüe, subsequently Air Minister in Franco's Government and now a General, broadcast from Ceuta the news that a certain number of Italian planes had arrived in Spanish Morocco. Some hours before, three of these planes had crashed in Algeria and it was the examination of their pilots by General Denain, former French Air Minister, that elicited the revelation that the expedition had been prepared before the outbreak of the rebellion. It was not until November 15— *four months later*—that the first Russian planes went into action on the loyalist side.

Thus Italian and German intervention came at the very outbreak of the rebellion in July (German planes began to arrive on July 28). And Russian "intervention" came four months later. The fact that four critical months elapsed between the appearance in Spanish skies of the first Nazi and Fascist planes in General Franco's service and the appearance over beleaguered Madrid of the first Russian planes is often, too often, ignored by those who persist in considering Russian "intervention" in Spain as no different from German and Italian intervention.

During these months the Soviet Government had repeatedly protested the violations of the Non-Intervention agreement by Germany and Italy. And it was the Moscow Government that was the first, and only, government to propose to the Non-Intervention Committee, long before a single Russian cartridge had ever been dispatched to Spain, the setting up of an effective control system over Spanish and Portuguese ports. If this proposal had been accepted, it would have made Non-Intervention a reality. But it was turned down.

Only after German and Italian intervention had been repeatedly but futilely denounced by the Russians did the Soviet Government at last inform the Non-Intervention Committee that it could no longer be bound by the agreement "to any greater extent than any of the remaining participants of the agreement." This declaration was made in a note handed to Lord Plymouth by the Soviet Ambassador on October 23, 1936. Because its terms are important I quote them in full:

"In adhering with other states to the agreement for non-intervention in Spanish affairs, the Government of the Soviet Union expected that the agreement would be fulfilled by its participants, that as the result of this the period of civil war in Spain would be shortened and the number of victims reduced.

"The time that has elapsed, however, has shown that the agreement is being systematically violated by a number of its participants—that the supply of arms to the rebels goes on unpunished.

"One of the participants to the agreement, Portugal, has become the main base of supply for the rebels, whilst the legitimate Government of Spain has turned out to be, in fact, under boycott, deprived of facilities to purchase arms outside Spain for the defence of the Spanish people.

"Thus, as the result of the violations of the agreement, a privileged situation for the rebels has been created, which situation was in no case within the purpose of the agreement.

"As the result of this abnormal situation there is a prolongation of the civil war in Spain and an increase in the number of its victims.

"The efforts of the representative of the Soviet Government to put a stop to the practice of violating the agreement have not found support in the Committee. The last proposal of the Soviet representative in regard to control over the ports of Portugal, which is the main base of supply for the rebels, has also not found support and has not even been placed on the agenda for today's meeting of the Committee.

"Thus the agreement has turned out to be an empty, torn scrap of paper. It has ceased in practice to exist.

"Not wishing to remain in the position of persons unwittingly assisting an unjust cause, the Government of the Soviet Union sees only one way out of the situation created—to return to the Spanish Government the facilities to purchase arms outside of Spain, which rights and facilities are enjoyed at present by the Governments of the world, and to extend to the participants of the agreement the right to sell or not to sell arms to Spain.

"In any case, the Soviet Government, unwilling to bear any longer the responsibilities for the clearly unjust situation created in regard to the legitimate Spanish Government and Spanish people, is compelled now to declare that in accordance with its statement on October 7 it cannot consider itself bound by the agreement for non-intervention to any greater extent than any of the remaining participants of the agreement."

Meanwhile German and Italian violations did not cease. Far from it! Throughout the month of October Germany and Italy poured in material to support Franco's great offensive that followed the capture of Toledo and that was supposed to end in glory with the capture of Madrid. Soviet Russia made good her word. Her answer to Non-Intervention, which had been turned into a sinister farce, was counter-non-intervention, if I may be permitted to manufacture the term. After all, what Russia did at that time was simply to revert to the normal practice of selling arms to a legitimate government. And arms continued to arrive from Russia. As Dr. Negrín pointed out in his address in May 1939 before the Council on Foreign Relations in New York: "Moscow tried to do for France and England what they should have done for themselves. The promise of Soviet aid to the Spanish Republic was that ultimately Paris and London would awake to the risks involved to themselves in an Italo-German victory in Spain and join the U.S.S.R. in supporting us. Munich, with its unnecessary surrender to the totalitarians, probably crushed this hope beyond repair. Moscow alone could not have saved us at any time. France and England never acted as their Imperial interests dictated. Some day there may be a rude awakening, and they will look for aid to the very people whom they helped to destroy through Non-Intervention.

"Of course we bought from Russia what, had the democracies observed international law and protected their national interests, we should have been able to buy from the United States, France, and England. Would you have asked us to refuse Russian arms when we could not get arms anywhere else?"

For Spain, Russia was a source of supply. For Russia, Spain was another dike to hold against the waves of aggression that were undermining the never too strong structure of collective security. In Spain and in China Russia gave material evidence of her policy of trying to give reality to collective security as she gave verbal evidence at the Disarmament Conference and at the sessions of the League.

At no time did the Russian Government attempt, as certain persons have charged, out of their ignorance or bad faith, to make use of the fact that we were dependent on the Soviet Union for arms, to interfere in internal Spanish politics. It may be recalled by my American readers that a letter from Stalin to Largo Caballero published in facsimile in the *New*

York Times in May 1939 urged the Spanish Premier to maintain a genuine popular front rather than to push revolutionary principles to the detriment of Spanish unity.

It would be an endless task to attempt to deal with the many and fantastic charges both from the Right and from various factions of the Left that Russian agents and Spanish Communists ran the Spanish Government during the war. This obsession has led its victims into several amusing contradictions. For example, there are those who insist that the Barcelona *"Putsch"* of May 1937 was provoked by the Communists in order to bring about the fall of Largo Caballero while on the other hand others insist that it was the Russian Embassy and the Communists who were responsible for what they term the "bloody repression" of the instigators of the revolt—that is, the members of the P.O.U.M. The Communists could hardly be at one and the same time the authors of the revolt and the prosecutors of the authors of the revolt. This is only one example of the ridiculous lengths to which the scaremongers of a Sovietized Spain have gone.

It is false to say, as some have said, that in March 1938 the Russians cut down their arms shipments to us in order to provoke the military disaster of the Aragon front and the fall of Indalecio Prieto, then Minister of Defence, and to replace him with Dr. Negrín, or that with Dr. Negrín as Premier and Minister of Defence in the fall of 1938 they pinched off supplies in order to provoke the fall of Barcelona. What happened is that after the sinking of the Russian freighter *Komsomol* on December 14, 1936 off the coast of Africa by the Italians, shipments of Russian material to loyalist ports by sea fell off and shipments overland depended entirely on the facilities of transit accorded us by the French.

If France or England, or for that matter the United States, had wanted at any time to counteract "Soviet influence" in Spain, they would have known what to do. "Soviet influence" in Spain was the result largely of the fact that when all the world persisted in denying us our legal rights to purchase arms for our defence, Russia restored us that right. In selling us arms the Russian Government was adhering to the normal practices of international law. Thus the British and French Governments, and the American Government, had they really desired to counteract "Soviet influence," had only to do likewise. Certainly there was no reason for them not to do so, once the fact that Germany and Italy were openly and repeatedly violating the Non-Intervention agreement had become evident. We bought arms where we could. We had no preferences. And certainly we had no prejudices against the excellent material of war manufactured in France, in England, and in the United States. France and Britain were themselves responsible for denying their arms-manufacturers our lucrative business.

There was one other country besides Russia that stood fast by its rights in relation to Republican Spain. That was Mexico. Under the inspired and energetic leadership of President Lázaro Cárdenas, Mexico gave to the Americas and to the world an example of honourable and intelligent and consistent conduct of international affairs. With the assistance of his Foreign Secretary, General Hay, and his young and capable Under-Secretary of Foreign Affairs, Ramón Beteta, President Cárdenas followed throughout the war in Spain a course of conduct which will stand in history along with his other statesmanlike achievements. Moreover, when the war was lost, Mexico not only refused to recognize Franco, but generously opened her doors to the Spanish Republic in exile.

CHAPTER V

The Great Ambition

IT WOULD BE ABSURD to suppose that the tremendous efforts made by Germany and Italy in Spain, and the placing of their men, war material, technicians, and best officers at the service of the rebels in the proportions which we have just seen, were due to caprice on the part of Mussolini and Hitler; or that the two dictators were merely anxious to have a new colleague with whom to celebrate the triumph of totalitarian ideology, and a few million Spaniards saluting, willy-nilly, in the Fascist style. Behind the scenes where one of the most ingenious comedies of the Fascist repertoire (which might well bear the title: "True love means possession") was being presented for public entertainment, the desire for expansion and hegemony inspiring the whole policy of the two totalitarian states was only too evident.

Neither of the dictators, certainly, ever lost a favourable opportunity to proclaim loudly that his assistance to the rebels was as altruistic as it was innocent. In the Appendix to the Anglo-Italian Agreement of April 16, 1938, there figures a letter from Count Ciano reiterating that "Italy has no territorial or political ambitions, and seeks no economic privileges in Spain, the Balearic Islands, overseas territories, or the Spanish Moroccan zone; neither has she any intention of maintaining armed forces in those regions." The Chancellor of the Reich, for his part, at the diplomatic reception in Berlin on January 11, 1937, gave the most categoric assurances to the French Ambassador that "it was not and never had been Germany's intention to violate the integrity of Spain, or of the Spanish possessions." Three weeks later, in his important speech of January 30, Hitler stressed even more firmly the disinterested nature of German sympathies for General Franco.

I do not deny that the two dictators are bound by an ideological link—the feeling that they must rise or fall together "defending the Fascist régimes," as Signor Virginio Gayda puts it; but only those who have understood nothing of the Spanish War and of Italo-German intervention could fail to see that Hitler and Mussolini were prompted to act by far more material and selfish motives. Their intervention in Spain was a further step towards European domination.

They could not have chosen a better moment for this intervention. With the conquest of Abyssinia, Italy had gained an unexpected victory. Faced with a hostile Great Britain (supported by fifty-one nations at Geneva), and with economic difficulties great enough in themselves to condemn a less ambitious enterprise to failure, Italy realized the long-cherished imperialist dream of Fascism. From his favourite rostrum, the balcony of the Venezia Palace, on May 9, 1936—four days after the entry of the Italian troops into Addis Ababa—Mussolini proclaimed to a multitude carried away by his fiery eloquence and the significance of the occasion: "The Italian people have created the Empire with their own life-blood. They will strengthen it with their work and defend it with their weapons. In this supreme assurance, legionaries, raise high your standards, your hearts, and your swords, to greet—after fifteen centuries—the reappearance of the Empire on these Roman hills where destiny has set its seal!"

An absurd policy of strong resolutions and feeble actions had delivered up an Empire into Italy's hands. Not only was Italy presented with an Empire at the cost of sacrificing an independent and sovereign state, but this also gave her a sensation of strength which, though illusory, encouraged her to follow the path she had chosen, a path which led directly to intervention in Spain. Any visitor to Italy during the last few months of the Ethiopian campaign must have heard the taxi-drivers in the streets and the waiters in the cafés boasting, not of having subdued the Negus, but of having defeated Great Britain. The fears expressed by Joseph Chamberlain many years ago, when France and Russia seemed on the point of forming an alliance against Great Britain, that the British fleet might one day have to abandon its traditional stations—"if it could manage to escape"—were, after a long and undisputed dominion of the seas, suddenly realized. What excited the Italians more than the entry of the royal troops into Addis Ababa was the sight of the British fleet hastily leaving Malta for a safer harbour.

But if the conquest of Abyssinia was a complete success for the policy of prestige on which the very existence of the totalitarian régimes depends, the new Empire in itself was very far from being the paradise described by official propaganda when Italy was being prepared for war. The photographs of Ethiopian cotton plantations dazzled the eyes of a population accustomed, through the extravagances and catastrophes of Fascist economy, to nourish themselves on dreams of grandeur rather than bread. In practice colonization met with tremendous obstacles. While at the beginning of 1937, when there was still enthusiasm for the new "place in the sun" which Mussolini's determination and ability had won for Italy, the number of Italian workmen in Abyssinia rose rapidly to 115,000, only a year later it had fallen to 36,000. In the meantime all that the colonists succeeded in doing was to disorganize agricultural production. An attempt to industrialize the country, in order to give the impression of Italian initiative and energy, meant that thousands of natives, attracted by the higher wages which were being paid in the new undertakings, were lured away from the fields. The failure of the attempts to substitute the lira for the thaler further complicated a situation whose real difficulty lay in the fact that, as was even admitted in Italy, "military must be in attendance on every convoy." The eight million bayonets on which the Duce, in his Milan speech of the autumn of 1936, offered an olive branch to the world were no doubt very useful to impress those who so effectively furthered totalitarian strategy by their own professions of fear; but they could not make a success of a colonization which was carried on in an entirely hostile manner and which for many years to come will not produce enough to free Italy from complete dependence on foreign countries for her oil, cotton, coal, and other important raw materials. Abyssinia could not content her. Abyssinia was the starting-point for her expansionist policy, and not the winning-post. Fascist Italy, with her gaze turned towards the European scene, realized that her upward flight would be safer if she took off from Spanish earth.

In the ambitious project of the two totalitarian states, carried out with impressive firmness and persistence (sometimes disguised as an ideological crusade and sometimes justified by the need for "living-room," but in fact aiming at world domination), one of the decisive blows must be the changing of the present situation in the Mediterranean. Not for nothing have the Italian publicists and Nazi geo-politicians given up most of their time in recent years to the problems of the Mediterranean. The title of one of their many books, *Weltentscheidung im Mittelmeer* (*World Determination in the Mediterranean*) says more than ten volumes put together. In the present struggle for power the Mediterranean seems to Germany and Italy the ideal place for inflicting final defeat on the democracies. Whoever holds the Mediterranean card wins the game. This idea is developed in the very interesting and well-documented book by Frau Margret Boveri, *Das Weltgeschehen im Mittelmeer* (*World Events in the Mediterranean*), in which the distinguished correspondent of the *Berliner Tageblatt*, after discussing the various reasons why the Mediterranean has become the favourite strategic zone, expounds the three possible causes of an extensive conflict in a region where the future of Europe—at the least—will be decided. First of all there is the antagonism between certain European nations with a desire for expansion and certain others who are unwilling to grant their just claims—Italy on the one hand and Great Britain and France on the other. "But Italy," adds Frau Boveri, "is not the only power who wishes to extend her influence in the Mediterranean." Secondly, there is the clash of interests between peoples subjected to a colonial or semi-colonial régime, with their natural longing for independence, and the exploiters with their determination to retain power. The third reason—which in the author's opinion introduces a modern factor and gives added interest to a sea which, though apparently calm, is so often the home of violent tempests—is "the conflict between the ideologies of the totalitarian powers on the one hand and of the democracies on the other."

It should be noted that in the case of each of the three conflicts foreshadowed, there is a clear division between the two camps—with Germany and Italy on the one side and Great Britain and France on the other. And midway between them is Spain, which, though no reference is made to her, will nevertheless be of no small importance when the time comes for her to throw her weight into the scales.

The two positions are not easily reconcilable. The Western democracies have every interest in maintaining the *status quo* in the Mediterranean, and the totalitarian powers in destroying it. The intervention of the latter in Spain represented their first serious attempt—and in the main a successful one—to put an end to an established situation which was in itself the main obstacle in their triumphal progress.

For Great Britain and France the maintenance of the *status quo* is, as everyone knows, of vital importance. The Mediterranean is the road to their possessions in Africa and in the Near and Far East. "If our Imperial routes were destroyed," said the French Prime Minister in October 1938, "there would be little hope for Alsace and Lorraine." The bulwarks of Empire are in the Mediterranean as well as in the mother country. France's enemies are the first to realize this. In the *Military Geography of the World Sea,* published a year ago by the War Ministry of the Reich, one can read: "By reason of the geographical situation of the mother country in relation to her colonies, the first task of the French navy is to carry out its protective mission in the Mediterranean and to maintain permanent communication between the French ports of the Mediterranean and those in Africa. It must not be forgotten that the French colonies in Africa—principally Algeria—are in a sense part of the mother country." The *Militär-Wochenblatt,* an organ of the same Ministry, also points out in its issue of February 25, 1938 that these observations apply not only to the north-south route, but also to the west-east route. "Not merely in Africa, but also in the Near and Far East and in Oceania, France owns territories of the greatest importance, which provide her with a large quantity of essential products; and all the routes between these possessions and the mother country converge in the Mediterranean. In consequence, France is as much concerned as Great Britain to maintain her maritime communications by way of the eastern Mediterranean, and to ensure, in the event of complications, that the western Mediterranean is free from all interference on the part of those powers which have not succumbed to French influence."

The memory of how the Moroccan divisions, sent at the eleventh hour to the front line by Joffre, became the deciding factor in the Battle of the Marne, is still very vivid in German minds.

The isolation of France was naturally Hitler's chief concern when, in the Bible of National Socialism, he laid down the principles of the foreign policy of Greater Germany. In *Mein Kampf,* after the famous definition of France—whether governed by the Bourbons or the Jacobins, the partisans of Napoleon or the bourgeois democrats, the clerical republicans or the Red Bolsheviks—as "the mortal enemy," the following passage occurs: [1] "A second war will come. It is essential to isolate France in such a way that in this second war Germany does not have to fight the whole world, but instead has to defend herself against a France who is disturbing the world and disturbing peace." Politically the attempt has failed. In spite of all the mistakes which have been made, France is not alone. The venture can therefore only be carried out in part, by isolating France from her African possessions and by preventing the transport of her troops from Africa.

It is not, however, merely the need to ensure the safe arrival of African troops that makes it essential for France to preserve the present balance of power in the Mediterranean. Any change in the present situation to the advantage of Germany and Italy would be a direct threat to her African positions. The Nazi experts Hans Hummel and Wulf Siewert point this out, with obvious satisfaction, in their work *Der Mittelmeerraum:* "It is an open question whether with the loss of Mediterranean hegemony Algeria and Tunis could be held for any length of time."

The Mediterranean is certainly of no less importance to Great Britain. Indeed, the Briton's consciousness of being a citizen of a great Empire brings the Mediterranean problem, from his point of view, into high relief. Until the "spontaneous" demands in the Italian Chamber for Tunis and Corsica—followed by a violent and continuous press campaign—opened her eyes to Italy's real designs, France had hardly troubled to interest the man in the street in her vast colonial Empire. The Empire attracted business men and certain Civil Servants delighted with the prospect of a wide field outside

[1] Page 765 of the German edition of 1935.

France for the development of bureaucracy. But to the majority of Frenchmen all this meant very little. When their colonial troops marched past on the 14th of July, they would cheer with great enthusiasm, and go back home proud of the fine bearing of these men, convinced that in any new war they would fight with the same courage as in 1914 to keep the Germans out of Paris. But the Frenchman does not share the deep emotion experienced by the humblest Englishman when he sees at the gates of Buckingham Palace a group of Indian officers in their splendid native dress—a love of Empire which is as strong as his affection for a favourite corner of London or the house in which he lives. For the Frenchman, the Empire is no part of his very being, something whose disappearance would mean the loss of a large part of the happiness which life has to offer. The French Empire-builders had none of that firmness of step of a Hernán Cortés or a Cecil Rhodes— of men who knew whither they were going and in whose name they were marching forward. Often, as in Indo-China, the conquest of Empire was due to the self-sacrificing and anonymous initiative of subordinate officials. Its loss would strike no chord save that of national honour, and even then might be made the opportunity for the exercise of the inimitable French wit. When in the eighteenth century, after the Seven Years' War with Great Britain, caused by the Family Compact, France lost Canada and the land on the left bank of the Mississippi by the Treaty of Paris in 1763, d'Argenson, one of Louis XV's ministers, said that he would give all the colonies for *"une tête d'épingle,"* while Voltaire marvelled that there could be any dispute with England over *"quelques arpents de neige."*

But lately things have changed. All at once fascinating panoramas were flashed on the cinema screens of regions divided from France by a waste of seas, but over which the French tricolour flies. Their development and progress, the fruits of French labour and initiative, were described in terms which aroused a genuine national pride. The promotion of officers from the military colleges was newly styled "promotion of the French Empire." A series of books was published on the various French colonies—no longer simple tourist manuals, or the literary effusions of writers attracted by the colour and exoticism of the colonial Empire, but books whose purpose was to create as rapidly as possible an imperialist mentality. All this, however, is a plant of but two years' growth. But every Englishman is born aware of the fact that the Mediterranean—especially since the opening of the Suez Canal—is Britain's route to the Indies and the Empire.

In the long discussions between the Cape and Mediterranean schools of thought, it was the imperialist point of view which was finally responsible for the triumph of the latter. From the commercial standpoint, Mussolini was right when he said: "For Great Britain the Mediterranean is merely one route among many, a convenient short cut." Whether the Mediterranean is dominated by Italy or Great Britain, British trade and commerce are not unduly affected. On the other hand, the prestige and future of the Empire are closely linked with this question. In 1936 Winston Churchill remarked that no one in possession of the slightest knowledge of strategy could fail to see that British domination in the Mediterranean was essential for the security and well-being of the British protectorates of Egypt, the Sudan, and Palestine. The Ethiopian experience decided the British Government to adhere definitively to the Mediterranean school, and in the summer of 1936, on his return from a visit to Malta and Cyprus, the First Lord of the Admiralty declared categorically not only that it was not a question of choosing between renouncing British positions and abandoning Malta, but that Great Britain was determined to face new and delicate problems and to reinforce her positions in the Mediterranean. Months afterwards Mr. Eden, at that time still Foreign Minister, stated that his country was ready to defend her interests in the Mediterranean as in every other part of the world. He added, however, that although the Mediterranean was an arterial road for Great Britain, there was nevertheless room in it for all.

There was a time when official Italy shared Mr. Eden's opinion. In 1913 the Italian Foreign Minister declared: "No one has the right today, or at any time in the future, to call the Mediterranean *'mare nostrum.'* It is, and must always be, an open highway for the nations." In those days *"mare nostrum"* for Italy meant the Adriatic.

Ten years later Fascism took the reins, and one of its first slogans was "The Mediterranean for Italy." Not only as an invocation of the past, but also as an indication for the future, Mussolini adorned the Via dell' Impero with the five marble maps representing the growth of the ancient Empire and the birth of the new. "Italy was powerful in the Mediterranean. It is my desire that she shall be so once again," said the Duce in Tripolitania to an assembly of Italians and Arabs, when he proclaimed himself the protector of Islam. It was a national movement which combined the lyricism of a d'Annunzio with the most practical methods of political and economic penetration, which took advantage of the troubles in Palestine (when it did not actually provoke them) to undermine British authority, which used the Bari radio station to encourage subversive tendencies—one of the "three possible causes of conflict" enumerated by the German writers—and which was given solemn and majestic expression in the magnificent Romanitá exhibition opened in the autumn of 1937 to celebrate the two-thousandth anniversary of the birth of Augustus.

"Today," writes the Nazi publicist Walther Pahl, "they talk of an awakening of the Mediterranean. This would have been impossible without an Italian awakening under the leadership of Benito Mussolini. The new Italy turns her gaze to the historic splendours of the Roman Empire; and so the great strength of Fascism is born."

As far back as 1923 Mussolini, in one of his speeches, spoke of the enemy who would have to be expelled from the Mediterranean. "The Mediterranean for the Mediterranean peoples," proclaimed the Duce, and when later he crystallized his thought in a phrase which has since been repeated a hundred times: "Italy is not willing to remain a prisoner in the Mediterranean," Gibraltar and Suez were the detested guardians whose collapse he foresaw on the day of Italy's liberation.

Italy took full advantage of the difficulties with which Great Britain and France were contending, difficulties due partly to the weakness of their own policy and partly to the varied racial composition of their protectorates and dominions. While, for reasons which are well known to all, her opportunities for stirring up trouble in Gibraltar, Malta, and Cyprus are not very great, the indecisions of London and the permanent rivalry between Jews and Arabs (whose racial passions prevent them from arriving at a *modus vivendi*—of obvious advantage to them both) give her in Palestine a fertile field for anti-British propaganda.

It is not liberty, however, that Italy covets, but hegemony in the Mediterranean. Even since Fascism came to power, it has—so far as one can discuss Italian policy in terms of straight lines—steered an even course. The definitive occupation in 1923 of the Dodecanese Islands, and their subsequent fortification; the Italian attitude—alternately "friendly" and violent —to Albania, from the Durazzo naval demonstration to the Pact of Friendship with Achmed Zogou and from the fortification of the Albanian ports to the total annexation of the country in 1939; the Corfu incident and the provisional occupation of the island; the secret treaty with Primo de Rivera's Spain in 1926; the spectacular visit of the Prince of the Undine to Tangiers, which, while only a timid echo of the Kaiser's *coup de théâtre*, achieved its main objective when the Statute of Tangiers was revised in the following year, and Italy was invited to share in the administration of that region as a consequence; the construction of a great strategic highway in Libya; the policy of perpetual menace whereby that garrison has been increased or decreased according to the international scene, so that today—in contravention of the assurances given to the British Government—there are 130,000 men at the very gates of the Tunisian frontier; the naval and air rearmament policy which has enabled General Valle, Italian Under-Secretary for Air, to state that the Italian air force at present controls "every corner of the Mediterranean"; the construction of an excellent seaplane base in the island of Pantelleria, between Sardinia and Tunis; these are the principal stages of this expansionist policy, a policy which aims at the domination of the Mediterranean, and of which the most recent phases are Count Ciano's visit to Spain and the announcement of a proposed visit by General Franco to Rome.

The conquest of Abyssinia was, as I have said, the first heavy blow aimed at British prestige in the Mediterranean. "The result of the Ethiopian enterprise," wrote the German publicist Edmund Schoppen in his book *Weltentscheidung im Mittelmeer,* "though it might have been the collapse of the Fascist régime, was in fact the foundation—or more correctly from a historical point of view the resurrection—of the Roman Empire. The King of the Empire finds himself face to face with the Emperor of the Empire. The curtain rises abruptly on the inexorable progress of events. The rupture between England and Italy is a fact. Their ways divide. The Mediterranean Empire arises from the tomb in which it has lain for fifteen hundred years."

But far from being decisive, this blow was only the first in the anti-British round which culminated in the intervention in Spain. "It is time that it was realized," wrote the Italian General Ambroglio Barlatti, in his review, *Il Mediterraneo,* of Rome, "that the Spanish campaign is a continuation of the Abyssinian one. Without Spanish collaboration we should never succeed in turning the Mediterranean into the 'Italian lake' of which the Duce has spoken."

This time it was no question of indirect action, but of a movement directly aimed at the very heart of the Anglo-French positions. The objective was the western basin of the Mediterranean, the place where the north-south and east-west routes meet.

"For years now," as *Annales Coloniales* (October 16, 1936) very truly observes, "the object of Italian naval manœuvres in the Mediterranean has been to cut the maritime communications between France and northern Africa." It was no doubt during these manœuvres that the Italian fleet realized that Spanish assistance would be necessary to attain this object.

Italy was not alone in the game. A deplorably mistaken interpretation of the contradictions of Fascist foreign policy during the past fifteen years has resulted in essential factors being confused with secondary ones. The zigzag of Mussolini's policy has, in reality, been systematic; he has inherited the methods which Italy's history has imposed on her statesmen. Francis I of France and Charles V of Spain are the symbols of this eternal pendulum.

In furthering his true national aims the Italian must always be a partner, never a leader. He does not possess that strong will which determines the objective, crushes the enemy, and imposes its own rule. The very success of the joint enterprise fills him with unsatisfied ambitions and fresh desires, and spurs him on to remedy new injustices. His mind fires his imagination and lures him on to a vast field of intrigue in which his artistic temperament finds an intrinsic beauty and value, irrespective of any prospect of success which the enterprise may have to offer.

Mussolini has always given very clear proof of this instability and restlessness. Eternally discontented, he finds on every front a wall of grievances and insults to be destroyed, and his friendships invariably leave in their wake a trail of disputes and resentment. From his former allies he has to claim Corsica, Nice, Malta, and Tunis, while the demands of his new "friend" for frontier and colonial compensation are still ringing in his ears. But these old tactics take on fresh life with the prospect of new struggles in which to intervene. History itself helps to broaden the field of conflict by creating new problems whose interplay, astutely directed, can fortify and extend positions which are due to a policy of surprise and cunning rather than to organic development.

The Spanish Civil War coincided with the cementing of Italo-German relations, and as Hitler was winning back the German territory of 1914, Mussolini was fighting in Spain a battle which helped him to forget the wounds inflicted by German expansion. While the Spanish people were struggling for their independence, their one desire being to determine their own national destiny, the scenes which preceded the Triple Alliance of 1882 and 1887 were being re-enacted in the Chancelleries of Rome and Berlin, with Hitler and Mussolini in the parts originally played by Bismarck and Crispi. The resemblance is not fanciful, so true to life are the details; the egoism and contemptuous arrogance of Bismarck are reproduced in his successor; the methods of Crispi and Mussolini are identical—the same ill humour, the same distrust, the same mutual suspicions mark the negotiations. Mussolini is the Crispi of his age, and history will decide whether he has acted with equal prudence, and whether the agreements signed with Germany offer the same guarantees and compensations as Crispi obtained through his Ambassador Robilant —"that most objectionable man," as Bismarck called him.

In his book *Les Frères ennemis*, Count Sforza draws a distinction between the policies of Crispi and Mussolini and suggests that they pursue different ideals and aims. No doubt the motives are distinct and are linked with different political ideas, but as regards the union of Germany and Italy in the international sphere, their objects are the same. The Spanish military rebellion, however—incited, encouraged, and supported throughout by Mussolini's army—added to the original Crispi policy a new strengthening factor absent from the Triple Alliance: the conquest of Spain for the Rome-Berlin Axis. Today the democracies are suddenly surprised by the sight of the powerful house of Austria rising up again before them—in a different form, it is true, but with the same dreams of hegemony and the same spirit which inspired Maximilian and Charles V. Must not the impartial observer bitterly regret that Richelieu—a man who has had no historical successor—is not living at this hour?

On the sand of this traditional Italian instability the British and French Governments, with an appalling ignorance of the changed circumstances, have built up their Spanish policy. In my conversations in Paris and Geneva I was able to realize to what an extent this factor militated against us. Spain was sacrificed to the illusion that it was possible to separate Rome from Berlin short of war. It was an illusion quite divorced from reality, since Hitler's own policy, when he ejected Italy from the Danube, drove her firmly towards the Mediterranean. This is as clearly reflected in daily events as the sun in a mirror. Once Italy ceased to be a great Danubian power, her *amour propre* and her desire not to seem to have suffered defeat at the hands of her ally forced her to support with all her might every German advance in central Europe, while Hitler in his turn assisted Italy in the Mediterranean, where Italian domination, with the aid of Spain, formed part of his plans.

The Italians and Germans have told all who are willing to listen that, as far as Mediterranean problems are concerned, their points of view are identical, and that no person or thing can prevent their combined efforts to alter the *status quo*. Along this road they march together in perfect unison. "No great European power," wrote Signor Virginio Gayda in the *Voce d'Italia* on September 5, 1937, "can remain on the margin of Mediterranean events. Side by side with vital Italian interests the legitimacy of German interests in regard to the future of the Mediterranean must therefore be recognized." And not to be outdone in politeness, the *Berliner Tageblatt* stated in its turn on January 8, 1939: "It is unnecessary to insist that the German conception of the Spanish question is in complete agreement with the Italian one, and that National Socialist sympathies have been with the Fascist Empire in the Mediterranean ever since the conquest of Abyssinia."

There are even some who believe that it is Germany who

is directing the game. This was the opinion of Colonel Jean Fabry when in 1937, during the Spanish War, he wrote: "A powerful German fleet, which will be even more powerful in 1939, is putting out to sea. It knows all the routes and harbours in the Mediterranean, while the tourists, the technicians, and the disguised agents of the Reich travel around the Canaries, Ifni, the Riff coast and the Balearic Islands. Once again Germany turns her gaze towards Agadir." These words of Colonel Fabry should at that time have been enough to awaken his Government from their slumbers; and today they are amply confirmed by Germany's growing ascendancy over Spanish policy. They are borne out by the insistence with which the official German press is inciting General Franco to launch his imperialist campaign with a demand for Gibraltar and Tangiers.

The whole Axis is concerned in the destruction of the *status quo*. Even Japan, which might have been considered too much absorbed in the Far East to trouble about the Mediterranean, is zealously aiding and abetting her two allies in this supreme attempt to deliver a death blow at the Western democracies in their most vulnerable spot. "If the Pacific is the vestibule for India," writes Herr Anton Zischka in *Italien in der Welt* (*Italians in the World*), "the Mediterranean is the vestibule of the West. England has to defend herself against two enemies, to fight in two continents, to reckon with both Italy and Japan. Everything depends on which of these two enemies enters the lists first, and on whether the London diplomats succeed in avoiding a simultaneous conflict with both." Edmund Schoppen, in *Weltentscheidung im Mittelmeer*, rounds off the argument: "England cannot abandon her old Imperial route in the Mediterranean. If the new Mediterranean Empire presses on towards hegemony before the Mongol-Anglo-Saxon question is settled, then there will be war between Italy and England. But Japan cannot remain passive. England would have to face Japan in the Pacific and Italy in the Mediterranean."

This war on two fronts, which has so much attraction for the Nazi authors—has it not begun already? There has been no state of tension in the Mediterranean during the past two years which the Japanese have not used in order to encroach on British and French interests in the Far East. There is a strong parallel between events in Spain and China. In the midst of the Mediterranean crisis, which was responsible for the Nyon Conference, the Japanese declared a blockade of the Chinese coasts. Twenty-four hours after the forced surrender of Minorca to Franco—which took place, it will be remembered, during a bombardment from Italian aircraft—Japanese troops landed on the island of Hainan. The capture of Canton, seriously endangering Britain's hold on Hong Kong, followed immediately upon Munich. The more recent Tientsin dispute broke out at a time when the situation in Europe and the Mediterranean had once again become disquieting.

All these demonstrations of totalitarian solidarity, however, are not in themselves enough to place Italy in a position to realize her great ambition. Italy has many vulnerable points —her communications with her east-African territories through the Suez Canal; her sea route between the home country and Libya; her long coast-line; her dependence upon overseas trade. If she had to rely on her own strength, and if present conditions persisted in the Suez Canal and the Strait of Gibraltar, her position would be very precarious. "Italy's strength in the Mediterranean of to-day," writes Elizabeth Monroe in her excellent book *The Mediterranean in Politics,* "is that of a blackmailer and potential destroyer. . . . She has the strength of a Samson who can pull down the pillars of Gaza, but she is ill-placed for securing benefits out of the wreck. . . . She therefore needs Mediterranean allies."

One ally at least Great Britain and France have given her— and that is Franco Spain.

CHAPTER VI

Storm in the Mediterranean

A FASCIST SPAIN was the only certain ally which could serve Italy in her policy of Mediterranean domination. None of the other minor powers could have given the same assistance, and with none did she enjoy friendly or confidential relations. When Mussolini included the Near East among Italy's "historic objectives," he revived a mistrust among the Western powers which had been smouldering since the war of 1911 and the occupation of Libya. While the pretext had been the abandoned state of the country and the obstacles placed in the way of Italians working there, the real cause of the occupation of Libya was Italy's determination to set up the banner of the house of Savoy somewhere along the African coast, where Great Britain, France, and Spain were extending their influence so rapidly. Italo-Turkish relations were poisoned as a result, and have remained so for many years.

When Giolitti decided to deliver his ultimatum to Turkey on September 28, 1911, Italian national pride, wounded by the failure of Crispi's Abyssinian campaign, revived throughout the country. From being the monopoly of a handful of writers and intellectuals, who reflected it in terms of an excessive nationalism and sank into despair on finding themselves alone and unsupported, this patriotic spirit spread to the people as a whole. The campaigns of the Italo-Turkish war, which ended in Italy's acquisition of Tripolitania, developed amid general enthusiasm. In Paris d'Annunzio momentarily forgot the theatre of Ida Rubinstein and his success as a French writer to sing the glories of the Italian victory in his *Canzoni.* Nationalist newspapers and reviews sprang up on all sides, from *Grande Italia* to the *Idea Nazionale.* It was the dawn of the "Third Rome"—ready to surpass ancient and Christian Rome, and inspired with the passion of Mazzini and the doctrines of the Risorgimento; a widespread movement aiming at Italian expansion and subsequently moderated by the forces of reality, until ten years later Fascism claimed it for its own.

All this resulted in an unnecessary humiliation of Turkey. A long time had to pass before the two dictators who succeeded to such a troubled heritage were able, through their realistic political conceptions, to sweep away the accumulated resentment of years. Attempts at a *rapprochement,* begun in 1928 by Mussolini and Mustafa Kemal, failed, and a new feeling of animosity arose when the Duce made his arrogant speech on the Near East and translated it into action by invading Abyssinia. Of recent years, the constant vexations to which the Turkish communities in the Dodecanese have been subjected—and which culminated in the expulsion of their most honoured leader from the islands at the end of July 1939, for the crime of having entertained some Turkish journalists in his house—have only served to increase the existing tension.

Italy has thus alienated a possible collaborator in the Mediterranean, a state with the power to prevent Italian oil supplies from passing through the Dardanelles.

Italian relations with Greece—on whose goodwill, in default of Turkish friendship, Italy might to a certain extent have

relied to improve her difficult situation in the Dardanelles—
have been strained ever since the occupation of Corfu in 1924.
If any evidence is needed of how that insult was received by
the Greeks, let me say that the occasion was the only one in
my long experience of Geneva when the intelligent and im-
passive M. Politis threw off the air of a frigid and sceptical
internationalist, for whom catastrophes and world injustices
are merely opportunities to exercise erudition and powers of
oratory.

The Anglo-Egyptian Treaty of 1936, particularly the clause
declaring the Suez Canal an integral part of Egypt—thereby
placing the keys of the Canal in the hands of Great Britain—
caused so much feeling in Italy that from that time onwards
England's new partner was considered as a further enemy.

So far as Yugoslavia is concerned, relations between the
two Governments are undeniably more cordial, but if war
should break out, the Yugoslavian people themselves would
not gladly fight on the side of Italy.

There remained Spain—the most valuable and decisive
factor in the furtherance of Italian plans. Thus it is that Spain's
incorporation in the Berlin-Rome Axis—and Spain will remain
tied to the apron-strings of what General Franco calls "our
Imperial Sister, Italy," Axis or no Axis—has extricated Italy
from her precarious political situation in the Mediterranean
and has placed her in a better position than ever before for a
fresh attack on British hegemony.

Before the Spanish War and the formation of a united front
by the aggressors, Germany and Italy were fighting separately
to destroy the present European order, an order based in part
on the *status quo* in the Mediterranean. Their expansionist
policy was directed, by the force of events, against Great
Britain and France. In spite of their continued attempts and
partial successes, however, Hitler and Mussolini had still not
succeeded by 1936 in seriously menacing Anglo-French
positions.

The Spanish enterprise represented the first complete and

united attack on the Western democracies. As the German and Italian aeroplanes took off—almost at the same time and in the same direction—on the outbreak of Franco's rising, they sealed an alliance which was at last to be put to the test. The Berlin-Rome Axis was welded in the open fire of a war against a people who value their own independence too highly to become willing tools in the destruction of the Mediterranean balance of power and in the removal of the chief obstacle to totalitarian progress. A greater bond than all the professions of faith of the dictators, however violent and well synchronized, was their joint campaign on the same battlefield. It was not a mere coincidence either that in the course of the Spanish War Hitler and Mussolini should have become openly allied through the Anti-Comintern Pact (a prelude to their military agreement signed at the end of the war), the anti-Communism of which was no more than another manoeuvre, as has been clearly proved by recent events.

The two dictators should be given their just due. They acted in Spain with decision, with indisputable logic, with a clear end in view, and without sparing their efforts or counting the cost. In this respect we share the opinion of Frau Margret Boveri, when in her book on the Mediterranean, already quoted in these pages, she writes: "The first conflict between Italy and England took place in Abyssinia; the second in Spain. In Spain, as in Abyssinia, Italy knows what she wants, England what she does not want. England does not want a Franco victory, but she does not want a Government victory either, nor does she want to take part in the struggle. That is the decisive factor. As long as England's will for peace is greater than her will to dominate, the prospects for Italy—whatever risks she may run—will continue to be favourable."

It would be hard to find a better exposition of the problem, a problem which is not only a Mediterranean one—Anglo-Italian rivalry and disagreement between one power and another—but which is also a European and a world problem, a conflict between democracies and dictatorships.

Italy and Germany certainly knew what they wanted when at the outbreak of the Spanish rebellion they gave every possible assistance to the insurgents. The prophets of Greater Germany had always looked upon Spain as a trump card. Bismarck referred with a certain pleasure to the "Spanish fly" on the French neck. The activity of German diplomats in Spain throughout the World War was due to this desire to use her against the "mortal enemy." The leading editorial in the *Temps* of August 17, 1917 stated in this connection: "German policy in Spain is more than a simple combination of propaganda or espionage. It has wider objectives. For the insatiable appetite of the Germans, Spain is a means as well as an end. In the spring of 1870, some time before the candidacy of the Hohenzollerns [for the Spanish throne] was officially presented, Germany was already trying to turn Spain into an instrument of aggression against us. One only needs to recall Bernhardi's mission. Today, as in 1870, Spain in German eyes is an excellent base of operations." With the advent of Hitler to power, the German imperialists returned to the Bismarckian policy of aiming at an "alliance with the neighbour's neighbour." And so we see that those who today protest against "encirclement" never had any other aim but to "encircle" France.

As far as Mussolini is concerned, he had abundant reasons to desire the restoration of a reactionary Spain—a Spain which in 1926 had complied with his request to place her bases and coast-line at his disposal in the event of a conflict in the Mediterranean. Like Hitler, Mussolini knew that a republican Spain could not be used for his plans, and that on the contrary there was always the risk, in the event of German and Italian aggression, that she would ally herself to the Western democracies, or that at least she would observe a stricter neutrality than that practised in 1914—with no submarine bases in the Balearic Islands and no Germanophil authorities to give a kindly welcome to foreign agents and spies.

Hitler and Mussolini made no secret of the extent of their activities in Spain. They explained—through their political and military mouthpieces, when they did not actually speak themselves—the real motives for their intervention, and the positive results which they hoped to gain from it. Thus the Nazi professor Max Gruen, in a lecture given in Constance on February 6, 1938, defined the Spanish War as a "European war for supremacy in the Mediterranean." Commander Berkeu, in the March 1937 issue of *Wissen und Wehr,* one of the foremost politico-military reviews of the Third Reich, wrote: "If events in Spain go in favour of the Nationalists, and the Social-Communist regime has to yield to an authoritarian regime on national lines, France will see on her southern frontier, which until now has always been free from complications, the rise of a state which will oppose her policy just as Germany and Italy have done." In the October 1938 issue of the same review Dr. Hermann Gackenholz expressed himself even more clearly. "Because of the civil war," he writes, "Spain has become the central point in the tension existing between the great powers. As this tension moves towards the western Mediterranean, Spain's importance as a potential ally becomes greater than ever. To this cause more than any other must be attributed the intervention of certain foreign powers."

In these three manifestations of Nazi thought, and in dozens of articles, speeches, and lectures on the same lines, the reason for Italo-German intervention was made crystal clear. There was no longer any talk of "common ideas," of the "Western civilization which must be saved." Vantage points for use in the next war, as the aggressors themselves declared, were what Germany and Italy went to seek in Spain.

Are the democracies ignorant of the perils of an attack

directed, first and last, against them? No; many voices have been raised in warning. In his book *Spain over Britain* Henry Blythe has written: "To the British Empire, the Mediterranean is essential as a trade route, a military highway and as a naval station. Though Italy can, as at present situated, threaten the British route through the Mediterranean, her own extremely weak defensive strategical position makes it impossible for her effectively to challenge Britain. Only by the control of Spain can Italy convert this weak defensive position into a strong offensive one. Therefore in any struggle in Spain Italy's strategic need demands that she intervene to secure, if she can, a military foothold on the Peninsula and in the Balearics."

At the very beginning of the Spanish War, Sir Abe Bailey in the London *Daily Telegraph* of August 18, 1936 called the attention of his countrymen to the danger that "the success of General Franco would bring nearer Mussolini's dream of transforming the Mediterranean into an Italian lake, and might also give Germany that foothold in Morocco for the realization of which she nearly plunged the world into war in 1911."

In France, too, there were significant warnings. In view of my resolve to quote, for preference, from enemy sources, I will say nothing of the continuous cries of alarm raised by the friends of the Spanish Republic and will cite instead one of the French publicists most hostile to the loyalist cause. "There is no doubt," wrote M. Vladimir d'Ormesson, "that leaving for a moment the question of Communism on one side, Germany has been attracted to the Spanish question for very different reasons, and that in Spain, as everywhere, her imperialist interests are well disguised. It is very probable that Germany is attempting to secure in the Peninsula bases other than purely commercial ones. It is possible that she is attempting in this way to reopen the Moroccan question. In any case it is certain that she sees in all this a means of interfering with our communications in the Mediterranean."

Fundamentally everyone was agreed in considering the Spanish problem an extremely important one and in giving due weight to the motives and aims of the interested parties. There was, however, one difference. While the dictators acted, the democrats were content merely to "take a grave view."

Were the hopes and fears of both sides exaggerated when they agreed that a Franco victory would bring with it a profound change in the Mediterranean and in Europe? Before replying to this question, one must consider the importance of Spain—with her coast-line, her islands, and her possessions —from a strategic point of view. Geographically the Peninsula is unquestionably in a most privileged situation. In the east, dominant positions in the western basin of the Mediterranean; in the south, ports on either side of the Strait of Gibraltar; in the north-west, an Atlantic coast-line whose port, Vigo, a naval base, El Ferrol, dominate the near-by trade routes; and in the north, a lofty Pyrenean frontier—these are the four faces of Spain. A closer examination of the strategic value of each will lead to an understanding of German and Italian desires and a realization of the disquieting consequences of their victory.

The Balearic group covers an area of less than two thousand square miles. What other archipelago of so small a size has had a history so rich in admirers? There is no Western power, no Mediterranean or European civilization, which has not coveted this small piece of territory. The Phœnicians and the Greeks, the Carthaginians and the Romans, the Vandals and the Visigoths, the Arabs and the Spaniards, the Germans and the Italians, the English and the French—all have had an interest in these islands, and all have occupied them successively.

These age-old disputes, this chequered history, are evidence of the immense strategic importance of the islands dominating the western basin of the Mediterranean. What could have been more significant than the execution of Britain's Admiral Byng for the loss of Minorca in 1756? Who is better qualified to an opinion on this question than Nelson, who gave preference to the Balearics over Malta?

All these struggles, events, and opinions, however, date from a time when there was no Suez Canal, and therefore no Mediterranean route to the Indies; before northern Africa was colonized by the European powers; and before the invention of aircraft and submarines. Far from losing, the Balearic Islands have considerably gained in importance during the course of the last hundred years. In order to appreciate this, one has only to recall the role they played during the first World War, when in spite of Spain's official neutrality, 3,200,000 tons of shipping were sunk by German submarines, who found in the islands and ports of Spain a "benevolent neutrality"—in other words, provisions and harbourage.

Since the World War the balance of power in Europe, and relations between the Mediterranean powers, have undergone frequent and profound changes. Attempts at *rapprochement* have been followed by suspicions, declarations of friendship by acute tension, dictatorships by democracies, democracies by dictatorships. "But in the midst of all these changes," Frau Margret Boveri observes very pertinently, "one thing remains constant, and that is that facing the French island of Corsica and the Italian island of Sardinia is the neutral group of the Balearic Islands, just where the most important French and British sea routes and an important Italian sea route cross. Hence the struggle to tinge Spanish neutrality with one shade or another, and the tremendous anxiety with which the development of the civil war is being followed in London, Paris and Rome."

My own impression is that in London and Paris the anxiety was not so tremendous as Frau Boveri claims. There were the best reasons in the world for uneasiness, but ever since Lord Plymouth, Parliamentary Under-Secretary of State for Foreign Affairs, and President of the Non-Intervention Committee, stated in the House of Lords on November 26, 1936, in reply to a question by Lord Cecil, that "on several occasions the Italian Government had given full assurances as to the absence of any Italian intention in regard to the Balearic Isles," the official position in both capitals was that, until such time as Rome should give notice of the annexation of these islands, there need be no occasion for anxiety just because Count Rossi or any subsequent *condottiere* might be preparing the way for an Italian regime in Majorca.

One of the phenomena of modern international politics is that words mean more than deeds, however much living reality may prove them false. Territories can be annexed, countries invaded, but until the aggressor considers that the moment has come to give official notice to the chancelleries, it would seem to the democratic governments and their diplomats to be a sign of bad form, incompatible with their high office, to question the correctness and disinterestedness of such proceedings. Members of the opposition, with their incurable vulgarity, may well concede some importance to the physical presence of a few thousand Italians in the Balearic Islands, but among educated people what matters is not what is done but what is promised.

The British Prime Minister was always of this opinion, and in his speech in the House of Commons on November 2, 1938, he stated that at Munich he had spoken on the subject of the future of Spain with Herr Hitler and Signor Mussolini, and that both of them had assured him "most definitely" that they had no territorial ambitions whatever in that country.

Therein lies the mistake—the mistake of not realizing that it was never a question of territorial ambitions or annexation of the Balearics or any other part of Spain, but of bringing Spain under the influence of Axis policy in such a way that results are obtained without the necessity of creating a second Fascist Chamber in Majorca, flying the Italian flag over Port Mahón, or appointing in the Canary Islands a German protector of the same standing as Baron von Neurath in Bohemia. Time and again I explained to the representatives of Great

Britain and France how well we knew that neither Hitler nor Mussolini would be so irresponsible as to risk unnecessarily their comfortable and certain position in Spain for senseless territorial ambitions, and that for those with any memory of international affairs a zone of influence was the same thing as open annexation—with all the advantages of the annexation and none of its risks.

In spite of the assurances given to the contrary by the Italian Government, the chief motive for their intervention was the Balearic Islands. It was a very understandable motive, for on the Balearics depends, to a large extent, the outcome of any Mediterranean conflict.

The naval and air bases of the Balearic Islands are of the first rank. On the island of Minorca is Port Mahón, fortified by the British, with ultra-modern English artillery, and, in the unanimous opinion of foreign military experts, one of the finest and best-protected naval bases in the Mediterranean; in the north is the small bay of Fornells, used during the Spanish War by Air France for its daily service between Marseille and Algiers, and a coveted seaplane base. On the island of Majorca are the two ports of Palma and Pollensa, in the improvement of which Italian and German engineers concentrated their greatest efforts during the two and a half years in which the Italians were the real masters of the island. Numerous aircraft bases, which were tried out during the course of the Spanish War, complete the defensive and offensive system of the islands, of which the smallest, Ibiza, is only fifty-five miles from the Spanish coast, while Gibraltar can be reached from the Balearics by plane in two and a half hours. In view of their relation to the Mediterranean ports of Spain (Barcelona, Valencia, Alicante, Almería), the powerful naval base of Cartagena, and the Italian bases in Sardinia, the Balearics are in the best possible position for severing at will the normal communications in the western Mediterranean.

Of these communications let us first consider the French line from Marseille to Orán, which passes between the

Balearics and the Spanish coast, and the lines from Toulon to Bizerta and from Marseille to Algeria, passing between the Balearics and Sardinia. The Balearics are the half-way house on all these routes; 250 miles from Marseille and Toulon on the one hand, and Algeria on the other; and 370 miles from Bizerta and Orán. Flanked by two coast-lines—the Spanish coast and the Balearics, and the Balearics and Sardinia— these routes, representing a journey of from twenty-five to forty hours, could be rendered useless for the transport of troops and material between France and her possessions in North Africa.

Is the west-east route, of vital importance to Great Britain, more fortunately situated? If it is borne in mind that for vessels on this route there is no British base between Gibraltar and Malta, and that in addition they have to pass within 62 miles of Cartagena, within 93 miles of the Balearics, and 37 miles of the most southerly point in Sardinia, it is easy to see how this important route between Great Britain and her Empire could be greatly obstructed by such a triangle, even if it were not rendered altogether impassable.

All these points were duly appreciated by the parties interested in the Mediterranean regime. France has hitherto had no grounds for anxiety. Her defensive system, dating from the distant days of the Triple Entente, was only built up on her eastern flank, between Toulon, Corsica, and Bizerta, since it was felt that her western flank was sufficiently protected by a neighbour whose policy—save for brief lapses during the World War when it was under the influence of the German-ophils of 1914 (the counterpart of Spain's present leaders)— had always moved in the Anglo-French orbit.

The triumph of Germany and Italy in Spain not only menaced France with a hostile frontier on the Pyrenees, but also exposed her flank in the Mediterranean, previously protected by a friendship in which common interests were allied to cultural affinities. As information on the growing Italian influence in the Balearics was confirmed, the anxiety of the French military and naval experts increased. In *France militaire* of October 21, 1937, there appears this disquieting comment: "The Balearics hold a position in the western basin of the Mediterranean in relation to the littoral of the Spanish Levant almost identical with that of Corsica and Sardinia in relation to the Tyrrhenian coasts of Italy. They are defensive advance posts, and in the event of an offensive they would be very effective in the flanking of sea routes. The Cartagena-Barcelona-Port Mahón triangle—like the two triangles Toulon-Boniface-Bizerta and Spezia-Cagliari-Trapani—has a defensive angle. If Spain should remain neutral, as she did in the Great War, the Balearics would regain their importance as positions, but this importance is to a certain extent negative. On the other hand, if Spain should ally herself with any other power—to be more precise, with Italy—this importance would become a positive one, by reason of the possible conjugation of the before-mentioned Spanish and Italian triangles—to the detriment of the French triangle. And this same conjugation, materialized in the line from the Balearics to the south of Sardinia, would also threaten the great British artery in the Mediterranean between Gibraltar and Malta."

In his very interesting work *The Defence of Britain* Captain Liddell Hart, whose reputation as a military expert is now world-wide, entirely shares the opinion of his French colleague. "The mere possibility that air and naval bases on the Eastern seaboard of Spain and in the Balearic Isles might be available for our opponents' use seriously complicates the problem of maintaining our traffic through, or even our forces in, the Mediterranean."

In effect, if the Spezia-Cagliari-Trapani triangle were combined with the bases of operations for naval and air forces in Barcelona, Cartagena, and Port Mahón, the region between Italy and Malta in the east, Gibraltar in the west, France in the north, and Morocco, Algeria, and Tunis in the south would be completely covered. There would be no access whatsoever for British sea-borne traffic in the west-east direction, nor for French in the north-south. There is a distance of some 1,000 miles between Gibraltar and Malta, and of about 450 miles between Marseille and Algeria. On the first route a ship doing 15 knots would take about 67 hours—that is to say, more than two days and three nights. The second route would take about 30 hours, or more than a day and a night. On the first route there are intermediate stations, which could be used, not as bases, but as emergency refuges. On the Marseille-Algeria route there would not even be these facilities. At least half the voyage between France and her large mobilization centres in northern Africa would have to be made during the day, and once Spain had openly joined a coalition against Great Britain and France, or had placed her "neutrality" at the service of their enemies, the shipping on this route would become a certain target for submarines and aircraft from enemy bases.

The Italians on their side have even popularized this strategic data in their schools. The military course given by General Ettore Grasetti at Milan University in 1938 included the following theme: "The western coasts of Sardinia and Sicily constitute, with the Balearic Islands, a system that, once under our control, will neutralize the British artery of Gibraltar-Malta. Thus with Italian influence in Palma de Majorca and German influence in Melilla and Ceuta, the Rome-Berlin Axis extends to the western Mediterranean (Majorca-Cagliari-Trapani), can sever the great British artery at its western source in Gibraltar, and can wield decisive influence in an easterly direction towards the island of Pantelleria. As far as France is concerned, the Italian Balearic-Sardinia line will cut the French lines between Marseille, Casablanca, and Orán in the west, between Algeria and Philippeville in the centre, and between Tunis and Suez in the east. In short, the whole French arterial system between the home country and French northern Africa, the basis of French general mobilization, can be severed."

This prospect consoles the Italians for their otherwise unfavourable situation. As we have already seen, if they had not found in Spain the ally they needed in the Mediterranean, they could not easily have challenged Great Britain and the world on the seas. The two thousand miles of coast which Italy has to defend, besides the two large islands of Sicily and Sardinia, would necessarily have had a moderating influence on her. No one can deny that Italy has made the most praiseworthy efforts during the past five years to compensate for the deficiencies of her geographical situation. She has completed the fortification of her own bases with that of the island of Pantelleria, which was discovered by Italian naval engineers in 1935 to be of considerable strategic importance; she has developed the speed factor with great success by building a series of light cruisers and very rapid destroyers, and she has created a powerful air force which had splendid schooling during its two and a half years in Spain. But of all that she has gained during the past five years, most important for her policy of Mediterranean domination is the use of Spanish bases and coast-lines, principally in the Balearics.

And the Germans? Seven months before the civil war broke out, *Die deutsche Wehr,* the organ of the German army, published in its issue of December 19, 1935 an article entitled "Spanish Anxiety in the Balearics," in which the author stressed the strategic importance of these islands. "It is well understood in Germany that a nation with a temperament such as the Spanish one should wish to be master of its own destiny. The measures begun in the Balearic Isles are very wise. If she perseveres on this path, Spain will one day become a real nation. Spanish neutrality in that case could assume a more beneficial form than during the World War."

In order that Spanish neutrality might be even more beneficial to German submarines than it was in 1914, Spain was plunged into a civil war. The Nazi press did not tire of praising the Balearic Islands and the service which they could render when the time came for a final settlement. In the opinion of the *Frankfurter Zeitung,* for example, they constituted "an ideal support in the next war." And the *Rheinische-West-phalische Zeitung,* organ of heavy industry, after pointing to the definite emancipation of Spain from Anglo-French influence as one of the positive results of the Spanish War, saw in the utilization of the Balearic Islands "the most certain method of severing all communications save wireless between Paris and northern Africa."

It is now, surely, quite obvious why one of the first things which the interventionist forces in Spain did was to occupy Majorca. Another event of equal significance, which took place some time later, disclosed the part which had been assigned to the Balearics by the Axis powers in case of a European conflagration. When for a moment in September 1938 war seemed inevitable, Italo-German aeroplanes, for the first time in a year, attacked the island of Minorca, occupied by the Republicans. Such sudden action was not justified by the development of operations in Spain. The London *Times* appreciated the real meaning of that seemingly untimely attack when it wrote that the Italian and German airmen from Palma and Pollensa were apparently preparing for a new phase of the war in which their first duty would be to place obstacles in the path of the French Colonial Army in the Mediterranean.

That is, in effect, the first duty of the Axis airmen. That is the capital role assigned to the Balearics, part of a Spain which is no longer free.

Before British and French ships on the west-east route from Gibraltar to Suez can be bombed and sunk by aircraft and submarines of the Cartagena-Baleares-Cagliari triangle, they have to pass through the Strait of Gibraltar.

Ever since Admiral Rooke, in 1704, hoisted the British flag over the Rock of Gibraltar, Great Britain has looked on this "key to the Mediterranean" as an essential part of the

Empire. One of the greatest figures in British liberalism, Charles James Fox, declared in 1782: "The fortress of Gibraltar is to be ranked among the most important possessions of this country." Great Britain has therefore repulsed all attempts to undermine her influence in that region; has resisted all the bloody sieges laid by the French and Spanish armies throughout the eighteenth century; and for 235 years has taken all necessary measures to adapt the defensive strength of the port and of the Rock of Gibraltar to the exigencies of fresh situations and the development of offensive weapons.

This British tenacity is explained by the fact that the Strait of Gibraltar is undoubtedly one of the most important strategic positions in the world. There are two reasons for this, both of capital importance. First, it is the only bridge between two continents, Europe and Africa, and secondly it is the only passage between two seas, the Mediterranean and the Atlantic. For Great Britain it is the decisive stage on the route to the Indies, both by way of the Mediterranean and by way of the Cape. And if in the event of a war with Italy the former route were closed to the British fleet, Gibraltar, from the British point of view, would still hold a most important position, whence the Italian fleet could be prevented from threatening Atlantic communications, and Fascist adversaries blockaded at a distance. The Nazi geo-politician Hermann Gackenholz undoubtedly had this in mind when he stated so categorically: "In a life-and-death struggle Italy will have to force a decision in the Strait of Gibraltar." The Italian and German admirals arrived at the same conclusion after the manœuvres of their respective fleets off the Spanish coasts in the summer of 1939.

A glance at the map will make the events of the last few years easier to understand. The Strait of Gibraltar is forty to forty-three miles long, from Cape Trafalgar to the Rock along the European coast, and from Cape Spartel to Ceuta along the African coast. It is at its narrowest, not at Gibraltar, but at Tarifa. At this point the two continents are separated by only nine miles. Save for the port of Gibraltar and the Rock, without hinterland, on the one side, and the international zone of Tangiers on the other, the Strait is surrounded by Spanish territory. Facing Gibraltar is Ceuta, the most strongly fortified port of Spanish Morocco, where, thanks to German co-operation, artillery has been considerably increased during the past two years. If the port of Gibraltar is dominated by the famous Rock, some 1,400 feet high, the port of Ceuta lies in the shadow of the Djebel Mussa, about 2,700 feet high. There is nothing between Gibraltar and the Spanish port of Algeciras save the bay of that name. Behind Gibraltar is La Línea a small Spanish town, but no smaller than the actual town of Gibraltar. The Strait is controlled at both ends by two important Spanish ports—Cádiz in the west and Málaga in the east. Remarkable improvements were effected in both during the course of the war, especially in Cádiz, where the majority of Italian troops disembarked.

Situated thus, could Gibraltar be defended if Spain should join an anti-British coalition? And even if enemy attacks were unsuccessful, could its impregnable position counteract the effects of a hostile Spain in the Strait? Since the end of the Spanish War these two factors have assumed an unquestionable importance.

In the World War Gibraltar was not able to prevent German submarines from passing through the Strait into the Mediterranean and sinking the *Britannia,* a warship of sixteen thousand tons, at the very base of the fortress. Five of the thirteen million tons of Allied or neutral shipping sunk by German submarines went to the bottom between Gibraltar and Port Said. And this in spite of the fact that Spain, save for the clandestine facilities given from the Balearic Islands, was neutral, and that Italy herself was on the side of the Allies. In any future war in which Italy and Spain were lined up together on the enemy front, with Spain a belligerent or (as is more probable and, as I shall subsequently prove, more dangerous) an active neutral obeying orders from Berlin and

Rome, things would be even worse.

Captain Liddell Hart is of this opinion.[1] "A significant feature of the last war was the high percentage of commerce destruction in proportion to the small forces employed in the submarine campaign there—there were rarely more than half a dozen submarines operating at any one time. A single one of them attained a total 'bag' of half a million tons of shipping. . . . Yet the campaign was carried out at an immense distance from the home bases of the submarines and under the great difficulties caused by the hazardous passage past the British Isles and the lack of convenient bases in the Mediterranean. Nowadays submarines have multiplied; new types of high-speed torpedo-craft have been developed; and the range of aircraft has been vastly extended. Moreover, we are now confronted with the ominous possibility that, if Italy should be an enemy, these menaces to sea traffic could operate from bases close to the traffic routes. It would be worse still if Spain were ranged on the opposing side, and her bases, both sea and air, were available for the enemy's use."

This is a subject which holds a great attraction for military writers on the other side. German naval historians—impressed by the remarkable possibilities which in their opinion the Mediterranean would hold if the difficulties confronting the German Admiralty in 1914 could through Italian and Spanish co-operation be overcome—have given it their pre-eminent attention.

In the *German Naval Annual* of 1938 Admiral Gadow prophesies a somewhat unpleasant future for Gibraltar if events turn out as it seems reasonable to expect. "Could a fortress such as Gibraltar, without any hinterland, and with a very weak neutral zone, be maintained and used as a war port of the first category?" The Admiral, no doubt bearing in mind the progress made in the mounting of artillery in neighbouring Spanish emplacements—thanks to the vigilance of his fellow-countrymen—was inclined to think not. "The air arm

[1] *The Defence of Britain.*

gives a negative reply. Long-distance batteries would consign the fortress and its fleet to a terrible fate. On the other side of the Strait, and facing Gibraltar, is the Spanish base of Ceuta, with powerful fortifications which can be made even more powerful. Would a Nationalist Spain, emancipated and conscious of her own destiny, decide to revive the old claim for a Spanish Gibraltar? Would she make use of the privileged position of those sentinels of the Strait, Cartagena and Cádiz, and so jeopardize the two-hundred-year-old British policy built up on the strategy of naval bases? There are many people in England who fear this."

The fears of some are the hopes of others. Italy, who according to the Fascist slogan does not want to remain a prisoner in the Mediterranean, sees a chance for freedom in a change in the present situation of the Gibraltar Strait. In his book *Wetterzonen der Weltpolitik* (*Storm Zones of World Politics*) Herr Walther Pahl indicates the direction of Italian efforts. "Up to now the obvious growth of Italian power in the Mediterranean has not sensibly weakened British positions. Their defences have not been impaired by the events of recent years. They are supported and strengthened by Gibraltar. But Gibraltar is a thorn in the flesh of the Italians, and signs and portents lead one to suppose that Italy will do all in her power to undermine British security in that zone of influence."

The first stage in the undermining of British security was to gain a foothold in Spain, and to help to power a general who would be willing to become the instrument of Italo-German policy. From the very beginning of the war, Germany and Italy strongly recommended—and took it upon themselves to put the recommendation into practice—the fortification of all Spanish positions in the Gibraltar area, especially on the coast of Spanish Morocco, from Melilla to Tetuán, from Ceuta to the Tangiers frontier, and from Arzila to Larache.

In Spain there was a firm conviction before the Spanish War that the transformation of Ceuta into a second Gibraltar could only take place "against England or under an English protectorate." It has taken place against England and under an Italo-German protectorate, and notwithstanding the Anglo-French Agreement of 1904, wherein "the two Governments agreed, in order to ensure a passage through the Straits of Gibraltar, not to allow the erection of fortifications or strategic works on that part of the Moroccan coast between Melilla and the heights dominating the right bank of the Oued Sebou."

This was not the only infringement, however. By the Franco-Spanish Agreement of 1912 Spain promised "not to give up, under any circumstances, even temporarily, her rights in the whole or part of the territory forming her zone of influence." The undisturbed movement of German agents in Spanish Morocco during the Spanish War, and the activity of German artillerymen and technicians all along the coast of the Strait, were common knowledge. At various times before and after the war this activity was responsible for a series of questions in the House of Commons, to which the reply always was that "no information" on the subject had been received. The special correspondent in Burgos of the Japanese paper *Nichi-Nichi*, however, had the good fortune to receive this information, perhaps because his reports were to be published at a safe distance. In one of his accounts, sent from Burgos in April 1939 and passed by the Franco censor, he described in great detail how "Italy and Germany, in collaboration with Spain" (!), "had constructed near Gibraltar a line of military bases placed zigzag along both sides of the Strait. Ceuta and Tarifa, Arzila and Cádiz are included in this line. The construction of the aerial bases of Lospapacio and Villafranca has been undertaken by German engineers. Those in Cádiz, Málaga, Tetuán, and Melilla are Italian. New forts are being erected behind Gibraltar. They are almost completed and are already fitted with batteries capable of bombarding the interior of the British positions. In Ceuta and La Línea the work of fortification is being proceeded with actively."

How far does all this justify the German and Italian contention that the new situation in Spain has entirely changed the Mediterranean scene, beginning with Gibraltar? Once again I prefer to leave the floor to so well-qualified an authority as Captain Liddell Hart. "We ought to be clear what this would mean. In the first place, Gibraltar would be untenable as a naval base. The anchorage there is narrow, as the sea-floor shelves sharply, and could not be used by our ships if it was under fire from hostile guns on the Spanish shore. A few mobile batteries, suddenly brought there, would suffice to make it unusable. We should then be left with no secure naval base of our own between this country and Alexandria, over 3,000 miles distant. In comparison with this fact it is a secondary question whether our ships would be able to pass through the Straits of Gibraltar into, and out of, the Mediterranean."

The Spanish War is over and the encirclement of Gibraltar complete. The *Popolo d'Italia* of July 30, 1939, in commenting on the air manœuvres which had just taken place, could allow itself the luxury of declaring that "in order to fly over the Mediterranean, it will in future be necessary to obtain Italian consent."

"For Great Britain the Mediterranean is merely one route among many; for us it is our very life!" exclaimed the Duce in his speech at Milan on November 1, 1936. Great Britain and France can certainly use the Atlantic route for their communications with Africa and the Far East. But on one condition: that the Atlantic is open to them. Spain, however, has a double sea-line, as the German writers whom we have just quoted recall with satisfaction. "In the case of both the Mediterranean and the Atlantic routes," write Herren Hummel and Siewert in their book *Der Mittelmeerraum,* "Spain must play a decisive part."

This is also the opinion of Captain Liddell Hart. "Nor does the risk end there," wrote the distinguished military correspondent of the London *Times*, when examining the situation created in the Mediterranean during the Spanish War. "The alternative route to the East round the Cape, and even the sea approaches to this country, would be jeopardized if hostile submarines and aircraft were able to operate from the north-western and south-western coasts of Spain. And this threat would be extended by an enemy's use of the Canary Isles. Thus, from a strategical point of view, the political outcome of the present struggle is not, and cannot, be a matter of indifference to us. A friendly Spain is desirable, a neutral Spain is vital."

In point of fact, not only is the Atlantic route two and a half times as long as the Mediterranean one—and this in war-time would involve an incalculable loss of time—but it would not be a particularly peaceful route either if Spain were allied to Germany and Italy (whether officially or secretly would make no difference). Ships making the trip from Bordeaux to Casablanca, on to Dakar, and round the Cape to Indo-China and the Indies, would have to pass near the north and north-east coast of Spain. Along these five hundred miles of Atlantic coast-line there are many naval and air bases threatening the Atlantic shipping of the Western democracies.

There is El Ferrol, the best war port of Spain, where according to Señor Araras, Franco's official biographer, "there is room for all the navies in the world." The author hardly needed to add that out of courtesy and gratitude the Italian and German navies would be given preference in this spacious harbour. "Inaccessible from the sea," writes Herr Franz Pauser in *Spaniens Tor zum Mittelmeer* (*Spain's Gate to the Mediterranean*), "protected by mountains and in the westernmost part of Europe, El Ferrol, the most important war port of Spain, can, with Vigo, flank all the Atlantic routes." From El Ferrol to Plymouth it is the same distance as from Hamburg to London—about 465 miles, or less than two hours in a bombing plane.

On El Ferrol in the north-west, Vigo in the west, and

Pasajes in the east, the Germans during the Spanish War showered their most delicate attentions, sending the best engineers of the Reich to fortify and prepare them for their future task in the reorganization of Europe. The most modern submarine bases and aerodromes have been installed there. On June 11, 1939 *Domingo,* the Franco review of San Sebastián, published a special number devoted to Vigo, which "with its magnificent airport—a gigantic work carried out in war-time—its emplacement, its area of 170 acres, its splendid tracks, has recently become of inestimable importance."

In what does this inestimable importance consist? It can be gauged from the factor quoted above; that is to say, its emplacement on the flank of Anglo-French communications.

If, however, the shipping of the democratic countries succeeded in avoiding the bombs and torpedoes launched from these well-placed bases of northern Spain, they would still have to pass farther south the Atlantic coast of southern Spain and Spanish Morocco. Here the ports of Cádiz, Arzila, and Larache are quite sufficient for offensive action, whether from sea or air, against Anglo-French shipping and French ports of embarkation—Casablanca, Rabat, and Port Lyautey. It should also be remembered that the roads and railway from Orán which join the Atlantic ports in French Morocco to Algeria and Tunis pass in their turn, for a distance of nearly 250 miles, very near to the Spanish protectorate, so that in addition to the sea menace to the Atlantic route, there is also the threat by land.

Still farther south, Ifni, Río de Oro, and, above all, the Canary Islands complete Spain's strategic system in the Atlantic.

The Canary Islands are under German control. German influence does not merely date from the Spanish War. Years ago German technicians and agents, in the guise of tourists attracted by the climate and beauties of these delightful islands, extended their influence throughout the territory, thereby causing serious concern to the authorities, who were forced to take certain restrictive measures. When the rebellion broke out, the Germans overran the islands. General Cugnac drew attention to this danger in *La France militaire* of October 26, 1937, when he said: "The Germans are entrenching themselves in the Canary Islands. But the Canaries are too near to our Casablanca-Bordeaux route, a part of the Dakar-Bordeaux itinerary, for their influence not to become a very serious problem in the event of our mobilization."

Ten years earlier Admiral Raeder, now Commander-in-Chief of the German fleet, reached the same conclusion, which he expressed, however, rather more categorically. "If one day a Vigo-Canaries-Azores triangle could be formed and placed under a single military command, the European situation and the relations between Europe and the other continents would be automatically and entirely changed. It would be a complete revolution in favour of the power which succeeded in occupying the angles of the triangle."

What then seemed a distant dream is now on the point of becoming reality. There is no question of Franco assuming this single military command, for he would obviously be incapable of opposing British and French sea power unaided. But as the *Military Geography of the World Sea* (Berlin, 1938) shows, everything has been well thought out beforehand. "Neither Spain nor Portugal, with their limited military resources, could use their valuable island possessions in the northern and central Atlantic to great advantage, in spite of their favourable military position. Left to themselves, these islands would at best constitute a supplementary menace. But in the hands of a strong power they could greatly obstruct the Anglo-French Atlantic communications on their flank."

This "strong power," it is hardly necessary to say, is Italy, guided and supported by Germany. With such a prospect before them, it is easy to understand how, immediately after the fall of Bilbao, the Rome newspapers were hardly able to suppress their joy. "Bilbao conquered: for the first time since the days of the Ancient Empire the Roman legions will have reached the Ocean where Britain reigns supreme!"

Two years later, at the beginning of August 1939, Spanish, German, and Italian generals met in cordial conference on board the Italian cruiser *Pola*, anchored in the Mediterranean. It was the very day on which the gold from the Bank of Spain, held in France, had been solemnly handed over to Franco's Government. But it was not, certainly, to celebrate this event that the distinguished guests, after a wide exchange of impressions, seated themselves at the Italian Admiral's table. It was more probably to drink to the success of a policy which promised to realize their great ambition—towards the fulfilment of which each one of those present had co-operated to the fullest extent of his powers—the ambition of dislodging Great Britain from her position as mistress of the seas, to the greater glory and profit of the totalitarian allies.

CHAPTER VII

Building Up an Army

THE BUILDING UP of the Republican army in a relatively short space of time—little more than a year—was one of the most impressive signs of the vitality latent in the Spanish people, and a clear proof that the role of a weak and backward third-class power which Spain had played for nearly half a century was entirely due to the incompetence and apathy of her rulers.

When the rebellion broke out, the Government was in the unique position of having to fight a war without any army at its command. The majority of the officers had made common cause with the rebels. Of 15,000 officers, barely 500 remained in the service of the Republic. Many of those 500 were Republicans by conviction; the rest stayed with the Government out of fear or in order to perpetrate acts of sabotage within the army ranks. Everything had to be improvised; practically nothing remained from the old army which could be put to any use. For many years the military organization in Spain had suffered from the defects of a class régime. Its object was not, as in other countries, to protect

122

and defend the State, but to maintain and increase the power of the officer class. Before the fall of the monarchy there existed in the Spanish army one officer for every seven soldiers and one general for every 660 men—apart from a very large number of generals in reserve. As there was no work in the barracks for all these gold-braided gentlemen, the officers' mess became the centre of conspiracy. The Spanish word *"pronunciamiento"* has now a universal significance, having become the synonym for a rising, bloodless or otherwise, of a group of officers in an attempt to seize power for themselves.

The defects of this military organization, which had been only partially remedied by the Republic, were also apparent for a time—in fact until large-scale German and Italian assistance began to arrive—in rebel territory. The rebels, however, had an army at their disposal for what it was worth, and within that army they could rely on at least two sections—the Moroccan forces and the Foreign Legion—who formed excellent shock troops, and whose fighting powers were considerably superior to those of the raw and inexperienced militiamen in Government territory.

In the first detailed plan of the rebellion communicated, on May 29, 1936, to the rebel leaders, neither of these two groups was mentioned. A certain feeling of shame at the idea of using Moroccan troops against the Spanish people, and, more particularly, the fear that their intervention from the very beginning of the war might have a bad effect at home and abroad, decided the organizers of the rebellion to rely chiefly on the Fifth, Sixth, and Seventh Divisions, quartered respectively in Saragossa, Burgos, and Valladolid. From these three points they were to march on Madrid and seize the reins of government.

This plan was soon discarded for another, in which the African garrisons were to be given a decisive role, while in the Peninsula the Second Division, with its headquarters in Seville, was to play the principal part, being responsible for ensuring the transport of Moorish troops and the Foreign

Legion. If the Republicans could have held Cádiz for eight days, this plan would have failed, and with it the whole rebellion. Credit must be given to General Franco, who was responsible for the second plan, for his wisdom in deciding that the centre and starting-point of the rebellion should be Morocco and not the Peninsula. The Moors, who had had long fighting experience, were the best soldiers of the old army—in fact, the only real shock troops; they were furnished with the most modern war equipment, immune from all political propaganda of a democratic nature, and led by the best officers of the Spanish army.

The Republic, on the other hand, had to build up its army in the very trenches and to begin at the beginning with fresh privates, sergeants, officers, General Staff, and supply services. The first militia formations were the nucleus of this new army. In those early days the structure of the fighting unit was usually determined by the means of transport. The men who succeeded in getting hold of a couple of cars, either through their organizations or on their own initiative, formed a section; the more fortunate ones who managed to commandeer three or four lorries formed a company. The incorporation of these separate units into battalions was the first step in the creation of the Republican army.

Another and more important step forward, was the formation of the Mixed Brigades, which had been at one time the favourite unit of the best military experts in Spain. Composed of various infantry battalions, with artillery, sappers, means of communication, and administrative staff, they comprised all the necessary factors and were a complete formation in themselves. For the first time these units were properly officered, instructed, and equipped, and formed a united and disciplined whole. They were organized by the General Staff in accordance with a plan which had taken into account the experience of the previous months. The time had gone by when the political parties had to carry the weight of the war organization on their shoulders. The existing militia lost their picturesque names—"Youth Guards," "October Battalion," "Red Lions," "Iron Brigade," "Pasionaria Battalion"—to become Brigades No. 8, No. 12, No. 17. . . .

Their efficiency was successfully put to the test in the attack on the Cerro de los Angeles (Hill of the Angels) on January 19, 1937. This hill dominates Madrid and, besides being an excellent observation post, was a perpetual menace to traffic on the adjoining highroad. After a brilliant attack, two of the Mixed Brigades placed the Republican flag on its summit. But the next day they were dislodged from their new positions. The People's Army had learned how to take objectives, but not how to keep them.

Six months later, however, the new army, which had given such brilliant proof of its attacking powers at Guadalajara—where it turned the Italian offensive of March 1937 into a second Caporetto—showed at Brunete that it had at last learned how to hold positions as well as to capture them. Although Brunete was afterwards retaken by the rebels, all the remaining towns and the hub of communications captured by the Republican troops remained permanently in their hands. The attack on Brunete, planned by the subsequent Chief of Staff, General Rojo, with a unified command and all the material necessary for a large-scale operation, in greater quantities than hitherto employed, was carried out with such secrecy, rapidity, and skill that among the prisoners taken were various medical officers from the rear guard and an artillery officer caught in his pyjamas. All the services functioned perfectly. Sixty miles from the nearest railway station an army of more than two hundred thousand men was provided for without the slightest difficulty.

There was still, however, a long road to travel. The chief difficulty continued to be the army command. In the beginning the militiamen's instinctive distrust of their professional officers had to be overcome. The failure of an operation, through whatever cause, was immediately attributed to disloyalty on the part of the commanding officer if he happened to have been a member of the old army. Every defeat meant the retirement of a professional officer, for whom it was generally hard to find a sufficiently able substitute. The retreat from Talavera to Madrid in the autumn of 1936 led to the displacement of General Asensio, unquestionably one of the most capable and intelligent officers in the Republican army. The distrust produced by his failure to hold up the rebel advance did not stop there, and even his subsequent appointment by Señor Largo Caballero to the post of Under-Secretary of War gave rise to serious political friction, which ended in his final retirement. Looking at the problem from a purely political point of view, and having decided that the fundamental factor was not one's own personal trust in the General, but the suspicion which he inspired in a large section of the troops, I was one of the Cabinet ministers who stood out most firmly for his dismissal. If in an England free from all the fears and hatreds inseparable from civil strife, Lord Haldane had to be sacrificed to public opinion during the World War, it seemed to me at the time that the continuance of General Asensio as the War Minister's closest collaborator was inadvisable from every point of view—primarily because a campaign against him might recoil on his chief, who besides being Minister of War was also Prime Minister. The fight waged by Caballero against what he thought was an injustice done to his Under-Secretary had a certain greatness. He deeply resented the fact that I, for the first time, took a position different from his, and from that day, to my great regret, I ceased to be his most trusted Minister. But in a struggle in which the whole future of the country was at stake, personal devotion had to give way. General Asensio could have become the greatest military genius. I still think that to have maintained him as Under-Secretary of War when the front mistrusted him would have been a grave mistake.

One of the reasons for forming the General War Commissariat in October 1936 was the need for improving relations between professional officers and militiamen. From that time until November of the following year I was in charge of this Commissariat, and remained so even after leaving the Government in the crisis of May 1937. The credit for its organization, erroneously attributed to me, belongs entirely to the War Minister, Señor Largo Caballero. It was a wise and successful measure, although of all the entities formed during the war the Commissariat was the one which came in for the severest criticism.

The point at issue was the relative strength of the various political parties composing the Commissariat. It was reproached with being preponderantly Communist, and it cannot be denied that for a considerable period this was so, at least as far as numbers were concerned. There were many reasons for this. The War Commissariat can claim an ancestry dating back to the French Revolution, when Dumouriez's treachery disclosed to Carnot and the Convention the acts of sabotage on the part of the Monarchist generals and gave an opportunity to Saint-Just to prove himself the most excellent and amazing political Commissar of all time. During the Russian Revolution the Commissariat became one of the fundamental supports of the Soviet Army. When it was formed in Spain, the Spanish Communists, attracted by an institution with such a history, took a greater interest in its development and expansion than the other political parties. The latter, for whom it had no particular meaning and who looked on it at first as something rather exotic and unnecessary, contented themselves with presenting lists of candidates drawn up with no special care. The Communists, on the other hand, sent their most active members right from the day of its inception. This inequality grew during the critical period of the defence of Madrid. The situation on that front during the months of November and December 1936 made it necessary to increase the number of commissars. Hundreds of provisional nominations were made, and these only served to increase the existing disproportion. These improvised Commissars acted at the time of greatest danger, sharing the grief of the fighters when Madrid seemed lost, and their joy when it was saved; after that they could hardly be deprived of a rank which they had acquired in the thick of the battle and which was held sacred by the troops themselves.

The only solution was to reorganize the Commissariat completely and to regulate its normal functions in the light of previous experience. Unfortunately for me, Señor Prieto, Minister of National Defence, did not approve my suggestions in this respect, and believing him to be sincerely convinced that I was the chief obstacle in the reorganization, I resigned my post, true to the opinion that in time of war one's first duty is loyal service to the Government, whether from a ministry or from the most unenviable position which it may be one's lot to fill.

But while mistakes were sometimes made in the War Commissariat, as elsewhere, no one can truthfully deny that the Commissars played a very large part in enforcing discipline in the army and maintaining morale when it was threatened by the serious scarcity of arms. True to their slogan: "The first to advance, the last to retreat"—words spoken by Commissar Belmonte as he fell at the head of a vigorous counter-attack— the Commissars not only carried out educational work at the front and tried to establish harmony between loyal officers and men, but also assumed temporary leadership of the troops when their commanders had been killed in battle. While many of the professional officers were suspicious of the Commissars in the beginning, as time went on the best of these officers came to look on their collaboration as most useful and desirable.

The work of the political Commissars on the one hand and the growing authority of the Government on the other gradually overcame these psychological difficulties. There remained, however, the problem of providing an army which was increasing in numbers, and which had to fight an enemy assisted by the finest German and Italian technicians, with officers competent to meet the fresh exigencies of the war.

Experience proved that it was easier to find a good army or divisional commandant than men capable of leading a battalion or company. A workman like Modesto, a composer like Durán, were capable of commanding large units, and were endowed with all the qualities of great leaders. On the other hand, more than one military operation, carefully thought out and successfully initiated, failed because subordinate officers were incapable of leading their men in an engagement.

Only after intensive instruction in the military colleges, and lectures given at the front, did these gaps become filled and the Republican army acquire that efficiency which enabled it to achieve such exploits as the crossing of the Ebro. On no other occasion was the tremendous effort made by the Republicans in the sphere of military organization more clearly seen than during the period covering the defence of the Levant and the offensive of July 1938, and a brief recapitulation of events may therefore not be out of place.

On April 2, 1938 the rebels in their offensive on the Aragón front achieved a notable success with the occupation of Gandesa, in the bend of the Ebro. Confident of their superiority in men and material, they attacked in the direction of Tortosa, but the Republican troops re-formed, held up the enemy, and finally drove them back towards the south. This sudden change in the situation made the rebels hesitate, but realizing that their attacking powers were not spent, they boldly decided to bring their left wing into action in a surprise attack, force their way through the loyalist lines, and advance towards the Mediterranean. On April 15 they reached the sea at Vinaroz, and Catalonia was cut off from the rest of Republican Spain.

The enemy offensive, begun on March 9 and carried out with enormous quantities of war material on a front 135 miles wide and in places 62 to 68 miles deep, was over.

The new front extended in a southerly direction from a point fifteen miles west of Andorra on the Pyrenean French-

Spanish frontier to Camarasa on the Segre, followed this river to its confluence with the Ebro, and then followed the Ebro to its mouth. In Balaguer the enemy held a strong bridgehead on the left bank of the Segre, and another at Serós on the lower reaches of the Segre, east of Fraga. From Mequinenza, where the Segre flows into the Ebro, to Amposta, on the Mediterranean, the two armies faced each other across the latter river.

The rebel advance towards the Mediterranean was one of the hardest blows of the whole war. Communications were cut with the Levant front and with the rest of the central-southern zone. It was impossible to transport troops and material from one zone to another, except by air and sea. The former route could only be used for the conveyance of officers and a small quantity of essential material. Owing to the lack of convoy ships, sea transport was very difficult, and the Government vessels were at the mercy of the rebel fleet, actively assisted by the Italian and German units which for eighteen months had been carrying out espionage and piracy in Spanish waters.

On the Levant front, therefore, the enemy gained both the initiative and an opportunity to carry out operations on inner lines. The rebel position, however, was by no means an ideal one. Between the Mediterranean and the main body of their troops was a stretch of difficult territory, with few roads, most of which were impassable. Only the Vinaroz-Cherta road, on which the two northern and southern routes converge, was fit for transport, and even that could be used for little more than peace-time traffic.

We had to face the fact, therefore, that the enemy, realizing their difficult and dangerous position, would not remain inactive for long and would attempt at all costs to break through our lines in an effort to improve their communications. On the north it would be difficult for them. The well-fortified Republican positions on the left bank of the Ebro made any attempt in that direction inadvisable. Their next push would have to be towards Castellón de la Plana.

As we had anticipated, they did not wait long. Without making the usual elaborate preparations—confident no doubt that the severing of Barcelona from Valencia had caused demoralization in the Republican ranks—and relying entirely on their artillery and air force, the rebels began their advance towards the Levant. The operation was a failure from the beginning and was not resumed until the insurgents, with the assistance of German and Italian warships, were able to reinforce their contingents in the Vinaroz sector and force the Republicans to rush troops to that part of the front.

It was now difficult for the enemy to go back. The new situation forced them to intensify operations, and what was at first merely an attempt to consolidate their coastal positions and extend their network of communications, became a general offensive, stretching from Teruel to the Mediterranean. By the end of April the focal point of the war was the Levant. For days a fierce battle raged, in which the Republicans, aware of their numerical inferiority in men and material, remained on the defensive.

Having met with continuous resistance on the coastal sector, and having gained nothing from their frontal attacks, the rebels rushed up fresh divisions and tried to force a way through between Montalbán and Morella. The Republican front had to be narrowed, and as a few miles of territory more or less in that sector were not of great strategic importance, the loyalist command very wisely decided to set up a line of defence well back, in a position from which their units could operate with greater freedom and from which they could at the same time prevent the enemy from using their cannon and tanks to the best advantage. So began the *"bataille d'usure"*— the war of attrition—in which, after sustaining great losses and using up an increasing number of men and arms, the rebels succeeded in advancing along the coast—the most important sector—a distance of less than two miles in five weeks.

Convinced that time was on the side of the Republicans, the rebels decided to change their methods, and, assembling all their available forces, launched one attack after another. Their object was to surround the loyal troops by means of their favourite *"bolsa"* ("pocket") manœuvre, which consists in finding the weakest spot in the opposing defences, driving in a wedge, and deploying in such a manner that the opponent has to retreat or run the risk of being cut off. This attempt was frustrated, however, by the disciplined fighting of the Republicans. At the end of May the General Staff voluntarily decided to narrow the Republican front from 90 to 75 miles, in order to give the troops a short breathing-space and to reorganize the reserves. This new front, however, did not remain stable for very long. The rebels renewed their offensive on May 29, this time with a definite objective—Sagunto and Valencia. They attacked along the whole front, from Teruel to the Mediterranean—their right wing in the direction of the Teruel-Sagunto railway, their centre in the direction of Viver-Segorbe, and their left wing along the coast. The troops in the left wing and centre were supposed to meet between Viver and Segorbe, about twenty-two miles from Sagunto, from which point they were to advance on the city.

This offensive, for which the rebel General Staff had set a limit of from three to four weeks, had to be carried out with the greatest speed. On its success, they hoped, depended nothing less than the end of the war. What could not be gained in the eastern offensive was to be obtained from the attack on the Levant. The cutting of communications, and the confusion caused by the severing of Catalonia from the central-southern zone, coupled with an advance in Andalucía and the capture of Almadén, would obviously create so much disorder that Republican resistance would rapidly crumble. It was worth a major effort. From the very first day of the offensive all available war material was employed and all the reserves were kept ready to intervene as soon as the first break should occur in the Republican lines.

The centre of Republican resistance was Mora de Rubielos. While that position remained in Government hands, the rebel troops carrying out flanking operations on the Teruel-Sagunto road were being constantly threatened. The fighting here was probably fiercer than at any other point in the course of the war. But Mora de Rubielos was held, and it was not until June 16, when the General Staff gave the order to its heroic defenders to retire to the new line, that it fell into rebel hands.

Between April 15 and June 10 the rebels had only gained two strategic successes in positions of secondary importance. They failed to break through the Republican defences on the coast, in the centre, and at Teruel. On the Teruel-Sagunto road they succeeded in advancing a few miles, but in the south their attacks were a complete failure, while on the rebel right wing, near Alcalá de Chivert, the Republicans regained the offensive and placed the enemy in a very difficult position.

Once again there was a change of tactics and direction. The advance along the coast to Castellón de la Plana, already attempted various times, was renewed, and this time Albocácer was taken by the enemy.

Ever since the end of May, Albocácer had been surrounded on three sides. With its capture the rebels found themselves only twelve miles from Castellón de la Plana. Castellón had suffered from air raids as few loyal cities had done. Two out of every three houses had been destroyed. The civilian population, who, with the many refugees in the town, had helped to build a subterranean city, had at last been evacuated. Castellón had ceased to be an economic factor and had become a heap of ruins, but around those ruins a fierce battle raged for five days, in which airplanes, warships, tanks, and artillery took part. At the end of the five days the loyalist troops evacuated the city.

The main body of Republican troops took up new positions on the River Mijares, about three miles south of Castellón. For three days other battalions held up the advance of an enemy ten times as strong and covered the retreat of the rest of the army. Only when the last man and machine-gun had crossed the river were the temporary positions on the Mijares abandoned. This episode, apparently of secondary importance, is an indication of the degree of discipline reached by the Republican army and of the fighting spirit of its officers and men.

In their task of resisting rebel pressure until the chain of fortifications in course of construction round Sagunto and Valencia was reasonably strong, the loyalist troops behaved magnificently. By July 8 the work of fortification was more or less finished. Thanks to the co-operation and enthusiasm of the civilian population and Valencian workers, the defences built up so rapidly were firm enough to withstand an enemy with superior resources. On that same day the General Staff gave orders for the evacuation of Nules. Protected by the new line, the Republicans repulsed all attacks, and did not yield another inch of ground. On July 24 the enemy was forced to abandon the offensive in that sector, in order, with reorganized reserves, to make a final attack on Valencia from Teruel and Viver.

On the same day, July 24, the Republicans began their amazing offensive on the Ebro. That morning Dr. Negrín had called a meeting of the Supreme War Council. Formed at the beginning of 1937, this council was composed of the most highly placed army leaders, and of four Cabinet Ministers— apart from the Prime Minister himself—representing the various political shades of opinion of the Government. After the previous Cabinet reorganization, the Ministers on this Council were Señor Giral, Minister without Portfolio, a Republican; Señor Paulino Gómez, Minister of the Interior, a Socialist; Señor Uribe, Minister of Agriculture, a Communist; and Señor Blanco, Minister of Education, a member of the C.N.T. In my capacity as Foreign Minister I also attended the meetings.

Questions of a purely military nature, which it was not necessary to bring up for general discussion in the Cabinet, or which by reason of their confidential nature it was advisable to confine to a narrow circle, were debated and resolved with the direct collaboration of the Chief of Staff and relevant experts and heads of departments. The fact that on this particular day Colonel Azcárate, Inspector-General of Engineers and brother of the Spanish Ambassador in London, was at the meeting led most of those present to suspect that some important operation was to be carried out. Few guessed, however, that it was to begin within the next few hours.

The Prime Minister briefly explained the critical position on the Levant front and said that unless extraordinary measures were taken, its natural consequence would be the fall of Sagunto and Valencia, and perhaps the loss of the war. The only way to prevent such a catastrophe was to attack the enemy at a point where they would be forced to withdraw a large part of their forces from the Levant. General Menéndez, Commander of the Levant Army, would then have time to rest his troops, which had been engaged in continuous fighting for three months, and to complete the defences round Valencia. Dr. Negrín began by enumerating the difficulties in the way of crossing the Ebro and pointed out that while in normal circumstances the territory gained would not justify the great risk involved, in the present situation the operation seemed to him to be one of overwhelming necessity. He then invited General Rojo to give a detailed explanation with the help of the map.

General Rojo's reports were always distinguished for their clarity and precision. This report was especially impressive. In his opinion the operation had some chance of success, always provided that the preparations were kept secret until the last moment. It was arranged that sufficient units to begin the advance on Gandesa, with all the necessary material, should cross the river overnight, so that if on the following day communications were cut, the troops on the opposite bank could hold out until the bridges were rebuilt. We knew, of course, that enemy aircraft would concentrate their attack on the bridges, and we also had to consider the possibility of some of these being carried away by floods, frequent on the Ebro at that time of the year. The surprise factor was the essential one, and in General Rojo's opinion the Prime Minister was completely justified in not calling the council meeting until the last moment, and in insisting that orders for troop movements should not be given until everything was ready.

Colonel Azcárate expressed anxiety concerning the scarcity of material for bridges, and reported on the measures which had been taken to ensure their rapid construction in a maximum of two hours, and their replacement, where possible, by others which were being built at top speed. The most reliable men had been chosen for this work, and, apart from two officers of the utmost confidence, not even the engineers themselves knew the purpose to which these bridges were to be put.

The terms in which the Prime Minister had stated the urgent need for extraordinary measures if the Levant front was to be saved left no room for serious objection, and subsequent discussion was confined to questions from ministers interested in certain aspects of an operation which was the first of its kind to be attempted during the war. We were all fully conscious of the danger that part of the army in Catalonia might be destroyed if the enemy reacted quickly enough and forced our troops back in disorder across a river where the bridges were few and none too safe. The threat on Valencia might then become a threat on Barcelona. It was perhaps a rash undertaking, but there was no alternative to running the risk, in the knowledge that we could rely on the fighting spirit and high morale of our troops. We separated after making a solemn promise not to disclose a word of what had passed at that meeting.

After the operation had begun, the Prime Minister called a Cabinet meeting and apologized for not having previously informed the members of the nature and imminence of the undertaking. He then read out the first war communiqué, which filled everybody present with the greatest jubilation. As on previous occasions, it was Premier Negrín himself who stated the position in what he considered were its just proportions, and curbed the excessive enthusiasm of those ministers who, through ignorance of the obstacles still to be overcome, were inclined to take the success of the offensive for granted.

The operations were carried out in perfect order. On the night of July 24–5 Republican troops on a ninety-mile front, between Mequinenza in the north and Amposta in the south, crossed the Ebro at six different points, taking the enemy completely by surprise. Only at Amposta, a point chosen by the General Staff purposely to divert enemy attention from the rest of the front, was there a slight resistance. The enthusiasm of our men was so great that many of them swam across the river, while the main body of troops, material, and supplies crossed by the bridges and pontoons. Once the majority of the men was across, the march on Gandesa began.

Forty-eight hours later, rebel aircraft, flown hastily from the Levant, put in an appearance. As had been foreseen, they concentrated their attack on the river crossings. They attempted to smash up the bridges, failed to destroy a single one, and lost various machines. Mass air raids did not succeed in holding up the Republican offensive. On July 27 our troops reached Villalabar de los Arcos in the environs of Gandesa. The next day they broke across the southern half of the Ebro bend, reached the outskirts of Bot, and occupied the highroad between Bot and Cherta. On July 30 the objectives mapped out by the Republican General Staff were reached with the exception of the village of Gandesa itself. In the space of six days an area of 270 square miles had been captured and 7,000 prisoners taken. The new Ebro front now stretched from Cherta in a northerly direction, leaving Bot on the east and encircling the Sierra of Pandols, a position of primary importance, which was now occupied by loyalist troops.

That same day the rebels began a strong counter-offensive, which reached its zenith on August 2 and rapidly declined as the Republican troops advanced from the Levant towards the Montes Universales, occupied heights threatening the enemy on his flank, and forced him to lessen his pressure on the Ebro and to retire hastily to Teruel with some of the divisions brought from that sector only a week before. The insurgents tried to fill up the gaps with troops drawn from the Lérida and Balaguer sectors, but this weakening of the northern front was taken advantage of by the Republicans, who crossed the Segre at Serós on August 9 and built a new bridgehead there.

The rebels were forced to employ their best troops in this counter-attack. Their losses were tremendous. Fighting in that sector lasted for more than three months. Not until November 15 did they succeed in re-forming their front on the Ebro. On the night of July 25 the Republicans had crossed the river; 113 days later they retired to their former positions. In the meantime the first snow had begun to fall in the Levant. We had accomplished our purpose. We had stopped the rebel offensive down the coast toward Valencia and forced them to prepare for a winter campaign.

The Republican army had reached a stage of maturity in which it was capable of carrying out the most difficult undertakings. Even the ranks of Tuscany—in the shape of German military correspondents of the Nazi press—could not forbear to cheer the operations on the Ebro. The prestige of the army increased in the eyes of the whole world. Not only was their courage admired, but their technical organization as well. And this stage of development had been reached in an astonishingly short space of time. When in the summer of 1937 I had the pleasure of lunching at his country-house with Mr. Lloyd George—a statesman more fitted to express an opinion on this matter than anyone else living—he recalled how long it took during the World War for the British army to complete its organization, and spoke of the many difficulties with which he and his colleagues had to contend. But a divided Spain, a Spain isolated by the policy of Non-Intervention, lacking the many resources which the British Government had at its disposal, cannot be compared with the British Empire. In one respect only can a parallel be drawn between the two peoples in two such very different sets of circumstances—in their love of country and their determination to fight to the end for their national independence.

Looking back on events in the spirit of calm and critical inquiry induced by our unhappy experience, I have come to the conclusion that loyalist Spain could have won the war on three separate occasions if certain conditions had been fulfilled on any one of them. Firstly, at Guadalajara, if we could have relied on a regular army such as the Republic succeeded in building by the end of 1937. Secondly, at Teruel, if there had been a system of reserves such as existed after the spring of 1938. At that time it was not only the scarcity of material, but, more than that, the lack of reserves, that prevented us from following up our success with fresh operations in another sector—operations which might have changed the course of the war. Lastly, on the Ebro. By this time we had organized reserves, but they could not be used because at the time of the offensive, begun in the difficult conditions already related, there was a greater inequality of material than had existed at any time during the war. This made it impossible not only to follow up the initial success, but also to carry out complementary operations on the Catalan front and a heavier offensive planned in the central-southern zone. The Ebro operations had to be restricted, and their repercussions were therefore limited as well.

This scarcity of material was caused by the closing of the French frontier, following a change of policy at the Quai d'Orsay. Nevertheless, advantage could and should have been taken of the Ebro success to carry out a series of operations in the central-southern zone planned by the General

Staff, with the approval of the Prime Minister. But owing to the weakness of certain army leaders in the central-southern zone, so tragically revealed during the last days of the war, these operations were all abortive, and no effort was made to take advantage of the intense disorder caused in rebel territory by an exploit of such high moral and military value as the Republican offensive on the Ebro.

Lastly, it should not be forgotten that the rebels were compensated for the setback administered to them by the Republican army on the Ebro by the victory of their allies at Munich.

CHAPTER VIII

Work Under Fire

WHILE LOYALIST SPAIN, undaunted by the many obstacles in her path, was building up an army, she did not neglect the great work of national reform begun in the early days of the Republic and suddenly interrupted two years later when the disloyalty of the President, Señor Alcalá Zamora, paved the way for a return to reactionary rule.

It is not until one reviews the work and plans of the Republic that one can understand the fervent zeal with which the Spaniards defended it for nearly three years, and can see through the petty motives which inspired a tiny majority to sacrifice the lives and possessions of the people, and the very independence of their country, on the altar of a wretched and unjust past.

It is common knowledge that Spain—perhaps alone of all the countries in Europe—was, before the advent of the Republic, in a state of economic, social, and political stagnation, which not only condemned the vast majority of Spaniards to a life of oppression, misery, and ignorance, but also formed the chief obstacle in the progress and development of the nation.

141

When the Republic was founded in 1931, it was faced with a gigantic task. It had to carry out a fairer and more rational distribution of land, give to millions of people their first opportunity for education, start a new drive in industry, improve the conditions of the workers, purify the public finances, and, in a word, regulate the life of the country in such a way that it could take its rightful place among the other nations of the civilized world.

One of the most difficult and urgent problems was that of land reform. The concentration of land in the hands of a privileged few had reached such proportions that, according to the figures of the Property Department in December 1930, 957,655 acres were shared among 14 landlords. In the central-southern region, out of a total of 38,782,040 acres, 15,971,192 were the property of 7,266 great landowners, and what remained was divided among a million peasants. While thousands did not even have enough ground to grow a few vegetables, in 1936 the Duke of Medinaceli owned 195,680 acres of land, the Duke of Peñaranda 104,345 acres, the Duke of Alba 89,625 acres, and the Marquis of Comillas 42,795 acres. From a summary of official statistics the following conclusion is reached: 14,721 landed proprietors absorbed approximately half the area under census; that is to say, 27,671,750 acres. The remainder, 28,415,975 acres, was divided among 1,755,305 people, the vast majority of whom owned less than two and a half acres each.

What, then, was the situation of the two social classes? One per cent of the total number of landlords averaged an annual income of 30,000 pesetas [1] each, while 95 per cent received in all only one third of the total land revenue, or about 200 pesetas per annum each. And the majority of this 95 per cent —that is, 980,850 peasants—averaged only 24 pesetas per annum each.

"In the Extremadura district," writes the distinguished agricultural engineer Don Pascual Carrión, in his excellent book

---

[1] A peseta, before the Spanish War, was roughly equivalent to twelve cents.

Los Latifundios de España (The Large Estates of Spain), "the great landowners in Badajoz absorb 60 per cent of the wealth of that province, and in Cáceres 57 per cent. The situation is much the same in Andalucía. The Penibetic district (Málaga and Granada) shows that 41 per cent of its wealth is in the hands of great landowners, the number of them being far less in Málaga than in Granada. In the valley of the Guadalquivir we find the most extreme cases of all Spain, for in Seville, where 5 per cent of the proprietors are great landowners, they share 72 per cent of the wealth of the province, nine times as much as in Castellón de la Plana. In short, in the Betic district, where the total number of proprietors and the total taxable incomes are 285,462 and 166,000,000 pesetas respectively, 6,015 owners receive 100,000,000 pesetas and 261,428 small proprietors have 42,000,000. Thus the annual income of the former works out at an average of 18,000 pesetas, and of the latter at 161 pesetas."

The result was that the peasant was obliged to rent land or to hire himself out as a day-labourer on the large estates. In either case he was the victim of the most iniquitous exploitation. In the matter of renting land, there was no special legislation protecting the tenant against the abuses and arbitrary impositions of the landlord. And as far as wages were concerned, in Extremadura a labourer was paid 2.25 pesetas for working from sunrise to sunset and in Salamanca 1.50 pesetas; while in some places he would get nothing but his food.

The Republic wanted to put an end to this state of affairs, which was not only thoroughly unjust, but also harmful to the national economy, since the large landowners, with their easy profits, did not trouble to organize the cultivation of their estates rationally and often let large tracts of them run to waste.

On April 29, 1931, a week after the proclamation of the Republic, the Provisional Government issued a decree concerning the leasing of land, which established a minimum of protection to the lessees and put a stop to some of the abuses. A further decree of June 11, 1931 granted to the lessees the right to apply to the *Jurado Mixto* (or "Mixed Jury," a body on which the workers' organizations were represented) for the revision and reduction of rents (which had been raised 300 per cent over those of 1913, although the sale price of products had only increased by 67 per cent). Both measures, it should be clearly understood, essentially benefited the middle-class peasant.

The Republic also wanted to improve the lot of the farm labourer. A decree of June 12, 1931 extended to agricultural workers the benefit of the laws regarding accidents at work, for in spite of the Geneva Convention of 1921, the Spanish agricultural proletariat had after ten years still not obtained this legitimate improvement in their conditions. At the same time an equitable rise in wages was arranged; the normal and the harvest wage, which in 1930 were 2.25 and 4 pesetas respectively, rose to 5 and 11 pesetas in 1932.

The fundamental problem to be solved, however, was that of the redistribution of land. The Republic, with great care and detail, drew up an Agrarian Reform Bill. The many difficulties placed in its way by the landowners, who went so far as to organize the rising of August 10, 1932, under the leadership of General Sanjurjo, delayed its approval until September 15 of the same year. The bill as finally approved merely aimed at increasing land production and strengthening the position of the small holder. The Agrarian Reform was based on the general principle of indemnified expropriation, save in the case of estates belonging to the grandees—since they were responsible for the August 1932 rising.

No sooner had the Republic begun work on Agrarian Reform, however, than the conservatives returned to power, and it was held in abeyance until, with the triumph of the Popular Front in February 1936, there was at last a chance to tackle the matter seriously. It was then that the insurrection of July 18 broke out, supported by the large landowners.

The rebellion, however, was not able to hold up Agrarian Reform. By a decree of October 7, 1936, the Republican State carried out the expropriation of the estates of all landowners who had taken part in the rebel movement, and these were distributed among the small holders and farm labourers of the respective localities, to be cultivated individually or collectively as desired. It was a strictly legal measure, based on Article 44 of the Spanish Constitution, which admits unindemnified expropriation in exceptional circumstances. The application of this article could not have been more clearly justified, for the great landowners had not only risen in arms against the legitimate State, but by abandoning their estates had also impaired the national economy.

From a political point of view this meant that the peasant identified himself with the Republican cause. On the loyalist side results were soon evident. Thousands of peasants went to the recruiting centres to join up. They knew that in defending the Republic they were defending their own land. In the rebel zone the consequences were no less important. The rural population of the invaded territory looked with envy on the peasants in Republican Spain, who were freed at last from the yoke of centuries. At the end of the war Franco annulled the decree of October 7 by a stroke of the pen. But the memory of those two and a half years when the Spanish peasant was master of his land can never be effaced, and it will be one of the certain causes for the downfall of the Franco régime, which, as was to be supposed, has re-established the wealthy landowners and the infamous system of exploitation—a system the Republic hoped to abolish for ever.

In accordance with the decree of October 7, 1936, the Spanish Government, during the war, distributed 10,000,000 acres among the peasants. This figure stands out in great contrast to that of preceding years. From 1907 to 1931 (twenty-four years) the corresponding figure was 170,377 acres; from August 1933 to February 1936, 410,666 acres; and from February 1936 to July 1936, 1,780,175 acres.

The number of peasants who benefited under this redistribution scheme, carried out in the midst of the war, was one and a half million.

But it was not enough to give them land. They also had to have the means of cultivating it. The life of the small farmer in Spain had always been a wretched one. In his previously cited book Don Pascual Carrión has described their sordid existence. "The small holder," he writes, "who is in want of capital to fertilize his land and maintain his livestock, usually has to resort to money-lenders, and when settlement day comes, he finds he owes everything in his possession—provisions for himself and his family; food for his horses; his fertilizers, and even his seeds—so that when the harvest is gathered, he has to sell it at a loss in order to pay his debts and the high rate of interest charged. He thus loses on both counts —by selling cheap and buying dear—since he mostly has to buy on a credit basis, paying an interest rate of at least twenty-five per cent. The following year he has to repeat the same operation—buying everything on credit or else borrowing the money; and as there are no adequate credit organizations, he has to repair again to the money-lender, who sooner or later is left in possession of his farm or forces him to sell it at a loss in order to pay his debts."

With these facts in mind, the Republic not only created a million and a half landowners after the outbreak of the rebellion, but also lent them the money necessary to cultivate their land and to free themselves from the clutches of the usurers. In spite of the urgent needs of the war, the Government set aside considerable sums for this purpose. The new proprietors received credits to the value of 110,046,876 pesetas, with more than 5,000 tons of seeds and 117,000 tons of fertilizers.

Neither did the Republic forget the existing small holders. These were given credits and loans to the extent of more than 14,000,000 pesetas, as well as large quantities of seeds and fertilizers. The Republican régime, overcoming all economic problems and the difficulties created by the blockade, made every effort to help the farmers, being well aware that the small holding was one of the pillars of Spanish democracy.

In the cultural sphere the work of the Republic was equally amazing. At the time of the fall of the monarchy there were only 37,599 school-teachers in Spain, all miserably paid, for a population of 23,000,000 inhabitants. For 3,000,000 of the children there were no schools at all, and illiteracy was a national plague. There existed grave defects in the system of secondary-school and university training, and the advantages of this type of education were reserved exclusively for a small social class.

In the first two years of the Republic, between 1931 and 1933, 10,000 schools were built and 20,000 teachers appointed. This work, interrupted during the time the Right was in power, was renewed and speeded up by the Popular Front Government after February 1936. It was during the war, however, that it reached its zenith. In the eighteen months from July 1936 to December 1937, 6,091 new schools were opened in the Republican zone, and teachers' salaries were raised to a minimum of 4,000 pesetas per annum. In their 1937 budget the Republican Government assigned the sum of 20,000,000 pesetas for scholastic material and furniture in the loyal zone, a figure more than twice as great as that budgeted by the last Monarchistic Government for all the schools in Spain. At the same time they devoted 7,250,000 pesetas to school clothing and canteens, as against 450,000 pesetas set aside for this purpose in the last Monarchist budget.

The struggle against adult illiteracy was carried on with great firmness and enthusiasm. Cultural militias and flying brigades were created. The former carried out their work in the barracks, and even in the very trenches, and thanks to their efforts 75,000 soldiers were taught to read and write. The flying brigades visited towns and villages and devoted themselves to the task of providing more than 300,000 adult members of the civilian population with an elementary education.

The Government also entrusted the *Consejo Central de Archivos, Bibliotecas y Tesoro Artístico* (Central Council of Archives, Libraries, and Art Treasures) with the task of improving and adding to the public libraries. In Spain neglect of these amenities was traditional. In one provincial capital the only public library had to rely for its entire maintenance on an annual revenue of 345 pesetas. Between March 1937 and April 1938 this council organized 22 municipal, 6 rural, and 79 school libraries, and, at a cost of 7,000,000 pesetas, bought nearly half a million volumes for the existing ones.

In spite of the difficulties created by the war, the Government not only paid due attention to secondary education, but did everything possible to make it available to all. With this end in view they established a system of scholarships from elementary schools for the cleverer children, and when necessary provided them with free text-books, and grants varying from 200 to 450 pesetas a month according to the age of the pupils and the income of their parents. At the beginning of 1938, 3,716 scholarships had already been awarded, and in that same year 25,000,000 pesetas were used for this purpose. Soon after the rebellion broke out, the Republic also created Workmen's Institutes, where young workmen were educated to matriculation standard so that they could later on study for a career. Six of these institutes were formed, and 16,-000,000 pesetas set aside for their upkeep.

As far as the Spanish art treasures are concerned, the whole world is a witness of the care taken by the Republic for their protection and safety. This was unquestionably one of the Spanish Government's most glorious achievements. At the very beginning of the rebellion a group of intellectuals, artists, poets, historians, and representatives of every political party, took upon themselves the defence of the national heritage of art in Madrid. This movement soon spread to the provinces. There can be no doubt that the great efforts which the Republic had made during its short life in sending lecturers and teachers with travelling museums and photographs of the artistic wealth of the country to the most remote corners of Spain had awakened in the people, if not a knowledge of their treasures, at least a respect for all manifestations of art. Posters designed by students of the School of Fine Arts warned the people of the approaching danger, recommending them to remove the threatened treasures to a place of safety and to gather in all scattered objects with the greatest care. There was such a general demand for action on these lines that all the Government had to do was to sanction the project and pass legislation to that effect. Soon afterwards the *Junta Central del Tesoro Artístico* (Central Board of Art Treasures, affiliated to the Central Council of Archives, Libraries, and Art Treasures) was formed, with vast ramifications in the provinces, and given the necessary grants for the construction of bomb-proof deposits and the protection of monuments of architectural merit.

When the Prado Museum, the National Library, and the Gallery of Modern Art were bombarded in Madrid, and when bombs falling on houses burst through eight storeys to explode in the basement, the Government arranged for the evacuation of the most important works in the Prado Museum, the Academy of St. Ferdinand, and all the various State and private collections. Shell-proof deposit vaults were constructed in Valencia, and there the art treasures remained in conditions of perfect safety and preservation until the offensive on the Levant front brought with it fears for the fate of the city. The Government then decided to remove them to the north of Catalonia, as far as possible from the scene of battle. Here the masterpieces of Spanish painting and other fine collections of art treasures remained until the fall of Catalonia, when the Government, well aware of the danger of exposing them to the hazards attendant on the last moments of defeat, decided, in agreement with international organizations, that they should be sent to Geneva.

The inventory drawn up at the League of Nations by the art experts of London, Paris, and Geneva, and signed by the Secretary-General, M. Avenol, constitutes the highest mark of appreciation of the work of the Government and the Central Board. It gives the lie direct to the fabulous stories of sales to foreign art galleries and transfers to the Soviet Union. And it is only thanks to the tremendous efforts carried out by the Republic that Spain is today in possession of thousands of paintings and other art treasures of inestimable value.

The work of propaganda was on the whole less satisfactory. In this sphere the Spaniard has to fight against his own temperament, for he is little inclined by nature to attempt to win over contrary opinion. Convinced of the justice of his cause, he finds it hard to realize that it is not enough to have right on one's side, but that one must also persuade others that this is the case. The origins of the Spanish struggle and the predominant fact of foreign aggression were so clear to the average loyalist Spaniard that he could not understand why such a tremendous effort should be necessary to convince the world of something as unquestionable as it was obvious. In the excellent posters displayed so lavishly during the first few months of the war, he saw not so much an argument which was to him superfluous, as the expression in line and colour of his own feelings and Republican zeal.

For some time, however, the poster was one of the most effective mediums of propaganda. Its lesson was a visual one. In a country where—until such time as the Republican work of education began to bear fruit—a large part of the rural population was unable to read, the poster took the place of the written word and carried to the remotest village the message of loyalist Spain. In the towns it helped to create a war atmosphere. With the rebel troops closing in on the city, the spiritual temperature of Madrid rose rapidly when posters were displayed on all her walls calling upon the people, with dramatic realism, to resist. When, mirrored in the posters, the women of Madrid saw themselves attacked by the invaders or separated for ever from their children, they rushed to the barricades to finish the work of building and fortification. Every militiaman dreamed of himself as that brave and resolute fighter in whom the artist had symbolized the counterattack which was to save the city. Every workman rebelled against the thought of working under the threat of that Fascist whip which lay outstretched across the poster as though its sinister work had already begun.

Some of these posters—in particular those of Renau, a Valencian artist who later held an important position in the Ministry of Education—were quite remarkable. No foreign delegate or writer who visited Republican Spain left the country without taking a set back with him. The finest artists offered their services for this propaganda work, and there was a good deal of friendly rivalry among the various organizations and political parties as to which could produce the best posters.

Radio propaganda was less effective. In the first place the Government stations were not powerful enough to be heard abroad with any regularity. The programs from the Madrid short-wave station reached America, but in Europe Barcelona could be heard in only a few places, and even then not very clearly. Towards the end of the war we succeeded in carrying out intensive propaganda in the rebel zone with our *"Radio Verdad"* ("Truth Radio"). Its effectiveness was proved by the speed with which the rebels replied to our broadcasts, and by the cruel measures which they adopted, on the advice and under pressure of the Gestapo, to prevent them from reaching the general public. Those who listened in to the *"Radio Verdad"* ran the risk of being executed on the spot. But deserters used to tell us how they would listen to the voice of their country from a small set concealed beneath blankets, and how our news spread over enemy territory in spite of the sternest attempts to prevent its doing so.

We also succeeded in overcoming the obstacles in the way of introducing Republican propaganda into the rebel zone.

Not only were leaflets dropped from airplanes, but other and more direct methods were utilized. We had to make many experiments and resort to the most ingenious stratagems. The insurgents' own literature served as a vehicle for our propaganda. A Phalangist leaflet would be exactly reproduced and our own news and commentaries inserted between the paragraphs. The secret of the success of this class of propaganda consisted in knowing how to direct it to the places where it would be most welcomed and put to best account. One single leaflet falling into the right hands would be freely copied. The program of the Government's Thirteen Points, the most important speeches of the Cabinet members, our notes to the powers denouncing foreign invasion, were all typed out and circulated in the rebel zone.

The most effective class of propaganda was unquestionably the war communiqué. There is no better tonic than good news from the front. While it is of paramount importance that the war communiqué should divulge no detail likely to be useful to the enemy, at the same time it should be as explicit as possible. The people want to be able to follow the events of the war for themselves. They do not expect to be told anything which is not for public consumption, but they resent any unjustified delay in the publication of news, good or bad, which will not prejudice the march of operations. While the rebels—whose men, with their low morale, could not bear to hear bad news—systematically denied the loss of important positions and even refused for some days to admit that the Republican army had crossed the Ebro, we, on the other hand, announced the fall of Málaga as soon as it was reported to us.

The result was that in the rebel zone the war communiqué was completely discredited, and sometimes even real rebel victories were not believed. I heard two men who had been taken prisoner by us three weeks after we had lost Teruel swear that the insurgents were still some miles from the city, and that their attempts to enter had failed. "But didn't you get the official news?" I asked them. "Yes," they replied, "but nobody takes any notice of what the dispatches say. It would be a fine thing if we believed everything we were told over there!"

There were times when our war communiqués went to the other extreme. During the eastern debacle, in the spring of 1938, it seemed as though a hidden hand took a delight in accentuating the pessimistic tone of their contents. It was the same when the Government moved to the central zone after the fall of Catalonia. The fronts were paralysed and there were no proper war communiqués, but in the dispatches sent by certain army leaders to the Ministry of Defence it was easy to detect their attempts to convince us that resistance was useless. The mere presence of half a dozen trucks on the highway would be interpreted as the herald of an immediate army offensive or the alarming advance of a motorized division. In both cases saboteurs and defeatists were doing their deadly work. In general, however, the tone of the Republican war communiqués was maintained at a level worthy of a people who had given abundant proof of their patience, understanding, and heroism and who had a right to hear the truth at all times.

While we cannot deny the defects of our propaganda system, from one point of view we have every reason for pride. Our propaganda never sank to the depths of vulgarity which characterized that of the rebels. Their broadcasts were a permanent challenge to good taste. I am quite certain that if the foreigners who supported the cause of the rebels in all good faith had listened in for a night or two to Burgos, Salamanca, or Seville, they would have been filled with shame at the way in which both the Spanish language and the most elementary sense of decency were abused. "Pasionaria" and her imaginary love affairs, the vices and crimes of the best-known loyalist leaders, the stolen fur coats and jewels with which the wives of the ministers were adorned—these were the favourite themes of the rebel broadcasts, interspersed with insults to foreign statesmen who were well known for their anti-Fascist attitude. As far as the Government broadcasts were concerned, however, only once during the period in which I was responsible for our propaganda did I have to dismiss one of our speakers for a misdemeanor of this kind; that was because, in defiance of the strictest instructions, he had made certain insinuations of an intimate nature concerning the character of General Franco.

The rebels, on the other hand, were in the fortunate position of having the vast machine of Nazi propaganda at their disposal from the very beginning of the war. Just as they entered the struggle with an army already in being (while we had to construct ours step by step), so from the very first moment of the war their propaganda batteries were drawn up on the emplacements ready to open fire. It would be dangerous for the European democracies to underestimate the work carried out during the past five years by Dr. Goebbels's departments, and the revelations concerning Nazi penetration in the French press, which in the summer of 1939 forced M. Daladier to arrest various highly placed journalists attached to certain Parisian newspapers, should be sufficient proof of their efficiency, if proof is needed. During the Czechoslovakian crisis the skill with which Nazi propaganda disseminated arguments so imperceptibly that the British and French public came to look on them as their own was remarkable. "Why should we fight because the Sudeten Germans want to go back to Germany?" To the man in the street the suggestion was absurd. Such was the watchword of Goebbels in September 1938.

In the case of Spain, Nazi propaganda worked on the aversion of many democratic circles, and all conservative sectors of opinion, from anything which savoured, however slightly, of Bolshevism. The stamping of loyalist Spain with the red trade-mark was an extremely clever move on the part of Dr. Goebbels's departments. To the majority of the foreign press the Government of Señor Giral in July and August 1936 was

"Red," in spite of the fact that it did not contain one Socialist minister. And even if the succeeding Governments had been presided over by the Catholic Minister Señor Irujo, it would still have been impossible to divest loyal Spaniards of their "Red" label. During my visit to the United States I was able to realize the effect of this propaganda to the full. Ardent Catholics who had been disgusted by the attitude of the Third Reich to the religious question began to sympathize with a Germany which was fighting to prevent the victory of a Bolshevist Spain.

It is only when one looks back over nearly three years of war that the efforts of the Spanish people and their legitimate Government are seen in their full proportions. With two thirds of their territory invaded and their principal industrial centres subjected to incessant air bombardment, production was not for one moment interrupted. Exports were maintained at the very highest level that the circumstances would permit. New industries were created. In the country agriculture was revolutionized by the introduction of machinery. While the war was still raging, the foundations of a new Spain were being laid. In juridical organization, in the making of new roads, in the preparation of a whole people for the future work of reconstruction, the Republic displayed an activity not unworthy of the work carried on in times of peace. It was in the financing of the war, however, that difficulties were confronted with the greatest resolution and clear-sightedness. The financial policy of the Republican Government in its struggle against invasion deserves a chapter to itself.

CHAPTER IX

Financing the War

THE REPUBLIC at its birth in 1931 inherited a legacy of financial sickness, from which it had to be nursed back to health and well-being. Since a republic, more than any other form of government, needs to follow a policy of austerity, the Spanish Republic carried out the financial tasks imposed upon it by historical circumstances as simply and naturally as possible. Careful foresight, cautious expenditure, well-planned reforms, and the most scrupulous administration of the public funds, together with a desire to put an end to the injustice of the existent fiscal system—which like all systems had its defects—such were the ideals inspiring the Republic in financial matters. In proceeding thus the Republicans merely aimed at rectifying the mistakes of the immediate past and made no attempt to pursue political tactics or revolutionary ends.

During the dictatorship of Primo de Rivera the control of public finances had been placed in the young and inexperienced hands of Señor Calvo Sotelo, who with the support, approval, and authority of a military Government had developed a rudely conceived "Statism" which was to nourish the whole economic life of the nation. The administration became an instrument for reviving the somnolent economy, which it was hoped to arouse with the cry of *"Enrichissez-vous."* This ponderous organism of the Spanish State was to dispel the desire for money, the atrophy of which had been stifling individual initiative, and was at the same time to further the progress of the nation. This tendency was partially inspired by the scheme of reform drawn up by Don Joaquin Costa after the Spanish-American War of 1898, with its saving formula of *Escuela y Depensa* ("Bread and Education"), preached by Danton a century before.

The Minister of Finance of the 1922–9 dictatorship believed that the progress of Spanish economy depended on the creation by the State of powerful organs for bankers' credits. Credit was essential for a period of regeneration and for the creation of wealth. This thesis has always had its partisans. In contemporary times it has been accepted and put into practice by various Governments, but it has long been current in Spain. The vision of Calvo Sotelo was the revival of an old misconception and an old habit.

From the earliest times Spanish local administration had lacked all political spontaneity. This lifelessness and absence of co-operation with the Government was, until the advent of the Republic, considered as one of the reasons for Spain's backwardness. Don Antonio Maura, one of the few Spanish statesmen of vigorous personality in the early twentieth century, made every endeavour to foster local initiative. His high powers of persuasion failed, however, in face of the inertia and apathy displayed by those who did not view the situation in the same light as the Conservative leader. The serious and fundamental nature of this problem was completely lost upon Señor Sotelo, who saw it only as a simple question of money. The credit showered on local corporations initiated a period of great urban reforms. The budgets of the Spanish provincial capitals swelled rapidly and there was not a single town of importance which did not issue loans and obtain ad-

vances from the local credit bank. The work was put in hand
on the basis of arbitrary and ill-conceived plans, whose exponents were to overcome all difficulties in the name of
progress. The urban reforms were financed by a series of bond
issues, and the issuing agencies were controlled by the same
people who controlled the public supply undertakings. This
rapidly growing demand by the supply undertakings meant
an increase in issues of credit, which in its turn resulted in
price inflation and inflated yields for these undertakings. So
was forged a whole chain of artificially promoted production
in which the normal movements of supply and demand ceased
in the atmosphere of harmony created by the distribution of
credit, without public works and service being in any way
increased.

By the time the Republic was formed, the local credit
banks had failed; the municipalities were insolvent and unable to pay the interest on their debts; buildings, only half
constructed and of poor material, were gradually crumbling
into ruins. But the damage did not end there. Healthy capital
—that is to say, capital emanating from national savings—
had been diverted from its normal course by an arbitrary
decree of Primo de Rivera's Government concerning public
works, which bore little relation to national needs. The result
was a complete dislocation of economic life and a fictitious
urbanism which seriously prejudiced the interests of the rural
population.

The credit lever was to assist foreign trade, prevented from
expansion by the private banks, which—against their own interests, it was said—had obstinately refused assistance. In
its desire to widen the impression of prosperity and wealth,
the dictatorship created a new bank, the *Banco de Comercio
Exterior* (Bank of Foreign Trade)—a State organization,
which, with its credit system, was to remedy the defects of
national production. Technical and cost problems, the readjustment of production conditions to foreign competition and

to the general level of world prices, became a simple matter of credit. The State and the Central Bank were the financiers of this new foundation of the dictatorship. Statistics show that the volume of exports remained, with normal fluctuations, about the same, but after the advent of the Republic the bank was forced to enter on a stage of open liquidation, and it was only by means of accommodating credits and computing assets on the basis of an assumed value laid down by the Government that it was possible for it to avoid the catastrophe of a bank smash.

Technically, public works were put in hand on a large scale with unreflecting enthusiasm. It mattered little that the existing railroad system had been suffering from a considerable deficit since before the dictatorship. Deficits amounting to hundreds of millions of pesetas were made up by the State in order to preserve a public service in which the concessionary undertakings had failed. The so-called "Railway Fund," a product of State intervention, was the State issuing agency of the so-called "Railway Debt." And it mattered still less that the cheaper transport provided by the new highroads was a powerful competitor of the railways. The plans in operation involved thousands of kilometres, and as they were all begun at once, it came about that when payment was forcibly suspended, nothing remained but levelled ground, unfinished bridges, stocks of railway lines, and locomotive factories; while the railroad system throughout the whole of Spain had not been increased by a single kilometre.

All over the Peninsula extensive irrigation works were begun. Schemes—some practical, some fantastic—which had been accumulating over a period of years, were put into operation. The firms carrying out this work were subsidized from the national budget, but they were able to mobilize not only the credits as such, but also the capital of those private interests standing to benefit from the public works, since the enterprises were authorized to issue securities on the guarantee of these credits. Such was the determination to transform the arable agriculture natural to Spain into an irrigation system.

The complement of this policy was the cultivation of new crops, such as tobacco and cotton, in order to improve the trade balance. This was done without counting the cost, the one desire being to create a self-sufficient economy. The only limit to expansion was that imposed by technical and credit possibilities.

The highroads were widened, improved, and straightened with so much zeal that the Government had to resort to foreign industry and to import every kind of building material.

The construction and improvement of harbours was carried on with the same fervour, and petitions from coastal towns were granted to the detriment of shipping routes. The manufacture of the necessary fittings increased the demand on the metallurgical industry, which was obliged to work to full capacity to produce them. The Harbour Boards mobilized credits and intensified their activities.

The Exchequer with its subsidies, the new banks, the "Credit Funds," the Boards, each one of these specialized organizations stimulated manufacture and public works, and financed a plentiful demand which was increased by an abundant credit.

This policy of inflation and growing public expenditure covered by the Extraordinary Budgets had its repercussion on the Exchequer, which was obliged to resort to credit in the form of repeated gold loans in both home and foreign markets. The effects on the exchange were catastrophic, exposing the artificial boom and the fallacies of the economic régime of the dictatorship. The *Centro de Contratación de Moneda* (Exchange Control Agency), was created with the object of protecting the peseta. Thus the exchange was ignored as a corrective symbol or index, and the violent fluctuations which would have represented the true situation were avoided altogether.

Defying the true demands of the situation, the *Centro de Contratación de Moneda* not only counteracted the tendency of the exchange, but for motives of national "prestige" raised it to a level impossible to maintain. The consequences of this went beyond the material losses caused by the intervention of the Centro. The Bank of Spain was forced to send a part of its gold reserve abroad, and this was hypothecated in order to cover loans from foreign issuing banks. Moreover, the internal capital market, already depleted by so many issues, was deprived of the foreign floating capital, which had taken advantage of the fictitious valuation of the peseta to realize a profitable placing, but which now fled hastily from a market showing signs of crisis.

Other Government measures, carried out under a régime which was anticipating Fascist autarchy, contributed to the drainage of the capital market. The nationalization of the petroleum industry, creating an import and distribution monopoly, cost the home market millions of pesetas in indemnification, and left in its train a multitude of claims which are still awaiting settlement. In the same way foreign enterprises were entrusted with the development of the new public services, which involved expensive large-scale installations of imported material, and so added to the debit balance of the nation. Such contradictions in the system necessarily shortened its life, and the attempt at autarchy was doomed to rapid failure.

On the overthrow of the dictatorship, and in the short interregnum of fourteen months between it and the Republic, criticism of the past conduct of the national economy was mainly responsible for the unanimous vote in the elections of April 12, 1931 condemning the policy of the past and forcing the King to abandon his throne and his country.

An account of the financial disaster of the dictatorship responsible for the downfall of the monarchy is of more than a mere historical interest. It throws into high relief the incapacity for government of the Spanish military caste. Al-

though the Finance Minister of the dictatorship was himself
a civilian, Spain was ruled at that time by a set of generals.
Some of the dreams of Imperial grandeur which have been
revived in Franco's régime recall so vividly the principles of
Primo de Rivera's dictatorship that at times it seems as though
they were identical.

The Republicans, on succeeding to power, fully appreciated the necessity for an austere régime, and there was a
repetition of the famous case of the liberal parliamentarians
of the Frankfurt Assembly, when, like their German predeces-
sors, the Republican deputies devoured works on economics
and public finance in an earnest desire to act correctly. The
new policy was a strong and vigorous one, a symbol of honest
citizenship; the classic measures for the promotion of financial
health were taken, and the necessary sacrifices made.

Spanish economy had to adjust itself to world economy,
and to renounce all expenditure beyond the financial resources of the nation. The *Centro de Moneda* was obliged to
abandon its policy of the "prestige" of the peseta, but this had
to be done judiciously in order to maintain that confidence
and stability necessary in all times of political change; the
situation was relieved by a fall in currency of those countries
in the strongest economic position. At the same time the
Centro initiated the import of goods on a barter basis, and by
placing obstacles in the way of acquiring foreign currency
prevented the superfluous or luxury importation which had
flourished under the system of fictitious valuations. These
measures helped to bring about a final readjustment of the
currency and at the same time protected the gold reserves as
the classic basis of international trade.

On the other hand it was a matter of urgent necessity to
alter the course of economic progress and to put a brake on
the previous credit policy. The issue of public loans ceased
until 1934, when the Right-wing parties, on regaining power,
began to revert to the practice. Issues from so many autonomous public-service bodies were also suspended. Unproduc-

tive construction was stopped—in particular, work on railways and those buildings which had been started in a delirium of urban aggrandizement. The Government did their best to find new uses for the mass of unconsumed material destined for this work. There was in fact no other way open, and as an illustration of the state of affairs existing at this time, it is enough to say that on the eve of the rebellion the Government was still having to instruct the Central Bank to discount bonds for public works begun before the establishment of the Republic.

The Republican Government was only able to avoid bankruptcy by a laborious task of recuperation and careful public expenditure. Though the Republic brought back the budget position to normal, made up all deficits, and met all liabilities, it was only by sacrificing its preconceived ideas and adapting its reforms to economic possibilities—possibilities considerably lessened by the previous political régime. It was able to finance the new agrarian and educational policies, but other projected reforms had temporarily to be put on one side in order not to unbalance the budget. Plans for social and health services had to be deferred, in the hope—as expressed by the political satirist—that if Rome lived for five centuries without doctors, Spain, whose hygienic conditions had never given cause for national pride, would also accept economies in this sphere.

The chief taxation reform had to do with the income tax. It was a judicious reform with all the characteristics of a trial performance. Not only was it necessary to find adequate personnel to administer the tax, but the habit of payment also had to be instilled in the contributors. The tax on high incomes did not exceed ten per cent, all associations being excluded from the charge. Reforms of the old direct taxes and of the death duties were carried out, in order to strengthen a Treasury which had abjured every type of loan as a means of revenue.

Indirect taxation was modified, firstly in order to compensate for the loss of revenue produced by the persistence of the regulated prices of Fiscal Monopolies in opposition to the inflation prices of free enterprise, the loss to the Treasury in this respect having represented hundreds of millions of pesetas; and secondly in order to tap the private expenditure of all social classes.

A return to the old system was planned by the conservative parties that came to power in 1933, which consisted of fugitive politicians from the Monarchist régime, and leaders armed by the Church to represent her in the Spanish lists. With the triumph of the Left at the elections of February 12, 1936, the régime of economic anarchy and waste was once again condemned.

The Treasury, in common with all branches of the administration, suffered immediate consequences from the rebellion of July 1936, and although the Government rapidly reassumed control of the other departments, it did not at first extend its intervention to the Finance Ministry, so that the fiscal machine—which up to then had been strong and invulnerable—began to break down. In order to relieve the situation the Government was obliged to reaffirm the principle of the legality of taxes, to adapt them to the changed circumstances, to create fresh sources of revenue, and to reorganize the system of collection. In the year 1937 the principal taxes—that is, land tax, industrial tax, profits tax, stamp tax, death duties, etc.—were restored, and in the second half of that year they brought in a revenue 130,000,000 pesetas higher than that during a similar period in 1936.

Customs revenues had been in a critical condition since 1936. The crisis, the policy of economy, and the high Spanish tariff walls had all contributed to this state of affairs. If it is added that at the beginning of the war frontier control was assumed by elements which certainly did not have the interests of the State at heart, the chaotic situation of the customs will be readily appreciated.

But once frontier control was taken over by the State, customs returns increased to an extraordinary degree. One need only compare the revenue in this respect during the period from July to December 1936—that is, 19,503,283 pesetas—with that of the corresponding periods in 1937 and 1938—52,897,819 and 98,747,000 pesetas respectively—to realize this.

The most important of the new taxes was the impost on war profits, which gave a very high yield.

Reforms were made in tax-collection by utilizing the subordinate staff of the old tax-collectors, the majority of whom had resigned or been dismissed for disloyalty or treason. The zeal of the new staff was reflected in the rapid increase in State revenue—to a level which was maintained throughout the last two years of the war.

Fiscal monopolies controlled by concessionary enterprises were disorganized in the first days of the struggle. The petroleum monopoly had to make extraordinary efforts to keep up supplies and to create reserves of gasoline and lubricants for the multiple needs of the army, the navy, the air force, and national transport. Through the close collaboration of the workers and that section of the Administrative Council which had remained loyal, it was possible to fill the large gaps caused by the defection and treachery of the technical and administrative staff; and management difficulties, increased by the action of the rebels, brought about a change in the structure of the monopoly, the concessionary undertaking becoming a monopoly directly administered by the State.

It was also necessary to increase State intervention in the tobacco monopoly—an organism of considerable importance for Spanish revenue—because of the mass defection of the Administrative Councils of the concessionary undertaking. The problem, however, was not difficult of solution, since the employees and workmen had been sufficiently educated by their trade unions to respond in full measure to the trust which the Government placed in them.

Throughout the whole war the Treasury was financed by the proceeds of taxation and its own credit facilities, without once having to resort to either forced or voluntary loans. The only credit operation in which the State intervened was the renewal of Treasury bonds issued on October 23, 1935 (during the period of conservative ascendancy). The Government offered bondholders the choice between redemption or conversion of their securities into a new Treasury loan, at the same interest and redeemable in two years' time. Of the 290,000,000 pesetas outstanding, requests were received for the redemption of only 2,000,000.

It is perhaps in matters of banking and public credit that the general policy of a country is most clearly reflected, and it is here that the finer shades of Republican policy can be best appreciated. During the first days of the rebellion, a moratorium was declared on all payments, at the suggestion of the bank directors and in agreement with the Supreme Banking Council, but it was raised shortly afterwards and only a few restrictions regarding the withdrawal of funds were retained. The banking mechanism of the country as an auxiliary of the Treasury was consistently kept in running order, and in spite of the desertion of many of their directors, councillors, and other technical staff, the private banks were thus saved from the effects of the catastrophe. The Ministry of Finance proceeded with the reorganization of the administration, in agreement with the Supreme Banking Council and by means of the creation of a Management Committee consisting of a representative of the Minister, and nominees of the stockholders, the current-account holders and the Bank Employees' Federation.

As regards the Bank of Spain, its administration, reduced to a governor, the sub-governors, and a few councillors, was faced in the first days of the war with the difficult situation created by the resignation of the most important members of the council. Once the vacancies for stockholding councillors were filled in accordance with the terms of the Banking Act, the Central Bank continued to function normally, and was throughout the war more closely identified with the economy of the Republic and the general interests of the nation than ever before. All that was done was to remedy abuses which tended to impede the prosecution of the war. The oligarchic organization and the system of privilege which before the re-bellion—and, in fact, ever since the days of the monarchy—had obstructed the working of the economic and financial machine, and which the Republic in its brief existence had only been partially able to destroy, had transformed the State into a client of the Bank of Spain, to which it was inferior in credit and privileges. In order to meet the new situation and to create a more equitable state of affairs, the Government was authorized to go beyond the limit established by the Banking Act for loans from the Bank of Spain to the Treas-ury—a faculty which was, however, used with discretion.

The Ministry of Finance maintained an anti-inflationist policy in order to conserve the national currency against the loss of purchasing power. This is reflected in the balance sheets of the Bank of Spain. Thanks to this policy, whereby the faculty of issuing twenty-five- and fifty-peseta Treasury notes as paper money (for which, as in other countries, authority was given to the Minister of Finance) was exer-cised with discretion, fiduciary circulation was not greatly increased in spite of the prodigious cost of the war.

The Spanish State discharged all its obligations in respect of the public debt. The payment of interest on the four-per-cent external debt, in the hands of foreign holders, was made in Paris and London just as usual, without the slightest delay and without giving rise to any claims whatsoever. The Re-publican Government fulfilled its commitments in respect of the public debt until it lost the national territory.

None of the precautionary and coercive measures taken by the Minister of Finance—from the restriction in the use of current accounts to the revision of the system of bank safes and the holding and exportation of jewels—affected foreign capital in any way whatever.

Foreign interests in loyalist Spain were scrupulously

respected. Even debts contracted before the war, known under the names of the "Moreno Plan" and the "Madlon Plan" (where delay in redemption would have been abundantly justified by the gravity of the Spanish situation), were conscientiously paid, although the efforts made to do this were certainly not appreciated in foreign financial circles, whose sympathy with the rebels was apparently stronger than their desire to take advantage of a situation favourable to themselves.

Since any large-scale disturbance such as that caused by the Spanish War must inevitably prejudice foreign interests, the Government issued a decree protecting all such interests, and created a High Commission to receive all foreign claims and to determine the amount of indemnity in each particular case. As president of this Commission, until my return to the Foreign Ministry in April 1938, I was a witness of its high-minded attitude and its resolve that the good name of the Republic should not be prejudiced by any of the decisions taken.

No number of statistics—whether or not they mean anything to the layman—could give any exact idea of the difficulties of financing a war for two and a half years on our own resources. The financial policy of the Republic can perhaps best be summed up as follows:

By exercising tact and avoiding clashes with those regional governments, local authorities, political and trade-union organizations and committees that had assumed the functions of government and created a chaotic situation, the State was soon able to regain firm control of the economic and financial life of the country.

The Government succeeded not only in preserving the banking system as an institution, but also in remedying the critical situation in which it had been placed and the damage caused by seditious activities on the part of certain high-placed officials.

The secrets of the success of the financial and economic policy of the Republic were as follows:

1. The exercise of absolute control over finance and economy in such a manner as not to create serious political dissension, and resolute and fearless attention to war needs without going a step further than was judicious or necessary.

2. Refusal to adopt any measure or carry out any operation without considering the possible repercussions on general war plans as constantly drawn up for six months ahead.

3. Absolute discretion. All efforts would have been in vain if the greatest circumspection had not been exercised. The plans of the Ministry of Finance and Economy, both in general and in details, were at no time the property of more than three people, all of whom enjoyed the complete confidence of the Minister.

In September 1936 the general opinion was that there was only enough money left to carry on the war for another eight, or at the most ten, months. Admittedly this would have been so if severe financial measures had not been taken. The constant demands of the various ministries, all of which had a legitimate right to receive as much assistance as possible, had to be resisted. Every army corps aspired to greater help than the rest. The tendency was to purchase all necessities outside Spain, and it was only by firm currency measures that the line of least resistance was cut and the people forced to buy in the home market or to create new industries—with consequent benefit to both the Treasury and the national economy. The watchword of the Minister of Finance in the matter of expenditure was: *Not to give money, but to cover needs.*

During the first months of the war the Minister was forced to yield to necessity and to buy war material abroad as and how he could, without following any strict purchasing plan. Many millions were lost in this way, and the enemy seized the opportunity to employ tactics of attrition and, through the intermediary of concealed agents, to force the Government to open numerous credits outside Spain, often for material which never reached us. It was one of the many fatal and disastrous aspects of Non-Intervention and of the attack it represented on the freedom of trade. But these dangers soon receded, and as an illustration of the efforts made to maintain Spanish economy and finance on a rational plane during such a difficult time I need only say that in foreign currency the Spanish War cost the Government less than the Spanish campaign in Morocco cost the Government of Alfonso XIII.

In order to maintain finance and economy during the war it was not necessary to carry out any new and original plans, but merely to put firmly into practice measures which are only too well known, but which are generally the last to be applied.

As from the end of 1937, a complete control of exports and imports was exercised by the Government, and a foreign trade monopoly created and placed in the hands of the State. This trade monopoly, directed by technicians and free from all political influences and private interference, was the most powerful factor in the maintenance of national economy and finance during the war.

The State monopoly of foreign currency, and raw materials with which it could be obtained, made it possible to carry on the war while it lasted; and in spite of the considerable frauds committed by private people and organizations, it could in fact have been carried on for longer at the cost of further restrictions and privations.

The policy of anticipating critical situations by making sacrifices before they became urgently necessary secured the Government against all contingencies. When on the capture of the hydraulic power station at Tremp in March 1938 the Minister of Defence, Indalecio Prieto, informed the Cabinet of the serious situation with which Barcelona was threatened by the cutting off of electric current—with the consequent paralysis of the war industries—Dr. Negrín, Prime Minister and Minister of Finance and Economy, reassured his colleague with the statement that the emergency power stations, which were steam-driven, were in working order and that there were coal reserves for two months. "But there isn't even any coal for the railways!" exclaimed the Minister of Public Works. "For that very reason there is coal for the emergency power stations," replied Dr. Negrín; "when I refused further supplies to the railways, I had this very contingency in mind." Similar situations arose in the case of gasoline and wheat.

The concentration of national economy and finance in the hands of one Minister made it possible for the State to create reserves and even to take full advantage in the world market of certain financial situations which had arisen.

Dr. Negrín, who almost since the beginning of the war had carried the burden of the war economy on his shoulders, invented for himself the following slogan: "The Minister of Finance who is niggardly during a war ought to be shot; the Minister of Finance who is wasteful during a war ought to be hanged."

It was thanks to the discovery of a happy medium between extravagance and parsimony that the war did not end in a year for lack of funds, as the defeatists had predicted with such certainty.

CHAPTER X

The Nameless Heroes

WHENEVER THE WAR weighed heavily on one's spirits, whenever one felt disheartened by the many difficulties with which the Government had to deal in the course of such an unequal struggle, the surest way of regaining strength and courage was to go to the front, or to a factory, and spend a few hours with the people. From them came that incredible vitality which amazed the world during two and a half years. The ordinary Spaniard—the farm labourer who had left his native soil to become first a militiaman and later a hard, disciplined soldier; the mechanic working in the munitions and aircraft factories with the enthusiasm of one who knew that on his efforts depended his comrades' ability to launch a successful offensive; the women who rose early each day to secure their meagre rations, and yet were never late at the factory nor too tired in the evening to knit and sew for the men in the trenches—these were the people who performed the miracle of Republican resistance.

The Spanish people were fully conscious of the greatness of their cause, and their constant desire to be worthy of it made them eager to excel. It was a moving sight in the trenches to see men whose lives depended on the course of a bullet, taking advantage of a quiet moment for a lesson in reading or writing. The "Cultural Militia," formed by the Ministry of Education, whose task was to abolish illiteracy by the end of the war, was one of the most popular institutions in the Republican army. The object of the War Commissariat Schools and the courses for non-professional officers was not only to make good soldiers and officers and commissars, but also to fulfil the deep desire of the people to make up for the time lost in those years when the education of the humble Spanish citizen was a very minor concern of the Government.

Whether they were being taught military or general subjects, the people's capacity for assimilation was remarkable. Many times I was questioned at the front on the international situation, and I can say unhesitatingly that those former farm labourers in the army who two years previously would have stood bewildered before a map of Europe, ignorant of the whereabouts of such a country as Czechoslovakia, had a far firmer grasp of general problems than members of certain chancelleries. In the summer of 1938 I had an interesting conversation on the very subject of Czechoslovakia with a group of soldiers anxious to know if it were really true that that country could, if necessary, mobilize forty-two divisions and count on fifteen hundred airplanes and an important munitions factory known as the Skoda Works. I told them that this was so. "Fifteen hundred airplanes?" a peasant from Extremadura, just promoted to the rank of corporal for brave conduct, asked in open-mouthed astonishment. And without waiting for my confirmation he exclaimed: "Then why are they letting Germany treat them like this? Why don't they declare war?" To that soldier of the Republic fifteen hundred airplanes was an astronomical figure.

This interest in international questions was born of a profound conviction that, just as the fate of the Republic would have great repercussions on the future of Europe, so the development of the Spanish War was closely linked to that of the external situation. But never at any time, not even when it brought the greatest havoc in its train, did the Spanish people become demoralized by the pernicious example of the policy of "appeasement." Directly after Munich, on my return from Geneva, I went to the front, not without a certain misgiving that this time the deplorable abandonment of a sovereign state to the aggressor nations might have had a disastrous effect on the morale of our people. But their reaction was magnificent. There was a certain disillusionment because the Czechs had not fought, but a greater determination than ever to go on defending the independence of Spain.

The healthy sense of humour of the Spanish people was a characteristic of the military campaign. It was evident in the plays written by soldiers and Commissars, and in the successful "Front-Line Guignol," whose chief characters were nearly always a German aviator, an Italian officer—and General Queipo de Llano, a bottle of sherry in one hand, a microphone in the other, and his speech betraying a weakness for any and every kind of liquid save water.

The war, which destroyed so much, did not rob the Spaniard of this sense of humour, a quality which has always been one of his strongest political weapons in defence or attack. The citizens of Madrid retained it throughout the length of a siege unique in history, a siege which might have shattered the nerves of any people less able to laugh in the face of death. The shells which for months rained down on the city with perfect Teutonic regularity at seven o'clock every morning were nicknamed "the alarm clock," and even the distressing lack of food, endured with such dignity, was sometimes joked about by those who suffered from it most. The foreigners who visited Madrid—Europeans or Americans, Parliamentary or trade-union delegations, writers or artists—were amazed to find that the theatres and cinemas had never been so full as in those two terrible years, and went back to their countries filled with admiration at the spirit of the people. Even after the war, when their sufferings were increased by the hideous and insane reprisals of the rebels, the people of Madrid, once they had recovered from the shock of finding the bandits in their very homes, began to make fun of them and to turn them into laughing-stocks.

The "Caudillo" (leader) was called "the deafest of the lot," because whenever his partisans, and others, acclaimed him, they had to shout three times—each time louder than before: "Franco, Franco, Franco!" When Neptune, whose statue in one of the avenues of Madrid had been protected by the loyalists against enemy aircraft and artillery, once more held up his "fork" after the bombardments were over, he was baptized "the last optimist," a subtle allusion to the fact that hunger had increased since the end of the war, a hunger which no military parades or proclamations of Spain's future Empire could appease. In the theatres and cinemas now the people stand up and make the Fascist salute whenever the National Anthem or the image of the Generalissimo demands homage to the new régime, and he who neglects to do so pays for his absent-mindedness with a heavy fine or a few months' imprisonment. But when arms are outstretched Roman-fashion, the fingers are still free to signal to friends in the hall, and sometimes to make signs of even greater irreverence. Beneath an immense poster which is displayed everywhere in Spain, even in the customs sheds, and which reads: "Franco is honour, Franco is heroism, Franco is faith, Franco is authority, Franco is justice, Franco is efficiency, Franco is intelligence, Franco is will-power," there appeared one morning, written in indelible ink, the following verse:

> *Menos Franco*
> *Y más pan blanco.*

(Not so much Franco and more white bread.)

In spite of the severe censorship, letters from Spain, written with true Fascist solemnity, are full of amusing hints and allusions, showing typical Spanish ingenuity in the art of describing the situation in Spain to anyone capable of reading between the lines.

Not only does all this reveal the indomitable spirit of the people, but it is also of great importance from a political standpoint. There has never been a régime in Spain—and General Primo de Rivera, if he were alive, could say something in this connection—capable of surviving for long the ridicule and derision of the people. The Republican Government was bitterly attacked by its enemies during the war, but rarely in the facetious tone which Spaniards now use towards the new régime and its leaders, and which in the long run will destroy the prestige and authority of those who consider that persecution and violence are sufficient protection against a popular reaction.

While there was great hatred of the invaders, and contempt for those who used them against the Spanish people and then proceeded to make them the real masters of Spain, the ordinary Spaniard in loyal territory harboured no feeling of revenge, nor did he regard a Republican victory as the signal for the massacre of former adversaries. I know that readers hostile to the Republic will ask: "And what about the 'Red atrocities'?" This is one of the aspects of the Spanish War on which, during a recent lecture tour in the United States, I expressed myself with the greatest frankness and freedom. I did not deny them. At the beginning of the war, in Madrid, Barcelona, Valencia, in nearly every part of Republican Spain, there were illegal executions and people were shot without trial and without the knowledge of the Government. It was a moment of great popular indignation, when anger against the traitors had let loose a tide of passion difficult to stem in such circumstances. (There is abundant precedent for this in the history of those very nations that hid their faces in horror at the events in Spain. This horror is more justifiable, however, when such things happen in a normal atmosphere.) It was also the moment chosen by those enemy agents who had penetrated the political and trade-union organizations, men who hoped to bring disgrace on the Republic and to use the righteous indignation of the people for their own provocative purposes. But, above all, the trouble was caused by the impotence of a Government which the rebellion had deprived of the means of administering authority, and to which the democratic countries had refused to sell the arms necessary to suppress the insurgents and to establish order. It was those same countries which were so shocked by the "Red atrocities," exaggerated a hundred times by Nazi and Fascist propaganda. When a government is forced to discuss at a cabinet meeting, as we were, whether the last five hundred rifles in Madrid, half of them without sufficient ammunition, should be sent to the front, where they were desperately needed, or kept in Madrid to protect the existence of the Government itself, it is a mark of the greatest hypocrisy to expect conditions of perfect law and order.

And yet not perhaps the greatest hypocrisy. The Spanish Republicans had lived through many bitter moments, but there were more to come. Franco's barbarous reprisals, condemned even by Monarchists and Right-wing Spaniards—people who have recently left Spain saying that it is impossible to live there—have not provoked a single word of condemnation from that Catholic hierarchy in the United States and those British and French reactionaries who had used the "Red atrocities" (calculated according to their own methods and then multiplied by a thousand or so) as their chief argument against loyalist Spain. This deliberate silence on the part of those who made such a parade of humanitarianism is a disgrace which it is beyond the power of words to describe.

The "atrocities" in Republican Spain ended as soon as the Government was able to reorganize the police, to stabilize the administration of justice, and to exercise its authority. Within a few weeks of the outbreak of the rebellion the political parties and trade unions were giving support to the Government in this connection, punishing any members who attempted to administer rough justice, and expelling suspicious and undesirable elements from their organizations.

The Republican Government cannot reproach itself with having, during the war, ordered or tolerated mass slaughters such as those of Badajoz and Málaga, and it would never have plunged Spain into a sea of blood after the war was over. We should have refrained from such a course not only because of its utter repugnance, but also because we were neither so stupid nor so ignorant of the feelings of the Spanish people as to believe that anything can be built up in Spain on a basis of terrorism and concentration camps. The policy of reconciliation on which the Negrín Government based its program of the Thirteen Points was inspired not merely by motives of generosity, but by the conviction that the only way to reconstruct the country and to ensure a happier future is to put aside all hatreds and differences and to reunite the people in a common task. This was and still is the only intelligent and the only possible policy.

I am absolutely certain that if the Republic had won the war, it would not have been necessary for half a million Spaniards to cross the frontier into France and to accept French hospitality in the hope of eventually starting life afresh in South America. The mere existence of these half-million refugees is in itself the greatest possible condemnation of Franco's régime.

At the front this policy of reconciliation was thoroughly understood and appreciated. The arrival in Republican trenches of deserters from rebel territory was one of the greatest delights of our soldiers. I have often been present at these brotherly reunions. The deserter, after interrogation by the authorities, would be immediately surrounded, and bombarded with questions as to how he managed to escape and what he had been doing since the beginning of the war. When, as was usually the case, he gave a hint of his penniless condition, the men were always ready to put their hands into their pockets. I remember one afternoon five hundred pesetas

being collected for a single deserter. Another day nine men
arrived at my sector. As a result of my work with the General
War Commissariat, I was practised in questioning deserters
and prisoners and had learned to distinguish at a glance
between men who had deserted in order to fight for our cause
and those who were fleeing from ill-treatment in the invaded
territory. There was not the slightest doubt about eight of
these men. They had for years belonged to parties and organizations of the Popular Front, and they had been determined
to cross over to our lines when a favourable opportunity
occurred. The ninth man kept a little behind the others, as
if he were conscious of a difference between himself and the
rest. There was a look of sly humour on his face as he turned
to me. From his accent and a certain southern wit I knew him
to be an Andalusian. "And you?" I asked him. "Why have
you come?" "Well, you see, it's like this," he replied. "The
Lieutenant said to me: 'I've got my doubts about those eight
men who are always about together. Don't lose sight of them.
Follow them wherever they go.' And as I always do what I'm
told, I started following them; and I went on following them
—and here I am!" Within a few days he was the most popular
man in the sector and a good soldier of the Republic.

There were always willing volunteers for the task of freeing as many Spaniards as possible from the rebels and winning them again for Spain. At night-time our soldiers would
talk to the men in the enemy trenches and try to persuade
them to join our ranks. More than once deserters have recounted how those calls across no man's land decided them
to make their escape. They knew that in loyal territory food
was scarce, and that two great powers, whose troops and war
material they had seen with their own eyes, were fighting
against the Republic. But they wanted to be in the real Spain
and to die for her if necessary. Their first request was to be
sent to the front. They came over to our lines whether things
were going well for us or ill. Even after the loss of Catalonia,
when the Government was in the central zone, scarcely a

day passed without deserters arriving at the Republican
outposts.

The time came when we had to alter our tactics and advise
them to stay where they were and help us by propaganda
or by sabotaging enemy activities as far as possible. That was
when the rebel command, uneasy at the growing number of
deserters, adopted the barbarous decision of shooting the
relations who were left behind, including children under ten
years of age. The execution of children of ten years old was
no novelty in rebel territory, where at that age they were
considered sufficiently advanced to be intoxicated with the
Republicanism of their parents.

In the factories, as at the front, there was the same indomitable spirit. The nameless heroism of those workers, both
men and women, underfed and suffering from lack of sleep
because of the nightly attacks from German and Italian airplanes (whose aim, according to the theories of totalitarian
war, was to demoralize the civilian population), is a proof
of the devotion and capacity for sacrifice of the Spanish
people. When one visited them they would rarely speak of
their privations and hardships, but were always ready to discuss the best way of intensifying production and of finding
new export markets which would bring in currency to carry
on the war. The management committees of these factories
often consisted of simple workmen—not because the Republic
had decided, for any doctrinal reason, to socialize industry,
but because in many cases the former directors of the factories had abandoned them in the early days of the war in
order to create fresh obstacles for the Government and to
dislocate the economic life of the country until such time as
the rebels should gain the victory.

Of the honesty of these workers—men raised by force of
circumstances to the posts of directors—in carrying out their
duties, I need hardly speak. Of the many legends of "Red
Spain," which, if they are a tribute to the efficiency of totalitarian libel methods, certainly do no credit to the intelligence

of those who believe them in all sincerity, the most absurd is that which represents all loyal Spaniards as possessed of a frenzy for riches and a propensity for stealing pictures and jewels and money. In the early days of the rebellion, when State and police control were quite illusory, we received at the Madrid Socialist Party's headquarters whole sheaves of thousand-peseta notes—discovered during the search for some dangerous Fascist or arms deposit—from men who could never have seen a single such note in their lives before. Sceptical of the loyalty of some of the local authorities, they would hand over to headquarters the money they had found, sometimes amounting to large sums, or valuables which it would have been unsafe to leave in houses abandoned by their owners. I shall never forget how in the rebel advance on Talavera three workmen rescued a sum of nearly four million pesetas, mostly in silver, which had been deposited in the local branch of the Bank of Spain, and after a veritable Odyssey brought it safely to Madrid. They reached the capital in a state of exhaustion, but their one great preoccupation on arrival was to explain that the thirty-odd pesetas which were missing had had to be spent on food during the journey.

The general ability of the people to deal with the requirements of the new situation was on an equally high level. Throughout the war the Spanish workers gave abundant proof of their competence. Just as they learned to become excellent aviators or divisional commanders with a speed which baffled foreign experts, so in the same way they took over factories abandoned by their former owners and ran them without any drop in production or slackening of internal discipline. It was a revelation for more than one foreign observer that people notorious for their indolence should devote themselves so wholeheartedly to their work, with no other coercion than a self-imposed one.

The strength and energy which had been submerged, it seemed for ever, in the morass of a routine economy revived with the feeling of responsibility evoked by the knowledge of a common destiny. The need for home-produced armaments to counteract the German and Italian war material sent over in such profusion to Spain acted in the factories as a constant spur and filled the workers with a fighting spirit stronger than hunger or death. In Sagunto all attempts of invading aircraft to force the workmen to fly from that fiery hell, bombed ten or twelve times a day, were a miserable failure. The comrades of a worker killed in an air raid would file past his dead body with clenched fists raised, pledging themselves in their silent homage not to cease work so long as a single machine was in running order. This pledge they kept until the very last day of the war. In the summer of 1938, with the enemy troops at the gates of Sagunto, the work of the factories still went on as though the front were hundreds of miles away. The presentation of a "Duty Medal" to the workers of Sagunto was made an occasion for offering national homage to the "heroes of the second line."

The dock workers were no less deserving of praise. I have seen them in Valencia gliding like shadows in the smoke and dust of the explosions to rescue sacks of wheat from some ship which had just been hit by enemy bombs. Not a single grain would be lost if they could help it. After unloading the cargo they would sweep up the wheat which had fallen on the wharf, for well they knew the value of every tiny roll of bread. They would shout words of encouragement to the crew, or, unmindful of the danger from shrapnel, would go to the help of some foreign sailor who had been hit during the bombardment. By the end of the war the Levant ports, which had suffered from hundreds of air raids, were a truly desolate sight. The enemy planes had left a long trail of destruction. Here and there a solitary derrick recalled the glory of former days; little else remained save air-raid shelters or the skeleton of some half-submerged ship in the harbour. Yet they were the scene of magnificent human strength and courage. Thousands of men risked their lives hourly to secure bread for people condemned by the Non-Intervention policy to a shameful blockade against which even the British flag was unable to protect its food-ships, ships whose arrival was awaited with an anxiety which could not easily have been appreciated by the members of the London Committee.

In the countryside there was the same enthusiasm. Wherever the young men had been called up, old men and women and children took their places. From dawn to dusk—sometimes even working by the light of lanterns when daylight was over—these country-folk would toil in the orchards, careful to see that not a single fruit was left to spoil. Everything was needed for the front. The defenders of the Republic were worthy of the best that could be given them. Whether or not there should be a return to the old days of feudalism, when the land belonged to one man and the people were his slaves—such was the issue dependent on their victory. Victory would mean a consolidation of the improvements in their condition made in recent years—small at first, but increasing greatly under a Government which realized that in the struggle for Spain's independence the hardest fighters had come from the country villages.

In the busiest days of the summer the soldiers from the nearest front would help with the harvest. In this spirit of co-operation between the army and the civilian population lies the true significance of the Spanish struggle on the loyalist side. The soldier who went to fight for his home and his village would lay aside his rifle and take up a sickle when the front was quiet for a few hours. The cause had need of both weapons, and he would wield them both with equal zeal. The farm labourer whether man or woman, who was not in the firing-line felt, in his or her way, none the less a soldier. It was a perfect brotherhood, united in a common destiny. Only with the victory of the ordinary Spaniard could a happier day dawn for all.

Thus the arrival of a new battalion in the village was more longed for than feared. Some of the hens, it is true, did not share in the general rejoicing, but their strange disappearance was soon forgotten. The old country-folk, anxious to learn to read in order to follow the war news in the papers, would attend the military school where the soldiers were finishing their education. In the summer merry bands of children would march in front of the sprinklers with which the soldiers, as a practical demonstration of the advantages of cleanliness, watered the roads. In the twinkling of an eye their clothes would be off and, heedless of the cries of protest from mothers not yet accustomed to the triumph of Mother Nature, they would be enjoying the delights of a communal bath. They were scenes of an innocent paganism which our enemies, had they witnessed them, would not have scrupled to use as a further pretext for accusing the "Reds" of creating a godless Spain.

But it was the Spanish woman who best proved her worth during the war. An absurd tradition had kept her on the fringe of national life and had confined her to the limited sphere of domestic work. The Republic gave her a vote, but this as a general rule simply meant doubling the political power of the husband or the confessor. The outcome of the women's vote in the 1933 elections was a reactionary one. The die-hards found some of their finest supporters in women under the influence of the Church. But by 1936 a change had begun to take place. The women had been deeply shocked by the savage reprisals following the October movement, and they registered their protest by voting for the Popular Front. Fundamentally, of course, it was an educational problem. Not more than ten years ago it was considered a remarkable event if a woman became a Doctor of Law at Madrid University. Subsequently many of the more ambitious women went to college, but their interest in a career was chiefly inspired by economic motives, an outcome of the desire of the poverty-stricken middle classes to forsake their narrow way of living and to rub shoulders with the aristocracy.

The women were attracted to politics chiefly by the powerful movement of the Young Socialists, which prepared them
for the moment when their remarkable qualities could be
placed entirely at the service of the people. That moment arrived on July 18. It was the Spanish woman who dominated
the magnificent mobilization of the people against the rebels,
and it was she who for two and a half years kept the flame of
resistance burning. Until the Government prohibited their
direct participation in the war, a good many members of the
Youth organizations took their places in the firing-line, where
they fought and died with a bravery which either put the
men to shame or fired them with new courage and enthusiasm.

No one suffered more than the Spanish woman from the
hardships of the war. No one endured them with greater
fortitude. If she lost a son at the front, she would hide her
grief for the sake of those left behind. When the others were
old enough she was the first to remind them of their duty to
their country. She brought up the young ones in a hatred of
that Fascism which had destroyed her heart and her home.
In the food queues, where she would wait long hours for a
meagre ration of lentils or rice, or perhaps, on more fortunate
days, a small piece of fish, she would turn like a wild beast on
any member of the Fifth Column who tried to exploit her
hunger by suggesting that there was no alternative but surrender. During the bread famines, which sometimes lasted
ten days in succession, the *agents provocateurs* never succeeded, in any part of loyalist territory, in organizing the
women for a single meeting of protest.

Whenever fresh soldiers were needed, the best recruiting
sergeants were always the women. (Sometimes they had to be
prevented from insulting, in a mood of patriotic fervour, the
young men on leave walking about the streets in mufti.)
They used up their remaining strength in organizing the dispatch of food to the front and to armament factories, and
after the international scheme of "Standard Parcels" was

adopted, it was the women who made up the packets and distributed them. At every meeting calling for resistance until the invaders were driven out of Spain, the women were the best propagandists. For members of the International Brigade it will be long before the memory fades of that afternoon when Barcelona bade them farewell, and of the multitude of girls who covered them with flowers, who flung their arms round their necks and kissed them with the gratitude of a country betrayed by the democratic Governments, but proud in the knowledge that the finest citizens of the world had gone out to fight and die in its cause.

But it was not merely in her capacity for emotion and sacrifice that the Spanish woman rose to the full height of her powers. For the first time in the history of Spain she undertook work of the greatest responsibility both in the Government and the Civil Service, thus giving the lie to those who had so long and so stupidly considered her as inferior to man in dealing with problems affecting the general well-being of the country.

Even the children, in their own way, set a touching example of dignity. I remember one day, in the summer of 1938, when enemy aircraft "bombarded" Madrid with small pieces of very fine white bread. The night before, the city had endured one of the customary savage cannonades intended to slaughter peaceable citizens and to raze a building or two to the ground. But on this particular morning the rebel command had changed its tactics and had decided to try the effect of dropping a few hundred kilos of bread on Madrid. This stratagem, as crude as it was insulting, was possibly suggested by one of the many German advisers who alternated their military activities with psychological studies of the civilian population during a foreign invasion. Their object was obviously a twofold one: to show that the bread, so scarce in Madrid, was plentiful enough in rebel territory to be given away; and to demoralize the inhabitants by accustoming them to the idea that the entry of Franco's army would mean the end of their sufferings. For the children of Madrid there could have been no finer present—better than the choicest packet of sweets which Santa Claus used to bring them every year before the war to make their Christmas Day a happy one. The first pieces which fell from the sky they picked up in wonderment. Mechanically they raised the bread to their mouths. Then they flung it to the ground as though it had burned their lips. Later one could see the children handing it in at the doors of the Police Commissariat—bread which they would never eat, no matter how hungry, because it was the gift of traitors. That same night the loyalist soldiers in the University City sent it back to the rebel trenches, wrapped up in paper on which was written: "Madrid cannot be bribed with this or with anything else. If you want Madrid, come and take it." It was one of the rare occasions when tears came to my eyes. Then I smiled as I remembered how during the election campaign of 1936 a very poor Castilian peasant, from whom the Fascists had tried to buy his vote, told me that he had replied: "Thank you, sir, but in my hunger I am my own master."

People with such qualities as these were not made to endure a régime based on treason and opposed to all that is best and finest in their nature. Franco's Spain may enjoy the hidden sympathy of the chancelleries, which with distinguished exceptions are all—even those representing the countries proudest of their democratic traditions—permeated with a certain aristocratic insouciance which inclines them to look kindly on dictators and totalitarian methods. But it is the other Spain, the Spain that for two and a half years gave the full measure of her spirit and her strength, who will conquer in the end. Until that time comes, the last episode of the struggle must remain unwritten.

CHAPTER XI

Military Lessons of the War

NOT ONLY was Spain the starting-point for the present international crisis, but, as has been clearly shown in the preceding chapters, she was also a vast experimental theatre where the Germans and Italians tested their arms and their tanks, tried out their air forces, and revised their strategic ideas in the light of practical experience. An examination, however brief and general, of the military lessons to be learned from the Spanish War must therefore be of especial interest in the present circumstances.

More than one foreign military expert has called the Spanish War "the pauper's war." By this they no doubt intended to convey that there were neither sufficient troops nor arms in Spain to allow of operations being planned and carried out on a large scale and in accordance with the principles of modern strategy. I need, however, cite only one case—that of the Republican offensive in the Ebro, already outlined in these pages—to prove that this conception of the war in Spain was a mistaken one. There were times when the fighting on the Ebro was proportionately harder and more intense than in the fiercest battle of the first World War.

Admittedly, the initial disparity between the length of the front and the number of defending or attacking troops existed, in a greater or less degree, throughout the war. Military experts estimate that, including reserves, there should be an average of at least one soldier for every yard of front. When this is not the case, the defences are likely to be considerably impaired, if not rendered useless, and it becomes extremely difficult to carry out engagements. The danger of surprise attacks, whether tactical or strategic, is considerably increased; breaks in the front line are inevitable; and the threat of flanking or enveloping operations, even in positional warfare, is the order of the day.

In relation to the length of the front, the numerical average of the Republican army was one quarter that stipulated by experts for purely defensive purposes. The usual proportion during the war was two and at the most two and a half men for every 10 yards of front—frequently not even that, especially when strong enemy attacks or Republican operations necessitated the concentration of heavy contingents in a particular sector. Man-power there was in plenty, and the will to fight, but arms were lamentably short.

The rebels were not faced with any of these difficulties. The proportion of men, including foreign troops, to the length of the front did not reach the figure laid down by the experts, and sometimes the disparity was even greater than on the loyalist side; but the lavish supplies furnished by their two powerful allies largely compensated the rebels, in the worst periods of the war, for their relative inferiority in numbers. Leaving on one side the tragic inequality between the resources of the two sides which characterized the last phase of hostilities, I will merely give two examples from an earlier stage of the war in support of this statement. During the great enemy offensive in the Levant (April–July 1938), the proportion of war material was as follows:

	REBEL	REPUBLICAN
Medium and heavy cannon	8–10	1
Light cannon	5–6	1
Bombing planes	10	1
Pursuit planes	8	1

In the rebel counter-offensive on the Ebro (July 30–November 15, 1938), the proportion was as follows:

	REBEL	REPUBLICAN
Medium and heavy cannon	12–15	1
Light cannon	7–10	1
Bombing planes	15	1
Pursuit planes	10	1

But in spite of the disparity on both sides between the number of troops and the length of front, and of the inferiority in war material in the loyalist camp, the Spanish War was rich in experiences and is deserving of attention from both experts and laymen. The value of lessons to be learned from a war is never absolute, but always relative. No cheap prescriptions can be made up from the experience of one war to cure the ills of another. Each war merely forms a valuable precedent which should not be ignored.

The first World War was immediately preceded by three others—the Boer, the Russo-Japanese, and the Balkan Wars. All three were "non-European"—to use a somewhat contemptuous expression more than once employed in the case of Spain—but each one of them taught lessons which are none the less important for not having been properly understood at the time.

The Boer War demonstrated the value of fortifications even in secondary positions, in spite of the tendency to depreciate them because—so it was alleged—they weakened the spirit of attack. Our own people were guilty of this error during the first few months of the war. The Russo-Japanese War proved the value of the machine-gun as a destructive weapon. It was ignored both before and after this war, as witness the fact that five years later—in 1910—the French Inspector-General of Infantry, replying to certain criticisms made in the Parliamentary Committee, stated: "We have manufactured machine-guns in order to please the public, but let us make no mistake, they are not going to change the situation in any way." The Balkan War proved that the class of artillery generally employed up to that time was useless against infantry operating on well-fortified ground, and that the howitzers and the Mausers were the best type of cannon for dislodging the enemy; both weapons already existed, but owing to a mistaken conception of their use they had not given the desired results and had been underestimated to such a degree that even at the beginning of the 1914 war there was still a tendency to consider them as a liability rather than as an excellent auxiliary to the infantry.

What, then, are the general lessons to be learned from the Spanish War? Perhaps the most important in the present circumstances is that the theory of the "lightning war" has been utterly discredited. And by that I mean a "lightning war" against real opposition. The sorry events in Poland in the fall of 1939 do not prove the contrary. What destroyed Poland was that same policy of appeasement which, as hopefully carried on for three years by Beck in his own country, had undermined Poland's capacity for resistance. Where there was real resistance, as in Warsaw—that had some of the quality of Madrid's resistance—*Blitzkrieg* had no lightning victory. The rapid development of aviation after the first World War, and the arms race caused by the appearance on the European horizon of certain states determined to extend their power by violence, were responsible for a great change in prevailing ideas and gave rise to the most fantastic forecasts. There were many military theorists, particularly in Germany and Italy, who considered that the country, or coalition of countries, with the greatest number of planes would automatically win the war merely by making full use of the air arm from the beginning of hostilities, thus dealing the enemy a blow from which he would not be able to recover. The main object of this aerial warfare, which was to be carried out in the space of a few days or weeks, was the total destruction of enemy morale through the mass bombardment of the civilian population and the principal centres of mobilization and industry. Other theorists advocated a combination of air and frontal land attacks on frontiers, with the object of surprising the enemy before he could complete his defensive preparations. In either case the surprise factor was the essential one. There was to be no declaration of war. A gigantic air squadron, sweeping over enemy territory like a cyclone, would be the only herald of hostilities.

This theory of warfare was well suited to the policy of intimidation practised by the totalitarian states. In the light of military knowledge it was untenable, but it could be used to frighten the man in the street. German and Italian propaganda had done its work, and in a state of tension, when people have already been subjected to a "war of nerves," the most absurd forecasts, the apocalyptic vision of a Göring or a Balbo riding on the clouds at the head of thousands of bombing planes, are capable of being taken seriously. Even if a healthy and vigorous reaction sets in, this type of propaganda has a temporary success, and there is no doubt that it exercised an indirect influence during the gravest moments of the Czechoslovakian crisis in September 1938. Even our films of the first bombardments of Madrid, which were merely intended to arouse public opinion in Europe against the horrible and unjustified slaughter of innocent women and children, sometimes provoked quite different reactions, which made us pause to consider whether we were not perhaps unintentionally presenting the defeatists and "appeasers" with a new argument for their demoralizing propaganda.

The Spanish War was responsible for exploding the new Italian and German theories of warfare—Douhetism and *Blitzkrieg* (or "lightning war")—and exposing them as mere scaremongering stories spread abroad to frighten the timorous. On the Spanish battlefield both these forms of warfare proved a complete failure.

Neither was the free aerial warfare *à outrance*—prophesied by German and Italian and other foreign writers—an unqualified success in the Spanish War. While it was no myth, its successful outcome depended upon a series of conditions difficult to fulfil and impossible to maintain long enough for any very intensive action. In practice this type of warfare did not last for any length of time. According to the doctrine of this free aerial combat, wars are decided in the air. The air force thus becomes the main arm. It must be given an opportunity to operate on its own account, free from all those restrictions imposed on other and less mobile arms by their very nature. This was most promising in theory, but it remained to be seen how far imagination went side by side with reality, and whether it had not in fact soared to heights far removed from the world which it hoped to destroy.

Experiments in operative air warfare were made on various occasions in Spain. The invaders carried out a "dress rehearsal," placing themselves in a similar situation to that which they would have to face when the time should come for a grand settlement, and arranging that the tests should take place in conditions resembling as closely as possible those of a European war. Thus the German air formations made careful experiments in the traversal of some hundreds of miles of enemy territory to reach a given objective. The Italian planes, on the other hand, followed the path marked out for them by Italy's geographical and strategical situation, and preferred to make attacks from their own coast on that of the enemy, without penetrating very far into loyalist territory.

The object of the Germans' "dress rehearsal" was to prepare for Continental warfare—for the war which eventually broke out in September 1939 against France, Poland, and Great Britain. As far as Britain is concerned, the conditions for an air attack on her were quite different. With the North

Sea and the Channel dominated by the British fleet, there is little chance for a surprise attack on London. The surprise factor is of course exceedingly important and the chances of its operating under such conditions as prevail around the British Isles seem to me slight.

For the Italians, however, the problem was very different. In their experiments in Spain they started with the fact in mind that the mountainous nature of the Italian land frontier would make large-scale operations very difficult for both France and Italy—especially for Italy—and that the use of a large air force over this territory would involve considerable risks and difficulties. For this reason the Italians—chiefly in order to test their aviation—confined themselves to attacks from their own coasts and islands against the coasts and islands of the enemy.

As a result of this "dress rehearsal" it was learned that the flight of airplanes far over enemy territory is subject to considerable limitations. Even in conditions most favourable for attack, such as, owing to the lack of anti-aircraft defences, existed in Spain, the average penetration of an airplane is not nearly so great as might have been expected from a calculation of its gasoline reserves and flying potentialities. In spite of the constant attacks on Spanish territory, only in very rare instances did planes—isolated and never in formation—succeed in penetrating more than seventy-five to a hundred miles. Any attempt to go farther involved the risk of heavy losses. In the Spanish War the German theory of permanent aerial warfare, in which the enemy could be struck at in the heart of his territory, was exploded almost as thoroughly as that of the "lightning war."

It would be going to the other extreme, however, entirely to ignore the part played by the air force in Spain. Without it the war could not have been waged nor the rebels have triumphed. Its influence cannot be measured by a mere summing up of the engagements in which it took part, nor by the number of aerial bombardments and of machines brought down. One has to have lived in Spain from August to November 1936 to realize the anguish of the men in the trenches who for hour after hour endured machine-gun fire from enemy machines without the sight of a single loyalist plane to cheer and encourage them. Every telephone call from the front was a request for airplanes. On every one of my visits to the militia I heard the same cry: "If only they'd send us half a dozen machines just for one week, we'd take back all the ground we've lost, and chase the Fascists to Burgos as well!" For those militiamen half a dozen planes was a fantastic dream. At the time the Republican command had little more than that number for all the fronts. When it *was* possible to send them, however—even though only for a couple of hours—there was no need to await the telegram from the commander of the recipient sector before writing in the communiqué to the War Minister: "Today the loyal troops in . . . Sector have fought with extraordinary courage."

In all the decisive phases of the struggle the air force played an extremely active role, and apart from its own activities it often had to carry out other functions as well. The scarcity of material, the rugged nature of the territory, and the lack of adequate means of transport meant that the air force was frequently resorted to in moments of difficulty and used for work which it would never have had to do in more normal war conditions. This was on the Republican side. But a calculation of the efficiency and limitations of the air arm can better be made from the side of the rebels, on account of their superiority in the air. As we have seen, from a psychological point of view the influence of the air arm was decisive. Particularly at the beginning of the war, and until our soldiers accustomed themselves to air attacks, a great deal of the progress made by the insurgents—a typical example is their rapid advance from Talavera to Madrid in the autumn of 1936 —was entirely due to the assistance of German and Italian airplanes. The actual casualties from aviation on the battlefield were no greater, but rather less, than those caused by artillery or machine-guns; during the critical period of the spring of 1938, when the whole of the eastern front was threatened with destruction, I read out, in a speech broadcast to the troops, the lists of casualties inflicted in various engagements, specifying which were due to aviation and which to other forms of warfare; and I well remember how amazed were the general public and even the soldiers themselves—notwithstanding the fact that they had been the nearest witnesses —to find that the number killed and wounded in air raids was relatively small. On the other hand, the moral effect was very great, and until an army has developed the fighting spirit shown by our troops in the Ebro offensive, the impression caused by a hundred airplanes flying over the trenches must necessarily determine the result of a battle.

In strictly military terms the experience gained in Spain was that the more the air arm is used for work outside its own sphere, the smaller is its contribution to the war, while the more it fulfils its natural function of auxiliary arm to the infantry, the greater will be its assistance in the prosecution of hostilities.

In the Spanish War the disparity in fighting conditions between the bombing and pursuit planes was far less than during the first World War. The average speed of the fastest bombers employed in Spain was between 250 and 280 miles per hour, and of the fastest pursuit planes between 280 and 300 m.p.h., as against 60 and 85–95 m.p.h. respectively in 1914–18. This means that in the Spanish War the best bombers were four times as fast as in the war of 1914, while the speed of the best pursuit planes had been little more than trebled. The bombing plane, therefore, no longer has the same relative inferiority to the pursuit plane and is now in a position to decide whether to accept a fight or to withdraw; nor does it have to choose the latter course on account of its comparatively low speed. If prudence is counselled, it is for other reasons—the bomber is more vulnerable than the pursuit plane, less easily manœuvred, and less mobile. It was often noticed, however, that because of the levelling-up in the speed of the two planes, at only one point in an engagement was the fighter in a position to open fire on the bomber with any likelihood of hitting its target, and that even in the most favourable conditions possible the time for firing was never more than two seconds. It should be borne in mind that a speed of 300 m.p.h. means that 147 yards are covered in one second, and as the Spanish War has proved that in aerial combat machine-gun fire is ineffective at a distance of more than 100 yards, it will be seen that the time for making a successful shot is extremely limited.

From an objective analysis of the aerial warfare in Spain, made on the basis of official reports, statements from captured pilots, and conversations with Republican aviators, the conclusion has been reached that the potential strength of the bombing plane not only has been quadrupled since 1918, but has also increased more rapidly than that of the pursuit plane. The time available for firing on one plane from another is now so short that the importance of the machine-gun in aerial fighting is no longer axiomatic. Our air-force leaders learned this lesson, and after the summer of 1938 they armed all pursuit planes with a light cannon, generally of 20 mm. calibre, with which they could fire a distance of half a mile in the relative certainty of hitting their target. Unfortunately the number of cannon available was too small, and the time for experimenting too short, for this innovation to make any appreciable change in the relation between our aviation and the powerful air arm of the enemy; but the impression of our experts was that the pursuit plane armed with a cannon is destined not merely to complement the machine-gun fighting plane, but to replace it. Experiments were also made in the arming of heavy and light bombing planes with a mobile or semi-mobile cannon, so that they could effect greater damage in engagements on the front and more easily beat off air at-

tacks. These experiments were satisfactory and had given rise
to great hopes when they were interrupted by the sudden end
of the war.

The efficiency of the air force in making ready for an
offensive was fully demonstrated, and the permanent shortage of guns and ammunition on the Republican side meant
that the preparation before an infantry attack often had to be
confined to an aerial bombardment on enemy positions. In
such cases the air force did not merely complement the
artillery, but rather replaced it.

The idea of employing the bombing plane—light, medium,
or heavy—as "flying artillery" is not a new one, but in the
Spanish War circumstances forced the Republicans to adopt
it on a scale which can certainly never have been foreseen.
It is a method with undeniable advantages. Fire can be concentrated on any part of the front, the choice of objective can
be made very rapidly, and the enemy can be easily surprised.
The radius of action of the bomber is four times that of
ground artillery. On the other hand, the activity of "flying
artillery" is chiefly confined to the hours between sunrise and
sunset, and even during that time a certain degree of visibility is essential. There is no way of escaping the tyranny
of the barometer. The bombing plane is soon put out of action
in bad weather, particularly if it has to operate over mountainous ground or along the coast. Land artillery can easily
fire to a depth of between six and nine miles; the range of
air artillery is shorter and its aim less accurate than the ordinary cannon when the objective is at a great distance. This
inferiority is not lessened by low flying, when the risk is
naturally greater and only partially compensated by an increased volume of fire. Moreover, the "flying artillery" can
be more easily silenced with a good anti-aircraft system than
can ground artillery by enemy shells.

There is no question therefore of deciding between one
type of arm and the other. Spanish experience has shown the
advantages and disadvantages of both and has proved that

the common-sense method is not to replace one by the other, but to combine the two in order to meet the varying conditions of the struggle.

Nothing during the Spanish War caused so much disillusionment as attacks by bombing planes. I have already referred to the excessive hopes which many military experts, chiefly German and Italian, had placed in this new method of warfare. Their calculations proved false. They were based firstly on a mistaken conception of the destructive effect of aerial bombs and of the extent to which an airplane could penetrate enemy territory, and secondly on an underestimation of anti-aircraft defences and of the moral resistance of troops at the front and the civilian population in the rear.

During the war hundreds of aerial attacks were made by German and Italian airplanes on Barcelona, Valencia, Cartagena, and Madrid. Thousands of projectiles were hurled on the civilian population, causing innumerable casualties. In not one single case, however, did the enemy succeed in paralysing the economic life of these cities for a period much longer than the duration of the actual bombardment—and then only partially. Panic among the civilian population was unknown, save during the last days in Catalonia when the refugees streaming towards the frontier were terrorized by the airplanes. But even then their fear of falling into the hands of the Fascists was far greater than their fear of air raids. The chance of a direct hit in a raid—even in the best possible conditions—was very small. And as there is no reason—rather the contrary—to suppose that the Germans and Italians sent their worn-out planes and their worst pilots to Spain, the fault must lie either in the system itself or in the method adopted.

From the beginning of the summer of 1938 to the end of the war, several thousand tons of bombs were dropped from the air on the two railway lines between Barcelona and the French and Spanish frontier. The stations and surrounding districts in Granollers, Gerona, Figueras, and Puigcerdá suffered considerable damage, and the number of victims was by no means small, but, in spite of this, railway traffic was never interrupted for more than two hours—the time needed to clean up the line and the platforms. The railroad track was not once destroyed. And yet the line of the railroad could not have been more favourable for the attackers. It is easily visible, and one part of it runs in an exposed position all along the coast. Surprise attacks could easily have been made, and anti-aircraft defences were very defective.

No less instructive is the case of Cartagena. In Cartagena Bay the warships of the Republican fleet were anchored for some weeks. Here also the enemy could make use of surprise tactics by attacking from the sea. Flying at a great height and then swooping down with the engines turned off, the rebel planes were able more than once, when the weather was favourable, to drop their bombs before the attack was detected and the anti-aircraft defences could be brought into action. The attacker thus had all the trumps in his hand, but never succeeded in sinking a single ship.

This failure of the bombing plane in air attacks was clearly shown in the loyalist offensive on the Ebro at the beginning of July 1938. The Republican bridges over this river had been built with insufficient material and were by no means strong. They were easily visible, and situated at a maximum distance of twelve miles from the enemy positions. For a period of four months they were used in the transport of supplies to an army of fifty thousand men fighting in continuous combat. During the whole offensive the enemy concentrated most of their air attacks on these bridges. In view of their vital function they were of course protected as far as possible with light cannons and machine-guns. Nevertheless, the rebels, with their overwhelming superiority in the air, were repeatedly able to direct their fire both on bridges and on anti-aircraft defences. During that period of nearly four months thousands of bombs, large and small, were dropped on the bridges without causing any serious damage. What harm was done was easily repaired on the spot by the troops themselves. Not once was the traffic interrupted. Until the night of November 14–15, 1938 when the Republican army returned across the river to their previous positions, the bridges remained standing. Having fulfilled their mission, some were dismantled and removed, while others were destroyed—but destroyed by the men who had built them and not by enemy aircraft.

Apart from isolated cases of small tactical importance, where luck played the most important part, the air arm during the Spanish War had to record more failures than successes in the bombardment of small objectives. The attempt to remedy this by an increase in projectiles merely led to a great waste of ammunition. Such small objectives as ordinary bridges, crossroads, railway lines (double or single), isolated buildings chosen as command or observation posts, and nests of machine-guns were rarely hit, and then only by chance. Objectives less than two and a half acres in area were safe, and in any case the attack, to have any chance of success, had to take place in conditions of perfect visibility and at a height no greater than three thousand feet. From a military point of view, however, it must be borne in mind that the most important targets come under the heading of small objectives. The inevitable margin of error in the reports of the aviator carrying out the attack must also be discounted. War dispatches frequently reported the destruction of a whole fleet of troop trucks by an enemy squadron. I have myself witnessed a spectacular air attack on a long line of Republican trucks—an attack so fierce that it seemed that not one truck could remain intact, nor any of our men—even those sheltering in the neighbouring fields—come out alive, yet when at last the raid was over and the procession set off on its way again, we found that not one single truck of the whole fleet had been touched.

With the deliberate and systematic persistence of the Prussian school, the enemy air force carried out various attempts at totalitarian warfare, with the object of completely destroying its particular target. In Guernica, Granollers, Nules,

Castellón de la Plana, Durango, and many other cities and villages in the Republican rear guard the rebels, completely indifferent to the question of whether or not the objective was a military one, proceeded, by means of intensive shell-fire or a certain type of projectile, to wipe out whole blocks of houses, or districts or villages, checking up the results by photography and treating the whole thing as a scientific experiment. Assiduously prepared reports from Republican airmen—compared with statements of captured enemy pilots—showed that a quarter to half a ton of bombs are needed to effect the total destruction of an industrial plant; one to two tons for town buildings; and four times the latter figure for military objectives.

The Spanish War proved that aerial attacks, though they cannot determine the result of a war, can cause serious damage in large cities. It also proved that in the bombardment of towns what really counts is not the civilian casualties but the material damage. Finally, it showed the limits of this material destruction. One to two tons of bombs are needed to turn two and a half acres of a city into a heap of ruins. The area of the city of Paris, excluding the suburbs, is about forty square miles. To destroy the whole city 10,000 to 20,000 tons of ammunition would therefore be necessary. And when it is remembered that a bombing plane can carry only 2 tons of ammunition, it will be seen that 5,000 to 10,000 machines would be needed for such an undertaking.

Admittedly, these machines would not have to attack Paris simultaneously, but could set out in relays, and many of them could return several times. Nevertheless, the bombing planes would have to be accompanied by at least twice as many pursuit planes, and the losses would be so great that before they had all succeeded in reaching Paris the attack could be broken—which would probably mean the end of the enemy air force. No air fleet exists which is capable of dropping sufficient bombs on Paris to destroy the city. And as far as London is concerned, three times more ammunition would be needed than for Paris. The idea is too absurd to be worthy of serious consideration.

Night attack by air on military objectives is an insoluble problem. Such attacks were frequent at the beginning of the Spanish War. Later on they were more and more confined to the large cities, where black-outs, however efficient, could never completely obliterate certain landmarks. Barcelona and Valencia, in particular, suffered from night bombardments, but in spite of the size of these two cities, and the fact that both were near the coast, where they could easily be located by night, the majority of bombs dropped on them during these nocturnal attacks fell in the sea or outside the inhabited part of the town.

The greatest obstacle in the defence against aerial attacks is panic. Once this breaks out among the civilian population, it is very difficult to control and often causes more victims than enemy bombs. Danger from panic can be reduced if there is an alarm system effective enough to inspire confidence in the people. On the Republican side the system of passive defence soon attained a very high degree of efficiency. More than once I have heard the British Military Attaché, Major Richards, and the French Military Attaché, Colonel Morel, sing its praises with great enthusiasm. Against overland attacks from land aerodromes, the pursuit plane was the best defensive arm. For attacks from airplanes flying over the sea—when as a general rule the bombs were heard before the warning sirens—anti-aircraft guns were the best means of defence. The 75 mm. cannon was most effective in repulsing attacks from airplanes flying at a great height. It frequently succeeded in dispersing an enemy squadron. Against attacks in the interior—night raids or bombardments on sectors of the front—the 20 mm. cannon was the most satisfactory method of defence.

The experience in regard to tanks in the Spanish War is also interesting. In the Battle of Madrid they were used on both sides, although there were very few in proportion to the

numerical strength of the two infantry groups and the length
of the front. Their use in this battle resulted in a technical
defeat for the rebels and a tactical defeat for the Republicans. The technical defeat of the rebels was the inevitable
consequence of a false conception of tank war and of the
use of material inadequate for its purpose. Not until the last
stage of the war did the enemy succeed in remedying the
technical faults brought to light in their first tank engagements. As far as the Republicans were concerned, they suffered a tactical defeat in tank warfare during the Battle of
Madrid, not because there was anything wrong with the tanks
themselves, but because they were used wrongly. An account of the operations may be interesting at this point.

When at the end of October 1936 the rebels were closing
in on the south and south-east of Madrid, the loyalist High
Command decided on a counter-attack, not only to relieve the
pressure on the city but also to form a basis of positive operations. The attack was launched against the right flank of the
enemy divisions, which were well entrenched and were preparing a fresh advance over a stretch of territory which was
becoming increasingly difficult for the Government troops.

The attack was preceded by a short artillery preparation.
Owing to the lack of artillery and ammunition, we could only
count on cannon of light calibre, and our fire was concentrated on the enemy's front line and a narrow line in the
rear where nests of machine-guns had been observed. The
positions of enemy artillery farther back were not covered by
our guns.

At the same time—though with little success—the enemy
positions were bombarded by the few airplanes at our disposal and fired at by machine-guns. Covered by this very inadequate preparation, the attack was launched over a front
of a mile and a quarter. From all appearances the rebels were
taken completely by surprise, so convinced were they that no
obstacle would be encountered in their rapid march on
Madrid. The first wave of attack consisted in a fairly well-

spaced line of forty tanks—one for every fifty or sixty yards of front. These advanced at a speed of eighteen to twenty miles an hour, and reached the first rebel positions without great difficulty, resisting and replying to the enemy fire. The tanks were followed by a second wave of attack from the infantry. When these troops found themselves at a critical point three hundred yards or so from the enemy lines, the tanks had already passed the first enemy positions. At this moment heavy machine-gun fire broke out from these positions, and the Republican infantry, although they attempted to continue their advance, found themselves fighting on exposed ground, where they suffered considerable losses and were finally immobilized. Thus the contact between the two waves of attack—the tanks and the infantry—was severed. The tanks, which had penetrated the enemy front with scarcely a single casualty, discovered that nobody was following them, and turned back. But on their return journey they were subjected to the whole of the enemy fire, and some of them were put out of action.

The result of this first large-scale tank attack by the Republicans, on October 29, 1936, was therefore a negative one. The Republican command had learned, however, that on the battlefield the speed of a tank is of limited value. The German theory that it is the best protection against enemy fire had been proved false. On the contrary, an excessive speed makes it difficult for the tank-drivers to find their bearings, lessens the effectiveness of their fire, and prevents the infantry from following them. Tank attacks should also be preceded by a well-planned and intensive artillery preparation. However great the firing-power of a tank—even if it carries a cannon, and even if aim is taken with great accuracy—it cannot replace artillery in the midst of an engagement. The essence of a tank attack lies in the infantry which follows. At no time during the attack must contact be lost between these two groups. The results may perhaps be different with very heavy tanks; in the Spanish War these were never used, and my observations are therefore limited to the type of medium tank of which we had experience. These observations, however, are sufficient to show that the tank can never constitute, as has been claimed, that "fourth arm" capable of deciding the result of a battle. It is nothing more than an auxiliary arm of the infantry. No subsequent experience in the Spanish War gave grounds for modifying the lesson learned from the first large-scale attack of Republican tanks before Madrid. On the contrary, it was merely confirmed by later tank engagements.

As regards the light tanks of German and Italian production employed by the enemy on a large scale up to the autumn of 1938, experience in Spain proved them highly unsatisfactory. A single machine-gun, properly handled, could put them out of action. Their failure thoroughly confirmed the observations of the well-known tank expert on the French General Staff, Lieutenant-Colonel Perré. In Germany and Italy, where the weight of the tank is reduced to a minimum in order to economize on material, it is easy to produce hundreds of them to make a good impression in military processions or in the news reels. But while these tanks can travel at a considerable speed, and while their armour-plating and cannon give them an awe-inspiring appearance, their importance on the battlefield is very small.

The problem to be solved was how far their weight could be reduced. It was found during the Spanish War that, however perfectly a tank is constructed, the weight must not be less than nine to ten tons if it is to make the most of its speed and to remain firm and steady on broken ground, if its arms are to be effective and its armour-plating to give adequate protection against enemy fire.

Neither the German tank P.Z.K.1., weighing about six tons, nor the Italian tank Fiat-Ansaldo 1933, weighing only three and a third tons, fulfils these conditions. The first forms part of the German armoured divisions (*Panzer Divisionen*), which were represented as irresistible; with the second the

Italians were able to subdue the unarmed population of Ethiopia.

Admittedly both types of tank are capable of a very high speed. It was proved, however, that on the battlefield this speed is practically valueless. A high speed potential can undoubtedly be very useful in accelerating the concentration of tank formations and in launching them rapidly against one sector or another, but in actual operations they are doomed to certain failure.

Spanish experience shows that the ideal type of tank is that of nine to ten tons. Its transport by rail or in specially constructed trucks does not entail any great difficulties, concentrations are easy to mask, its construction is simple, and it can easily be replaced in case of loss. In certain circumstances a 75 mm. shell is sufficient to destroy a tank of twenty tons, while at least two such shells are necessary to destroy two tanks of ten tons.

In the Battle of Guadalajara of March 1937 the rebel tanks were an utter failure. Here these German and Italian pseudo war-chariots and the illusory "light but very rapid tanks" met their fate.

The situation was as follows: After the rebels had lost the Battle of Madrid, the Republican front was stabilized in the south, south-east, and east-by-south of the capital, and since there was no longer any prospect of their advancing in those sectors, even with the assistance of unlimited material, they tried to force their way through on the north-east. The blow had to be struck rapidly, and surprise tactics employed.

With this object in view the rebels assembled all their available tanks and motorized formations. On a relatively narrow front they concentrated 280 to 300 light tanks and three Italian motorized divisions, with four or five supporting divisions of infantry. The enemy attack was carried out with extraordinary violence. After a hard combat the loyalist troops withdrew in accordance with instructions. The insurgents continued their pressure, and after a few days they succeeded in penetrating Republican territory on a comparatively narrow front to a depth of twenty-five to thirty miles. Then the Republicans counter-attacked. At the head of the loyalist troops a small group of tanks—not more than forty—of nine and twenty tons, armed with machine-guns and assisted by the air arm, attacked the enemy tanks and destroyed about a hundred of them. Next they engaged the Italian infantry—thereby exposing the weakness of motorization, for as soon as motorized troops are overcome as such, they have little chance of reaction and can soon be routed. The Government troops then made a flank attack on the Italian divisions, which fled in disorder to positions considerably in the rear of their original lines. If the Republicans had had abundant reserves, a couple of relief divisions would have sufficed for the rebel retreat to have reached catastrophic proportions.

On the battlefield remained the Italian and German tanks, some destroyed and some captured. The occupants who had been taken prisoner all acknowledged that in the thick of the fight they had completely lost their bearings, and that the abrupt movements of their tanks often prevented them from distinguishing between their own men and those of the enemy. And as a result of the continual jolting, it had soon become not merely difficult, but impossible, to use their arms. We had, in fact, noticed during the fight that the enemy tanks were zigzagging from one side to another in an aimless manner, that they had not been able to avoid the ditches and natural obstacles in the road, and that even at short range their machine-guns were inactive.

The rebels lost the Battle of Guadalajara chiefly because of the military inadequacy of the Italian and German light tanks, and also because these tanks did not keep the necessary contact with the infantry and were therefore isolated in the face of enemy fire. The Republican command took firm advantage of these defects, being hampered only by the shortage of contingents.

The relative importance of the defensive and the offensive during the Spanish War was seen most clearly in the case of Madrid. The city was defended by bodies of improvised troops, poorly equipped and officered, with weak positions, hastily constructed fortifications, practically no artillery, only two airplanes, and no reserves. But these men knew that the outcome of the war was in their hands and that they must keep the enemy from the gates of the capital or die in the attempt. Faced with an army superior in every respect, an army supported by a powerful air force and equipped with the most modern war material and artillery of every calibre, they won the victory of the last months of 1936. This is the great lesson of the Battle of Madrid. In the worst possible conditions the defensive triumphed against an enemy numerically five times superior and with far greater material resources. Nor was their success shortlived. During the thirty months which followed, the enemy carried out a series of well-planned and varied attacks between the south and east of Madrid. On all the sectors fresh reinforcements were constantly arriving; batteries of light, medium, and heavy cannon were tried out; Italian and German tanks were moved up; hundreds of airplanes were brought into action; the extreme of totalitarian warfare, in the form of daily artillery bombardments, was waged on the civilian population; the roads were bombarded in order to cut off the supply of food to the capital; but the defences still held. The defence triumphed; the fighting soldier, with his insuperable moral qualities—the essential factor in every defence—remained firm, and nothing could shake his resistance. It is the proud achievement of Madrid never to have been conquered by force of arms.

CHAPTER XII

Behind the Scenes in the Cabinet

IT WAS NOT till the end of July 1936 that I arrived in Madrid, after a week of fruitless attempts to reach the capital without having to go back through France. Our hopes that in the first forty-eight hours of the rebellion there would be no serious control of the roads were dashed almost before we had left San Sebastián on Sunday the 19th, in a car which the local Socialist organization had placed at our disposal. There were six of us in all—three Socialist deputies, and three leaders of Youth groups whom we had met in Irún returning from an international conference. Two trucks in a bend of the high-road, blocking the imagined advance of rebel troops from Navarre, forced us to make a detour to Bilbao, where the news—equally imaginary—that the enemy was already in Ochandiano had caused such a disturbance that it was impossible to get the necessary gasoline to continue our journey.

The next morning it was too late. Making our way—more at a venture than by the map—along secondary roads which we supposed would be less closely watched, we would arrive at a village only to be stopped by comrades on Government patrol and told that the next village was in the hands of the Fascists. Ready for any unpleasant surprise, we journeyed in this way all over the province of Burgos, until at last we had to admit ourselves beaten, and, rather than go back on our tracks, made for Santander. After three days of anxious waiting in this town, we set off again for Bilbao, our return being less easy and more eventful than the outward journey.

Rumours were circulating that some Italian Fascists were driving about in a car of the same colour as ours and committing all kinds of outrages. A chase of the phantom car was immediately organized. Shots were fired at us from a truck full of militiamen which we met on the road, and only thanks to my speed in opening the car door and showing my Socialist Party card was a serious incident avoided.

A few miles farther on, however, we were stopped by a patrol of Basque Nationalists, certain that they had at last captured the "Italian car." Covering us with their rifles, which in those disturbed days used to go off almost of their own accord, they forced us to put up our hands and get out of the car one by one. Neither our documents nor our explanations were of any avail. "It's the car all right! They're the people. Don't let's waste any time—take them away!" shouted the member of the group who seemed to be their leader. "*You* Alvarez del Vayo!" he exclaimed when I showed him my Deputy's card. "This Fascist guy must think we're a lot of idiots." Finally they agreed that one of their number should go to the village to find some Socialist who might be able to identify us. Fortunately a few minutes later a group of militiamen drove up, one of whom recognized us. The same rifles which had been pointed against us a few moments before now formed our guard of honour as far as Bilbao.

There was nothing for it but to go back to France and from there to return to Spain via Barcelona. The rebel radio hastened to broadcast the news of our flight. But the night after crossing the frontier we were in Madrid.

The whole of August was taken up with frequent visits to

the front and work in the Madrid Socialist group. At the end
of the month the Prime Minister, Señor Giral, on meeting me
one day in the War Ministry, told me that he wanted to
broaden the basis of the Government. He wondered how
Señor Largo Caballero would welcome this proposal, and
how far he would be willing to participate in a Cabinet
reorganization.

There is no doubt that it was only the two most prominent
Socialist leaders, Largo Caballero and Indalecio Prieto, with
whom Señor Giral wished to share his grave responsibilities.
But in the meantime the military situation had deteriorated
to such an extent that a complete change in the administration of the war seemed inevitable, and Señor Giral decided to
resign. Very generously he took it upon himself to persuade
the President of the Republic to dispense with his services,
although Señor Azaña was reluctant to part with a man to
whom he was bound by close political and personal ties and
who had taken over the Government at such a critical time.

For various reasons I was entrusted by Señor Largo Caballero to take the first steps in the formation of the new Cabinet.
The rivalry between the various parties and organizations—
which at a later stage of the war was to cause such difficulties
—had already begun to make itself felt, and efforts were
needed to overcome the obstacles which the formation of any
coalition government invariably creates. The Communists
did not want to enter the Government. The C.N.T., which
claimed a membership of two million in its trade unions
(organizations of an Anarchist tendency), wanted a greater
representation than seemed justified by its strength in the
country. Within the Socialist Party, Indalecio Prieto's political friends felt that he should be the new Prime Minister.
Señor Prieto himself, when, in the name of Señor Largo
Caballero, I asked for his collaboration, told me quite frankly
that he doubted if the new Government would be the right
one in the circumstances. "In time of war," he said, "governments are soon discredited. Caballero is our last card; why

play him so soon?" As for the Republicans, it was not pleasant for them to have to exchange a position of exclusive responsibility for one in which their influence in the Government was to be considerably diminished.

Agreement was finally reached in regard to the most difficult point, that of proportionate representation, and from the names proposed by the various parties, Señor Large Caballero dictated to me the list of the new Cabinet. "Prime Minister and War Minister myself; Foreign Minister—you" . . . this was the first intimation I had of my entry into the Government. During the whole period of preliminary negotiations Señor Largo Caballero never once said whom he intended to appoint as Foreign Minister and Minister of the Interior, portfolios which, together with those of the Prime Minister and War Minister, he had reserved for the Socialist group which he represented.

The new Government was welcomed with great enthusiasm, particularly at the front. The very name of Señor Largo Caballero was enough to ensure its popularity. His splendid personal qualities, his scrupulous honesty and his tremendous capacity for work, which had apparently not lessened with the years, were well known. If the enemy advance on the Talavera front could have been halted, and if a military success, however small, could have followed the formation of the Government, the position of the Cabinet would have been so strong that all danger of those political differences which arose again a few months later would have been avoided.

The Government was put to one of its severest tests when it was forced to leave Madrid. Ever since the fall of Toledo the question of an eventual transfer to Valencia or Barcelona had on various occasions been discussed by the Cabinet. While Indalecio Prieto, supported by the Republicans, had, from the beginning of October, advocated the removal of the Government to a town farther from the front. Señor Largo Caballero, the Communist Ministers, and myself thought that a premature departure would be a mistake. We each of us had good reasons for our opinions. The partisans of an immediate Government transfer based their arguments on questions of a general nature, and also on the fear that the absence of direct contact between the Government and the President of the Republic would create a dangerous situation. Reports reaching us regarding the attitude of Señor Azaña, who had taken up temporary residence in Barcelona, were by no means reassuring. We feared that his habitual pessimism, exacerbated by isolation, might lead him to make some irrevocable decision. Those who thought that the Government should not wait until the last moment, but should make its departure in comparative calm, were proved right by subsequent events. The rest of us, on the other hand, feared that the premature removal of the Government would add to the confusion and dismay caused by the rapid advance of the rebel troops. But Madrid recovered her morale in an amazing fashion and proved herself ready to meet all difficulties.

I spent the three days preceding the transfer of the Government to Valencia in the War Ministry. In the office of General Pozas, who was in command of the Central Army, the officers of the General Staff were working all through the night trying to find a way of breaking the enemy ring which was closing in on the city. Suddenly someone announced that he had found the solution. "Yes, that's it—all we have to do is to bring over *these* battalions to *this* position and make an attack on the flank." General Pozas, a typical cavalry man who liked to have everything cut and dried and who had the greatest contempt for academic strategy, retorted: "But where are those battalions? That's what I should like to know. They ran off years ago and haven't left so much as their tails behind them." After this explosion, however, this old Republican, whose indignation with the militiamen was like that of a disappointed father whose son has not come out at the top of his class, put on his spectacles and set himself again to study the map with great care and attention.

Everything was in a state of confusion. Only in the Minister's office was there an atmosphere of calm. Completely imperturbable, concealing his thoughts even from his intimate friends, Señor Largo Caballero, Prime Minister and Minister of War, did not for one moment let himself be affected by the prevailing nervous tension. As usual he went to bed at eleven, and as usual he was at his desk again by seven in the morning.

Only on the night of November 4 did Largo Caballero ignore this time-table. The grave problems created by the encirclement of Madrid and the urgent necessity of avoiding internal disorders had decided him to bring the C.N.T. into the Government, thereby forming a bloc of all the anti-Fascist forces of the country. Señor Azaña raised serious objections, however, to the appointment of two of the four candidates proposed for the ministerial posts—Señora Montseny and García Oliver, both members of the F.A.I. (*Federación Anarquista Ibérica,* Iberian Anarchist Federation). Señor Giral had returned by plane that very morning to inform us of the President's opposition. In different circumstances the natural course would have been to yield to the will of the President or to give him time to change his mind. But in those dark days through which Madrid was passing, any indecision would have been fatal. Already the prospective Ministers, two of whom had come expressly from Barcelona, had begun to suspect that their entry into the Government was not well considered in high places, and were talking about returning to Catalonia and breaking off relations between the C.N.T. and the Government. Twice I had to leave the Prime Minister's study in order to quiet and reassure them.

A telephone conversation between the President of the Republic and the Prime Minister, not lacking in a certain dramatic quality, put an end to an embarrassing situation. Although we were unable to hear his voice, the rest of us could almost feel the exasperation of Señor Azaña coming over the wires. Within a few moments, however, Señor Largo Caballero was given authorization to send to the official *Gazette* the notice of the appointment of the four C.N.T. members, duly sanctioned by the President.

Those Ministers who did not agree with us that the C.N.T. members should be admitted into the Cabinet had further reason for indignation when their new colleagues—with all the vehemence and heroics of their Anarchist oratory—contended that the Government should stay in Madrid and defend the capital in street-fighting at the barricades in the manner of the Paris Commune. Following a detailed exposition by Premier Caballero of the military situation in its relation to the necessity of transferring the Government to Valencia, the four Anarchist Ministers withdrew from the meeting to discuss the matter among themselves. In the silence that followed while they were out of the room, those Ministers who had opposed the incorporation of the Anarchists in the Government exchanged significant glances as if to make clear to Largo Caballero and me how utterly wrong we had been to insist on inviting the Anarchists into the Cabinet. But this, in our view, had been unavoidable. In Madrid's critical situation, had the Anarchists not been allowed to share the Government's responsibility, it is more than likely that they would have seized the opportunity afforded by the Government's departure for Valencia to try to set up a local Junta of their own. This would have only produced confusion and disaster throughout the loyal territory.

After a long period of deliberation the four ministers returned and expressed their willingness to vote for the transference of the Government. The danger of a split in the Cabinet at this crucial hour was avoided. The Government's decision to move from Madrid to Valencia was approved by a unanimous vote of the Cabinet. Unanimity was important in order that no party or political organization could later claim to have opposed the decision.

During Largo Caballero's premiership a Cabinet vote on

important decisions was the general procedure. Whenever energetic measures were required for the defence of the Republic it usually happened that, while the majority of the votes were cast in support of the Premier's position, the Prieto group in the Cabinet inclined to vote with the moderate Republicans whose policies were more hesitant than Caballero's. When Dr. Negrín became Premier he introduced a different practice. Votes were taken only on death sentences. On no other matters was a division of Cabinet opinion allowed to coalesce. Each minister was free to express his point of view and the final decision was made by the Premier on the basis of the discussion, but no vote was taken. This assured a more vigorous leadership.

When the departure of the Government was decided upon, the enemy was less than two miles from the capital. It was agreed that, in order not to attract too much attention, the Ministers should leave Madrid separately. I remained behind for a few hours, preparing contacts with the diplomatic corps and organizing the evacuation of the Code Section, the only department which I was interested in taking with me.

On arriving at Tarancón, forty-five miles from Madrid, we were informed by one of the road patrols that they could not give us any gasoline without a special permit from the military commander, to whose headquarters we were conducted. There we found that Tarancón was in the hands of the "Iron Column," behind whose fine-sounding name a whole series of undesirables, armed with rifles and obeying no law but their own, were sowing terror on all sides and preparing the installation of the "new social order" by a series of thefts and murders. The local chief was a man whom I had known ever since the revolutionary movement of 1930 which preceded the Republic, and whose connections with the police of that time had given grounds for suspecting him of being nothing but a common informer. In an aggressive tone, obviously savouring the pleasure of paying off old scores, he informed me that he had instructions not to allow any minister to pass, and that in Madrid it had been decided "that the Government should return to their posts." I retorted that the Government took orders from no one, and turning to the three or four scoundrels who had surrounded the chief of the Code Department and me, and who were ostentatiously handling their sub-machine-guns, I told them what I thought of their behaviour, adding that their rightful place was at the front.

At this moment the Ministers of Agriculture and Education entered the room. They had been through the same experience as ourselves, and having learned of my enforced arrival had come to find out what was happening. As the most important thing was to make contact with the rest of the Cabinet in Valencia, we decided to take the road to Madrid with our escorts, but to stop at the first crossroads and give the occupants of the "Iron Column" car to understand that the joke had gone far enough. This plan we put into effect, and in view of our attitude our pursuers evidently considered that the most prudent course was to turn back and leave us. After our arrival in Valencia, the dispatch of a few truck-loads of soldiers to the place of the incident put an immediate end to the domination of the "Iron Column" over Tarancón.

This "Iron Column" was one of the armed and uncontrolled groups which were formed in the early days of the rebellion. Until their activities were suppressed by the Government reorganization of the militia, they were responsible for a series of excesses which, suitably exaggerated by the foreign anti-Republican press, did much to arouse prejudice against loyalist Spain and stamp her as the perpetrator of "Red" atrocities.

As soon as the situation in Madrid became stabilized, one of the most urgent matters which the Government in Valencia had to consider was the control plan drawn up by the London Committee. At first the majority of the Cabinet was opposed to its acceptance. The subject provoked more heated discussion than any other question in my two terms of office as Foreign Minister. It fell to my unhappy lot to defend a highly unpopular point of view. Indalecio Prieto had an easier task. His patriotic indignation and his powers of eloquence—of which he made full use—carried away the majority of my colleagues, who refused to accept a plan so obviously unjust, partial, and contrary to all the tenets of international law. My own feeling was that there was no alternative but to play the diplomatic game into which my predecessor in the Foreign Office had entered, accept the plan in principle and at the same time do everything possible to delay the date of its application. After all, the Republic had accepted the Non-Intervention proposal as it was made to us. We had abandoned our legal right to purchase arms for our defence. We did so—my predecessor did so—through a letter addressed to the French Government by our Ambassador in Paris, Don Alvaro de Albornoz, early in August because we were assured that the rebels would get no help either. Perhaps it was unwise to abandon our rights in the first place. I think it was. But it had been done, under duress, and there was nothing left to do but play the game into which we had entered even though we knew by this time that the dice were loaded.

In the end my point of view on the control plan prevailed. But in the course of this long controversy, which lasted for several Cabinet meetings, I was on one occasion obliged to hand in my resignation. What happened was this:

As I foresaw a difficult situation in the Cabinet, I set down on paper, rather against my custom, the broad lines of what I intended to say. I showed my notes to the Russian Ambassador, who called at the Foreign Ministry that morning. He read them carefully and expressed something like agreement with my argument. His Government's stand on the London Committee was for acceptance in principle of the control plan. From my office M. Rosenberg went directly to Señor Prieto and tried to win him around to my viewpoint. This was a perfectly normal thing for him to do, especially in view of the fact that since the very day of his arrival in Madrid he and Señor Prieto had been very close to each other. In fact, Señor Prieto had spent some time after the Ambassador's arrival showing him around Madrid. They were on the very best of terms. So that afternoon when I expressed my views it was not surprising that Señor Prieto noticed certain similarities between what I said and what he had heard a few hours before from M. Rosenberg, who was, of course, merely repeating what I had said in the notes I showed him. Then Señor Prieto rose to accuse me of being the mouthpiece of the Russian Ambassador and of actually working for the Soviet Government.

Next morning I handed in my resignation to Largo Caballero. On the one hand I felt that there was no object in prolonging a discussion which had already lasted too long, while on the other a categoric rejection of the control plan would constitute, it seemed to me, such a serious mistake that I was not ready to assume the responsibility for it. My resignation was not accepted.

The authority of the Prime Minister helped considerably in getting the plan accepted in principle, and, as I had foreseen, two months had to pass before it came into force. Its application was only one of the many sterile attempts of the London Committee to give the semblance of impartiality to a policy which in reality operated in favour of Germany, Italy, and the rebels and to the prejudice of the Spanish Government.

There was no further serious dissension in the Cabinet until the crisis of May 1937. The conflict caused by the appointment of General Asensio as Under-Secretary of War ended with his replacement by an official enjoying the confidence of the War Minister.[1] But criticism of General Asensio—whose loyalty Señor Largo Caballero considered above suspicion— had created a tense situation between the Prime Minister and the Communist members of the Government. A speech

[1] See page 126.

made by José Díaz, Secretary-General of the Communist Party, attacking the military policy of the Government aroused latent antagonisms. In this tense atmosphere the breaking-point was reached during the discussion of measures for suppressing the seditious movement which had just broken out in Catalonia, provoked by extremist elements of the F.A.I. and the P.O.U.M. (*Partido Obrero de Unificación Marxista*, United Marxist Workers' Party), the latter, an organization hated by the Communists as a Trotskyist stronghold which had for weeks been preaching open rebellion against the Government in its newspaper *La Batalla*.

On the day in question I had been invited to dine at the British Embassy. I waited until the very last moment, in the hope that the heated discussions, which had already lasted some hours, would die down. It had always seemed to me that the Cabinet meetings were unnecessarily long. During the Premiership of Señor Largo Caballero the length of these sessions gave evidence of a lack of personal consideration for a man who, in spite of a physical resistance which enabled him to preside over the debates for five or six hours at a stretch, was, after all, seventy years old, and who bore on his shoulders the tremendous responsibility of both the Premiership and the conduct of the War Ministry. But the Cabinet was composed of eighteen Ministers, the majority of whom felt it necessary to speak at length in every discussion, and the Prime Minister found it difficult to impose any time limit for speeches of individual members. In my opinion Cabinet meetings in time of war should never last longer than two hours.

The occasion of the British Embassy dinner was the coronation of King George VI, and it was essential for me to be present. After making a brief attempt at conciliation, I left the Cabinet meeting, certain that on my return it would still be in session. But when, an hour and a quarter later, I did return, I met the Prime Minister on the stairs. He had just called on the President to inform him that the Cabinet had resigned. During my short absence the resignation of the two Communist Ministers had produced a crisis.

Señor Largo Caballero was once more entrusted with the task of forming a Government. The stumbling-block was the portfolio of the War Minister. Everybody agreed that Señor Largo Caballero should continue as Prime Minister, but whereas certain members considered that the two posts of Prime Minister and War Minister should not be in the hands of one man, Señor Largo Caballero demanded for himself not only the War Ministry, but also the Air and Naval Ministries, to be combined with it under the title of the Ministry of National Defence. It was impossible to obtain the consent of the various parties for this proposal, or to persuade Señor Largo Caballero to be content with the Premiership alone, and Dr. Negrín was therefore appointed Prime Minister, with Señor Prieto as Minister of National Defence and Señor Giral as Foreign Minister in place of myself. The political tension caused by the May crisis, the outcome of which ran counter to the interests of the two trade-union organizations, the U.G.T. and the C.N.T., was hardly eased where the former was concerned when Señor Largo Caballero resumed his leadership of the U.G.T. after ceasing to be Prime Minister. But the situation was improved thanks to the spontaneous support given to the Government by the anti-Fascist masses, for whom the chief concern was not who should win the war, but that it should be won.

In time of war it is wrong to feel indispensable. General tension and the dynamism of the front admit of no pause, and nothing can save a man, however powerful, from being swept away to destruction if the current of national feeling turns against him.

The May crisis, however, widened the existing differences between the parties and marked the beginning of a vast campaign against the Communists, who were blamed for the fall of the Largo Caballero Government. Press controversy became more and more heated. All this created a lamentable impression at the fronts and made us fear that frictions and disagreements in the rear guard might spread to the army.

For months this growth of the political struggle was for me a constant torture and anxiety. I could never understand how it was possible so far to forget the supreme interests of the war. Since I too had been dismissed from the Foreign Ministry and obliged to resign from the General War Commissariat, I was able to preach by my example unconditional support of the Government; and by means of an intensive propaganda in the press and on the platform I endeavoured to re-establish the anti-Fascist front, of which by this time only the name remained. Twice I refused the offer of an ambassadorship made to me by the Prime Minister. I considered that it was more important to work inside Spain to eliminate the dissensions which were undermining our resistance and robbing our struggle of its early fire and enthusiasm.

If in times of peace it is difficult for a coalition cabinet, representing opposing forces, to work smoothly, it is an almost superhuman task to satisfy political parties when the exigencies of war take precedence over other interests. A large part of the Government's time was taken up in listening to complaints from the various political groups, all fearful lest one of their number should gain some advantage over the rest. I personally never felt less of a party man than during the war. The best Spaniard was he who fought the hardest for victory, no matter to what party or organization he might belong. Victory meant freeing Spain not only from foreign servitude, but from the fearful régime of hatred and persecution which a rebel triumph, we knew, must bring in its train. Not only was the political future of Spain at stake, but her very existence as a nation capable of regaining full sovereignty and internal peace. Before the magnitude of such an aim the private interests of the political organizations sank into relative insignificance. The great mass of the Spanish people understood this, but the strong desire for unity in the rank and file was not always reflected in the higher spheres. It would be untrue and unjust, however, to say that the political parties were responsible for the defeat of the Republic. Until the time of the Casado rising, the ranks of Government Spain always closed behind the Government at every moment of crisis.

It is no demagogic flattery, however, to say that in this great historic trial to which Spain was subjected, the Spanish people as such proved themselves of greater worth than many of their leaders. Some of these leaders have since stressed the difference between themselves and the people by carrying on petty controversies even in exile—behaviour unworthy of a struggle of which all those who fought on the loyalist side should be justly proud. Today, as yesterday, one would unhesitatingly give up one's life for the Spanish people. But for these others, with their personal ambitions, their underhand manœuvres, their attempts to dispose of imagined rivals in the fight for leadership—all the ruses regarded by the old-time politicians as a proof of political skill—for all such unworthy politicos I would not risk so much as my little finger.

One of the greatest difficulties with which the Government had to contend was the rival claims of the various parties and organizations for official positions. The problem of finding the right man for the right place was made doubly difficult by the need to create an entire administrative organization, and to replace thousands of Civil Servants who on the outbreak of the rebellion had gone over to the enemy or who were not sufficiently trustworthy. From the army leaders and the magistrates on the Supreme Tribunal down to the customs officials, we were obliged to replace the majority of the personnel who until July 18, 1936 had been in charge of the machinery of the Republican State. In the Foreign Ministry alone, ninety per cent of the former diplomatic corps had deserted. It will not be hard to imagine how difficult it was to find men with some knowledge of languages and a certain experience of international problems to render effective service to the Republic abroad. The same difficulty existed to a greater or lesser degree in the other branches of the administration—more particularly in the Ministry of National Defence, where on the choice of army leaders depended to a large extent the outcome of the war.

The tendency of the Government to take into consideration the personal qualities, ability, and keenness of a candidate rather than his political affiliation was not always appreciated by the various parties, who thought that they had been slighted if appointments were not made in strict proportion to political representation.

The chief target of the critics was, of course, the appointment of the army command. I will not go so far as to say that the choice of these officers was always a fortunate one, but I do know that throughout Dr. Negrín's term of office as Defence Minister he made every effort to find the best man for the job, irrespective of political affiliations. The difficulty was to find experienced and competent commanding officers. On many occasions—and in spite of his contention that the appointment of army leaders was his sole responsibility as Defence Minister—Dr. Negrín would put forward a list of names at the Cabinet meetings, asking us to give our opinion and to tell him if we knew of anyone better suited to the post. Sometimes we would spend half an hour trying to think of a better candidate, and if we were successful Dr. Negrín would invariably sanction our choice.

In any case the problem was not peculiar to the improvisation of a new army and the consequent shortage of suitable commanders. In his remarkable book *Le Ministère Clemenceau*, General Mordacq, *Chef de Cabinet* of the great Premier, recounts how that extraordinary man—who did not hesitate to pass sentence of death on the "Bonnet Rouge" traitors and to bring the all-powerful former Prime Minister Caillaux to trial, and whose answer to all the demands of the politicians and the intrigues of the Chamber was: *"Je fais la guerre"*—had to bend all his energies for a period of several months to the task of putting younger blood into the army and of retiring incompetent generals who had been sheltering behind the spirit of camaraderie in General Army Headquarters.

The serious military situation created by the rebel advance towards the sea at the end of March 1938 put an end for a time to the tiresome complaints of the discontented. As always happens in times of peril, backs were straightened and shoulders squared. On April 1 the Prime Minister told me that he was going to carry out a complete Government reorganization, and that he wished me to return to the Foreign Ministry. I confined myself to saying that I was ready to serve in whatever post might be assigned to me. This time Prieto's stand was the chief obstacle in the formation of the new Cabinet. Sincerely convinced that Señor Prieto's pessimism, which had spread beyond the walls of the Ministry of National Defence, was impairing the vigorous prosecution of the war, Dr. Negrín decided to take upon himself the responsibility for the conduct of this Ministry, in addition to the Premiership. All the same he had no wish to lose a collaborator whom he held in the highest esteem. Señor Prieto, however, refused to remain in the Government either as Minister of Public Works or Minister without Portfolio, and finally the Cabinet had to be formed without him. Señor Prieto's animosity towards Dr. Negrín, which in exile was to flare out into open conflict and to cause tremendous difficulties in the work of helping the refugees, dates from this time.

In the formation of his first Cabinet, Dr. Negrín broke with the tradition of allowing the political parties to nominate ministers. As Prime Minister he wanted to reserve to himself the right of choosing his colleagues. As a general principle he asked each party or organization for a list of names, from which he made the final choice. His first Cabinet consisted of only nine Ministers, including himself. In the new Government of "National Union" the number was increased to twelve, and in this the two trade-union organizations were represented. The Republican parties had five members in the Cabinet, including the representative of the Catalan *Esquerra;* the Socialists four, including the leader of the party, Señor González Peña, who represented the U.G.T.; the Basque Nationalist Party, the C.N.T., and the Communists one representative each.

It was a far cry to this Cabinet from the one in which I had had my first experience as Minister. Between the two periods a whole year of general stabilization had run its course. Some of the problems which had caused so many anxious discussions in the Largo Caballero Cabinet had in the meantime been solved. Public order had been restored sufficiently to allow the Government to carry on in a more normal manner. The Republican army was by now a reality. The early attempts at collectivization and the independent action of the various organizations had been followed by a harnessing of the country's economy in the service of the State. Time, a sense of responsibility, and the conviction that Spain was engaged in a war, calling for a superhuman effort, against two invading powers, had all helped to smooth away the difficulties with which in the first few months we had had to contend.

Dr. Negrín was no more successful than his predecessor in limiting the Cabinet meetings to two hours. It is true that he would sometimes let two weeks go by without a session, but no time was gained, and the practice gave an opportunity for malcontents to accuse the Prime Minister of exercising autocratic powers. He begrudged the time wasted in too much talking in time of war. His disinclination to express his own views, at least at any length, may have been due to this desire to get on with the job, though as time went on he overcame this psychological aversion to talking. From a very poor orator he succeeded in making himself within a few months an effective speaker. But as long as he had Señor Prieto in the Cabinet he very rarely made public addresses. When asked to do so he would reply, with the dry humour characteristic of him: "No, I believe in a division of labour, and when it comes to speech-making I have assured myself of the collaboration of the best orator to be found." After Señor Prieto's departure from the Cabinet, however, he resigned himself to the necessity of speaking in public and improved his delivery rapidly. It was with some surprise that his audience in the Cortes on a day in October 1938 heard him, after reading a weighty but rather monotonous speech, deliver, in answer to objections from the opposition benches, one of the best parliamentary impromptu speeches ever heard in the Cortes. The eyes of the whole House were fixed on him as if he were transformed into a new being. But in spite of this success, he still preferred to write his speeches, and whenever he had to make an impromptu address, for instance to the army, one could feel his profound dislike for improvisation. A professor of physiology can become the best of fighters and administrators, but he will always feel a nostalgia for the methods of the lecture-room.

I could well understand Dr. Negrín's dislike of spending three or four hours discussing death sentences. While Señor Irujo, representative of the Basque National Party, was in the Government, it was impossible to escape the consequences of his excessive desire to examine every report with the most scrupulous care. A brilliant lawyer, in whom a passion for justice and a fine human kindliness were combined with an instinctive tendency to consider every condemned person as a victim of the new tribunals set up during the war, he took up a large part of our debates with his interventions. If any foreigner believing the myth of a Red and bloodthirsty Spain, whose leaders were resolved to exterminate all those who did not agree with the ideology of Moscow, could have been present at one of those Cabinet meetings, he would have been amazed at the sight of twelve Ministers discussing one death sentence with a thoroughness worthy of the Hague Tribunal. Sitting at Dr. Negrín's right, I could see how painful it was for him, when it came his turn to vote last, to give the deciding vote on occasions when the Cabinet had divided equally.

I remember one such dramatic moment when it was a question of passing the death sentence on one of the closest friends and colleagues of his university days. Without hesitating an instant he cast his vote for confirmation of the sentence. But all of us were aware of the tension under which he was suffering and of the effort it cost him to continue the meeting and deal with the other questions pending.

Apart from this, in the Cabinet meetings there was an atmosphere of perfect understanding between the Government and the Prime Minister. Three sessions of my second Ministerial period are engraved in my mind to the smallest detail.

About two weeks after the second reorganization of the Cabinet, the rebel advance to the coast cut the normal communications between Barcelona and Valencia and Madrid. A Cabinet meeting was urgently called at eleven o'clock that night. Before the assembled Ministers, Dr. Negrín read a series of decrees which he intended to submit at once to the President of the Republic for signature. All the necessary precautions had been taken some days before, and every means of securing contact between the two zones had been carefully studied, down to the smallest detail. As Dr. Negrín was speaking, an adjutant came into the room to inform him that General Miaja was on the telephone. We had been waiting for this call, put through as soon as advice had been received from the General Staff that the rebels were about to sever communications. At any moment the telephone lines would be cut. Dr. Negrín read to General Miaja the decree entrusting him with the military command of the remainder of Republican Spain, of which he had already been informed. He had just had time to add a few words of encouragement and confidence when the conversation was suddenly interrupted. We were all conscious of a break which, although it might be technically repaired, would seriously prejudice the unity and cohesion of the Republican front.

Thanks to the energy and fortitude shown by the Prime

Minister during those anxious days, the consequences of this disaster were considerably less than they might have been. No one with an elementary sense of justice can withhold from Dr. Negrín the credit of having saved the situation in April 1938, and of having made it possible for the war to continue for nearly another year.

The Cabinet afforded a very different scene on the day when the Prime Minister announced that the Republican troops had crossed the Ebro. It was useless to attempt, as was Dr. Negrín's custom, to minimize the importance of the operation. "Gentlemen, I beg you not to be over-elated at this success, because tomorrow morning we may have to come back over the river again and God alone knows how we shall be able to do it." In moments of difficulty Dr. Negrín grew in stature; on happier occasions he would always look ahead and make provision for any future difficulties which might arise.

This time, however, his appeal for moderation had no effect. The operation in itself was so brilliant, and the spirit of our soldiers so magnificent, that the Ministers could not contain their enthusiasm. It was probably the only occasion when even President Azaña believed in a Government victory. Dr. Negrín told me how animated the President was when he called to inform him of the details and the course of operation, and how he had tried to warn him, too, against an excessive optimism. The fact was that the shortage of war material, of which Dr. Negrín better than anyone else was aware, acted as a constant brake on the Prime Minister and became an anxious obsession only known to those who enjoyed his greatest confidence.

Another Cabinet meeting of considerable interest was the extraordinary session held to discuss and approve the program of the Thirteen Points. Convinced that the simple slogan: "For a democratic and independent Spain" did not give sufficient idea of the Government's attitude to the most important problems caused by the struggle which had been forced on us, the Prime Minister and I agreed that it would be advisable to draw up a short program of Republican "war aims." Together we made a note of the basic points, which, with some small additions, were approved by the Cabinet.

The discussion of these Thirteen Points underlined the unanimity of the Cabinet regarding the terms of a peace designed to reunite Spaniards for the good of the nation rather than divide them into opposite camps. Even the point which held small attraction for the C.N.T. representatives—that ensuring Catholics a position for which, in view of the participation of the Church leaders in the rebellion and the hatred shown by the Spanish episcopate to the Republic during the course of the war, they could scarcely have dared hope—was approved without great difficulty. It was a Cabinet meeting which did credit to the Government and to the country, and which in itself gave the lie direct to all those who tried to represent loyalist Spain as a country dominated by foreign influence, demagogues, and revolutionaries.

The social life of the Government was naturally very much limited. When any important delegates arrived they were generally invited by the Prime Minister to his residence in Barcelona, where an annex was reserved for the hospitality of foreign guests. As far as I personally was concerned, I carried out my most essential social duties in the Foreign Ministry itself. Ever since we had left Madrid our establishment had been of a somewhat temporary nature, and we had had more serious preoccupations than that of setting up a comfortable home. From a top flat in the Calle del Ciscar, Valencia, which was scarcely big enough for my wife and me, and whose magnificence can be gauged by the fact that in peacetime the rent was the equivalent of about two dollars and a half a week, we would listen on the radio to rebel descriptions of the Oriental luxury surrounding the Ministers of the Republic.

Some of our distinguished visitors, nevertheless, found themselves in a somewhat embarrassing position when at any of the Prime Minister's dinners of a more or less official nature they discovered that Dr. Negrín and his Spanish guests were in dinner jackets or uniform. It must have seemed very strange that a "Red" should be capable of wearing a black tie. The atmosphere, however, was always so simple and friendly that any small and involuntary breaches of etiquette were soon forgotten by those who had most reason for embarrassment.

Behind the scenes in the Cabinet was no hidden mystery. Merely a strong determination on the part of the Ministers to serve their country by every means in their power.

CHAPTER XIII

In the Foreign Ministry

DURING THE MOST CRITICAL PERIOD of its existence the Republic remained steadfast to the high principles which had inspired its international policy since its creation—the loyal observance of commitments, support of the League of Nations, and a firm determination to serve the cause of peace. Apart from these general principles, the Republic clearly realized that it was united to the two great Western democracies by common interests and geographical situation, and therefore sought a *rapprochement* with Great Britain and France by every means in its power. In spite of the attitude of reserve shown by both those countries, collaboration with Great Britain and France was throughout the Spanish War the guiding principle and ruling ambition of the Spanish Republic in so far as its foreign policy was concerned.

In pursuit of this aim great sacrifices were made, beginning with the acceptance in principle of "Non-Intervention" in August 1936. It would be difficult to conceive a greater violation of the rights of a sovereign state than the Non-Intervention scheme. In such a vital matter as that of the purchase of war material it placed the Republican Government on an equal footing with the Rebel generals. Nevertheless, the Republic could hardly refuse to co-operate in the policy of Non-Intervention when it was presented to the world by Britain and France as an effort to localize the war. This was made clear in a letter sent by the Spanish Ambassador in Paris to the French Government on August 10, 1936.

When after innumerable difficulties the British Government finally succeeded in getting the Non-Intervention control plan adopted by the London Committee, the Republic accepted it in principle and declared itself ready to collaborate in its application. In order to do this it had first to overcome justifiable opposition and once again to sacrifice its own inclinations and interests, since the plan—which was drawn up with obvious partiality—furthered rather than hindered Germany and Italy in their policy of assisting the rebels, while at the same time making it very difficult for the legitimate Government to obtain supplies.

This desire for collaboration was shown in a hundred different ways and could form the subject for a whole book. No sooner had Great Britain and France, at the beginning of February 1938, announced that they were making a joint *démarche* to prevent the bombing of open towns than the Spanish Ministry of Defence, in a decree dated February 5, made known its resolve to limit the offensive operations of the Republican air force, during the period of the negotiations, to "co-operation with the land army at the front, and vigilance and reconnaissance operations in the rear." The British Commission for the Exchange of Prisoners and Hostages in Spain, of which Field-Marshal Sir Philip Chetwode was chairman, and the British and French members of the International Military Commission entrusted with the verification of the withdrawal of non-Spanish combatants in Spain —General Molesworth and Colonel Bach—can bear witness to the spirit of co-operation of the Republican authorities.

It was the Spanish Memorandum of February 9, 1937, however, that gave the most conclusive proof of the Republic's desire for an understanding with Great Britain and France. Though it could not, in view of the existing circumstances, take the form of a pact of mutual assistance or an alliance, it was to all intents and purposes the same. With the statement contained in its first paragraph that "the Spanish Government visualized Spain's future international policy, so far as western Europe is concerned, in the form of active collaboration with France and the United Kingdom," the two powers were promised that their specific interests, both military and economic, would be taken into account, and that the possibility of Spain's helping Great Britain and France to avert the danger of a general conflagration would be jointly discussed.

This Memorandum was therefore something more than a mere declaration. After it had been approved by the Spanish President and Prime Minister, I sent it to London and Paris and thereby offered the British and French Governments a concrete basis for building up their position. The only condition to our willingness "to consent to certain sacrifices and to induce the country to renounce the policy of neutrality which has so far had the support of the majority of the political parties" was that the Spanish Government should be given the opportunity to spare its people unnecessary bloodshed. The Government therefore suggested a formula which could not have been in greater harmony with the policy of Non-Intervention: "The re-embarkation, on a date to be fixed by the London Committee, of all foreigners, without exception and whatsoever their function, at present taking part in the internal struggle in Spain."

As this Memorandum shows, the foreign policy of the Republic was based on an entirely new conception of Spain's function in international life. Instead of resigning herself to a purely passive position and to the role in peace-time of witnessing the agreements and resolutions of other powers—

which were often contrary to her own interests, in which she had no share, and which in time of war compromised her by forcing her into a position of illusory neutrality—Spain claimed the place to which she was entitled by her strategic situation, her material resources, and the qualities of her people. On resolving to renounce the policy of isolation and neutrality at any price which had brought her increasing discredit in the international sphere, Spain took up her position by the side of those two powers which, with her, form a natural system of defence against any attempt to violate the present European order. The desire for collaboration with Great Britain and France was not the result of a mere whim, nor even of kindred sympathies or ideological affinities. Geography and a community of interests were the governing factors. All Spanish policy which rejects this collaboration, or attempts to run counter to Great Britain and France, is doomed to hopeless failure.

On the other hand we were convinced that with the end of foreign intervention and the consequent suppression of the rebels, Spain would emerge from the war with so great a vitality and faith in her own abilities that her collaboration could not be lightly ignored.

We were not so foolish as to think that by imitating the language of the two modern Cæsars and the haughty and theatrical gestures of Greater Germany and Fascist Italy we could make Spain into an imperial power. But we did feel that our country's active participation in European politics would bring with it a recognition of legitimate Spanish interests and would prevent Spain from being regarded as a second-class power. We considered that the period in which Spain had been a mere satellite of Great Britain and France was definitely over. Hispano-Anglo-French collaboration could only be effective if due recognition were given to a country which had shown its heroic determination to defend its liberty, which had proved itself capable of meeting the greatest difficulties, which in a matter of months had converted a few militia groups into a vigorous army, and whose strategic importance was proved by the sacrifice of money and men which the Germans and Italians had made in order to secure influence in the land. Once this western bloc had been formed, Great Britain and France would have been the first to benefit by the prestige, consolidation, and economic reconstruction of their new ally. Spain, moreover, would have been particularly valuable in attracting the sympathy and support of Spanish America to the side of the European democracies. From the Argentine to Mexico the Spanish epic was followed with unprecedented enthusiasm, and the victory of the Republic, whose Hispano-American policy, unlike that of the rebels, reconciled a close collaboration of the sister races with the highest regard for the United States and for the Latin-American policy of President Roosevelt, would have carried to the New World, not the intrigues of the Phalanx in the cause of Nazi propaganda, but the voice and the spirit of a triumphant democracy.

But of what use is it for one side to make an attempt at *rapprochement* if the other persists in holding itself aloof? The friendly attitude of the Republic could only have borne fruit if the British and French leaders—at a time when Spain's international policy was at the crossroads—had been ready to act with that same decision and speed which during recent years has been the characteristic and the merit of the totalitarian states.

In Messieurs Eden and Delbos I found two agreeable colleagues whom I had no difficulty in convincing that the outcome of the Spanish War was of vital interest to their respective countries. But their pleasant words and their undoubtedly excellent intentions were never translated into firm and practical action. While Mr. Eden was stating in the House of Commons that "Spain should be left to the Spaniards"—a perfect formula which, if adopted, would have meant a speedy victory for the Republic—and M. Delbos was sending cordial messages from the French democracy to democratic Spain, the Italian divisions and German "technicians," without hindrance from the London Committee, were advancing on Spanish territory, and in the rebel ports war material from Hamburg and Genoa was being unloaded by day and night.

Neither of the two Governments received the Republican initiative favourably, and the intentional "leakage" by which the text of the Spanish Memorandum was made known to the public gave evidence of an active hand behind the scenes which was doing everything possible to frustrate attempts to help the cause of the Spanish Government. In London, more than in Paris, there were many supporters of the theory that once the rebel generals were in power, it would not be difficult to win their favour, either through financial interests, or by diplomatic negotiations which would help them to shake off the "protection" of their former allies.

This conception of Franco as a "prisoner" of Germany and Italy, to be liberated at all costs—however grotesque it may appear to those who know his pro-German sentiments and his devotion to the totalitarian régimes—was widely held in British political circles by men who were sincerely convinced of its truth. It was only after long and continuous attempts at enlightenment, in which Señor Azcárate, the Spanish Ambassador in London, gave characteristic proof of his tact and perseverance, that the supporters of this thesis were reduced in number to those who placed their Fascist sympathies before the interests of the Empire.

Although the February Memorandum was an official statement of the Republic's foreign policy during the war, it must not be thought that it represented the extent of our efforts to persuade Great Britain and France to adopt an attitude more in keeping with their own interests. By every relevant argument, by communicating reports on Italo-German activity to both Governments, by the submission of concrete proposals for combating the Italian menace in Majorca—by every means in our power we endeavoured to bring about a change of attitude in London and Paris.

We were not crying for the moon. We made no request for armed assistance. We only asked that in strict accordance with the policy of Non-Intervention—which Great Britain and France had imposed on us and should for that very reason have enforced—"Spain should be left to the Spaniards"; and that if those two democracies did not feel able to prevent Germany and Italy from continuing to intervene in Spain, they should make honourable recognition of the failure of their policy and re-establish in full the right to freedom of trade. In a word, we asked that international law should be respected.

The way in which the British and French Governments ignored our warnings, suggestions, and requests was truly heartbreaking. At one point I began to wonder whether those among us were not right who held that this inconceivable apathy was due to the composition of the Spanish Government, and whether a Cabinet excluding members of the extreme Left—particularly the Communists—would not be welcomed with more sympathy and understanding in London and Paris. The annexation of Austria and the development of the Czechoslovakian crisis, however, convinced me that the Anglo-French lack of interest in the fate of the Republic had wider causes. The policy of peace at any price, a policy which must inevitably lead to war, had so demoralized the Western democracies that even the sacrifice of their most important positions seemed justified if the hunger of the totalitarian states could be momentarily appeased thereby. Although German propaganda represented him as a Moscow agent, it is not to be supposed that in British Government circles Dr. Beneš was looked upon as a very virulent Communist; neither can Dr. Schuschnigg be considered as any great friend of Stalin. At the time that Czechoslovakia was flung to the German wolves, M. Hodza's Government could not have been more moderate, but this did not prevent it from suffering the same fate as the "Red" Government of Republican Spain.

One of the many obstacles in the path of the Republican Foreign Ministry was the fact that it had to deal with a foreign diplomatic corps consisting mainly of chargés d'affaires or young and inexperienced secretaries far below the standard which such an exceptional situation demanded. Nearly all the heads of missions made Saint-Jean-de-Luz a winter as well as a summer residence. With the exception of the U.S.S.R., Mexico, Chile, and Brazil, no country was represented in Madrid by an ambassador or minister. This abnormal situation was particularly inexplicable in the case of France, which had at the time a Popular Front Government. Until M. Herbette was replaced by M. Erik Labonne, who took up his post at Barcelona, France for more than a year was represented inside Spain by various chargés d'affaires, one of whom (whose name I do not even remember) behaved with such impertinence and animosity, and so much like an authentic member of the *Croix de Feu*, that I had to refuse him admission to my study.

To make matters worse, the *doyen* of the diplomatic corps was the Chilean Ambassador, Señor Nuñez Morgado, a fervent rebel supporter, whose Embassy had become one of the principal strongholds of the Fifth Column. My predecessor, Señor Barcia, in the midst of his many preoccupations, had not realized the necessity for fixing a limit from the first upon the exercise of the rights of asylum. Although Spain was not obliged under the terms of any agreement to respect these rights, it was natural, in view of the bonds of friendship uniting her to her sister republics, that she should honour a practice so deeply rooted in South American tradition.

These rights of asylum, however, quickly became the subject of great abuse and gave rise to a continual series of conflicts. It was only thanks to the patience of the Government and the discipline of the people of Madrid in face of the provocation caused by the presence of more than twenty thousand "refugees"—well fed, often armed, and only awaiting the rebel entry into the capital to come out of hiding and turn on the Republicans—that serious consequences were avoided.

On receiving the portfolio of Foreign Minister, I sent a note to the dean of the diplomatic corps reminding him that the right of asylum, in accordance with American tradition, could be claimed only in the case of those who had played a prominent part in a subversive movement, and even so only on condition that within the space of twenty-four hours the head of the mission sent a list of the people under his protection to the Government to whom he was accredited.

But the damage had been done. Embassies and legations were filled to overflowing with "refugees," and a large number of annexes were leased during the month of August to house what had become a veritable rebel army. The French Embassy alone had more than two thousand under its roof. The choice with which we were faced by this *fait accompli*, and which I had to present to the Cabinet at one of our first meetings, lay between demanding the surrender of all these "refugees" at the risk of breaking off diplomatic relations with nearly all the American countries or keeping a careful watch on the legations in order to prevent any addition to their numbers. The Government finally decided on the latter course.

Two Embassies, those of the United States and Great Britain—the latter at any rate while Mr. (now Sir) George Ogilvie Forbes was Chargé d'Affaires—refused to take in any refugees. Not only in this but in every respect the conduct of the United States Embassy towards the Republic was exemplary. The attitude of the majority of the North American people to the Spanish War was faithfully reflected in that of their Ambassador, Mr. Claude G. Bowers, for whom Republican Spain will always feel a profound gratitude. His purpose and outlook were very different from those of the majority of his colleagues, and from his observatory in Saint-Jean-de-Luz he was no doubt able to keep his Government well informed on all that was happening in Spain, while his opinion that the

peace of Europe depended largely on a Republican victory
is by now an open secret.

Of the two Soviet Ambassadors, Rosenberg and Gaikis
(succeeded by M. Marchenko, as Chargé d'Affaires, who remained in this post until the end of the war), it was naturally
the first who attracted the most international attention. He
was hardly a man to pass unnoticed. In his work as Chargé
d'Affaires at the Paris Embassy before the conclusion of the
French-Soviet Pact, and in his important post in the League
of Nations Secretariat, he had given proof of extraordinary
intelligence and never failing activity. The atmosphere was
propitious for Nazi and rebel propaganda to represent him as
the real dictator of "Red" Spain, and certain "revelations"
made in exile by former members of the loyalist diplomatic
service (as part of the campaign against the "Communist
servitude" of the Negrín Government) have helped to
strengthen the impression that during Rosenberg's term of
office as Ambassador he directed the foreign policy of Spain.

If it were not both vain and despicable to enter into this
class of polemics, I could quote a whole series of facts to
prove the baselessness and absurdity of these assertions. They
will be given their answer on the day—may it come soon!—
when each one of us who held a position of responsibility in
Spain is called upon to give an account of himself to his
country.

With the appointment of M. Erik Labonne as French
Ambassador, the long period in which France had been vir-
tually unrepresented in Spain came to an end, and a natural
solution was found for some of the small but vexing questions which had been so long outstanding. I had had pleasant
official relations with M. Labonne during my term of office
in Mexico, to which country he was accredited a few months
after my own arrival. Both his original personality and the
loosely knotted ties which gave an unmistakable stamp to his
appearance were apt to mislead those who had not had the
opportunity of appreciating in him a diplomat moulded by

the severe discipline of the French consular and colonial service. He was an excellent diplomat and functionary, pleasant and punctilious, a man whom I should not like to have to oppose in any negotiations where conflicting interests were at stake, but who was of sufficiently independent outlook to be able to form his own judgment and to maintain it firmly against opposition. Reduced to the position of "Non-Intervention" Ambassador in Spain, from which he was appointed to the high office of Resident-General in Tunis, M. Labonne carried out his duties with cordiality and goodwill, but his work was not what might have been expected of him if the Quai d'Orsay had shared his opinion as to where French interests really lay. M. Labonne could have done much to help France profit by the rebirth of Spain and the Republican Government's desire for a policy of open collaboration with the two great Western democracies. Every time I touched on this theme in our frequent conversations I seemed to feel, behind the reserve which his Government's attitude imposed on him, a complete agreement with my point of view. The day the loyalist troops crossed the Ebro was a happy one for M. Labonne; and his pleasure was evident in his spontaneous congratulations and in the satisfaction with which he wrote down in his notebook (generally used only for small claims or complaints about military airplanes in the Air France aerodrome, or the detention of some suspicious French subject) all the details which I was able to give him of this remarkable military operation. His departure coincided with the arrival of the new British Minister, Mr. Ralph Skrine Stevenson, who must still remember with what discernment his distinguished French colleague gave an opinion on the problem with which the two allies were faced by the development of the inadequately styled "Spanish question."

In September 1936, a few days after my entry into the Cabinet, Mr. Ogilvie Forbes arrived in Madrid as British Chargé d'Affaires. Judging by the change in Mr. Forbes's attitude after he had taken stock of the situation, he must have come to Madrid with the impression that the Republicans were some kind of fierce sans-culottes or incendiaries. My first interview with him, on his visit to the headquarters of the general Union of Workers to meet Señor Largo Caballero, impressed me most favourably. He was a man of charming manners, intelligent and broad-minded; endowed, too, with great quickness of perception and a strong human kindliness. I shall never forget his emotion when the Getafe Hospital was destroyed by German planes and a number of children met a most horrible death. He arrived at the hospital almost before the authorities and made personal arrangements for assistance. Mr. Forbes enoyed a popularity, not only with officials, but with all who came into contact with him, which must have been the envy of his colleagues. He knew exactly how to gauge our difficulties and could appreciate our efforts to restore public order and put an end to the inevitable excesses which followed the outbreak of the rebellion and the Government's temporary loss of control. One morning in Valencia, Señor Indalecio Prieto, the Air Minister, telephoned me in great disgust to say that our anti-aircraft batteries, in beating off an enemy raid, had fired accidentally on the *Royal Oak* and wounded some of the crew. When I proffered my Government's sincere regrets for this incident to the British representative, I could not help contrasting his courteous behaviour with that of certain other diplomats, who would besiege the Ministry in a state of great excitement if so much as one of their cars was detained a little longer than necessary by the patrols controlling the highroads. Not only did we greatly deplore Mr. Forbes's departure, but we were driven to fear that it was partly due to the fact that his impartiality did not please those who wished to preserve the impression that in loyal territory all was chaos, violence, and abuse. It so happened, however, that when Mr. Forbes's successor, Mr. Leche (who also came to Republican Spain rather as though he were descending to the nethermost pit) left us in his turn, he expressed himself, if my information is not incorrect, in terms which won for him the reputation of a rabid Bolshevik among his friends in London.

Continuous appeals to the League of Nations had shown us the degree of importance to which the Geneva institution had been reduced by the desertion of those governments whose interest it should have been to preserve the League's prestige and strength.

Born out of a reaction against the international anarchy which had been the principal cause of the World War and against the "prestige" policy of the great powers which characterized pre-1914 diplomacy and left millions of dead and disabled in its train, the League of Nations was hampered from the first by the lack of adequate machinery for imposing its decisions. The Covenant was a compromise between the extremes of a world federation—or an association of nations within a super-state resolved to command respect for international law—and the principle of unlimited national sovereignty. In spite of its terrible lesson, the world of 1919 was not ready for the creation of a super-state and had to begin with a more modest experiment on the basis of an inter-state system, in which the nations bound themselves not to resort to war until they had exhausted every means of conciliation, and to give assistance to any member state who should be the victim of aggression.

The League represented, however, an advance towards a new international order. Although in its early days its strength was seriously impaired by the refusal of the United States to be represented at Geneva, during the twelve succeeding years the idea of the League gained greatly in popularity and met with the enthusiastic support of large and influential sectors of public opinion, even in North America. It won its spurs in the Corfu incident, when Mussolini was prevented from consummating his *coup de force,* and when the war between Greece and Bulgaria was rapidly and skilfully avoided. Between the great days of the Geneva Protocol of 1924 and the inauguration of the Disarmament Conference in 1932, the League had its ups and downs, but it was able to resist the current of nationalist tendencies caused by the world economic and financial crises of 1929 and 1931, which affected practically every nation and led each to seek its own salvation in a series of protectionist measures entirely opposed to the spirit of internationalism.

With the revival of the old ideas of absolute national sovereignty in a more virulent form than ever before, the growth of Fascism caused the rapid deterioration of the League. The totalitarian states saw in the Covenant an obstacle to their expansionist policies. The destruction of the League of Nations became their main objective. Geneva was for them the danger spot where Great Britain and France could unite the forces of peace in a concerted action against aggression, and their hostility increased with the entry into the League of the Soviet Union, which from the first followed an energetic and consistent policy in defence of collective security. Opposed to every form of international negotiation which might tend to eliminate the threat of war and so stabilize the European situation, Hitler and Mussolini became the irreconcilable enemies of the League of Nations.

Until the advent to power of Pierre Laval, France, though increasingly interested in the conclusion of separate military pacts, continued to look on Geneva as one of the main supports of her foreign policy. In Great Britain pro-League feeling took concrete form on the occasion of the celebrated "Peace Ballot," which was held on the initiative of Lord Cecil, and which led Mr. Baldwin, at that time Prime Minister, to declare that "the Covenant of the League of Nations is the sheet-anchor of British policy." The return of the conservatives to power in the general elections of 1935 was primarily due to their announced support of a firm foreign policy based on the strengthening of the League.

The Japanese invasion of Manchuria was the first brutal challenge to the Covenant. The League did not come very well out of the test. But its prestige was soon restored by the firm attitude adopted at the beginning of the Italo-Ethiopian conflict. Four days after the Italian troops invaded Abyssinia, the Council denounced this act of aggression, and four days after that the Assembly voted sanctions. It was deplorable that Article XVI was then only applied half-heartedly and that the oil embargo—the one purely economic measure which could have had a decisive effect—should have been excluded from the list on the grounds that its inclusion would have incited Italy to declare war. But more fatal still was the fact that this policy of temporizing with the aggressor, a policy which became so dominant that it threatened the very life of the League, should have been carried out, as far as the Italo-Ethiopian conflict was concerned, behind the back of Geneva. M. Laval had the honour of initiating it. The first attempt to apply sanctions failed at a time when the League states had all the cards in their hand. The small states which had followed the great powers in their action against the aggressor, at so much sacrifice to themselves, lost all confidence in Geneva.

Up to 1936, however, collective security could have been made a reality. Hitler had done no more than sketch out his plan for militarizing Germany. The great mistake of the French Government in allowing the reoccupation of the Rhineland could have been remedied. This is proved by the fact that the mere condemnation by the Council, on April 17, 1936, of the violation of the Versailles Treaty resulted for a time in Germany's refraining from further infractions of the Covenant, or of any other international agreement. And when the Germans did invade Spain a few months later, they went about it so furtively that one can only conclude that they were afraid. Throughout August 1936 the German Ambassadors in Paris and London were making almost daily trips to the British and French Foreign Offices to deny that German help was being sent to Franco. Everything they did at that time indicated clearly that they thought there was a risk of arousing the sleeping democracies, and they stepped carefully in order to avoid this. There was of course no risk, as it turned out, unhappily.

Even after Germany's withdrawal from the League, it could still count on a sufficient number of powerful states to oppose any policy of aggression. Winston Churchill realized this. His advice, however, was not followed. On that day in February 1938 when Mr. Chamberlain, after sacrificing Mr. Eden on the altar of the totalitarian states, definitely rejected the idea of sanctions and destroyed the last illusion of the small powers in British support of the League, the totalitarian press hailed his words as the epitaph of a dead institution. Their joy, however, was premature. In the Committee for the Application of the Principles of the Covenant—the Committee of twenty-eight—Spain, together with sixteen other countries, opposed the tentative efforts made to bring back Germany and Italy into the League, which would have meant a complete disregard for fundamental principles, and would have transformed the League into an organism "without obligations or sanctions"—that is to say, an entity for screening and condoning all aggressive violence.

In this disintegrating process Spain represented the last opportunity to save the League from final collapse. But, in the happy phrase of Señor Azaña, the only effective non-intervention applied to Spain was the non-intervention of the League of Nations. The Council and Assembly confined themselves to voting resolutions exhorting the London Committee to speed up the withdrawal of "volunteers" and systematically ignored the fundamentals of the problem. The policy of yielding to the aggressors reached such scandalous extremes that the mere possibility of denouncing aggression made the solid columns of the lordly Palace of Nations tremble to their foundations. Each further request for the "Spanish question" to be included in the agenda was regarded almost as an impertinence. The Spanish Government never lost a single opportunity, however, of making the League of Nations and the governments directing its policy realize their responsibilities.

While we were under no illusion regarding the practical result of our appeals, our sense of duty, the fact that Spain was one of the most loyal members of the League (and the only country which had embodied the principles of the Covenant in her Constitution), and our desire to proclaim the justice of our cause before such a representative tribunal decided the Spanish Government to have repeated recourse to Geneva.

In September 1938 collective security was given an ignoble burial. Never had a League Assembly been subjected to a greater humiliation than when the one vital question, on whose solution depended the future of peace, was excluded from its deliberations. While the hand of war was knocking on the portals, the representatives of nearly fifty countries—seated in the resplendent armchairs of the new and luxurious Conference Hall, which under the artistic direction of M. Avenol had been converted into a mortuary chamber—silently swallowed their indignation at being made the laughing-stock of the whole world. When the discussion of the Secretary-General's report languished—after M. Litvinov, the Mexican and Colombian delegates, and myself had broken the rule against even alluding to the burning question of Czechoslovakia, and had stated our opinion on the matter in no uncertain terms—interest was diverted from the Conference Hall to the lobbies.

The general conviction was that if Paris and London remained firm, Hitler would have no alternative but to yield. This impression hardened on the day that Litvinov, in the Sixth Committee—countering the manoeuvre of the capitulators who were hinting that the Soviet Union had taken up an indecisive position—declared that his country was ready to fulfil its obligations under the French-Soviet Pact and the Czech-Soviet Pact if France, in the event of German aggression, would go to the assistance of Czechoslovakia.

For me this statement came as no surprise. Although we had never looked upon a general war as a solution of the Spanish problem, it was my duty to keep myself and my Gov-

ernment informed on the development of the situation, and
it was natural therefore that I should have made every attempt to discover the true attitude of the Soviet Government.
To the clever but fruitless attempts of those responsible for
the 1938 capitulation to excuse themselves on the grounds
that it was not clear that the Soviet Union would have gone
to war for Czechoslovakia even if France had fulfilled her
obligations, I am in a position to reply categorically that there
can be no doubt whatsoever on this point. This is also the
opinion of Dr. Beneš, expressed both in public and in private
during his stay in the United States.

It is absolutely certain that Russia at the time would have
fought against Germany on the side of Great Britain and
France. But not Russia alone. The Czechoslovakian crisis was
followed in the Rumanian and Yugoslav delegations with the
very greatest interest, and, but for the Munich disaster, a
favourable regrouping of the Balkan States would have been
possible. Even the Assembly revived for a few hours on September 28 and plucked up courage to vote a resolution supporting the messages of President Roosevelt to Dr. Beneš
and Hitler.

The whole propaganda of the Munichois, designed to prove
that resistance would inevitably have led to war, has been
invalidated by the reports subsequently received from Germany regarding the circumstances surrounding the dismissal
of General Beck, Chief of the German General Staff, on
September 3, 1939. The Reichswehr was opposed to a war on
two fronts. They knew the worth of the Czech army, concerning which the French army leader General Faucher (who, as
its chief adviser for a period of seven years, should be qualified to hold an opinion on the subject) has stated: "Even if
Czechoslovakia had had to face Germany unaided, I feel sure
that the struggle would have lasted for some months. It must
be borne in mind that the Czech army had forty fine divisions
at its disposal, which means that in proportion to the total

German forces it was no worse off than the French troops at Verdun." [1]

There would have been no war. September 1938 was the time to check Hitler in his ambitious attempt at European domination. To start with, Germany stood alone against Great Britain, France, the Soviet Union, and Czechoslovakia. In Spain the Republican army was still fighting with great courage on the farther bank of the Ebro. Italian intervention in favour of Germany was at that time more than doubtful. Mussolini talked very loudly, but while other countries were taking the preliminary precautions necessitated by the gravity of the situation, everything went on in Italy just as though Europe was enjoying a period of the greatest peace and tranquillity. The lack of military preparations on the part of some of the powers in the democratic front was more than compensated by the extension of this front, which was not unlikely to be joined by Rumania and Turkey as well as other of the Balkan States. There would have been no war. But even at that risk, anything, in the opinion of the French General Staff, was preferable to capitulation. Léon Jouhaux has recounted how General Gamelin's report, shown to him by M. Daladier, ended with the words: "In spite of all the difficulties, we must intervene."

It was on the road from Geneva to Paris, at Ancy-le-Franc, where our car had broken down, that I listened stupefied to the news that, on the invitation of the Duce, Mr. Chamberlain and M. Daladier were to meet Hitler and Mussolini in Munich the following day. A few moments before, I had been talking with some reservists in a café while we were waiting for our car to be repaired. I can hardly say that they were overwhelmed with joy at the idea of having to leave their families and their work to go and fight. But their morale was good, and the weakness of the French people at that time is not a very safe argument with which to justify the incal-

[1] From an interview published in the Paris *Époque* on December 24, 1938.

culable harm inflicted on the interests of France by the capitulators.

On my arrival in Paris I was slightly reassured to learn that M. Bonnet, at least, was not going to Munich. It could still be hoped that M. Daladier would be able to resist the arrogant claims of the Führer untrammelled by the presence of a Foreign Minister who in his room at the Hôtel des Bergues, Geneva, on the eve of the Assembly, had—as I myself had heard, not to my surprise—expressed himself on the Sudeten problem in exactly the same terms as the Nazi press. But alas, this, too, was merely another illusion.

When Hitler pointed on the map to the places in Czechoslovakia which he intended to attack (thus indicating by the disclosure of his plans his feeling that British and French capitulation was an accomplished fact, and giving his guests an excellent opportunity for breaking off the interview), he was not met with any firm response. If at that moment Mr. Chamberlain and M. Daladier had closed the conversation and returned home, Hitler would have known that if he marched against Czechoslovakia he would be faced with a war on two fronts, and would have thought twice before taking this final step.

There have been few defeats in the diplomatic history of the great powers so shameful and unnecessary as the defeat of Great Britain and France at Munich. Munich could only have been remotely justified if it had fulfilled the irresponsible prophecy made at the time that war would be prevented for two generations.

September 29 was a day of great anxiety, and, with the single exception of M. Georges Bonnet, there was not one person to whom I spoke who was not filled with foreboding and a certain feeling of shame. The Foreign Minister, however, was radiant when I visited him at the Quai d'Orsay, in company with our Ambassador in Paris, Dr. Pascua. In his obvious satisfaction he ventured to insinuate more strongly than on previous occasions that it was our duty to consider how best we could put an end to the war in Spain. One Munich was not enough. He wanted, apparently, a Spanish one as well. He must have realized from the tone of my reply, however, that the climate of Barcelona was not the most suitable for another Lord Runciman, for he rapidly changed the conversation. As always when this subject was being discussed, I took great care to make it clearly understood that our one desire was for peace, but that its attainment depended more on the British and French Governments than on ourselves. As soon as both Governments, in fulfillment of their obligations, should succeed in getting Germany and Italy to withdraw from Spain, the question of arriving at an understanding with the rebels could safely be left to us.

Some of our French friends believed in all good faith that the defeat inflicted at Munich would be compensated by a change of British and French policy in regard to Spain. Once Czechoslovakia was lost, they considered a victory of the Spanish loyalists more essential than ever for French security. The announcement made by the Spanish Government a few days previously at the League Assembly that all foreign combatants fighting in the Republican army were to be withdrawn from Spain rightly seemed to them to afford an excellent opportunity for demanding the total repatriation of German and Italian troops and "technicians" and the cessation of shipments of war material. If this last step should not be successful, there would be other ways of assisting the Republicans.

But the policy of "appeasement" was at its zenith, and the Munich peacemakers were not willing so much as to listen to anything which might run counter to the wishes of Mussolini, to whom they could not be too grateful for his noble action in preparing the way for an interview with Hitler—an interview wherein the tiresome problem of Czechoslovakia, which had given months and months of work to the diplomats, was "finally solved" in the space of a few hours. Or at least they had Hitler's word that it was solved.

During the whole of the month of October attempts to arrive at a speedy settlement of the Spanish question—not by the withdrawal of the Germans and Italians from Spain, but simply by pressing the Spanish Government to make peace at any price—were multiplied, and I had to give instructions to our ambassadors to be doubly on their guard against any manœuvre such as that which had been used so successfully against the Prague Government. I advised our Ambassador in Paris that if the French Foreign Minister submitted any concrete proposal, he should confine himself to taking note of it and replying that it would be placed before his Government. For a long time I had been very sceptical of M. Bonnet's pretended friendship for the Spanish Republic, and his attitude during the Czech crisis had merely increased my distrust in the uprightness, or at any rate the clear-sightedness, of his policy.

A visit to Barcelona from the Socialist ex-Minister M. Vincent Auriol confirmed us in our impression that—perhaps as a result of the extra-official conversations in Munich—Spain was the next victim to be sacrificed on the altar of the totalitarian states. Although his visit was an unofficial one, we knew, and he made no attempt to conceal the fact, that before leaving Paris he had conferred with important members of his Government. They could not have chosen a better emissary. Throughout the war, and before it, M. Auriol had been one of the most loyal and sincere friends of the Spanish Republic. He was assured of a cordial reception in Barcelona.

It was therefore very easy to talk to him confidentially. He seemed surprised at the firmness with which I stated that if the French Ambassador should ever approach us in the same manner as the British and French representatives had visited Dr. Beneš on that tragic night in Prague, my reply would be to hand him his passports. But he nevertheless entirely understood our reason for not entering into any peace discussions which did not fully guarantee the independence of Spain, so long as there was any hope of resistance.

This firm stand against all appeasement manœuvres did not mean, however, that we were adopting a purely negative attitude and that Spanish foreign policy was to consist in saying no to every peace proposal.

When, after Munich, it became clear that the British Government had decided to follow very closely the policy of friendship with Rome which had already been initiated with the Anglo-Italian Agreement of the previous April, the Spanish Government—in spite of its tremendous opposition to Italian intervention in Spain—did not hesitate to inform the British Government categorically that if the latter would put an end to this intervention, the victory and consolidation of the Republic in Spain would afford no obstacle whatever to a policy of collaboration with Italy in the Mediterranean. They even went so far as to declare that they would themselves be willing to collaborate with Italy on the basis of mutual respect for the integrity and political independence of either state. This declaration, which I communicated personally to M. Fouques Duparc, the French Chargé d'Affaires in Barcelona, was also ignored by the British Government.

In the last stage of the war, between the fall of Barcelona and the fall of Madrid, the Republic endeavoured by every means in its power to persuade Great Britain and France to take the necessary steps for ensuring that the end of the war would not be marked by a reign of terror and political reprisals. But on this point I will write at greater length in a later chapter.

CHAPTER XIV

Did Democracy Fail in Spain?

THROUGHOUT THE WAR the Republican cause had the support of the majority of the Spanish people. If this was obvious in loyalist Spain, it was no less so in rebel territory. Our hopes of winning the war were never based solely on a military victory. The fact that Franco was receiving unlimited supplies from Germany and Italy, while we were faced with the difficulty of providing the Republican army with the mere essentials of war material, made it unlikely, we knew, that in the purely military sphere the fight would go in our favour.

To win the war we relied not only on the bravery and enthusiasm of our own men, but also on the growing hostility of the Spaniards in rebel territory to those generals who had delivered up their country to invading armies. This hostility accounted for the low morale on Franco's side. Whereas the morale of the Republicans improved with misfortune, the rebels needed continual successes to keep up the spirits of their people.

Republican Spain endured the fall of Málaga, the loss of the northern regions (including Asturias and the Basque country), and the cutting off of Barcelona from Valencia and Madrid when the Italian divisions reached the sea in the spring of 1938, all without losing heart. Any one of these military reverses would have produced immediate collapse in the invaded territory. We were therefore justified in relying for ultimate victory on the efforts of a Republican army fighting for national independence, and the process of decomposition on the rebel side, a process inevitable among people who have become the instrument of foreign intervention.

The Republican Government showed its conviction that the majority of the Spanish people were on the side of the Republic by advocating a national plebiscite to take place immediately after the war. The idea of such a plebiscite, whereby all Spaniards in both loyalist and rebel territory should determine the political régime of their country, took concrete form in the program of the Thirteen Points in which Dr. Negrín's Government made known its "war aims."

We were determined that the plebiscite announced in the Thirteen Points should be held as soon as possible after peace was declared. It was the only way to bring about a reconciliation in Spain and to prevent resentment and past differences from precipitating a new civil war. Besides, we were sure that the vast majority of the Spanish people would vote for a democratic Spain, just as they would do now if Franco allowed his countrymen to express their views freely. Those in the United States and Great Britain who must find it difficult to reconcile their enthusiasm for the new European dictator with their loyalty to the principles of American and British democracy not only would be more consistent, but would also do the Spanish people a great service if they tried to persuade their idol to do no more than adopt one of the Negrín Government's Thirteen Points—that relating to a national plebiscite.

If the vast majority of the Spanish people was in favour of a democratic form of government, why has democracy failed in Spain?

In order to answer this question one must differentiate between two periods: first, the months from the elections of February 1936 to the outbreak of the rebellion; and secondly, the war period.

In themselves the elections of February 1936 in Spain were a triumph for democracy. The Spanish people went to the polls in conditions worse than at any time in their history. The electoral machine suffered from all the defects of a system in which official pressure and the purchase of votes made any expression of the national will extremely difficult. The working-class organizations, which had been among the chief supporters of the Republic ever since its foundation, were still suffering from the effects of the defeat of two years before, when the dictatorial Government of Gil Robles, after the 1934 revolt, had crushed and persecuted the Spanish proletariat in an attempt to eliminate them from the political life of the country. Nevertheless the Popular Front was victorious. Democracy triumphed over the combined elements of corruption and force.

It was when democracy took up the reins of government after its victory that it failed in Spain. This was certainly not because of its program. Nothing in the Popular Front program on which the Azaña Cabinet rose to power after the elections could have justified the revolt of the Right. It was in many respects more moderate than the New Deal. Democracy failed in that period (February–July 1936) because of the extreme and naïve confidence of the members of the Government. Señor Azaña still lived in the memory of that easy morning of August 1932 when, standing on the balcony of the War Office and calmly smoking a cigarette, he superintended the arrest of the Sanjurjo conspirators. That cigarette of Señor Azaña's was to prove fatal to the future of the Republic.

No, the failure lay in not realizing that the reactionary forces defeated at the elections would have recourse to violence against the Republican régime if they were not forced to behave. Right from the very day of the elections the reactionaries could think and talk of nothing but a *coup d'état*. Spanish Fascists made no attempt to disguise their determination to break up the régime which had allowed the control of the nation to be wrested from their grasp. At meetings, in the press, in Parliament, their language became more and more aggressive. Whereas Republican newspapers had been suppressed every other day during the previous two years, the Fascist press was now allowed to preach open rebellion. The army generals conspired freely. Instead of discharging or arresting them, the Government merely sent them to distant posts where, free from official control, they could plot behind the scenes without fear of disturbance.

The Republic had learned nothing during the five years in which its existence was at the mercy of its enemies. In 1932 it covered itself with eternal glory (in its own estimation) by saving General Sanjurjo from the firing squad after he had been condemned to death for military insurrection. (This officer would have been the leader of the rebellion in 1936 in place of Franco if he had not finally met his death in an airplane crash on July 20 on his way to Spain from Portugal, where he had been engaged in the conspiracy against the Republic.) In 1934 the dictatorial Government of Gil Robles and his army generals repaid this generosity by imprisoning the Republican leaders, among them Señor Azaña, and sending Moroccan troops to practise their notorious cruelty on the Asturian miners. But when Spanish democracy regained power in 1936, instead of making a stand against its enemies, it preferred to let them grow in power, for fear of being accused of intolerance or undue severity.

It was in the period between the elections and the outbreak of the rebellion that democracy failed. No recourse to dictatorship of any kind would have been necessary to ensure respect for the Republican régime and to nip the insurrectionist movement in the bud. If half a dozen generals had been imprisoned, or even one or two of them shot, Spain would have been spared much bloodshed and three terrible years of war. Even at the beginning of July 1936 when all preparations for the rebellion had been made, the Republican Government could still have saved the situation by disbanding part of the army, as had been suggested, or by arming the most reliable members of the trade unions, as we Socialists had asked. A firm attitude at that time would have made the rebel leaders reflect, and abandon their project. All documentary evidence, including the subsequent biographies of Franco and Mola (which should be read by those in the United States and Great Britain who sympathize with the rebels through ignorance of what really happened in Spain), proves that the insurgent leaders were convinced that forty-eight hours after the insurrection they would be the new rulers of the country. They never contemplated a civil war because they did not expect resistance. If the Government had armed the country or disbanded part of the army, the rebels would have realized that the Republic was ready to fight for its rights and they would have retreated before this prospect. Even if some of the conspirators had in fact rebelled, the situation would have been very different from what it actually was on July 18, when thanks to the passivity of the Government, rebel military commanders in many places simply arrested the civil authorities and gained entire command of the town.

The Government undoubtedly believed that Fascism could be disarmed with kind words. But events in other countries, beginning with Germany, should have taught them to know better. Those who, like myself, had watched at close range the long agony of the Weimar Republic in Germany and had witnessed the fabulous growth of National Socialism (whose chief allies were, unintentionally, the German democrats) unceasingly drew the attention of the Republican Government, both at public meetings and in Parliament, to the profound mistake of believing that democracy means giving its enemies carte blanche to destroy it.

Our warnings were unavailing. The chief efforts of the

Government were directed towards convincing the Left-wing parties that they should give the reactionaries no excuse to rise against the Republic. In point of fact, none of the parties of the Left had the slightest intention of steering Spanish policy towards radical extremes. In drawing up the Popular Front program they had voluntarily sacrificed many of their legitimate aspirations. It was only natural to insist that this program, so moderate in itself, should at least be carried out with decision, especially so far as the defence of Republican institutions was concerned. The sole object of the militia, which the Socialist Party, after many difficulties, had formed, and which was chiefly composed of Youth organizations, was to support the Government and keep watch on the subversive activities of the enemies of the Republic. In the months which followed the elections the Socialist militia, practically without arms, and trained by a few army officers who were, by reason of their position, well aware of the military plot against the Republic, spent many nights out of their beds when immediate danger threatened. The enthusiasm and discipline of these young men—self-appointed policemen of the Republic, who never provoked a single incident—were amazing. They did their job quietly and without ostentation, and they were well enough educated politically to know that Spain was not ready for either Socialism or Communism, but for a democratic Republic, whose disappearance could only lead to a Fascist régime. The Government, however, was more concerned with the Youth organizations than with the comings and goings, too obvious to pass unnoticed, of the generals planning the rebellion.

Democratic Spain was again triumphant on July 18. The magnificent popular response to the generals, who during five months of plotting had forgotten the very existence of the Spanish people, was a further victory for democracy. The State collapsed and the Republic was left without an army, without a police force, and with its administrative machinery decimated by desertions and sabotage. But the people re-

mained—alive, determined, and purposeful, the supreme exec-
utor of that national will which in the February elections had
voted against the Fascistization of Spain.

In Madrid it was the people who attacked the Montaña
Barracks. Wherever the authorities failed for want of foresight or decision at the critical moment, it was the people
who took upon themselves the defence of the Republic; who
filled the posts temporarily left vacant, so that they could
maintain order and keep down those excesses which are the
necessary corollary of any social upheaval on such a scale.
It was the people who sent the first soldiers to stem the rebel
advance, who disarmed the naval officers when they would
have handed over the fleet to Franco. It was they who organized the control of the roads and kept watch for sabotage on
the part of speculators and spies. In the factories, abandoned
by their owners or managers, it was the workers' committees
who saw that the machinery was not destroyed and that the
work carried on. Until the Government had recovered from
the terrible blow struck by the rebels, it was the democratic
masses of the country who alone were active, efficient, and
trustworthy—who were, in fact, all that really counted.

Throughout the whole war democracy did not cease to
work efficiently in Republican Spain. The unity of the Spanish
people during their two and a half years of war, without
which they could never have withstood the combined aggression of Germany and Italy, was achieved by the will of the
majority of loyal Spaniards, who placed the defence of their
country's independence above party interests. Government
authority made itself increasingly felt and had the genuine
support of public opinion, a support obtained not by repression and terror, but by the Government's decision to resist
until the invaders were driven out of Spain. We have been
charged by some with having prolonged the war only to
serve the interests of Moscow, who, according to our accusers,
wanted to use the Spanish people in a war of attrition against
the aggressive forces of Nazi Germany, the better to be able

to face the Hitler menace in the east. This charge is as absurd as it is groundless. The truth is that if any Republican leader had protested publicly, at any time before the rebels' Barcelona offensive in December 1938, against the policy of resistance pursued by the Negrín Government, he would have aroused violent opposition from the vast majority of loyal Spaniards. This is the only plausible explanation of the fact that although Señor Azaña, the President of the Republic, had been for some time disposed to abandon the struggle, he was unable to form any cabinet favourable to capitulation.

Democracy inspired Republican policy during the whole war and greatly altered the position of certain Left-wing elements in face of many of the fundamental problems created by the hardships and difficulties of the struggle. The Anarchists, opposed in principle to the idea of the State and to the existence of a regular army, became during the course of the war disciplined soldiers and even showed a certain unexpected pleasure in the exercise of authority. Their acceptance of the need for a regular army in place of the early militia (an organization which naturally appealed more to their temperament and conception of a people in arms) was a democratic concession to the opinion of the majority, which held that a militia system is not sufficient to oppose invading armies. Anarchists and Communists, in their support of the program of the Thirteen Points, withdrew their doctrinal opposition to the preservation of private property, and both parties agreed with the guarantees for freedom of worship offered by the Government to the Catholics. The Government, in fact, was able to issue a decree authorizing Catholic priests to administer spiritual comfort to any soldier at the front who desired it, without any fear that such a measure would arouse opposition or friction. I know of many cases where Anarchist commissars, at the request of a mortally wounded comrade, have sought out a Catholic priest and brought him to the side of the dying man. I myself, as a member of the Government, have presided at the Catholic

funeral of a Basque captain and have walked behind the
clergy and the crucifix from one end of Barcelona to the
other without detecting on the faces of the many workmen
who were watching the procession the slightest suspicion of
surprise or reproof.

On the other hand, the Right-wing elements who supported
the Republic and fought with us to defend the independence
of Spain also made the necessary concessions in order to
arrive at that central point of agreement where all loyal
Spaniards could meet. They knew that it was impossible that,
after the war, the privileges of land and capital should not be
curtailed in some degree. They could not expect that the
peasants who had been fighting shoulder to shoulder with
those Spaniards of the liberal bourgeoisie who placed their
country above personal interests should return after the war
to a life of exploitation by their landlords and a wage of forty
cents a day. Neither were the industrial workers, men who
had not only showed a spirit of great patriotism, but who had
also given ample proof of their skill in munition factories, who
had quickly learned to become aviators and had risen to the
highest ranks in the people's army—neither were these prepared to see Spain remain the country with the lowest wages
and the hardest working conditions in the whole of Europe.

On this basis of mutual concessions the Government had
no need to resort to force in order to lead the country in its
fight for independence. The same dissenting voices which
now accuse us of having exercised a dictatorship imposed, in
its turn, by Moscow are the best proof that, if we were guilty
of any excesses, we erred on the side of generosity and goodwill. We were well aware of the existence of these small
opposition groups, men who during the war placed politics
above the supreme need for defeating Fascism. In the same
way, now that the war is over, they employ their time not in
attacking Franco or denouncing the brutal reprisals against
the Republicans, but in informing the world that the aggressors in Spain were not, as some people had innocently thought,

Hitler and Mussolini, but Stalin, Dr. Negrín, and myself. We knew that they spent their time criticizing the Government, but we were convinced that they would be isolated by public opinion and that there was no need to take action against them.

Democracy, Spanish democracy, did not fail in Spain during the war. It was European, and to a certain extent American, democracy that failed in Spain, and failed lamentably.

The British and French democracies, in particular, failed to recognize in time that the battle between democracy and Fascism was being fought in Spain, and that the result of the struggle would have a profound effect on the political development of Europe. Their behaviour throughout the Spanish War was characterized by that same slowness and inability to oppose the firm and rapid action of the totalitarian states which has brought Europe within two years under the hegemony of the Axis. They invented Non-Intervention when the Italian and German airplanes were already known to be on rebel territory. In the London Committee they were the constant victims of, if not connivers at, the facile manœuvres of the aggressor states. Throughout the two and a half years of German and Italian intervention in Spain, Great Britain and France made no serious attempt to put an end to it. When the Spanish Government protested in Paris, it was told confidentially that London would not make any move. When London's attention was drawn to the situation, the blame was put on Paris. In this way the responsibility for a policy of suicidal passivity was flung backwards and forwards between Paris and London, as though it was not the vital interests of Great Britain and France that were at stake. And all this time Hitler and Mussolini were extending their sway in Spain.

The reason given to justify this insane and fundamentally anti-French and anti-British policy of the London and Paris Governments was that it would avoid a general conflagration. In the case of Spain, just as in that of the Czechoslovakian crisis in September 1938, it was against all reason that the choice should be between surrender and war. A firm policy could have avoided both. The Spanish Munich was as unnecessary as the other. The Spanish Munich did not assume the theatrical form of the celebrated conference in the birthplace of National Socialism (the choice of which, as meeting-place, must have given Chamberlain and Daladier food for thought), but the principle of capitulation was the same. The London Committee was the equivalent of Munich. It was the finest example of the art of handing victims over to the aggressor states while preserving the perfect manners of a gentleman and at the same time giving the impression that peace is the one objective and consideration.

It was not only the governments of the great democracies who failed to understand that the loss of Republican Spain would mean a crushing defeat for the cause of democracy. In these countries it was democracy itself that failed to impose its point of view on the governments.

In Great Britain, France, and the United States the majority of public opinion strongly supported the loyalist cause. The evolution of British public opinion is particularly interesting. In the course of the war a number of British delegations visited loyalist Spain. The Spanish Government opened its doors to all, and the more conservative our guests, the more interest did their visits hold for us. Among others, I will quote here the case of Field-Marshal Sir Philip Chetwode, president of the British Commission for the Exchange of Prisoners and Hostages in Spain. In spite of his delightful courtesy, Sir Philip, on his arrival in Barcelona, had difficulty in hiding from us how profoundly he had been affected by anti-Republican propaganda. Our first interview in the Spanish Foreign Office, and his subsequent conversation with the Prime Minister, Dr. Negrín, must have been a great surprise for the famous General. He found the Spanish Government not only filled with a spirit of human generosity, but also resolved to suspend all death sentences on enemies of the régime during the period of negotiations. It was a commitment which the

Government kept until the end of the war, although the British Commission, in spite of continuous efforts, never succeeded in obtaining a promise of reciprocity from the rebel authorities. When Sir Philip Chetwode left Barcelona, he frankly admitted to his friends that his prejudices against Republican Spain were based on a mistaken conception of events, and I am sure that there must be more than one confirmation of this change of opinion in the archives of the British Foreign Office. By the end of the war there were various distinguished conservative members among the Parliamentary group of friends of Republican Spain, such as Winston Churchill and others, whose attitude is already public knowledge.

There can be no question but that in France the majority of the people sincerely desired a loyalist victory. Not only the working classes, intellectuals, university men and women, and that wide section of the French bourgeoisie which sets the standard for democratic France, but also those French conservatives who placed the nation's interests above political animosity and who were well aware that a third front in a Spain dominated by Germany and Italy was a grave menace to French security. It is an open secret that the two most conservative Ministers in the Daladier Cabinet—Mandel, who inherited his clear foresight and energy in defending French interests from his former leader Clemenceau, and that very intelligent statesman Paul Reynaud—were the most consistent supporters of the loyalist cause.

In the United States the last Gallup polls showed that not only were the vast majority of the American people on the side of Republican Spain, but that even a large number of Catholics had begun to realize that the real interests of their Church would be better protected in the long run by a Republican rather than a Franco régime. The Catholic hierarchy in the United States certainly did not share this opinion, partly perhaps through ignorance of facts which were known to some far-sighted European prelates (such as Cardinal

Verdier, Archbishop of Paris), whose proximity to Spain and consequent knowledge of the situation made them desire a Republican victory. And why did they desire this victory? Because they realized the danger of the Catholic Church's becoming inseparably united to a régime detested by the majority of Spaniards.

They were right. While Franco remains in power, and if Germany does not extend her growing influence in Spain in order to introduce that neo-paganism so contrary to Catholic interests, the Catholic Church in Spain will enjoy a privileged position which it would never have held under the Republic. But it is to be feared that when the Spanish people rise up once more, the Catholic Church, which is now looked upon as the chief ally of Spanish Fascism, will suffer the consequences of a strong national reaction against all that the Franco régime represents. On the other hand, the Republican Government, while it would not have celebrated victory surrounded by archbishops and foreign divisions and Moroccan troops, as did Franco's Government in the Madrid parade, would certainly have accorded the Catholic Church a position of respect and tolerance much more secure, and freer from future complications, than Fascist Spain offers her.

Although the majority of the people in Great Britain, France, and the United States were in favour of Republican Spain, they failed to force their respective Governments to put an end to the dishonest policy of Non-Intervention and to raise the embargo on war material. It was only a question of proceeding in accordance with international law and the tradition of over a hundred years. Throughout the nineteenth century intervention in the affairs of one nation by others met with round condemnation. Great Britain fought over the intervention of Napoleon in Spanish affairs. The later intervention of the Holy Alliance in Spain—I refer to the Holy Alliance of a century ago, not the one of today—was condemned by Great Britain and by the great American President James Monroe, and by Thomas Jefferson as well. The independence of Belgium and the existence of a united Italy were due to the refusal of France and Great Britain to tolerate intervention in the name of autocratic ideals. But in 1936 the sound and healthy principle of non-interference was abandoned—was in fact reversed—by democratic countries of western Europe when they devised this strange thing called Non-Intervention, which became, in fact, a unilateral intervention in favour of the rebels and against the Republic.

As soon as the war was over, Germany and Italy entered into a friendly dispute as to which of them had given most help to Franco. This has been a most edifying spectacle, holding for us a strange irony. All the reports which we presented to the Foreign Office and the Quai d'Orsay over a period of two and a half years, and which were invariably considered as fantastic exaggerations, have since been brazenly confirmed by Berlin and Rome. While Hitler boasts of his foresight in placing a powerful air force at the disposal of Franco in the first day of the war, Mussolini allows no one to estimate the army which he sent to Spain at less than a hundred thousand men. The records of the glorious activities of the London Committee which that body leaves to posterity will not be complete if they fail to include these official declarations of the two dictators responsible for Franco's victory.

No, it was not Spanish democracy that failed. It was the other democracies who failed to save democratic Spain, as they will one day learn to their cost.

The tragedy lies not only in the loss of a million lives in Spain, and the destruction of an old civilization which had many beauties and irreplaceable values. The damage done to Spain cannot be repaired, for the dead will not come back to life and the old values cannot be restored; but Spain will shake off the Fascist yoke sooner than many people believe. The damage done to Europe and the whole world will be plain to the democracies when they find out who Franco is and what he represents.

CHAPTER XV

The Collapse of Catalonia

HAVING WON the Munich round, Germany and Italy were free to deliver a knock-out blow to Republican Spain. No longer was there any need to play for safety; neither the position in central Europe—where maintenance of the military machine at the trigger-point of readiness, an indispensable factor in the totalitarian game of bluff, had become unnecessary after the absorption of Czechoslovakia—nor the general European situation, in which the appeasers were sinking into a slough of defeatism, called for any policy of caution.

Arms and munitions retained in the neighbourhood of Prague, not so much for use as for the benefit of those governments which had shown such a kindly tendency to be impressed, could now be sent to Spain, where, since the Battle of the Ebro, the fortunes of the totalitarian states had been suffering an eclipse.

There was every need for rapid action. Successes such as Munich, due to the indecision of one party rather than the superiority of the other, can last only as long as it takes the former to realize that there is no justification for his retreat.

A reaction inspired by national dignity set in against the unsavoury policy of "appeasement," and the desire to recover from an unnecessary defeat placed the nations on their guard and lessened the prospects of further attempts at intimidation. Nor were the arms factories idle in Great Britain and France. The Axis was worried that within one year's time their arms superiority over the Allies, especially as regards aircraft, would be lost, and the relative strength of the two totalitarian states would decline.

A few months still remained to Germany and Italy in which to settle the Spanish question in a manner satisfactory to themselves, but there was no time to lose. On the other hand, they would have complete liberty of action during those months and would run no risk whatever. After tolerating their barefaced intervention for more than two years, Great Britain and France, who had just delivered up another sovereign state to the dictators, were not likely to put any serious difficulties in their way merely because they were doubling their war material in Spain or postponing the withdrawal of troops until Franco's final victory. In any case, the Anglo-Italian Agreement of April 16, 1938 had given the totalitarian states carte blanche as far as the latter question was concerned.

The situation in the rebel zone would not permit of the war dragging on for another winter without a final solution. Reports received in Rome confirmed the existence of growing disintegration in rebel territory. The number of people arrested for listening to the "Red" radio broadcasts increased daily. The dissensions between Phalangists and Requetés had spread to the army, and in Orense, Segovia, and San Sebastián there had been serious insubordination and many officers had been punished. Hatred of the invaders grew after the Negrín Government began to carry out their decision to withdraw all foreign combatants from the Republican army, and as the people realized that this was not—as the Burgos press claimed —a mere *coup de théâtre* staged for the benefit of simpletons in Geneva, but a solemnly contracted obligation to be fulfilled at all costs. A system of food supplies whereby, in the midst of plenty, only the privileged few had enough to eat, increasing taxes, restrictions on movements in the "liberated zone," fines imposed at will and on the slightest provocation -all these hardships increased the sum of grievances of a people whose morale had never been very high, and who could only be kept down by a military success heralding the end of the war.

Such were the reasons, both internal and external, which at the beginning of November 1938 decided the German and Italian General Staffs in Spain to prepare the final grand offensive.

In the following six weeks there was constantly increasing activity in the rebel ports. In Vigo alone thirty thousand tons of war material were landed during the month of December. Italian officers and men arrived in Cádiz in sufficient numbers to counteract the effects of the "symbolic withdrawal." The S.S. *Brescia* brought a thousand men and twenty-four officers from Genoa. The S. S. *Calabria,* proceeding from Spezia, landed 310 cases of war material and a few hundred gunners. So it went on. The Spanish Embassy in London sent all the information at its disposal regarding this intervention to the British Foreign Office. This information was confirmed, after the fall of Barcelona, by the Italian press—the only difference between the two versions being that the Italian figures were higher than our own.

Movements and concentrations of troops observed in the early days of December on the Pamplona-Logroño line indicated that an offensive was imminent and that it would take place in that sector. On December 11 Dr. Negrín, Prime Minister and Defense Minister, addressed the army in terms which constituted a warning to the whole of loyal Spain. "The enemy is preparing to attack on the eastern front. An Italian army corps is to take part in the offensive. Spain calls for a further effort from you and is confident that you will not yield an inch of Catalan soil."

It was not the front, however, that gave us the greatest anxiety, but the rear guard. The people themselves were as magnificent as ever, but small disagreements and political intrigues had lowered powers of resistance which in Catalonia had never been very high—perhaps because this region had not suffered from the rigours of war so intensely as other parts of Spain. Only a few days before Dr. Negrín's address the possibility of a Government crisis had been the inspired theme of those who were wont to take more interest in such matters than in the progress of the war. I remember Dr. Negrín commenting on these rumours with his habitual good humour. "If they only knew what was in store for us," he remarked, "they wouldn't be in such a hurry to change places"; and he added dryly: "This time I think it's my turn to provoke a crisis!"

The enemy was in fact to find that the Catalan troops were in possession of a splendid morale—as was to be expected of men who on the Ebro front had time and again given proof of their courage and ability—but that they were insufficiently equipped to stand up to an offensive carried out with far greater supplies of war material than anything hitherto employed in the war. The hermetic sealing of the French frontier towards the end of the spring of 1938 had not only disorganized the system of Republican provisions, but also made it essential that the receipt of fresh supplies by the Spanish Government should involve no risk of international complications. M. Georges Bonnet had made his entry into the Quai d'Orsay.

After many difficulties and frustrations, and by dint of great effort and striving, we at last obtained a promise that the French border would be opened to the passage of arms from wherever we could get them. It was certain that unless fresh obstacles were created through unforeseen international contingencies, the Republican army would be able to count on the necessary arms by the spring of 1939. The loyalist fleet would have at its disposal two dozen ultra-rapid torpedo-boats, capable of neutralizing the action of enemy warships—including those of "unknown" nationality operating in the Mediterranean. The number of airplanes, all manned by Spanish crews, would be increased to five or six hundred, a figure hitherto undreamed of during the war. But alas, the material began to arrive after the fate of the Republic had been sealed, and some of the consignments fell into the hands of the enemy before they were even unpacked. It is not outside the realms of possibility that the prospect of having to face an army which would have been properly equipped for the first time since the beginning of the war was one of the factors which decided the foreign General Staffs assisting General Franco to advise a rapid launching of the offensive.

If the frontier had not been closed in June 1938, the arms which had been ordered and which were in course of shipment would have been sufficient to supply the needs of all the units by July or August—in any case not later than September. As things developed, however, the High Command found that the gigantic efforts which had been made to increase the army to more than a million men, to create fresh cadres, to instruct and prepare reserves, and to train hundreds of air pilots, were all rendered useless by the non-arrival of sufficient war material.

In such a situation it was more than ever necessary that the morale of the people, which had been forged on the anvil of a terrible and unequal struggle and in which lay the whole strength of Republican resistance, should not be crushed. Before the offensive began, the Government approached the authorities and the leaders of political parties and trade unions, both national and regional. Without going into any details likely to have an undesired effect, they explained the situation and advised the formation of a "resistance bloc," and an appeal to the people to be ready for the greatest sacrifices and to show a calm and disciplined front whatever the hazards of war might bring. If, by means of general collaboration, the phenomenon of the previous April could be repeated, when a healthy reaction saved the Republic from collapse after many people had given Barcelona only another week, this fresh attack might also fail; and if it failed, the war would be won.

On account of bad weather the offensive expected for the first fortnight of December did not begin until the 23rd. Those who knew of the delay in the arrival of war material would gaze anxiously at the skies and pray that the rain would last for a few weeks longer. On the other hand, the general feeling on the front was that the enemy could attack when he liked. There were even certain manifestations of impatience as day after day passed without any sign of the offensive. "If it weren't for this damned weather," said Colonel Modesto to the correspondent of *Ce Soir* on December 17, "the fun would have started by now."

With all the means at their disposal the rebels launched their attack. For the first time since Guadalajara all the Italian troops were employed at once. The "Littorio" division again appeared, although it had been announced two months before that it was to be disbanded. The Italian General Staff was also in command of a new and completely Italian unit, the "9th of May," while Franco's best division, composed of Navarrese troops, was reinforced with two Italian brigades. Besides the five Italian divisions led by General Gambara, the "regrouping of cars," under the command of Colonel Olmi and consisting of three battalions of armoured cars, a special company of tanks, and two companies of motorcycles armed with machine-guns, also took part in the offensive. All the divisions were motorized and their artillery transported by mechanical means.

The fighting was even fiercer than in the Battle of the Ebro. Even greater was the heroism of the Spanish infantry, who attacked and captured the Italo-German tanks with hand-grenades; who, face downwards on their native earth, suffered massive bombardments such as had never been known before; who forced the enemy to carry out five or six attacks of this kind before gaining an inch of ground; who put up such a magnificent defence that some of the positions were lost and recaptured twenty times over.

But no heroism could save such a slender front, where, for want of armed reserves, the loyalist command was unable to make good any breach in the defences. A break finally occurred in the Segre sector. The other units succeeded in holding up the enemy for more than a week and in preventing them from making the most of their initial gains, but with the evacuation, on January 4, of Borjas Blancas, situated on the Lérida-Tarragona road, the position of the Republican army became critical.

The night before, Dr. Negrín and I had attended a meeting urgently convened at the headquarters of General Rojo, the Chief of Staff. In a small bell-tent hidden by trees from enemy aircraft—always very active on moonlight nights—we followed on the map for the space of an hour General Rojo's exposition of the progress of operations. The choice before us was to stake our all on resisting the enemy during the next forty-eight hours, with a ninety-per-cent chance of losing everything—or to sacrifice a considerable tract of land and retire to new positions in the mountainous district between the Ebro and the Pyrenees. It was then that the desperate situation of an army for whom there were no more munitions, but who—so their leaders had told us—were still fighting after days of unequal struggle with the same courage as before, was borne in upon me in all its tragedy.

One of the army leaders at the conference, General Sarabia, proposed to reinforce the sector most directly menaced by withdrawing two brigades here, two battalions there, and sending them to the crucial area. No, there's no objection—take as many men as you like; but those two brigades have only eight hundred rifles between them, and those two battalions less than three hundred.

At last someone asks the dreaded question: "How many rifles have we got in all?" "Thirty-seven thousand for the whole army of Catalonia," is the reply. Further discussion is useless.

It is decided to withdraw the troops to the new line. Through-out the journey back to Barcelona the Prime Minister did not once open his lips.

But it was not only rifles which were lacking. The scarcity of material was so great that in Igualada two battalions of machine-gunners, well organized, trained, and officered, had to retire upon sighting the enemy for want of a single machine-gun or rifle. They made use of airplane machine-guns which, for land purposes, were practically worthless—because they need as swift a current of air to cool them as a plane creates in flight—and which were put out of action almost immediately. Material which the militia councils and trade-union commit-tees had thought useless and left in the artillery fields during the first weeks of the war was sent to the front, not so much for any real military purpose as to give some encouragement to the troops.

The enemy, on the other hand, had in some parts of the front a cannon stationed at every twenty yards. The propor-tion of loyal and rebel arms during the various phases of the offensive was as follows: aviation—between 1 to 10 and 1 to 20; heavy artillery—abundance of material in rebel territory and none whatsoever on the loyalist side; artillery of medium and light calibre—between 1 to 20 and 1 to 30; tanks and small tanks—1 to 30; light infantry arms, including automatics —1 to 10. If it were possible to establish any comparison as far as ammunition and shells were concerned, the disproportion would be seen to be greater still.

The army continued its retreat in the hope of being able to hold the enemy behind Tarragona. In the meantime negotia-tions were begun to obtain an advance delivery of some of the arms for which we were waiting and whose arrival could not be long delayed. Before I left for Geneva, where the League of Nations Council was to examine the report of the International Commission set up to supervise the withdrawal of foreign combatants from the Republican side, the Prime Minister told me of the efforts made to obtain this advance delivery. It was an absurdly small quantity in relation to all the issues at stake in Spain—the democratic future of Europe, the safety of Great Britain and France, and the probabilities of a general war, which a further victory for the totalitarian states would increase tenfold.

A hundred thousand rifles and two thousand machine-guns would have saved the Catalan front. With a hundred and fifty thousand rifles, three thousand machine-guns, and two groups of light artillery we could have saved this front and also have ensured a successful outcome for some of the operations undertaken in the central-southern zone.

The civilian evacuation of Barcelona began while I was making a last-moment effort in Paris. All we asked was what one might term a loan of arms, to be returned within a month or six weeks. It was impossible to obtain it. Yet in Paris everybody had suddenly become aware of the tremendous error committed in regard to Spain. Henri de Kerillis, who is one of the most intelligent exponents of French nationalism, but who had nevertheless, in his own vigorous fashion, upheld the cause of the rebels throughout the war, wrote that at such a time a Franco victory "was a catastrophe for France." Army generals, members of the Daladier Government, begged me to assure them that Barcelona would hold out for at least another couple of months, since in a very short time there would be a change in the whole European position. Noble sentiments, a perfect understanding of the situation, but no effective assistance.

The French Government had once again been paralysed by London. Mr. Chamberlain had just returned from Italy, and the totalitarian tactics of confronting the Western democracies with a *fait accompli* had succeeded again all along the line. A few days before, I had had a talk with Lord Halifax in Geneva. I had then gathered the impression that when in the Rome conversations the Spanish problem was mentioned, Mussolini, with a comment worthy of his realistic policy, had cut short the feeble attempts of his distinguished British guests to draw his attention to the ill effects produced on British public opinion by the decisive participation of Italian divisions in the Catalan offensive. "That matter," said the Duce, "has already been settled. Franco has won and there is no point in pursuing the question further."

During the weeks preceding the visit to Rome the British Prime Minister had expressed himself in the House of Commons in somewhat disquieting terms. The whole of the diplomatic battle raging round the Spanish problem was now concentrated on the question of belligerent rights. Franco and his allies were claiming from the Western powers authorization to murder the Spanish Republic by a blockade. The war of starvation which Spain, in common with all civilized countries, had proscribed as despicable and criminal in the London Declaration of 1909 was now demanded with the most barefaced insistence. They were trying to obtain international sanction to impose on Republican Spain, not an effective blockade consistent with the principles of international law, but a fictitious blockade carried out in the form of modernized piracy. In reply to a question in the House, Mr. Chamberlain reaffirmed the official standpoint which he had always taken: belligerent rights were to be granted only under the conditions enumerated in the Non-Intervention plan; that is, withdrawal of foreign volunteers. He added, however: "So long as no other solution has been found."

The way was once more left open for bargaining. Hitler and Mussolini knew that either their offensive in Catalonia would break down Republican resistance or that the *fait accompli* created by the advance of Italian troops towards the French frontier, and the consequent desire of the appeasers to avoid all possible complications, would force the latter into granting belligerent rights to Franco.

For the moment, however, this was not necessary. The situation in Catalonia was deteriorating rapidly. With our best shock troops exhausted after three weeks of incessant struggle, and subjected to the demoralizing process of a retreat of which no one could foresee the end, the new front planned by the Republican High Command on January 20—forming an almost straight line from the sector east of Vendrell on the Mediterranean to the Tremp-Sort sector—also broke before a superiority of arms. In the meantime Barcelona was subjected to constant punishment from Savoia planes, which, taking off from the Luigi Nerieri aerodrome near Palma in Majorca, would drop as many bombs as they could carry, fly back, and then return to attack the centre of the city; Heinkels from the German seaplane base in Pollensa, also in the Balearic Islands, would complement the daily activities of the Italian aviators by night raids, spreading panic along the coast and machine-gunning the cars in which citizens of Barcelona were leaving the town in increasing numbers. Between January 20 and 22 Barcelona was bombed fifteen times. The morale of the city was breaking fast.

Nevertheless when, in view of reports which were reaching Paris, I left everything on January 24 and set off for Barcelona, I did not think that all was lost. While I did not share the opinion of the high-placed French friends who had that day honoured the Spanish Ambassador's table and who refused to see any difference between Madrid in November 1936 and Barcelona in January 1939, at the same time I never foresaw such a landslide.

Barcelona should have remained in our hands at least for the time necessary to form echelon lines of defence; that is to say, a minimum of three or four days more. The cause of the sudden collapse was threefold. First, the lack of co-ordination between the local command and that of the retreating troops, due to the fact that the army leader appointed to defend the city was detained in Port Mahón, Minorca, where he had held his former post, and only arrived in Barcelona a few hours before the enemy entered the city. Secondly, the withdrawal of Assault Guards entrusted with the defence of the town, who, through some misunderstanding still to be explained, received instructions to retire to Gerona. And lastly the atmosphere in the city itself. In spite of the efforts made by the Government to raise the morale of the civilian population, Barcelona, which had endured continual attacks from enemy aircraft with heroic stoicism, did not react at the decisive moment with the same determination as other Spanish cities had done at the beginning of the war.

The General Staff had always considered that it would be impossible to defend Barcelona for an indefinite period once the army had been forced to retire towards the north of Catalonia, with no prospect of a counter-offensive. In the first place, all the light arms on the Catalan front would have been necessary to defend a city the size of Barcelona, and, as we have seen, on the day of the fall of Borjas Blancas three weeks before, these only amounted to thirty-seven thousand rifles. Secondly, the food supplies in Barcelona were so meagre that the town, once isolated, could not have withstood a prolonged siege even on iron rations. Lastly, the enemy aircraft, operating from aerodromes close to the city, and with their land artillery dominating the port, would have completed a blockade which the rebel fleet alone was not strong enough to carry out.

The contention of foreign technicians that Barcelona could have been defended for some months more, was due to the fact that while they were aware, at least to some extent, of the defensive and technical ability of the Republican army, they were ignorant of the terrible scarcity of material, and the lack of food caused by air raids on the ports and by the insufficiency of land transport.

The fall of Barcelona had placed us in a desperately difficult position. In addition to the tragic situation on the front, there was now the new factor of dislocation of the whole administrative machinery. At Figueras the Government continued to be a Government more by virtue of their moral authority and the confidence which they still inspired in the people than on the grounds of any normal functioning of the administration.

It was touching to see how loyal the people remained to the Republic and its leaders in the midst of a catastrophe which involved the collapse within a few weeks of the whole of Catalonia. I well remember a certain afternoon when the French Ambassador and the British Chargé d'Affaires in Perpignan had expressed an urgent desire to see me and, being unable to come to Figueras because of transport difficulties, had arranged to meet me in Le Perthus. From La Junquera to Le Perthus, both frontier customs posts, it is only a matter of five minutes in a car. On that memorable day it took me practically an hour to thread my way through the tremendous multitude which had been waiting for hours to cross into France. It was useless to stay in the car, and I made nearly the whole journey on foot, between thousands of men, women, and troops, all jammed so tightly together that they could scarcely move. It might have seemed the easiest thing in the world for an *agent provocateur* to have incited those poor suffering people—men and women who had left everything behind them and who were in a state of nervous exhaustion after waiting for so many hours without food or sleep—to demonstrate against a "fugitive Minister." But their healthy intuition told them that there must be some justification for my journey and that perhaps the opening of the French frontier was dependent on its outcome. And by dint of superhuman efforts they forced a way open and made room for me to pass.

An even less ministerial journey awaited me on my return that night from La Silla, a small French frontier town, to Agullana, where the Prime Minister and my Cabinet colleagues were awaiting the result of my negotiations. For four hours I journeyed on foot along a mountain path over which I had never been before. In the opposite direction a continuous human stream flowed down towards France, a stream of people who were convinced that it would take an eternity to cross the frontier at La Junquera and who were trying another route in the fear that any delay might mean their falling into enemy hands. There were a few soldiers with rifles, some not knowing why they carried them, others hoping to be sent back from France to Madrid via Valencia, in order to carry on the fight. So we walked on, Señor Méndez Aspe, the Minister of Finance, and I, until at five o'clock in the morning we finally reached our destination. Somehow I do not think that it was ever the impression of foreign correspondents in rebel territory that the best-known of the Franco leaders could have moved about so freely, even in less abnormal circumstances, without the slightest protection or escort. But if this was a further proof that we could rely on the people, it only served to increase the feeling of impotence of a Government forced to carry on in such conditions.

In the purely military sphere, there existed the possibility, after the fall of Barcelona, of an intermediate line of resistance between Gerona and the French frontier. Lines from the River Ter to Puigcerdá and from Figueras to Camprodón had been thought out, planned, and constructed; but the few armed forces arriving from the fronts to occupy them met with unarmed reserves, and instead of support being forthcoming, panic ensued, a panic created rather by the civilian fugitives than by any enemy action. Nevertheless, in the last days of the struggle in Catalonia the troops succeeded, with practically no material, in re-forming an elastic front, which facilitated the evacuation of the civil population and the withdrawal of the army and its material.

On February 9, from the last Spanish cottage on the frontier, we saw the Republican army pass by on its way to France. It was heartbreaking to watch that procession of men who had been defeated merely because the means of defending the country and the cause which they loved so passionately had been withheld from them. Well-known forms passed by, the finest fighters of the army, men who had defied death a hundred times, men who had known the excitement of the advance, who had held on for long hours among the ruins of positions demolished by shell-fire; men who still saw before them the faces of comrades who had fallen without losing the hope of victory, the memory of home, and the ideals and emotions which spring from a free conscience.

Watching them pass, I lived again through the whole drama of the Spanish people in their long struggle for a régime of liberty and justice. I have never known people with a greater gift for happiness and enjoyment; a people easier to govern— even though politicians with nothing to offer but their stupidities and vanities have told us the contrary. The one failing of these people is perhaps that they are over-generous, and that their historical memory is too short—which explains why in the Second Republic of 1931 the errors of the First Republic of 1873 were repeated, and why between 1931 and 1936 they made the fatal mistake of not following up their victory by destroying the forces of reaction for ever.

For thirty years of political life I have taken part in this constant struggle to obtain for the people what in the majority of countries has for more than half a century been a normal state of affairs—a democratic régime, with many imperfections perhaps, but one in which it would have been difficult to find —as one could find in Salamanca in 1930—a farm labourer working from dawn to dusk for sixteen cents a day (and sometimes only his food); a régime in which the most elementary rights of the individual would not be in constant peril.

For thirty-three months the one ambition of this people had been to safeguard the independence of their country and to hold up the advance of Fascism and European war. They had put up with conditions which no other army in Europe would have borne for so long. They had fought at times practically without weapons. And after so much sacrifice and so much bloodshed they had been defeated, and branded by hostile public opinion as fugitives or criminals, in a country which, though it opened its doors to them, forced them to return to their pariah-like existence. It will not, therefore, be hard to understand that I could not wish my worst enemy to suffer what we suffered in that last little Spanish cottage on the frontier as we watched our men pass by. . . .

Those of us who still remained in Catalonia left with the troops. The other members of the Government were waiting in Toulouse for permission to fly to the central zone. The last two days in Catalan territory will not easily be forgotten. No one knew where the front was. Dr. Negrín's residence in Agullana, revealed to the rebels by an indiscretion—unintentional or otherwise—on the part of the local Perpignan newspapers, was frequently honoured by visits from enemy aircraft, which could at any time have dropped down low and destroyed it without the slightest risk. On the second raid the enemy must have thought the house was empty, although it was from there that the Prime Minister issued forth to take leave of the troops—with a very narrow margin of time and only after the General Staff had sent various messages urging his departure.

In spite of its exposed position, however, the President's house at least had a telephone. On the other hand, in the office of the Abajol mining engineer whose last guests were Señor Méndez Aspe and I there was no fear of our sleep being interrupted by any call, save that of some motorized enemy patrol which might have been disrespectful enough to awaken us. Two very young soldiers who remained with us— whether through devotion or because we gave them abundant supplies of cigarettes was not altogether clear—formed our bodyguard. The question was who would form it next morning—these faithful companions or some less amiable Requetés or Phalangists. So exhausted were we, however, that this problem was scarcely given the careful and critical consideration which it deserved. Apart from all our other anxieties, we had been up for two nights in succession personally directing the evacuation of the pictures from the Prado Museum.

One is by now so accustomed to read and hear the most inaccurate and extravagant versions of every single event

connected with the magnificent struggle of Republican Spain
that it has not surprised me in the least to see how many
people—directors of museums, Fascist painters, League of
Nations functionaries, Swiss customs officials, insurance
agents, garage proprietors—dispute the honour of having
saved the masterpieces of Spanish art from destruction. The
facts, however, are very simple, and are confirmed by a document signed in Figueras on February 3, 1939 by the Sub-
Director of the Louvre, M. Jaujard, and myself. As soon as
the Spanish Government realized how slender were the
chances of holding up the enemy advance, one of their chief
anxieties was to place the Prado treasures in safety. Their
preservation in perfect condition in the midst of tremendous
difficulties—as those who have since admired them in Geneva
can bear witness—is one of the Republican Government's most
legitimate grounds for pride. Their removal from Madrid,
where they were in grave danger of destruction from enemy
aircraft, first to Valencia and then to Catalonia (it is to be
presumed that those who now claim the honour of having
saved them do not include this careful attention among their
services to universal culture), showed how far the Republican
authorities carried their zeal in preventing the barbarous rain
of enemy bombs from depriving Spain and humanity of some
of the most exquisite productions of art which the world has
known.

The proximity of rebel troops, led by the Italians—who as
they passed through Valencia had torn up the orange trees
by the roots, and who could hardly be considered the most
trustworthy guardians of Spain's beauties—added to the natural fear that these art treasures might be destroyed in air
raids or last-moment skirmishes, decided us to advise the
Comité Internationale pour la Sauvegarde des Trésors d'Art
d'Espagne of the danger, through the medium of the Spanish
Embassy in Paris. I, for my part, also informed the British,
American, and French Governments of our desire to evacuate
the Prado pictures, and had more than one interview on the

subject with M. Jules Henry, the French Ambassador, and Messrs. Stevenson and Thurston, the British and American Chargés d'Affaires.

The promise obtained from the representatives of the Comité Internationale, with whom in Figueras I had discussed ways and means of evacuation, was only partially kept. It was arranged that the pictures should be removed in French lorries. We scarcely had a single truck at our disposal, and while it was asking a good deal of the hundred thousand refugees who had been waiting for three days piled up like cattle at the French frontier that they should make way—as they did without the slightest incident—for a caravan of seventy-five trucks, it was, we felt, quite out of the question to take trucks from a General Staff which was at its wits' end to find sufficient means of transport for withdrawing its own troops.

Not one of the seventy-five French lorries arrived. Nevertheless the Prado pictures left after two incredible nights spent in assembling a train of cars one by one. For forty-eight hours carabineers were bringing up the pictures from the various places, many miles apart, where they had been deposited. It was touching to see these men on the second night —their strength failing through lack of food and sleep— loading the pictures on the trucks and then following like shadows to make sure that no irreparable damage should be done before the main road was reached. So, followed by the sad gaze of Señor Pérez Rubio, Director of Art Treasures, and his efficient collaborators, Señores Giner and Bolivar, who had done so much in the two and a half years of war to safeguard the treasures of the Prado, the *Maids of Honour* left Spain for the first time since Velázquez painted them at the court of King Philip IV.

It was only after a long discussion with the representatives of the Comité Internationale that I succeeded in adding this last clause to the signed document: *"Ce reçu comportera l'engagement de ne rendre, le jour où la paix sera rétablie en*

Espagne, les œuvres et les objets d'art confiés au Secrétaire-Général de la Société des Nations, qu'au Gouvernement de l'Espagne pour rester le bien commun de la nation espagnole." [1]

The extent of Franco's debts to his Axis allies made this condition one of vital necessity.

[1] "This receipt involves an obligation, once peace has been re-established in Spain, to return the paintings and art objects entrusted to the Secretary-General of the League of Nations only to the Spanish Government, in order that they may remain the property of the Spanish nation."

CHAPTER XVI

Why We Continued the War

EVER SINCE the transfer of the Government to Figueras the question of its further removal to the central-southern zone had more than once been discussed in the Cabinet. Not only were we faced with the difficulties of organizing resistance in the north of Catalonia and of trying to save at least a small strip of territory from which to hold the frontier, but we were also in the distressing situation of being entirely cut off from the rest of Republican Spain. Every day our isolation grew. By dint of continual journeys to Perpignan it was possible for me as Foreign Minister to maintain some kind of contact— although a very irregular one—between the Government and our foreign representatives. The Minister of National Defence, however, had no means of getting into touch with the High Command in Madrid. On the other hand, the General Staff considered it essential that the Premier and some of the Ministers should stay in Catalonia until the last moment in order not to increase the panic which had begun to cause such havoc among the civilian population, and to ensure that their evacuation and the orderly withdrawal of the army towards

France were carried out in the best conditions possible. There was nothing for it, therefore, but to split up the Government, and as there were no planes in which to fly direct to the central zone, it was finally decided that the majority of the Ministers should leave for Toulouse and from there go by air to Valencia or Alicante. On arrival in France, they had to seek the necessary permission of the French Government to travel to Spain, and when on February 9, after watching our troops march through Le Perthus, the Prime Minister, the other two Ministers who had remained in Catalonia, and I left for Toulouse, we found our colleagues still there awaiting a favourable reply.

The Cabinet met in the Spanish Consulate at Toulouse. Our pilots had told us that it would be impossible to leave that night in our own planes. There was no time to lose, and after discussing various proposals we finally hit on a plan. Two members of the Spanish Cortes who had been waiting a week to proceed to the central zone had finally managed to get seats in the Air France plane which was carrying on a regular service between Toulouse and Casablanca. Though keenly disappointed, they immediately agreed to our suggestion that the Prime Minister and I should take their places in the machine. (In spite of a previous decision that, in view of the special nature of our mission, the Finance and Foreign Ministers should remain in France, I had succeeded in getting the Prime Minister's permission to accompany him.) Our chief object—to gauge the powers of resisting in the central zone until such time as humane peace terms would be granted, would be doomed to instant failure if the rest of Republican Spain collapsed. We therefore considered that even from a diplomatic point of view it was essential to retain the one card left in our hands, and after a short discussion our colleagues came round to our way of thinking.

In the aerodrome various reporters who had been dogging our footsteps were keeping close watch for the departure of the Spanish planes. Fortunately they did not "cover" the Air

France plane so carefully, and we were able to take our places in the machine unnoticed. It was a splendid flight. . . . As we flew over Barcelona—the city lights shining with a brightness to which we were unaccustomed after two and a half years of war—the feeling of her nearness was so intense as to waken us from sleep. . . . Then came the fair countryside of the Levant, all the more beautiful in our eyes for being still part of our own Spain. Near Alicante the pilot, without giving our names, radioed the arrival of two Republican officials. In the aerodrome the local authorities were awaiting us. At once we began telephoning from the Civil Government office to the provinces, Dr. Negrín calling the various army leaders, and I the provincial Governors. In ten minutes some of the tremendous harm caused by three weeks of isolation had been repaired. Enemy planes did not waste much time in showing themselves over the Civil Government buildings, and it was a splendid opportunity to test the morale of the people. Absolute calm reigned, and there was not the slightest sign of disorder. Arriving from Catalonia, troubled and oppressed by the memory of a multitude panic-stricken at the thought of falling into the hands of a hateful enemy, we were heartened and refreshed by this evidence of calmness and self-control.

But when we reached the harbour a truly desolate scene met our gaze. The whole port seemed to have been stripped bare by machine-gun fire. A ship with French colours painted on her funnel, to all appearances deserted, lay forlorn at the quayside surrounded by grisly reminders of the enemy bombardments. The problem of food supplies for the central zone arose before us in all its gravity. We had discussed it fully in Toulouse and had taken the necessary measures for organizing the dispatch of the most indispensable supplies in ships small enough to run the blockade. The difficulty lay in providing for the months of February and March; after that the early harvest in Andalucía and Extremadura would help to make conditions more or less supportable. But in spite of the great obstacles to be overcome, the supply of food to the central-southern zone was not only possible but ensured. Even after the desertion of the fleet, on whose protection we had naturally relied, it was not interrupted.

But what depressed me even more than the sight of Alicante harbour was the morale of the military leaders. In a conversation held that afternoon at General Miaja's headquarters in Valencia with the army generals who had called to pay their respects, the Prime Minister and I were able to realize the effect which the Catalan landslide had made on them, and to see their scepticism regarding our ability to continue resisting until such time as the rebels should promise to respect the lives of our fighters. I could not but be aware that while our arrival had raised the morale of the people as a whole, for some of these gentlemen it was not exactly a happy event. Although outwardly we were greeted with every possible sign of loyalty and respect, I felt that we were being considered as two unexpected guests whose arrival had upset a program drawn up carefully and in secret. Our words of encouragement found no echo in their hearts, which were dead to all vigorous reaction, and longing only for an early end to hostilities. The one obsession of these men—scarcely veiled by the conventional language of discipline—was to put an end to the war, no matter how. Before we parted that night, Dr. Negrín said to me: "Did you see that? The rebels don't need motorized divisions against people with such a morale. A few bicycles would be enough to break up the front. The first thing to do is to strengthen the army command. Tomorrow we must go to Madrid and call a meeting of the parties and organizations. If they agree to carry on the fight, we'll go ahead."

On the road to Madrid we passed army units who cheered as we drove by. The will to fight, although impaired by recent events and by the attitude of certain elements which made little attempt to hide their defeatism, was latent in the people and only needed some evidence of strength from the leaders to be galvanized into action. We did not want an endless and blind struggle, but we were not willing to die a dishonourable death without so much as attempting to secure a peace guaranteeing the lives of those who had committed no other crime than that of defending their country's independence. Certain signs showed, however, that the growing apathy of the leaders had given rise to an increasing desire for capitulation in circles which had never been distinguished for their firm attitude. More than once on our journey we passed by houses which had recently been whitewashed, less out of a desire for cleanliness than in order to efface the anti-Fascist signs which in the early days of the war were to be seen on all sides. In the villages the old "political boss" and his wife and daughters, who up to then had gone about in an exaggeratedly proletarian garb, were little by little taking out their Sunday clothes from the trunks in which they had lain throughout the war, and were preparing themselves for a worthy reception of the victors. In some places the Republicans reacted promptly to these signs of impatience. In others they began to fear that any bold action might mark them out even more clearly for the terrible vengeance awaiting them after a rebel victory.

On entering the capital I was overcome with an emotion which, for the time being, clouded my critical sense. I could not believe that Madrid would ever yield. The streets were full of reminders of her epic struggle, and it seemed impossible that the people we saw around us could ever be forced to a condition of surrender or servitude. It was torture to think that this city—a city without counterpart—might soon be subjected to the irreverence and frivolity of those who had so often proved themselves incapable of showing that respect for a brave opponent which is the mark of a true soldier. Since the enemy's law was a law of hate, it was not difficult, although inexpressibly painful, to foresee the extent of the reprisals when the time should come to surrender. No government with a clear conception of duty towards its people could do less than defend the city until the great democracies which were ready to recognize Franco should promise to impose the condition of humane treatment, nor could they do other than go on defending it if this guarantee were not given.

After conversations between the Prime Minister and representatives of the political parties and trade-union organizations, the conclusion was reached that, however desirable a speedy peace, an essential condition was that there should be no reprisals. Not one responsible leader expressed himself—either then or afterwards—in favour of unconditional surrender. There may have been some who thought that the whole question could have been solved by transporting a few dozen prominent persons out of the country by plane, but if such an opinion existed it was not likely to have been disclosed to us, seeing that we had just arrived from France with very different proposals.

Once this essential point had been cleared up and the whole of the Government reunited in Madrid—with the exception of the Minister without Portfolio, Señor Giral, who had been asked to accompany President Azaña after his departure from Catalonia—the various Ministers proceeded to reorganize the services, while the Minister of Finance and I were ordered to leave for Paris.

Before setting out in the plane from Albacete we visited the Prime Minister at Los Llanos, a splendid country-house and game preserve belonging to the Marquis of Larios, which —doubtless as a mark of consideration to its owner—had not been bombed once during the whole war, in spite of the fact that for some time it had been an air pilots' hostel. Here Dr. Negrín had called a meeting of army, navy and air-force leaders. Among those present were General Miaja, Commander-in-Chief of the army in the region still in the hands of the Constitutional Government, Colonel Casado, Commander of the Central Army, General González Escobar and General Menéndez, commanding the other two armies, Colonel Briones, Commander of the Naval Base, and General Matallana, Chief of General Staff of the Land, Sea, and Air Forces. The object of the conference was to examine the military situation in all its aspects and to make a careful study of the possibilities which still remained open to us. The meeting, which lasted nearly five hours, was not over when we arrived, and during dinner I remarked a certain attitude of hostility and reserve on the part of my companions, which hardly augured well for the future.

That night the Prime Minister informed us that at the meeting with the army leaders he had made a clear statement of the Government's attitude and the negotiations which were being carried out to secure an honourable peace. These negotiations officially dated from February 6. But before that date and the meeting of Parliament, and as soon as the adverse course of the war made it necessary to take certain soundings, I had had a discussion with Mr. Stevenson, the British Chargé d'Affaires, regarding the position of the thousands of compromised Spaniards in the rest of Republican Spain who would be cut off from all means of escape if, contrary to our hopes and our decision to continue the struggle, defeat in Catalonia were followed sooner or later by defeat in the central-southern zone. Mr. Stevenson agreed that such a contingency should be taken into account, and offered to suggest to the Foreign Office that they should study a plan for evacuating the civilian population with the assistance of the British and French navies, which two years before had been so effective in transporting Basque women and children to France.

On February 6, however, the Prime Minister in my presence informed Mr. Stevenson and the French Ambassador, M. Jules Henry, at the Agullana Presidency, that the Spanish Government was ready to end the war on the conditions which had been laid down by Dr. Negrín before the Cortes in Figueras on February 1, and which had received the unanimous approval of the Chamber.

The day before, I had had a meeting with both diplomats at Le Perthus, in the course of which the British Chargé d'Affaires informed me that he had received instructions from his Government to ask if we would consent to Great Britain's using her good offices with General Franco to put an end to the struggle on conditions acceptable to us. With the reservation that the French Government, not being represented in Burgos, could not directly second any such action on the part of the British Government, M. Henry associated himself with the attempts of his colleague to hasten the end of the war. Both representatives insisted that their proposals were inspired by the highest motives, that there was not the slightest desire to force the issue, and that the decision rested solely with ourselves. I confined myself to stating that these proposals would be placed before my Government. The next day I invited them to Agullana to discuss the whole question with the Prime Minister and me.

Dr. Negrín began by expounding the scope and significance of the three conditions for peace contained in his Figueras speech, which were as follows:

1. Evacuation of Spanish territory by all foreign elements.
2. The Spanish people to be allowed to determine their own political régime freely and without foreign pressure of any kind.
3. No reprisals to be taken.

The first condition we considered indispensable to our national independence, and as far as the second—stipulating the free decision of the Spanish people—was concerned, we knew, as the Prime Minister acknowledged, that we were not in a position to demand the necessary guarantees. It was possible that Franco would refuse so much as to consider these first two conditions, and that he would allege that he himself represented the country's will and would therefore be the guarantor of its liberty and independence. But even in the unlikely event of his accepting them at that actual point in the hostilities, we knew that such an acceptance would be purely formal.

The Prime Minister went on to explain that under the

circumstances the first two conditions were of a theoretical importance. We were convinced that the rebels had been and continued to be the instruments of Germany and Italy, and that in the event of a victory—which they would owe exclusively to these two powers—they would fall completely under totalitarian domination. We could not therefore regard any guarantee from General Franco of Spanish political and territorial independence as anything more than an empty promise, whatever importance the British and French Governments might attach to it. From the point of view of internal policy it would have been somewhat ingenuous to believe that the rebels would propose to hold the wide national plebiscite promised by the Spanish Government in the program of Thirteen Points in the event of a Republican victory. Both demands had to be sustained, but in effect the real point at issue was that concerning reprisals.

If they gave us effective guarantees that there would be no reprisals—and by that we meant no execution or imprisonment of Republicans because of their ideals and because of their defence of a legal government against rebellion—and, along with such guarantees, facilities for evacuating from Spain all those for whom existence under the rebel régime would be materially impossible and morally a torture, then the cessation of hostilities could be considered. But if these guarantees were refused, then the struggle would continue to the last man and the last cartridge. Here Dr. Negrín naturally stressed the powers of resistance of the central zone, giving as many details as could be properly divulged, and the Government's determination not to lay down arms unless on this third point it was given the satisfaction which humane principles, common sense, and European dignity demanded. Moreover, a war to the death might bring about a change in our attitude, whereas an immediate settlement would mean the avoidance of further bloodshed and destruction, and the salvation of the fleet and of that part of the State possessions in the hands of the Constitutional Government.

When the army generals at Los Llanos heard from the lips of the Prime Minister of the efforts which had been made, even those who were most firmly set on a speedy end to the war agreed that what the Government had been trying for weeks to obtain was the very minimum which could be asked in exchange for a surrender of arms.

Besides the task of carrying out these negotiations in Paris, I was also entrusted with a very important and delicate mission. The Cabinet had decided at a meeting held the day previously in Madrid that the President of the Republic should return at once to Spain, and I had been instructed to communicate this decision to him. All the political parties, including that of the Left Republicans of which Señor Azaña, until his appointment as President, had been the leader, shared the Government's desire for his return to national territory, a desire which had also been respectfully expressed by the chief army leaders during the meeting at Los Llanos. It was, one might say, a call to the President from the nation, and it seemed logical to expect that it would be answered as soon as it reached his ears. Nevertheless, before leaving Albacete, I voiced to the Prime Minister my doubts as to the successful outcome of my mission. We had both been witnesses of a painful scene on the day of the President's departure from Catalonia.

In the very modest dwelling-house in Abajol which Señor Azaña had occupied during his last days in Spain—a residence in every respect inadequate for the President of a Republic, but which by reason of its distance from the front was not likely to be the object of a surprise attack by the enemy—the Speaker, the Prime Minister, and I were discussing with His Excellency the last details of his journey and the form in which his entry into France should be communicated to the French Government. Suddenly the President announced his intention of not returning to Spain under any circumstances while the war lasted. I waited for an adequate reply from the Prime Minister, but it seemed that he did not pay very serious attention to a remark which, as he afterwards told me, was characteristic of Señor Azaña, who was temperamentally disposed to brusque and disconcerting outbursts, which he would retract as soon as he had had an opportunity of bringing his customary intelligence and good judgment to bear on the situation. I confess that I was not much reassured by this explanation, and it was with the vivid impression of that last interview in my mind that I made ready to carry out the task which had been entrusted to me.

The recollection of those four days spent at the Paris Embassy trying to convince Señor Azaña that his place was in Spain by the side of his people is not so pleasant that I should wish to dwell on it unnecessarily. "My one duty is to make peace. I refuse to help, by my presence, to prolong a senseless struggle. We must try to get the best possible guarantees for humane treatment and then finish everything as soon as we can,"—with these words the President of the Republic received the communication which I made him in the name of the Government.

I took the liberty of reminding Señor Azaña that a considerable part of this program had been the aim of the Government since before it left Catalonia, and I recapitulated the efforts made to carry it out. I told him of the negotiations initiated twenty-four hours previously by our Ambassador in London, the success of which largely depended on our being able to give the impression that we were ready—if the essential peace guarantees were refused—to continue resistance, and explained that this impression could only be given if the President returned to loyalist territory. "Nobody believes in our powers of resistance," was the reply, "and the most sceptical of all are our own generals."

I was well aware of the reason for this remark. Before my arrival in Paris the President had made unsuccessful attempts to obtain from Generals Rojo, Jurado, and Hidalgo de Cisneros a written report which he could use against the Negrín Government to justify his refusal to return to Spain.

The incident deserves to be briefly narrated. The three generals in question had called separately at the Paris Embassy to discuss with the Ambassador, Dr. Pascua, various matters connected with the situation of the Republican troops in France, and having learned of their presence, Señor Azaña sent out an adjutant to invite them to pay him their respects. Various matters were discussed, among them the position in the central-southern zone. To the President's questions regarding the military situation, the generals replied frankly as befitted a private conversation, and made no attempt to conceal the difficulties of resistance. To the great surprise of the army leaders, Señor Azaña then asked them to send him a written report of all they had just said. "You will thus be doing a great service both to Spain and to myself." General Hidalgo de Cisneros answered that he regretted he could send such a report only to his immediate chief, the Minister of National Defence, or through the latter's intermediary. In reply to Señor Azaña's remark that it was perfectly constitutional for the President of the Republic to ask for the official opinion of the army leaders who called on him, General Cisneros explained clearly the reasons for his presence in the Embassy and the merely incidental character of his interview with the President. Generals Rojo and Jurado subsequently wrote a letter to Señor Azaña asking to be excused from sending the report.

When I realized that there was no hope of persuading Señor Azaña to return to Spain, I decided to leave for Toulouse, from which town I was able to maintain contact with the ambassadors.

Meanwhile the diplomatic activity which had begun two weeks before, and which now centred on London, was developing rapidly. On February 13 Señor Azcárate, the Spanish Ambassador in London, informed the British Foreign Office that his Government, having carefully studied the situation in Spain, was confirmed in its impression that in the central-southern zone it could dispose of the necessary factors to allow of resistance for a certain period. The Ambassador also recapitulated the terms on which we would be willing to consider a cessation of hostilities.

"The Spanish Government," added the Ambassador, "without making any concrete demand or petition, is confident that the British Government will take the necessary steps, either by persuasion or by pressure, to arrange a settlement on that basis, permitting of a speedy cessation of the struggle. If this should not be the case, the Spanish Government would not hesitate to continue resistance to the last; for, on the one hand, with the necessary elements at its disposal in the central and southern area, nothing could justify, nor could anyone reasonably expect, its unconditional surrender; and on the other hand, the moderation and justice of the three points mentioned as representing the basis for a possible settlement cannot be doubted by anyone who examines them in an objective and impartial spirit of inquiry."

Señor Azcárate, in accordance with a previous arrangement, came over to Paris to give me a verbal account of his negotiations. As a result of the wide exchange of impressions which took place in the Paris Embassy between Señor Azcárate, Dr. Pascua, and myself, and of our fear that unless the President of the Republic returned to Spain quickly Great Britain and France would recognize Franco, thereby making it much more difficult for us to take any effective action, we came to the conclusion that it would be useless and even detrimental to continue to demand as a condition for any future settlement the evacuation of foreigners and the right of the Spanish people to establish their own political régime, and that we should concentrate on the point concerning reprisals and the obtaining of facilities for the evacuation of those in the greatest danger, whether civilians or soldiers.

That same night Señor Azcárate returned to London, and on the following day he informed the British Government of the fresh attitude adopted by us in Paris. As a result of his conversations—of which he kept me informed in detail—I was convinced that the British Government would have been willing to take the initiative of submitting extremely interesting proposals to the rebel authorities for the immediate termination of the war if the Spanish Government could have authorized the British to inform the rebels of their own readiness to abandon the struggle on the condition that there should be no reprisals. We repeatedly telegraphed the Prime Minister to this effect in order to obtain his consent to such a communication.

Something quite extraordinary now occurred, which was later explained by the deplorable events which subsequently took place in Spain. No reply was received from the Prime Minister to any of our telegrams. It would indeed have been difficult for him to send a reply, seeing that not one telegram came into his hands. The Ambassadors in Paris and London were able to assure me, after a careful investigation, of their speedy and correct dispatch. The key to the mystery must have lain in Madrid, where—as Dr. Negrín afterwards supposed—subversive elements, acting on instructions from certain army leaders who, under Colonel Casado, were preparing a military rising, had intercepted the cables sent by Señor Azcárate and myself. The first communication from the Prime Minister, which was not received until the eve of the recognition of Franco, was the reply to a letter which I had sent him from Toulouse by General Hidalgo de Cisneros, who was returning by plane to Madrid.

Since the recognition of Franco by Great Britain and France was now about to take place in the form which it was finally given, and which included a vague promise that the British and French Ambassadors in Burgos would press for a renunciation of reprisals, and since President Azaña's resignation was imminent, nothing further remained for me to do in Paris, and I began to count the minutes until I could get back to Spain and throw in my lot with the rest. I was convinced that as matters had developed, a policy of resistance could secure humane peace conditions and would at the same time enable us to evacuate those who under no circumstances should be abandoned to rebel reprisals.

After a long telephone conversation with the Ambassadors in Paris and London, in which we agreed upon the line to be followed after the recognition of Franco, I set out for Spain in the last airplane of the Spanish Government authorized to leave Toulouse. In case its departure might be delayed by bad weather or any other cause, I made a hasty review of the possibilities of a sea journey or an alternative flight by Air France via Orán and Alicante. But happily it was in a plane carrying the Republican colours that I landed in Albacete on the morning of February 27, after a journey not made any pleasanter by the fact that the rebels were perfectly well aware of the departure of the last loyalist machine from France.

CHAPTER XVII

The Last Days of the War

EXTERNALLY THE SITUATION in the central-southern zone had not changed during my absence. The civilian population and the army were still suffering from the deplorable effects of the defeatist campaign, which were even greater than the natural weariness caused by the length of the war. Nevertheless, authentic reports from the front showed that in spite of the many attempts to disillusion the people, they were still prepared to fight to the end because, their instinct told them, there was no other way out.

Transport was in a lamentable condition, but not beyond hope of remedy, since the fault lay, not in lack of materials, which were readily available, but in disorganization and sabotage. War material, in spite of what had been brought over during the last weeks of the struggle in Catalonia, was still as scarce as ever, but it was at least more abundant than in the Catalan zone, where the eastern debacle and the Ebro offensive had made considerable inroads on supplies. The army could count on nearly eight hundred thousand men, and there was every hope that the Government's negotiations for securing essential war supplies would be successful. The Republican fleet was composed of three cruisers, a dozen destroyers, and various torpedo-boats, and we were in possession of five hundred miles of coast, with four important ports—Almería, Cartagena, Alicante, and Valencia.

Resistance for a further six months was no idle dream. It only needed the strengthening of public morale, the reorganization of services, and the removal from posts of authority of certain unreliable and defeatist elements, to say nothing of accomplices of the enemy. Both Madrid and Valencia could have held out, but even if those two cities had fallen, a line defending part of the province of Albacete, the province of Murcía, part of Almería, the province of Alicante, and the south of Valencia could still have been maintained.

The attitude of mind of an enemy who considered the war over was a factor in our favour. No one views with pleasure the prospect of falling in the last battle, and however weak they may have considered our military situation, the memory of the defence of Madrid—if nothing more—must have weighed on the minds of the rebels and made them think twice before risking the loss of fifty thousand more of their men when the alternative was merely to respect the lives of the Republican soldiers. If we had insisted on such of our peace terms as were of a purely political character, the rebel command might easily have justified a continuation of the war. But the demand that there should be no reprisals was so reasonable, and so essential in any case to the normal development of the new régime, that to prolong the war by refusing it must have seemed madness to those on the rebel side who had not completely lost all sense of responsibility. We were not therefore indulging in wild speculations when we decided that the necessary guarantees would be obtained by firm resistance on our part. There was in any case no other solution, save that of abandoning the struggle and leaving the rebels to ravage the central zone with fire and sword and to murder the defenceless population with impunity.

But while the external situation had not changed in the central-southern zone, the underground movement of conspiracy against the Government, furthered by the desertion of the President of the Republic, had been growing rapidly. The people in general received the news of the resignation of Señor Azaña with natural indignation, but without realizing to the full the tremendous consequences which such a terrible blow to the Republic would bring in its train. They were relying on the speedy arrival of his successor, Señor Martínez Barrio, Speaker of the House, who, in accordance with the Constitution, automatically became President of the Republic; and in the midst of so many other grave anxieties, they did not attach any unusual importance to a change of personalities. On the other hand, the leaders of the new rebellion used the resignation of the President, and Señor Martínez Barrio's hesitation to take his place, as a pretext for rejecting the authority of the Government on the score of its unconstitutional character. Fundamentally, hostility against the Negrín Government had stronger roots than these juridical niceties; the Negrín Government was, in fact, the chief obstacle in the path to capitulation.

The conversation held on March 2, 1939 at General Miaja's headquarters on the Alameda de Osuna [1] between General Hidalgo de Cisneros, Chief of the Republican Air Force, and General Casado, Chief of the Central Army, throws a strong light on the criminal rising which was to take place three days later, when the new rebels, after a brief pretence of resistance, unconditionally delivered up the army and the people of the central-southern zone to the fierce reprisals of Franco.

On the day in question General Casado had invited General Hidalgo de Cisneros to have lunch with him. In the course of conversation General Casado expressed his conviction that Franco was not willing to negotiate with the Negrín Government and that so long as it rested with the latter to enter into

[1] On the eastern outskirts of Madrid.

peace discussions, nothing could be done. On the other hand, there was no more time to lose. It was essential to arrive at an agreement "in two or three days." "And only we soldiers can do this," added General Casado. He then referred to the interviews which he had had in Madrid with British officials. "I can't go into any details, but I give you my word of honour that I can get out of Franco much more than the Negrín Government ever can." Later he said: "I'm quite certain—and I'll pledge you my word of honour on this too—that it will be possible to make Franco promise that no Germans, Italians, or Moors shall enter Madrid, that there shall be no reprisals, that anyone can leave Spain who wants to, and that the military rank of the majority of us soldiers will be recognized."

Chief among the arguments advanced to prove that there would be no difficulty in the matter of recognizing military ranks was that Franco would be forced to maintain a strong army after the war and would therefore need Republican officers to make up for the tremendous losses suffered on the rebel side. General Casado undoubtedly considered the recognition of these military ranks as one of the strongest cards in his hand; he knew that it would attract many of the young men who in a brief space of time had risen from sergeant to lieutenant-colonel and who would not hesitate between the prospect of an uncertain emigrant existence and the chance of remaining at a good post in Spain.

Never dreaming for one moment that Casado was about to launch a rebellion, General Hidalgo de Cisneros took his leave, advising him to see Dr. Negrín and to waste no more time on idle nonsense.[1]

The tenor of this conversation establishes the real motive of the Casado rising—which was none other than Casado's frenzied desire to play the role of leading figure—and throws into relief his lack of balance and critical sense. Moreover, it

---

[1] In view of the importance of this conversation, I sent General Hidalgo de Cisneros, at present in France, the record reproduced here, and have received from him a confirmation of its authenticity.—J. de V., October 1939.

disposes once and for all of the legend that the second rebel movement grew out of indignation aroused by the supposed handing over of the army command to Communists by the Negrín Government. This allegation has, in any case, no foundation in fact whatsoever. With the exception of the appointment of Lieutenant-Colonel Galán as Chief of the Naval Base of Cartagena—in view of the alarming reports reaching us from that city—and a change in one or two of the military commands near the Government Residence, necessitated by the danger of a surprise attack, no important military appointments had taken place at that time.

The move for capitulation had in fact begun when the Government was still in Catalonia, and no one was more surprised and disappointed than Casado by our arrival in the central zone. He was anxious to take personal credit for setting the peace machinery in motion. After having accepted the rank of general with alacrity (on the very day that General Cisneros lunched with him he had, in the latter's presence, given orders for his new insignia to be placed on his uniform), he relegated himself to the rank of colonel on realizing that promotion might be an obstacle to the consolidation of his position when General Franco's "promised" recognition of the military ranks took place. Not until then did he suddenly discover that his promotion to the rank of general had not been legalized by the President of the Republic and was therefore unconstitutional. His anti-Communism was only revealed when the Communists, and other soldiers who were not Communists but who were unwilling to be the victims of his personal ambition, rose in Madrid against a policy of unconditional surrender and in defence of the legitimate Government. But once in exile, and bearing on his shoulders the tremendous responsibility for having divided the anti-Fascist front, broken down resistance, executed innumerable comrades, and delivered up the central-southern zone without obtaining a single one of the conditions laid down in his "peace program," he decided that anti-Communism was the surest platform from which to win the sympathy and support of certain British circles.

Treachery, irresponsibility, or ambition? By whatever motive he was actuated, it is certain that Casado is not a leader in whom the Spanish people could ever place their trust.

In their policy of resistance, both during the period following the collapse of the eastern front in March 1938 and in the last phase of the war, the Government always acted on its own initiative. It is absurd to suppose that in this respect its members were prisoners of the Communist Party, and an incident which occurred shortly before the Casado coup is sufficient to prove the baselessness of such a contention. On the day in question the Prime Minister told me that he had informed the Central Committee of the Communist Party that he reserved to himself full freedom of action irrespective of any decisions which the political parties might make on their own account. It had come to his knowledge that at a meeting of the Central Committee the Communists had agreed to oppose any peace moves which were not based on the three conditions laid down by the Prime Minister in his speech before the Cortes. During the course of his interview with the Central Committee, Dr. Negrín reminded them that it rested with the Government alone to determine such a question. "Always providing that you are its leader," observed the Communists. "Either I myself," replied the Prime Minister, "or anyone else whom I may consider suitable in the circumstances, for while the Presidency of the Republic remains vacant, the responsibility for a decision rests with me. And if at any time I should decide that someone else ought to take my place, I want to be quite sure that there will be no difficulty in making the change." "But who *would* take your place?" asked the Communists. "Besteiro, for instance," replied Dr. Negrín. An exclamation of horror followed the mere pronouncement of

Señor Besteiro's name, but the interview closed with a vote of confidence in the Prime Minister and a promise to respect his decisions.

On March 5, to the cry of "Long live Franco!" the artillery-men in the Cartagena coastal batteries rose in rebellion, forced the Republican fleet to put out to sea under the threat of firing on the ships, and sent a radio request to the Franco zone for assistance and airplanes.

The news that the Government—entirely on account of the suspicious attitude of the artillery and garrison officers—had appointed Lieutenant-Colonel Galán as Chief of the Naval B se had not been at all well received by the fleet. Neverthe-less they reacted with dignity to this ultimatum of the new rebels and rejected it amid cheers for the Republic.

We telephoned to the new Chief of the Naval Base to inform him of the immediate arrival of reinforcements. In the middle of a sentence his voice suddenly ceased; there was every reason to fear that he had been arrested in his study. The scarcity of trustworthy officials was once again in tragic evi-dence. After a rapid perusal of names, Rodríguez, the Com-mander of the Eleventh Lister Division, recently returned from France, personally received orders from the Minister of Defence to take command of a brigade which had been con-centrated in the outskirts of Cartagena, and to put down the rebellion at all costs. I can see him now as he went off that day, in civilian clothes, his army greatcoat the only sign of his soldier's calling—full of energy and calm determination.

By that afternoon the Cartagena rising was almost com-pletely subdued. Our only cause for uneasiness was the action of the fleet, which had set off for an unknown destination. We little thought, however, that it had gone never to return, thus depriving the central zone of an important means of resistance, and a valuable aid if we should be faced with the unfortunate necessity of evacuating the population.

A meeting of the Cabinet had been called to discuss the general lines of the speech which the Prime Minister was to broadcast on the following day. In this speech the Government's position in regard to the peace question, and the steps taken to obtain an armistice free from persecutions and reprisals, were to be clearly stated. The majority of the ministers telephoned the Prime Minister and me from Madrid, urging us to take a plane to the capital, and saying that General Casado was of the opinion that a meeting of the Cabinet in Madrid would help to allay the nervous excitement which had taken hold of the people during the last few hours, and especially after the news of the Cartagena rising. But the very fact that the suggestion came from General Casado decided Dr. Negrín to send an airplane to Madrid, in order to bring the ministers to his residence some thirty miles from Alicante.

There were abundant reasons to distrust the persistent suggestions that the Government should meet in Madrid. Ever since the early hours of that morning the Prime Minister and the Defence Minister had been asking Generals Miaja and Casado to come and assist them in carrying out measures rendered advisable by events in Cartagena, but in spite of these continuous requests neither of the two Generals had called on Dr. Negrín or given any satisfactory explanation for their delay. The explanation was to be forthcoming a few hours later.

The Cabinet meeting broke up for dinner. In the dining-room of the Presidency were gathered all the ministers, General Matallana, Chief of General Staff (the only one of the High Command to answer the summons), and General Cordón, Under-Secretary of War, with their respective assistants, when we were suddenly startled by news from Valencia that an attack on the Government was being broadcast in Madrid. At first we thought it might be one of the Franco stations broadcasting on the Madrid wave-lengths. A telephone call from General Cordón to General Casado to ask if it really was the Madrid station brought us the news that he had risen in rebellion.

The Prime Minister telephoned to Casado.[1] "What is going on in Madrid, General?" he asked. "What is going on is that I have rebelled," was the reply. "That you have rebelled! Against whom? Against me?" "Yes, against you." "Very well, you can consider yourself relieved of your command," answered Dr. Negrín quietly. After all, he was still Prime Minister of Spain and Commander-in-Chief of the armies. Very soon he was to discover that the steps he could take to assert his authority were few.

This brief dialogue was followed by a series of telephone calls. The ministers who had been with Casado that afternoon and who had defended him at the Cabinet meeting against the suspicions of the Prime Minister refused to believe the news. "I'm coming over this very moment. Don't do anything until we have had a talk. All this can soon be settled"—this friendly request from the Minister of the Interior, Señor Paulino Gómez, merely provoked from General Casado the warning that not only would his journey be in vain, but that he would run the risk of being arrested on entering the capital.

While the rest of us returned to the meeting, the Prime Minister instructed the Under-Secretary of War to telephone

[1] In his book *The Last Days of Madrid* (London: Peter Davies), pp. 149–50, General Casado gives another and fanciful version of this telephonic exchange with the Prime Minister.

There is striking comparison to be made between this conversation, particularly as Casado reports it, and a historic telephone conversation between General Mola in Pamplona and Don Diego Martínez Barrio in Madrid in the early morning hours of July 19, 1936.

Martínez Barrio, Speaker of the Cortes, was designated by President Azaña to form a Government to succeed that of Casares Quiroga. This Government lasted only several hours. But Martínez Barrio's first act, it seems, was to telephone General Mola to ask what his projects were, with rebellion breaking out in Morocco and Andalucía. General Mola, who we later learned had been in charge of plans for the rebellion on the Peninsula, announced that he was in revolt. According to Mola's secretary, José María Iribarren, Martínez Barrio attempted to dissuade him. But the General was committed to the rebellion, and the consequences were what the world knows. By July 26 he thought himself beaten (Iribarren, op. cit., p. 132). Casado did a comparable thing, with disaster ensuing even more promptly.

the various chiefs of army corps in order to discover their attitude. A report from Cisneros, who on the news of the Cartagena rising that morning had been sent by Dr. Negrín to bring back Generals Miaja and Matallana by plane, was not very encouraging. Tired of waiting in the aerodrome for the two Generals, General Cisneros had driven over to Valencia, and had found General Miaja in his study with General Menéndez, leader of the Levant Army, and General Matallana, Chief of General Staff. All three were in a mood of great excitement, accusing the Government of a criminal "war-to-the-death" spirit, and proclaiming loudly that they were going to put an end to hostilities within twenty-four hours.

"But how?" asked General Hidalgo de Cisneros. "By surrendering?" "Yes, by surrendering. There's no other way out," replied General Matallana. A few hours later, however, this General—a man of fine character and a stern and disciplined soldier, who had fallen a victim to the manœuvres and capitulatory tactics of his companions—placed himself at the disposal of the Prime Minister in order to assist in carrying out the necessary measures for the suppression of the Cartagena rising.

The result of General Cordón's soundings was not at all satisfactory. It was obvious that the movement, which had been in course of preparation for some weeks, was a widespread one. Some of the army leaders, when called up by telephone, answered that they would remain with the Government, but only on condition that no proceedings were taken against Casado and that there were no clashes between the various military forces. General Menéndez, doubtless in the belief that we intended to hold General Matallana as a hostage, contented himself with demanding the latter's immediate "liberation" under the threat of fetching him himself and "shooting the lot of you." A sudden break in the telephone communication, no doubt engineered from Madrid, warned us that our situation was becoming increasingly precarious.

Every possible means was tried to get in touch with the outside world, but it was not until two o'clock in the morning that a call from Casado to General Hidalgo de Cisneros put an end to our isolation.

On our instructions General Cisneros used all his diplomacy to re-establish communications, a matter of prime necessity. "But how was it you did this without letting me know?" he asked Casado, pretending to be offended. "I'll explain it all later; everything has happened so quickly. The reason I'm ringing now is to say that the Governor of Alicante informs me that the air force is all ready to bombard him." "They are carrying out my orders," replied Cisneros coldly. "But this is absurd," answered the other; "at all costs we must prevent any shots being fired." "Agreed," said Cisneros, "but in that case it is essential for me to get in touch with the aerodromes." In this manner contact was at least partly re-established.

There was, of course, no way of getting into touch with the two chiefs of army corps who had remained completely loyal —Colonel Bueno, who on account of his standing and authority was best suited for the Madrid command, and Colonel Barceló, afterwards executed by Casado. They were even more carefully watched and isolated than ourselves.

After five fruitless hours spent in attempting to make the contacts necessary to oppose Casado's coup, the Government set about making such preparations as the situation demanded. To remain there meant that we ran the risk of being cut off and arrested at any moment. Our forces consisted of a hundred guerrilla fighters brought over a few days previously to the Presidency—a building exposed on all sides and entirely unprotected. While orders were being given for the transfer of two airplanes to a new aerodrome whose whereabouts were not very well known to the authorities, I made use of the opportunity to give a full account of events to the only two foreign correspondents who had come to the Presidency--

William Forrest of the London *News Chronicle*, and Marthe Huysmans, correspondent of the Brussels *Peuple* and daughter of the former Speaker of the Belgian Parliament. Both were trusty friends of Republican Spain, and up to the very last moment they worked loyally and well in their task of reporting the struggle of the Spanish people, a struggle of which almost any end might have been foreseen save the tragic one they were now forced to witness.

When I returned to the Prime Minister's study, General Matallana—whose situation was a very difficult one and whose embarrassment Dr. Negrín saw no real reason to prolong—was taking leave of his chief. Conscious of the approaching disaster, and bitterly regretting the break in the loyalist ranks, he said good-bye to us both with tears in his eyes and set off on the journey to Valencia. His departure forced us to hasten our own. While we had nothing to fear from him personally, any denunciation or indiscretion on the part of the chauffeur or one of his assistants might lead to our speedy arrest.

While we were waiting in the aerodrome at nine o'clock in the morning for the airplanes which were to arrive at any moment, Dr. Negrín called me to his car, and under pretext of exploring the district we drove out in search of the one army headquarters where there was a chance of finding some of the loyal leaders.

This was the Dakar base, but a base in name only. It was a house on the highroad, exposed to the view of the whole countryside, and filled to overflowing with people, who had turned its terrace into the most public and democratic of meeting-places.

Here were assembled Generals Hidalgo de Cisneros, Cordón, and Modesto, Colonel Nuñez Masas, the Under-Secretary of Aviation, Lister, "Pasionaria," and a considerable number of army chiefs and officers. They were joined later by Señores Uribe and Moix, the Ministers of Agriculture and

Labour, who had been entrusted by their organizations with the task of reassembling their respective members in the event of evacuation.

Dr. Negrín set about drawing up a message for Casado; it was a last appeal for agreement and our final attempt to avert the tragedy which threatened to overwhelm us all. Once again it was General Hidalgo de Cisneros who took it upon himself to telephone Casado, sending him the message over the Teletypewriter. By disclosing our whereabouts we ran the risk that troops might be sent from Valencia to arrest us, but we felt in the first place that the prevention of a break in the anti-Fascist front must necessarily be our first consideration, and secondly that the constant coming and going of people to and from the house, to say nothing of the guerilla fighters posted at the door, had divested our meeting-place of any secret character it might once have possessed. Dr. Negrín's message to Casado, of which I believe the only copies are the original and the one which I took away with me, ran as follows:

The Government over which I preside has been painfully surprised by a movement in whose aims of a swift and honorable peace free from persecutions and reprisals, and guaranteeing the country's independence (as announced by the *Junta* in its manifesto to the country), there appears to be certain discrepancies. My Government also considers that the reasons given by the *Junta* in explanation of its actions are unjustifiable. It has consistently laboured to retain that spirit of unity which has always animated its policy, and any mistaken interpretation of its actions can only be due to the impatience of those who are unaware of the real situation. If they had waited for the explanation of the present position, which was to have been given tonight in the Government's name, it is certain that this unfortunate episode would never have taken place. If contact between the Government and those sectors who appear to be in disagreement could have been established in time, there is no doubt whatever that all differences would have been removed. It is impossible to undo what has been done, but it *is* nevertheless possible to prevent serious consequences to those who have fought as brothers for a common denominator of ideals, and—most particularly—to Spain. If the roots of mischief are pruned in time, they may yet grow a good and useful plant. On the altar of the sacred interests of Spain we must all offer up our weapons, and if we wish for a settlement with our adversaries, we must first avoid all bloody conflict between those who have been brothers in arms. The Government therefore calls upon the *Junta* which has been constituted in Madrid and proposes that it should appoint one or more persons to settle all differences in a friendly and patriotic manner. Inasmuch as it is of interest to Spain, it is of interest to the Government that, whatsoever may happen, any transfer of authority should take place in a normal and constitutional manner. Only in this way can the cause for which we have fought remain unsullied. And only thus can we preserve those advantages in the international sphere which still remain to us through our limited connections. In the certainty that as Spaniards the *Junta* will give heed to our request.

JUAN NEGRÍN

No more could have been asked of a Government which, in the most difficult situation that ever men intent on serving their country have had to face, had been so basely betrayed. It was a document full of concessions. We knew perfectly well that one of the reasons which had decided the new rebels to speed up their plans was the desire to prevent Dr. Negrín from broadcasting his speech that night, as had been announced since the previous Friday. For from this speech the whole population of the central-southern zone would have learned of the pending negotiations and the efforts made to obtain an honourable peace. Casado had heard all this from the lips of the Prime Minister himself. The broadcasting of the speech would have deprived the Casado movement of its whole *raison d'être*. Hence the determination to stifle the voice of the Government.

But stronger than the indignation aroused in us by the resort to such methods at such a serious time was the need to maintain unity among those who had fought under the same flag. We could foresee the disastrous effect that a breach in the anti-Fascist front would produce in the minds of millions all over the world who, inspired by their nobility and heroism, had supported the cause of the Spanish people. We could foresee the sudden collapse of all resistance, and the disorder and confusion in which evacuation would take place. After the great sacrifices which had been made we could hardly allow ourselves to be swayed by mere considerations of personal pride. We were ready, for we had no other choice, to cede to others a by no means enviable position, if we could do it in such a way as to conceal the fact that a monstrously absurd *coup d'état* had taken place in the course of a struggle originated by a military rebellion. But we were only ready to do this on condition that matters developed normally and that the transfer of powers should not take the contemptible form of a mere *Putsch*.

While this message was being sent I stood on the terrace gazing out over the Levant countryside, clear and lovely on that early spring morning—a countryside made for men to live in contentedly and at peace. Every tree, every stone, every movement of light and shade, held for me a meaning unknown in other and happier days. With a cold feeling at my heart I watched the little children playing in the meadows below. Would their youth be enriched by the gift of freedom, or were they doomed to grow up in a régime foreign to the spirit of the country, from which all true liberty and happiness had been banished? During those last few days we had dreamed of a Spanish stronghold in which, however small it might be, we would make our stand until the hour of reconquest arrived. The memory of those Spanish liberals of the early nineteenth century, who from their island siege-house had for six whole months resisted the assault of reactionary forces,[1] seemed

---

[1] At the siege of Cádiz by Napoleon in 1812.

especially inspiring at a time when the whole course of European politics was undergoing a rapid change. While we had never looked upon a general war as an easy means of escape, it was obvious to the sober judgment that if the inevitable conflict between the Western democracies and the totalitarian states broke out while there still remained a Republican redoubt in Spain, the tremendous sacrifices of the Spanish people would not have been in vain. The thought that we might lose all merely because our defeat came a few months too soon added to the bitterness of parting; and the green meadows, the trees, the stream winding through the valley until it was lost to sight in the distance, engraved themselves on my mind with an even greater clearness as the time drew near when I must bid them farewell.

Until half past two that afternoon we waited for Casado's reply. From the aerodrome we were warned several times that if the planes were delayed any longer they would fall into the hands of the Casadist forces; it was only by a miracle that this had not happened already. There was not even a cup of coffee for us to drink. Dr. Negrín fell asleep after thirty hours of unbelievable tension, while General Modesto, two other officers, and I sat down to cards to kill time. Ever and again the rumbling of a truck passing by loaded with troops would break in on our silence.

At half past two a telephone call announced the capture by the Casado forces of the military command at Alicante, the last loyalist stronghold. If we were to get to France our departure could not be delayed a moment later than three o'clock. On account of the precautions we had to take on the road, when we arrived at the aerodrome it was already past the hour. This worried me, for I wanted at all costs to avoid the humiliating fate of being taken just at the point when we were about to make good our departure. But no one tried to intercept us.

In the aerodrome we were greeted by the justified, if restrained, indignation of our colleagues, who like ourselves had had nothing to eat, and who had, besides, been waiting for six hours in the blazing sun. It was the first long flight over rebel territory that the Douglas had made by day. But our grief at leaving Spain blinded us to all other anxieties.

From France we continued provisioning the central zone with all the means at our disposal, organizing the dispatch of food and chartering ships for evacuation. We were not turned aside from our duty either by the insults of the Casado broadcasts or by the news that the Madrid *Junta* was treating some of the loyal fighters worse than if they had been Fascists, and shooting them for the crime of not having wished to surrender. When the Director-General of Supply, Trifón Gómez, came to Paris from Madrid to order the necessary provisions, he found on interviewing Dr. Negrín that some of the measures decided on by him had already been taken.

The reason that more people did not leave the central-southern zone was the terrible disorganization which took place after our departure and the incomprehensible attitude of the port authorities, who instead of facilitating evacuation, threatened to fire on at least one of the ships if she did not leave the harbour. A minimum of thirty thousand people could have been evacuated in certain vessels which had been chartered by us for several voyages. That only about two thousand actually left, and that those two thousand were not selected in a fair or intelligent manner, is a matter for which the responsibility rests entirely with Casado and his accomplices. I myself went to London to ask for the protection of the British navy, and met with the greatest sympathy and friendliness on the part of the trade-union and Labour Party leaders. A joint delegation from both organizations was sent to the Foreign Office, from which it obtained a promise of help in the evacuation of Republicans most endangered. Unfortunately this promise remained, like so many others in this unhappy age, only a promise. As far as I know, the only Spanish Republicans who were evacuated with British help were Casado and his associates, for whose safety the British Government apparently felt itself morally responsible.

With the anti-Fascist front miserably divided, the defences broken, and a feeling of defeatism rife throughout the country, matters developed quickly, and all the central-southern zone fell into the hands of the enemy without any attempt at resistance being made. The repeated statements of the Madrid *Junta* that the struggle would go on to the death if their basic demands were not met were seen to be nothing but another deception.

Two days before Madrid was delivered up to Franco, I spoke in the House of Commons—on the invitation of the Parliamentary Committee of the Friends of Republican Spain —to a large group of Members of Parliament representative of all the various political parties. In my speech I was careful to give more weight to the splendid struggle of the Spanish people than to our internal dissensions. When one of those present asked me how I could explain the conduct of General Miaja, who had won so much sympathy among progressive circles in Great Britain, I replied that I preferred to forget his recent attitude and to remember only his two years spent in the defence of Madrid.

In England, as in France, everybody suddenly realized the tremendous mistake which had been made in allowing Germany and Italy to convert Spain into one of their zones of influence, and the repercussions that their Spanish victory would have on the whole of European politics, especially in the Mediterranean. Only a few hours before, the German threat to Rumania had once again increased the general tension and had banished the last illusion of Munich. It was no doubt with this in mind that, after I had finished speaking and answering questions, a Conservative member made the following disconcerting inquiry: "Don't you think, Señor del Vayo," he asked, "that Madrid and the rest of Republican Spain could still be saved if France and England sent out sufficient forces immediately?" "I'm afraid," was my reply, "that it is now just a little too late."

CHAPTER XVIII

Under the Fascist Yoke

ON DECEMBER 30, 1938, Mr. Winston Churchill wrote:

> But it must be admitted that if at this moment the Spanish Government were victorious they would be so anxious to live on friendly terms with Great Britain, they would find so much sympathy among the British people for them, that we should probably be able to dissuade them from the vengeance which would have attended their triumph earlier in the struggle. On the other hand, if Franco won, his Nazi backers would drive him to the same kind of brutal suppressions as are practised in the Totalitarian States.

Mr. Churchill's assumption is correct, and shows that his view of the Spanish problem was as clear-sighted as his analysis of the European situation as a whole, as given in the remarkable book [1] from which the above quotation is drawn.

If the Republicans had won the war, Spain and the rest of the world would have been spared the fierce reprisals which followed Franco's victory. More than once, in discuss-

[1] *Step by Step* (New York: G. P. Putnam's Sons; 1939).

ing with Dr. Negrín the attitude to be adopted towards the rebels after the war, we had agreed that it would be best for the half-dozen generals most implicated in the insurrection to flee the country, thus sparing us the necessity of executing them. We had not the slightest desire to make martyrs of them, and the likelihood of their organizing a fresh plot against the Government from abroad did not give us a moment's uneasiness. We were certain that as soon as the Spaniards in rebel territory came into contact with their brothers in the loyalist zone—as soon as they convinced themselves of the absurdity of the tales of a Government subjected to the tyranny of Moscow, and saw with their own eyes how the Italo-German air force had destroyed their country—the men who had brought Spain to this pass would be condemned by popular indignation to perpetual exile and would be prevented from taking any further part in work of an actively political nature.

So far as the rest were concerned, we did not so much as consider the question of bringing them to trial. We naturally did not intend to repeat our mistake of allowing them access to positions of authority. But given an effective system of control, all the technicians and professional men of any worth who had fought on the rebel side would gradually have been absorbed in the work of general reconstruction. If the country was to enjoy a real and lasting peace, this was the only sensible policy to pursue.

As Mr. Churchill prophesied, exactly the opposite took place after the victory of Franco. Only those who have lived through them can realize the horror of those first days of the "victorious" entry of Franco's troops into the central-southern zone. I have since talked with some of the men who managed to escape, and from their accounts I have been able to reconstruct a fairly accurate picture of events too horrible even for the brush of a Goya. Even that famous artist's *Estampas de la Guerra* (*Sketches of the War*) give no idea of the cruelty of which fanatical hatred and lack of political imagination could be capable a hundred and thirty years later. But even more than heartlessness it was a case of stupidity. Nearly all the refugees with whom I talked were agreed that if Franco had shown himself only slightly more intelligent, he could, in those moments of desperation, have won over the majority of the loyalist population.

Casado's treachery had demoralized even the strongest of the Republicans. At first many saw in him a man capable of ending the war, but the execution of the two loyalist leaders Barceló and Conesa created a terrible impression, and there was widespread disillusionment when it was realized that Casado had failed to come to any agreement with Franco and that he had no intention of going beyond the first item on his program—that of playing the role of peace arbiter and "leader" of the central zone for a few days.

All the people then asked was that they should be left alone and given bread. On the other hand, reports of the miserable existence of the refugees in the French concentration camps, which the Franco press took care to publish, had shattered all remaining illusions in the Western democracies. From every point of view it was Franco's hour. That he did not take advantage of it is a measure of his inability as a statesman.

Abandoned to their fate by Casado and his "ministers," who had not taken any serious steps to organize the evacuation of those in the greatest danger, thousands of prominent Republicans rushed to the Levant ports on the news that a neutral zone was to be reserved for all those who wished to leave the country. There they were hunted down in the most infamous manner. An American who, after having been in hiding for some months in Spain, eventually managed to reach Paris about the middle of June has recounted in the *News Chronicle* of June 26, 1939 the terrible odyssey of which he was a witness:

> That night in Alicante was, perhaps, the most terrible of the whole war. I made my way there from Valencia with hundreds

of others because we had been told that in a neutral zone we should be safe from Franco and would be able to leave the country.

The harbour was under the control of the International Commission [1] and it was immune. The Franco delegate had promised that all who wished to leave could do so in Spanish ships.

When the ships did not appear a feeling of despair came over the camp. In one night 50 people committed suicide. Some of them killed themselves with their penknives. Four women died that way during the night.

We spent two days waiting for the boats to come, but on the second day the Italians arrived. They drew up their guns on the road facing the harbour and we knew it was all over.

Franco's promise of ships for evacuation was a trick to prevent any other ships coming to our aid and to trap these men and women whom he had listed for death and punishment. It was a successful trick. It caught in that neutral zone hundreds of people who might have escaped.

While Franco's troops were advancing towards the loyalist cities, the Fifth Column came out of their hiding-places to settle outstanding accounts for themselves. Within an hour the balconies of the houses were covered with Monarchist flags and religious images. Crucifix in hand, the *beatas* [2] wended their way through the streets calling on the Phalangist youth—who were going off in trucks to hunt the "Reds"— not to spare the life of a single heretic. Republican soldiers who had begun to straggle in from the fronts were lying in the squares, hungry and exhausted, some of them having tramped more than fifty miles. Here they were left, jeered at by the crowd, until the new authorities ordered them to be sent *en masse* to the bull-ring, where they were herded like cattle and kept for days in the open without so much as a

---

[1] A Commission formed of Members of Parliament from various countries, sent to Spain to assist with the evacuation.

[2] The Spanish word *beata* means an over-pious woman, and generally implies bigotry and prudery.—*Translator*.

single blanket. Their only food was a soup made of water and a few beans. At dawn shots would be heard, repeated shots— but they did not come from any isolated source of Republican resistance. Franco's purification campaign had begun.

A week later the rejoicings were over. In great panic people continued to give the Fascist salute, but those who were not on the winning side showed signs of grave anxiety. In the food shops the supplies held back by the Fifth Column shop-keepers during the period of the Republic made their appear-ance. It was a further challenge to those who had not had the privilege of fighting with the Phalanx. Men, women, and children stood spellbound before the shop windows, devour-ing with their eyes the hams, sausages, preserves, chocolate, which were spread out before them and which they could not buy because one of the first decrees of the new régime ren-dered all Republican money worthless. Not only the notes issued during the war, but also all previous currencies, with the exception of a few very old and scarce series, lost all their value overnight. It therefore came about that even those among Franco's own sympathizers in loyalist territory who had kept their pre-rebellion notes could not celebrate his victory and were obliged to swell the queues waiting before the doors of the banks in the hope of being able to change their money into Franco currency.

"A week after the entry of Franco's troops," said a foreign lady who had spent many years in Spain and who from hav-ing been critical of our cause had, as she herself put it, been turned into a "Red" by the rebels, "Valencia was like a carnival. But a gloomy and faded carnival. You can have no idea of the misery of Spain"; and here she quoted the remark of an old common friend, a doctor, also of conservative ten-dencies: "Since peace broke out, life has become impossible."

The evacuation trains took an eternity to reach their des-tinations. The more fortunate spent two days and a night getting from Madrid to Valencia. Sometimes the coaches would stay in a station for a whole week. "I shall never forget," said this same lady to me, "the sight I saw in one station. A woman was going along the platform holding one child by the hand, with three others dragging behind, and a huge sack of bread on her shoulder. By some accident the sack slipped and the bread fell to the ground. The children rushed to pick up the biggest pieces, leaving only the crumbs behind. Scarcely had they moved away when three Republican soldiers, who had been huddled together in a corner, fell on these crumbs of bread like hungry wolves. . . . You have no idea what an impression this made on me."

For months the former loyalist territory suffered greater hunger than during the worst period of the siege of Madrid. In their hatred of everything connected with us, the Franco authorities had discarded our distributing system, which, with all its defects, was the result of two years' work, and it therefore came about in some places that while there was more to eat than before, the people went hungrier than ever. The bread was appalling. With their typical Spanish humour, the people of Madrid would say, "In Negrín's time the Reds gave us a bread ration of 200 grams; then they lowered it to 150; then to 100; now comes Franco and all is *bran*." [1]

There was no room in the prisons for the thousands of prisoners. Other buildings had to be requisitioned. The Residencia de Estudiantes, in the Calle del Pinar, Madrid, which before the war had housed so many British and American students, was turned into a women's prison. Many convents suffered a similar fate.

In accordance with the "Law of Political Responsibility," decreed by Franco in February 1939, and consisting of no less than eighty-nine Articles, no Republican could escape reprisals. It is a piece of totalitarian legislation, some of whose measures—for example, those dealing with the political responsibility of associations—are likely to interest professional lawyers on account of their novelty, but which taken as a whole are enough to disgrace any régime. Omis-

[1] "Bran" in Spanish is *salvado*, which also means "saved."—*Translator*.

sions are punished as severely as actions. Article I established the political responsibility (physical or moral) of all those who between October 1, 1934 (the date of Gil Robles's advent to power) and July 18, 1936 helped to promote "subversive activities," and of those who subsequently opposed the national movement either actively or by a "serious passivity." Thus not only are past actions punished, and acts which were perfectly lawful when they took place represented as crimes, but the penal vocabulary has become enriched with new terms, and passivity, abstention, and omission raised to the category of offences against the State.

Not only are the leaders of parties and organizations since declared illegal punishable under this law, but also those who have merely been members of them or have given them moral or economic support. Everyone who in one form or another helped to bring about the Popular Front victory of 1936 is therefore involved. Only by a careful study of this law can one get any idea of the régime of persecution, denunciation, and vengeance of which it is a product. In all, it must have been responsible for hundreds of thousands of arrests and trials.

In order to follow the proceedings of the tribunals, I have had to wade patiently through the Franco press for the last six months. For those who retain their love of journalism a regular perusal of this press is by no means a pleasure. It would be hard to find any less attractive newspapers in the whole of Europe. The Press Law of Señor Serrano Suñer will not allow the slightest deviation from dogmatic orthodoxy. The Chief of Press—that is to say, the Minister of the Interior—appoints the newspaper directors. One of his most recent appointments was that of Don Luís de Galinsoga to *La Vanguardia Española* of Barcelona; on taking up his new post Señor Galinsoga explained in the June 8, 1939 issue of his paper that the duty of every Spaniard who desires to be worthy of his country's redemption is "to think like Franco, feel like Franco, talk like Franco."

The Franco press is hampered not only by the monotony of a totalitarian régime, but by the lack of good journalists. Save for the articles of Manuel Aznar and Julio Camba, both fugitives of the old liberal press, and a few others, the Spanish newspapers, apart from their news reports, are boring in the extreme.

All this is but another consequence of the emigration of the Spanish intellectuals. There are few professors, scientists, writers, or artists who have not been obliged to leave Spain. This state of affairs is reflected in the difficulties which the Franco administration has encountered in providing universities and schools with the necessary staffs. "Cases have occurred," states the Madrid correspondent of *Diario Vasco* (June 18, 1939) "where for lack of lecturers it has not been possible to begin the preliminary courses."

Once more the Church has been able to take charge of the country's education. A decree of the Ministry of Education has re-established the *Juntas Provinciales de Primera Enseñanza* (Provincial Councils for Elementary Education), on which the Church, the State, and the family are represented. All the privileges enjoyed by the religious congregations in the secondary schools, and which the Republic curtailed, have been restored. This, however, has not solved the serious problem caused by the lack of qualified staffs.

The exodus of the intellectuals has been so great that the pro-Franco Spanish colony in Mexico, which like all the Spanish colonies in America is deeply patriotic, was greatly disturbed when well-known men of science and literature began to arrive as political refugees, and even went so far as to entrust one of its most prominent members, Señor Rivero Quijano, with the delicate task of making its uneasiness known in Burgos.

But if the press is meagre in some respects, in two of its departments, which often run into entire pages, it is second to none. I refer to the sections dealing with Public Order and Tribunals. These represent a return to the darkest periods of the Spanish nineteenth century. "Not only a Red but also a Freemason"; "The Protestants, enemies of order and family life"; "A Red monster, the author of 1,000 assassinations"— these are the headlines which are to be seen daily in the Franco papers.

In order that nothing may be wanting from the prison-like background of the Franco régime, the Civil Guard has reappeared in Spanish life, with all the unrestrained brutality for which it was notorious in the past. It is not hard to imagine the impression caused in the towns and villages of loyal Spain by the sight of these feared and hated forms—men who have appeared from rebel territory as from a world of nightmares. Their name is linked in people's minds with every bloodthirsty episode of Spanish political history during the thirty years preceding the rebellion of July 1936. Popular tradition has always portrayed the sinister representative of this supreme police force of the monarchy as the most hated figure in Spain.

I well remember how the peasants' delegations who had come to Madrid on the proclamation of the Republic insisted on the Government's dissolution of this force. They could not conceive of a Republic with a Civil Guard. When I told them that for the time being it was impossible, since General Sanjurjo, Commander-in-Chief of the Guard, had accepted the new régime—even helping to remove obstacles in the way of its installation—and since its officers and men had given no cause for mistrust, the peasants, only half-convinced, finally and reluctantly decided to condense their demands into a minimum request. "At least," they asked us, "do away with the three-cornered hat!"

This three-cornered hat of the Civil Guards—the symbol of persecution and violence—was to be seen everywhere, particularly in Andalucía and Extremadura. The peasants would leave the country roads to hide behind the trees as soon as it appeared in the distance, and the old women would cross themselves when its owners passed them, as though the devil himself had come into their path.

As was to have been expected, the majority of the Civil Guard went over to Franco's side on the outbreak of the rebellion. The small force which remained with us, apart from a few honourable exceptions—among whom was General Escobar, leader of a Republican army corps in Andalucía, subsequently executed in the post-war reprisals—were either guilty of treachery during the course of the campaign, or else were incorporated into other and more reliable units. But in every case we had to change their uniform, beginning with the hat.

Today the three-cornered hat of the Civil Guard has once again become the outstanding symbol of a Government system built up on repression and terror.

When, under the pressure of a public opinion horrified by so many executions and arrests and by the crisis of production caused by a labour shortage, Franco decided at the end of September to proclaim a partial amnesty, the repression had been responsible for thousands of executions. On May 20, 1939, the following notice could have been seen tucked away in the local news column of the *Levante,* Phalangist organ in Valencia: "Justice. During the first fortnight of the present month, the work of the courts martial has proceeded normally. Apart from other punishments, 270 death sentences have been passed." And this in the space of two weeks and in a single locality!

The *Diario de Burgos* (May 10, 1939), in an article entitled "How Franco's justice Is Administered," states:

"A fortnight after the Liberation the number of courts martial has already grown from 100 to 200 a day, and it is soon expected to be 300 and possibly 400. . . ."

"There are more than 1,200,000 index cards," adds the correspondent, "all of which were checked before we arrived in Madrid, and made out after scrupulously careful work among the thousands of prisoners captured during the course of the war." (It is not difficult to guess the nature of

the "scrupulously careful work" of investigation—the tortur-
ing of prisoners until they were ready to say anything required of them.)

"Special courts of justice," the newspaper goes on to explain, "attached to the private and public banks, the press,
the railways, the telephone company, the Civil Service, the
Madrid municipality, the College of Lawyers, etc., are also
in session, in order to prevent all those responsible for repul-
sive crimes during the Red period from escaping the arm of
Justice merely because they are lucky enough not to have
been informed against."

In other words, general incitement to private and professional revenge.

Side by side with organized reprisals go mass executions,
such as those which followed the murder on July 29, 1939,
on the Extremadura highroad, of Señor Gabaldón, the Madrid
Inspector of Police, when fifty-three people were shot for
having "instigated" the crime.

In the villages there was scarcely need for Franco's justice
to intervene. The local Phalanx took upon itself the task of
carrying out "cleaning-up" operations. Everything savouring
of committees was radically suppressed. The mere fact of
having been a member of a committee for a few days was
enough to seal a man's death warrant. Anyone who had expressed a hope during the war that the Republic would win
met the same fate. The "señoritas" in rebel territory, however, were more fortunate. No punishment was meted out to
them if, on being accosted in the street by Italian officers,
they answered contemptuously with the one word: "Guadalajara!"

But, with all its severity, the repression cannot provide its
authors with any feeling of security. The authorities and the
press are constantly lamenting the survival of the democratic
virus, whether Masonic or Red. "The war is over, but the
enemy is not dead," said General Franco in his Málaga speech.
"We must be on our guard against those who work craftily

and untiringly when our back is turned to disseminate their propaganda in the new institutions and organizations," warns the *Vanguardia Española* (May 31, 1939), referring to the loyalist elements in the Phalangist ranks. The press frequently writes of the "Sixth Column" of the Reds, which cannot be "touched" but can be "sensed." And the radio announcer ends the evening's program with a salute to the fallen which begins with the words: "Spaniards, beware! Peace is not a comfortable and cowardly refuge! . . ." and ends with a declaration of war on "the enemy without and within."

Franco and his Ministers would never walk in the streets, as we used to, without protection or escort. (I remember in this connection an amusing *faux pas* on the part of the Republican police during my term of office as Foreign Minister. I had arrived in Madrid in General Miaja's airplane and had asked him to keep my arrival secret until the following day. I wanted to experience again the pleasure of wandering at will in the streets of Madrid. During the afternoon I was recognized in various places, and the Police Headquarters sent out agents to look for me. They finally tracked me to a cinema where documentary films of the war were being shown. The inspector was both relieved and puzzled. He telephoned to his superior officer to tell him that I had been found, but that I was with a "blonde" and he did not dare to intrude. "Then keep discreet watch and don't lose sight of him," were his chief's instructions. Later on the police discovered that the Foreign Minister's adventure did not call for the exercise of any great discretion. The mysterious "blonde" was Madame del Vayo.)

To be surprised by the police in a cinema like any ordinary citizen is not a risk to which the leaders of liberated Spain are exposed. The London *Daily Telegraph* of June 6, 1939 gives the following interesting details in this connection:

Rigorous precautions are taken to safeguard Serrano Suñer. At the Ministry of the Interior in Burgos, if two acquaintances pause to chat on the stairs or in a corridor, they are immediately approached by guards and asked to move on. Señor Suñer does not alight from his car in the street. Instead the car is driven over the pavement and into the rather confined hall of the Ministry, where there is just room for it, jammed against the stairs. On more than one occasion, soldiers, police and visitors have been nearly overcome by fumes from the exhaust.

Under the guidance of the Church the purity campaign is responsible for a good deal of official activity. "No immoral dances, no indecent frocks, no bare legs, no heathen beaches," is the slogan. More than one foreigner daring, in her ignorance of these Government orders, to appear on the sands in beach trousers has had to pay for her immorality with a fine. In the case of Spanish girls the penalty is much more severe. In Valencia this summer the Phalangists cut the hair of the young girls who appeared on the beach in "immoral" bathing-suits. In Madrid those who went about with bare legs suffered the same punishment. The hair is cropped close to the head except for one piece which is left long in the front; and worse than the disfigurement is the fact that the victims are "branded" for several months. One girl of eighteen—daughter of a very distinguished family—who, thanks to diplomatic intervention, was able to get authority to join her parents abroad, told me of the panic with which she was seized one morning when, wandering bare-legged through the streets of Madrid, she came upon some Phalangists stopping other girls for the same crime. Immediately there flashed through her mind a picture of herself with cropped hair and long fore-lock—a coiffure which would certainly not have been the best of safe-conducts with which to pass the frontier.

Bare heads, too, are included in the list of Phalangist taboos. "The way in which young men and women of good families go about without hats," observes the Madrid *Informaciones* of June 29, 1939, "reminds one of the Soviet Revolution." In point of fact, the habit of men going bareheaded dates back to pre-rebellion days, and was introduced by those same "young men of good families" of whom the Madrid newspaper complains so bitterly, but that does not prevent it from being attributed to Republican degeneration. The hatters have taken advantage of this, and in advertising their new models they employ a virulent rhetoric against those who "show their hostility to the glorious national movement" by going about without hats.

It would seem, however, that a certain coquetry is permitted to the girls of the Phalanx. Dressed in blue blouses, with black skirts and red berets, they can often be seen, with members of the other women's organization, "Front and Hospitals" (these latter in white and wearing a soldier's cap with a visor), well made up and rather less willing to hide their charms than the Spanish bishops could wish. They are, however, victims of the wrath of the "Good Press," for which cocktails and Lucky Strike cigarettes are irreconcilable with the modesty and decency expected of the women of the new Spain.

With the abolition of divorce, decreed by the Minister of Justice, Don Estéban Bilbao—a former Carlist who, though repudiated by the Requetés, is able, by reason of his office, to give the impression of Carlist participation in Franco's new Government—the Spanish episcopate has gained a great victory. Civil marriage had already been abolished. On October 5, 1939 the Phalangist organ *Alcázar* celebrated with enthusiasm the disappearance of "those two juridical monsters which, generally speaking, were only made use of by hysterical and vicious subjects or libertines."

As in Germany and Italy, the Youth organizations include small children, divided into groups under the names of "Margarita" and "Pelayo." They are dressed in uniform on the Balilla model, and carry out a similar program. Suffice it to quote some of the twelve points of their aims and beliefs:

3. The Phalanx founded by José Antonio is the Guardian of Spain, and it is my greatest desire to belong to it.
4. The Leader is my chief; I will always love and obey him.
8. Life is warlike.
12. By land, sea, and air we will build our Empire.

The cult of José Antonio Primo de Rivera has a strong religious flavour. His remains, his memory, and his words are venerated as though he already figured as a saint in the Roman calendar. At some of the religious ceremonies a huge portrait of him, side by side with an equally large one of Franco, stands on the altar. The press reports on the Easter Mass in the Central Prison at Burgos state that each of these portraits is twelve feet high and that they add to the impressive dignity of that great act of redemption in which the Red sinners, including those sentenced to death, fulfil their duty to the Church. During the first six months of the Franco régime the firing squad and the altar have been the two poles between which Spanish life has revolved.

This religious worship of José Antonio is another instance of the strength of the Phalanx. From the crisis of August 1939—the first political event of any importance which exposed existing differences and antagonisms—the Phalanx emerged stronger than ever. *"Una granitica organizzazione totalitaria,"* as Mario Appolius, the Burgos correspondent of *Il Popolo d'Italia* termed it, it put an end to the slight traces of independence on the part of dissident generals, Requetés, and Monarchists.

By the decree of unification published on August 4, 1939, the Phalanx became the executive organ to which all Spanish politics were to be subordinated. "The *Falange Española Tradicionalista y de las J.O.N.S.* (Spanish Traditionalist Phalanx of the National-Syndicalist Councils) represents the discipline by which the people, united and orderly, ascend to the State and by which the State instils in the people the virtues of service, brotherhood, and hierarchy." The Council of fifteen members which acts as a permanent executive committee in the name of the National Council of the Phalanx, but which in the last resort replaces it, shares the power of the Government. In practice the Phalanx, the Government, and the State are one. In order to get any important post one must belong to the Phalanx. The Phalanx owes obedience solely to the "Leader," who in his turn is responsible only "to God and to History."

The foreign journalists who represented the outcome of the August crisis as a compromise between the army and the Phalanx—a victory shared among those army leaders who were hoping to snatch Spain from the grasp of the Axis and Señor Serrano Suñer, the passionate admirer of totalitarian ideology—forgot that the generals, before they could become ministers, would have to pass through the archway of the Phalanx, and that the Minister of the Interior himself was appointed President of the Political Council.

Monarchists, Requetés, former capitalists and landowners, in whom the demagogic language of the Phalanx inspired a certain terror, all were vanquished by the partisans of totalitarian Spain. Nevertheless, the idea of a restoration of the monarchy had taken root in the country in those months. Loathing for the Franco régime, and disillusionment caused by its incompetence and cruelty, had brought many people to look upon a return of the monarchy as the only solution to the Spanish problem. "Alfonso, or his son, or whomever you like—so long as they do something to restore order out of this chaos and get rid of these Phalangists"—in these terms many Spaniards expressed themselves in the privacy of their homes. Various foreign observers who have their finger on the pulse of public opinion have confirmed this state of affairs, and the many refugees who—until the guard was doubled on the French frontier after the outbreak of the war with Germany —continued to escape into France were unanimous in their reports that universal hatred against the Franco régime and its supreme representative, the Phalanx, had resulted in a growing pro-Monarchist feeling. But with their victory of August 4, 1939 the Phalanx succeeded in stemming this rising tide of agitation. As the sole party, with complete control over Government appointments, and forming part of the State machinery, the Phalanx is in a better position than ever before to suppress its detractors and its enemies.

"Produce, produce, produce!"—with this triple command the "Leader" replies to the triple salute: "Franco, Franco, Franco!" The slogan corresponds to the policy of autarchy. So that she shall not be inferior to Germany and Italy, Franco Spain also desires self-sufficiency. It is said that she is likely to concentrate on the production of machinery, electrical materials, wood pulp, pharmaceutical products, cellulose and its derivatives. Cotton—key product in the import balance—is treated by apologists of Spanish autarchy as a separate problem. Up to now a mixed system has been advocated—the rational intensification of its cultivation in Spain, and artificial substitutes so far as is convenient and possible.

A vast plan of public works has been drawn up, in which harbours are given the importance assigned to them by the strategic situation of the country, by some not entirely disinterested advice of General Franco's former comrades-in-arms, Germany and Italy, and by the repeated assertions of the "Leader" that Spain cannot live with her back to the ocean. Many thousands of miles of roads are to be built or repaired, and all together more than a hundred million pesetas had been set aside for the remainder of the year 1939. A supplementary public-works plan has still further increased the budget for road-building. Besides a "General" ten-year plan, an "Economic" ten-year plan has been drawn up. All this is reminiscent of the period of magnificence, prestige, and rank extravagance of Primo de Rivera's dictatorship and seems likely to lead to the same condition of bankruptcy.

On the other hand, the Franco State has spent little on social services. Apart from the *Auxilio Social* (Social Assistance)—a section of the Phalanx of whose incapacity the Quaker delegates and other humanitarian workers who went out to both sides during the war and who remained in Spain afterwards, are well qualified to speak—the institutions for giving relief to the poor and needy could be counted on the fingers of one hand.

When Franco's troops entered loyalist territory, all the children's homes set up during the war by the Republic were closed. A few hundred children were kept back by "Social Assistance" for a series of collective baptisms which were to contribute to the splendour of the "Feast of Victory." The rest, however, were sent back to their villages as "Godless children" and there left to their fate. For the representatives of foreign assistance organizations, which had given such magnificent aid to the civilian population in both rebel and loyalist territory, life was made impossible. Miss Fernanda Jacobsen, who as Commandant of the Scottish Ambulance Unit did such splendid work in Madrid, and whom I had to defend against accusations of giving too much help to Franco supporters (all that she did, in fact, was to carry out her mission in an excellent and impartial manner), was arrested and narrowly escaped imprisonment.

Humanitarianism is apparently excluded from the Phalangist creed. "Social reforms," declared *Arriba España* on June 26, 1939, "are of no use whatsoever. A totalitarian policy, a self-sufficient economy, and a Syndical organization are the demands of these Fascist times—in this order of subordination and importance."

The Phalangist newspaper is careful to lay down the order and to place the Syndical organization last, for in spite of repeated promises, the National Phalangist Council has not yet been able to issue the Charter of Syndicates which, according to official statements, is to form the basis of "National-Syndicalist Spain."

The international position of the new régime deserves separate consideration.

Not long ago Count Sforza recalled the phrase with which Alfonso XIII was wont to welcome the distinguished Englishmen and Frenchmen who came to pay their respects to him during the World War: "Here in Spain only I and the canaille are pro-Ally." "A statement," observed Count Sforza, "entirely correct as far as the 'canaille' was concerned, but somewhat less exact as regards the King."

The shrewd Italian ex-Minister for Foreign Affairs was absolutely right. In Spain only the people were on the side of the Allies during the Great War; the King, the generals, the army officers, the great landlords, the high clergy, all the reactionary classes of the country ardently desired a German victory. It was a reality fully accepted at the time by the British and French press themselves. It will not be difficult for Mr. John Walter of the London *Times,* whom I had the pleasure of knowing in those days in Madrid, to recall this. *Le Temps,* for its part, was writing on December 28, 1914:

> The Rights in the Iberian Peninsula are openly pro-German, and their enthusiasm is fired by German propaganda. . . . Spanish papers represent us as the enemies of all tradition and moral principles. We are the "reprobate and infidel" nation, cursed of God and lower than the Moslem and the pagan. Feudal Germany and clerical and bureaucratic Austria, on the other hand, have for them the merit of representing the pillars of State religion, absolute authority and caste privileges, all of which constitute, in their eyes, the basis of social order.

Between 1914 and 1918 there was so much feeling between the pro-Allies and the pro-Germans in Spain that at times it seemed as though their differences could only end in a civil war. From their pulpits the priests coerced the faithful into giving financial assistance towards a German victory. "Whoever refuses to pay this new type of war tax will have to atone for his sin in the next world," [1] proclaimed the high Spanish clergy, while collections were taken in the churches for the Central Powers. In the reactionary press hatred of the Allies reached such a point that the sinking of the *Lusitania* was attributed to Mr. Churchill—just as twenty-five years later he was credited with the torpedoing of the *Athenia.* In practice this powerful pro-German feeling, against which the

[1] *Le Temps,* August 7, 1915.

people formed a united front, translated itself into such a benevolent "neutrality" towards Germany as to allow her to sink 3,200,000 tons of Allied shipping in the Mediterranean.

Between the World War and the Italo-German War in Spain, the Spanish Germanophils remained faithful to their tradition.

During this interval of time Spanish history can be divided into two main periods: (1) the dictatorship of Primo de Rivera from 1923 to 1930, and (2) the Republican stage which followed the change of régime in 1931. It is not difficult to see where the international sympathies of the two régimes lay.

The advent to power of the army generals in 1923 marked the beginning of an Italo-Spanish *rapprochement* directed against France. The 1926 agreements between Mussolini and Primo de Rivera were hailed by the Madrid newspaper *El Sol*, at that time an organ of the dictatorship, as an expression of "the common interest of Spain and Italy to prevent Mediterranean domination by a third power." They were a foretaste of the solidarity of interests between a Franco Spain and a Fascist Italy opposed to the Western democracies. Two years later the diplomacy of Primo de Rivera openly urged that Italy should be represented on the International Commission of Tangiers.

The Republic, on the other hand, during the period in which it was governed by the Republicans, followed a policy of *rapprochement* with Great Britain and France. This is one of the accusations appearing in works on Spain by Nazi authors. According to the Hitler propagandists before the rebellion, the task of snatching Spain from the Anglo-French orbit, and freeing her from "democratic servitude" was "to be attempted at all costs." The cost was a war of two and a half years, at the end of which the *Frankfurter Zeitung* (February 4, 1939) wrote jubilantly: "For years Spain has been a Republic spiritually and politically united with France. But a sudden change took place from the very moment that the

Nationalist colours were flown over the Pyrenees."

The rebels of 1936, the victors of 1939, are the Germanophils of 1914. To appreciate this one need only turn the pages of the Franco newspapers published during the Spanish War. From their almost daily statements, all identical in tendency, I will quote but a few examples, in order not to tire the reader unduly.

Directed against France:

"Spaniards are filled with a feeling of hatred when they gaze over the Pyrenees, and they look on France's enemies with sympathy." (*Correo Español*, Bilbao, May 20, 1938.)

"Among the miserable specimens of countries who have ceased to exist stands France, which was in our time our historic neighbour, and which is today no more than 'contiguous' to us, like a stinking and infected hovel which adjoins us in a courtyard." (*Hierro*, Bilbao, April 8, 1938.)

"Those Spaniards who intend to go to France for any other reason than to spit in the faces of the French for their revolting crime, are no Spaniards." (*Unidad*, San Sebastián, June 18, 1938.)

Directed against the Anglo-Saxon democracies:

"The individual is what we possess passively in common with the species. Its distinction is purely numerical and physical; individuals are the species cut in bits. The cows of a herd are individuals. . . . The English are 'individualists.' . . . With individuals anxious to amass a small bundle of selfishness disguised as 'individual rights' one can, for example, carry out extensive colonization. What one cannot do, because it is a work of civilization, is create an Empire." (José María Pemán, in *Unidad*, April 9, 1938.)

"For many years England has only produced ordinarily discreet, not to say mediocre, personalities." (*Heraldo de Aragón*, Saragossa, May 27, 1938.)

"With a cynicism which breaks all world records (what felicity for the land of records!) the United States of America, from the mouth of him whom they call the first citizen of the world, have set themselves up as the defenders of the moral values of the West. *Risum teneatis amici?* (Can you keep from laughing, friends?) The country of divorce, of lynch law, of the 400 sects, of the universities where a doctor's degree can be bought for a song; the country whose national monuments have to be destroyed after 20 years because they are on the verge of collapse; the country of the gangster, of the thieving mayors, of the odious race distinctions; the country of Malthusianism, of the protection of dogs and the persecution of Negroes; is this country to be the defender of the culture and values of the West? Of what West?" (*Voz de España,* San Sebastián, December 7, 1938.)

After insults, threats:

"Not only can we do without France; we can even march against her. . . ." (Queipo de Llano, in a radio broadcast, November 1937.)

" . . . Germany, Italy, Spain, will leap over the Rhine, over the Alps, and over the Pyrenees, to put an end to France." (Giménez Caballero, National Councillor of the Phalanx, in a speech made in April 1937 in Palencia.)

"The victory of the Leader will mean stark death for the democracies." (*El Correo Español,* Bilbao, March 31, 1938.)

But: Long live Germany and Italy!

"O Germany! Our sister in the finest of the Spanish destinies —the Imperial destiny. We understand your romantic cry of the last century, when you apostrophized our traditional ballads and our prowess of the 2nd of May in the words: '*Sie sind Brüder*'— 'They are brothers.' In these days of your triumph in the face of all the secret societies, we greet you, not with the interlocked grip of the Masons, but with our hands open, our arms well raised, as with the stentorian voice of brothers we cry: '*Heil Hitler!*' (*El Correo Español,* Bilbao, October 15, 1938.)

" . . . This salute of the 'open hand' which makes us look upon the Duce as the supreme pontiff of the new and resuscitated Rome. The Rome of which our Franco and our Spain, fanatical for the faith, will once again become the right arm." (Giménez Caballero, in *Arriba España,* Pamplona, August 16, 1938.)

"If the Franco-German declaration is to fulfil its function of *rapprochement* and friendship between the two countries, it will be on condition that, at the appointed time, France gives back the German colonies to their rightful owner." (*La Unión,* Seville, January 10, 1939.)

"The cries of 'Corsica, Nice, Savoy!' uttered by those who listened to the Italian Foreign Minister, have only a symbolic value. . . . On the other hand, the Italian claims on Tunis, the Suez Canal and the Somali coast, are most specific and topical; they deserve to be upheld by a strong public opinion in all those countries which, like ours, have taken friendship with Italy as a maxim of their foreign policy." (*Domingo,* San Sebastián, January 8, 1939.)

But even more categorical and startling than these press comments were the official speeches made on the departure from Spain and the arrival in Italy of Italian troops. The most representative political and military leaders of Franco Spain took it upon themselves to deal a final blow to the illusions of the democratic "realists." Let us listen to them on the Cádiz quay on May 31, 1939.

Serrano Suñer, Minister of the Interior, speaking "in the name of my country and my Leader," cried:

> Every time that a war- or battle-cry resounds on the Italian shores of the Mediterranean, the Spanish people from the Iberian shores of that sea will answer with the shout of "Rome, Rome, Rome!" In this immortal word is our common destiny, both Latin and Mediterranean. If Italy were threatened, a forest of Italo-Spanish bayonets would defend our common spiritual inheritance, which is the essence of our lineage.

General Queipo de Llano, whom later they tried to turn into the champion of Spanish independence, added:

> As a representative of the Spanish army I tell you that from now onwards our two countries will follow a united destiny and our two armies will always fight together on all the battlefields which Fate may have in store for us. If in different circumstances Latin civilization should be threatened on land or sea by no matter what barbarism, we Spaniards would fight by your side as you have fought by ours. . . . Let but one of your sentinels utter the alarm, and the Spanish people will muster as one man to the cry of "Duce, Duce, Duce!"

And Señor Giménez Caballero, addressing the Italian troops in their own language, ended his harangue with these words: "Good-bye, and until the next battle!"

As for the "Leader" himself, he sent his "dear **Duce**" a telegram in the following effusive terms:

At this moment when your valiant legionaries are leaving Spanish soil at the end of our glorious crusade I wish to express to you once again my gratitude and that of all the Spanish people for your efficient and intelligent aid which has forged unbreakable bonds between our two peoples stop My Minister of the Interior conveys to you the feelings of our Spain in addition to my personal greeting until such time as I can establish the personal contacts I desire to have with you stop Receive my greetings of friendship and deep affection stop.

The feelings of Franco Spain conveyed by the Spanish Minister of the Interior to Italy were expressed as follows:

Across our sea furrowed by our splendid ships, our feelings, anxieties, and joys will from henceforth be mutual, and our brotherly ties, which have been sealed with blood, will never again be broken.

Messages and speeches, telegrams and interviews followed hard on one another . . . with no essential difference between them. And by an ironic turn of events it has come about that the departure of the foreign troops, so impatiently awaited by the democracies, was a great disillusionment for Great Britain and France, who have now been forced to realize that this universally demanded Spanish independence merely means for Mussolini, Hitler, and Franco a Spain independent of the democracies, and of them alone.

On his return from Rome, Serrano Suñer repeated in the port of Barcelona his assurance of the "absolute, intimate, and affectionate friendship" between "the two great sister nations in Rome," and stated in terms of contempt and pity for the democratic illusionists: "I know that certain foreign circles are consoling themselves for the Italo-Spanish demonstrations in Rome by saying that the feelings which I have expressed do not reflect the attitude of the Spanish people. Barcelona has today replied to these circles. . . . Europe must get used to considering Italo-Spanish friendship as an indestructible reality, cemented by the blood of their two peoples, by the strong affinity of their lineage, and by the identity of ideas of the two revolutions."

The Minister might have added: "Let those who find such easy consolation in our official and semi-official words now watch our actions. For even if one refuses (as is usual) to find any active value in political speeches, our foreign policy ever since the moment of victory should be enough to make the most sceptical understand our feelings and our intentions. For:

"Did we not, in *January,* two days before the capture of Barcelona, conclude with Hitler a cultural agreement such as the world has never seen?

"Did we not, in *February,* sign the Bérard-Jordana Agreement, which imposes unilateral engagements on France, and which only binds us to two things: firstly to demand recognition, and secondly to receive gold?

"Did we not, in *March*—on the very day of the entry of our troops into Madrid—adhere to the Anti-Comintern Pact, of which the true political, military, and strategic significance is well known?

"Did we not, in *April,* reject the general instrument of arbitration for the pacific settlement of international differences?

"Did we not, in *May,* leave the League of Nations, thus following faithfully in the footsteps of our Japanese, German, and Italian friends?

"Did we not, in *June,* send political and military missions to Berlin and Rome to take part in conversations at the Venezia Palace and the Wilhelmstrasse, conversations whose wide scope has been stressed by the whole of the international press?

"Did we not, in *July,* receive an official visit from Count Ciano, whose conversations with our Leader—judging by the words of the toasts and of the final communiqué—have shown 'complete solidarity of viewpoints and intentions' and 'the indissoluble friendship of the two nations'?"

Such is the appreciable balance-sheet which Serrano Suñer could have drawn up under the seven headings of Franco's foreign policy.

In the régime which owes its life to aggression, the aggressors' front finds the understanding and support which spring from common sympathies.

During the war against the Republic the rebels upheld all the claims made by this aggressive front, and applauded each *coup de force* of the Berlin and Rome dictators. And ever since they gained complete control of Spanish territory, the applause has grown louder; the annexation of Czechoslovakia and Memel by the Reich was warmly acclaimed by the whole of the Franco press, and a telegram of congratulations was sent from the "Leader" to the Führer. The invasion of Albania by the Italian troops aroused the enthusiasm of the "new Spain." On the Danzig question, the Franco-inspired press entirely supported Hitler's point of view and glorified "the will of a man who could sacrifice Alsace and Lorraine while his unquestionable right to Danzig is disputed" (*Arriba España*, Pamplona, April 30, 1939). The aggressive and anti-British policy of Japan in the Far East meets with the entire moral support of "National-Syndicalist" Spain, which rejoices royally over all the difficulties of "perfidious Albion." And so, untiringly, the official and semi-official newspapers of the Peninsula proclaim the legality of the colonial claims of Fascist Italy and the Third Reich. And while they have upheld, both during and after the war, the expansionist policy of the totalitarian powers, the rebels have received in return the encouragement of those powers in their imperialist ambitions.

For a very long time the Spanish policy of Berlin and Rome had but one object in view—the creation of a Spain hostile to the democracies. The surest way to attain this aim was by inciting and fostering an imperialist sentiment among the Spaniards. To this end a whole Italo-German literature was published during and even after the Spanish War, urging the resurrection of a "strong," "proud," "active" Spain, "conscious of her historical greatness." As early as 1934 the famous German professor Ewald Banse wrote in his book *Raum und Volk in Weltkrieg:*

Spain is the natural ally of Germany against France, just as she was in the sixteenth and seventeenth centuries, and the resuscitation of the two powers depends on the collapse of France. This being so, it is of primary importance for us to re-create a strong Spain.

On these lines, the whole German and Italian press during the Spanish War foretold the coming of a "great and Imperial" Spain. Once the war was over, this same press no longer hesitated to speak out even more clearly. The *Popolo d'Italia,* after the capture of Barcelona, said:

National Spain has vanquished by force of arms. Spain is a warrior nation returning to the warlike tradition of her historical greatness. . . . National Spain, daughter of victory, comes forward as an Imperial nation demanding of the modern world a place in the sun. Franco's Spain therefore takes up her position in the new Europe against the old Europe of London and Paris, which had unjustly assigned her to the rank of secondary power.

And when the Italian troops left the Peninsula, the *Telegrafo,* organ of the Ciano family, observed (June 8, 1939):

Spain must aspire to an important role in European politics, and must attain the position which should be hers in virtue of her warlike qualities. . . . A national régime such as Franco's cannot last if it does not satisfy the instinctive need for power and grandeur.

In their campaign for the rebirth of an Imperial Spain, Berlin and Rome did not preach to deaf ears. Studious and obedient disciples, good apprentice dictators, the rebels followed to the letter the example and suggestions of their master. From the very outbreak of the rebellion their watchword, or rather their war-cry, had been: "For Catholicism and the Empire!" Catholicism, however, not being indispensable to a totalitarian régime, was very quickly relegated to second place, while the Empire became the chief aspiration of the rebels.

The Imperial watchword figured in the decree regarding the structure of the sole party (August 4, 1937) and in the twenty-six points of the Traditionalist Phalanx program, and since the war it has become the rallying-cry which resounds from end to end of the "new Spain." There is not a solemn ceremony, not an official proclamation, not a ministerial speech which does not contain this phrase: "The Empire." The "Leader" himself never allows an occasion to pass for propagating this chief ideal of "his" Spain. "In these hours of triumph and glory, of the victory of a vigorous Spain against international intrigues," he cried at Cádiz on April 19, 1939, "you must remember those *conquistadores* who propagated in the world the faith and the will of a people. We must have an Imperial will, for with this youth, with these sailors who gave brotherly unity to Spain, our glory will reach even greater heights, and the strength of Spain will increase."

What is the meaning of this cry of "Empire" repeated unceasingly by the insignificant as well as by the great leaders of Spanish Fascism? It should not be believed, as the craftiness of some and the naïveté of others would have it, that it is to be a "spiritual" or "peaceful" Empire. The Franquists themselves have fully explained to us the real sense of their chief watchword.

One of the most prominent university professors of Franco Spain, Señor González Oliveros, who enjoys the personal confidence of Serrano Suñer has expressed himself clearly on the subject. In his book *Phalangists and Requetés, an Organic Whole* (Valladolid, "2nd triumphal year") he describes the "Imperial idea" as the "conductor-wire and objective of the new Spain." He adds that the "Imperial idea implies by definition the adoption of an attitude of expansion."

Another Franquist of note, Professor Bañuelos, who holds a

chair in the University of Valladolid, has explained even more clearly the meaning of the Imperial slogan as it is proclaimed today from the Pyrenees to Morocco. "Our conception of nations as organisms which are born, grow, decline, and die," says Señor Bañuelos in his book *Political Revolutions and Human Selection,* "leads us to consider this problem from the postulate that Spain has changed her ideology and is no longer content to live within her present frontiers—since this would imply the state of decadence inevitably preceding decay and disappearance."

And here is the conclusion of Franco's neo-Darwinist:

> Let us prepare to hold and enlarge our frontiers. Let us take up a defensive position until we are ready to launch an offensive with certainty of victory. Today the limits of my Spain are her present frontiers; tomorrow I hope that her bounds will be wider and her dependencies vaster. And if this should not be so, if our people do not feel within them the desire for fresh conquests, then they must make ready to disappear, for the feeling and instinct to possess and dominate are innate in mankind.

Claims, conquests, domination: in these three words lies the essence of the Franco neo-Imperialism. Thus are the dreams of Hitler and Mussolini realized: a Spain mobilized on the side of the aggressive nations against the "satiated plutocracies."

"Since the day of victory," wrote M. Bertrand Allard, a notorious Franquist, in the *Revue Hebdomadaire* of Paris, "the men in Berlin have not ceased to 'run' the Phalangist Party. Making the most of that natural well-being born of victory, they have inspired it with the irredentist spirit, a spirit most propitious for a *rapprochement* with the Axis."

It should be said that these "men in Berlin" have succeeded in their task. It is therefore not surprising that Franco is not content merely to proclaim the idea of Empire, but that he so often adds scarcely veiled threats. "I assure you," declared the "Leader" to the Italo-German-Spanish aviators at a meeting in the Barajas aerodrome, "that this present force will be increased a hundredfold by the material which is later to be launched in the air. The air force must be ready. It constitutes the muscles of steel which will build the Empire, which will make Spain once more a great nation."

A few weeks later, in the most strongly fortified Atlantic port of Spain, he said: "Ferrol cannot turn her back on the sea; in her arsenals we will build up the war units which are to give Spain back her Empire."

No, it is of no "spiritual" and "pacific" Empire of which the Franquists dream. Neither have they left any doubt as to the conquests which they are preparing by "increasing their air force a hundredfold" and by "building up their war units." Their claims are already clearly formulated and only await the "propitious moment" for official presentation.

"To what will Spain lay claim?" asks Professor Oliveros. "Better not to talk about the matter," he begins in a sudden access of prudence, but he does talk about it all the same, for the passage continues:

> Everybody knows that we can claim what is "ours" and what is unfairly held in the hands of others. Let us place ourselves at once in a position to be able to take back what is "ours" by right, as soon as the opportunity presents itself. "Ours" by occupation, or by our blood and sweat. . . .

And in order that there shall not be the slightest possibility of misunderstanding on this subject, he entitles the second chapter of his book: "Remember Gibraltar!"

> Let us remember Gibraltar, key to our history for the past four centuries. Our privileged strategic situation on the intercontinental routes and in Europe constitutes both our greatness and our danger. . . . When in 1704 Admiral Rooke captured Gibraltar by gangster tactics, his Government wrote that he was to hold it at all costs, because Gibraltar was as important to Great Britain as Scotland. Let us recapture it!

And finally:

> Let me repeat, however, in imitation of old Cato: I consider that at all times and in all places the sessions of the Phalangists and the Requetés, whether convoked for deliberations or resolutions, should begin with this ritual watchword, followed by a minute's silence: "Remember Gibraltar!!!"

Need one add that this is not a private hobby-horse of the Franquist Cato? His ideas are in complete harmony with all that has been said or written in the speeches and press of the "new Spain." Not once but a hundred times the Franquists are pleased to repeat that phrase of Ganivet in which the Spanish writer refers to Gibraltar as a "continual offence" to the Spaniards. And it has not been forgotten that Serrano Suñer, on passing through the Strait of Gibraltar at the beginning of June 1939, apostrophized the Rock in these terms: "You are still there, bristling with arms; but your end is near, and your days are numbered!"

Here, then, is one of the first objectives of Spanish neo-Imperialism: Gibraltar.

Another and even more immediate objective is Tangiers. Already part of the Franco press has begun a campaign in favour of a change in the International Statute. Just as the Hitler group prepared all their *coups de force* by a violent campaign against the Versailles Treaty, so the Franquists have begun by attacking the Treaty of Algeciras of 1906. The Phalangist journal *España* said on May 6, 1939:

> This unfortunate treaty was imposed by France, and our neighbour has appropriated the better part of our recognized zone of influence, has converted Tangiers into a French vassal state, and has taken advantage of the war in Spain to cease to fulfil her obligations under the treaty. And now we, too, are free from international engagements in Morocco and are in the best possible situation for determining our own rights and guaranteeing those interests which derive from our geographical situation and our possessions on the African coast. The Treaty of Algeciras—or rather the scrap of paper which remains—is even older and more

useless than the Versailles Treaty. We must begin negotiating afresh. But this time our diplomacy will not be forced to follow wrong paths because its eyes are blindfolded and its hands are tied.

A month later the same journal returned to the charge. On June 8, 1939 it said:

> Reality once again proves the truth of the old historic axiom: Tangiers, enclosed within our territory, dominating our routes, hinders the Spanish Protectorate in its work of civilizing colonization. This town remains an obstacle for the completion of pacts, engagements, and international obligations.

For other Franco newspapers, Tangiers is the natural stepping-stone "to the just aspirations of the new and glorious Spain, which wishes to take that place among the European nations which is hers by virtue of her historical past." The statement made in an article in *L'Œuvre* that Tangiers represents "the threat of a new Danzig to the extreme south-west of Europe" is by no means an exaggeration.

But one would be underestimating the Franquists' ambitions if one believed that on the other side of the Strait they will stop at the territory of Tangiers. There was an *arrière pensée* to General Franco's statement at an interview granted to the special envoy of the *Popolo d'Italia* in May 1939. "The Moroccans," said the "Leader," "love Spain; and we love these great and loyal warriors. Spain has a future in Morocco; she understands Islam. With the rebirth of an Imperial sense, the love of Africa also is reborn in the Spanish people. . . ."

The idea behind these words has, on the instructions of the "Leader," been expressed by the most authorized members of the inspired press. "Our international future," wrote Professor Bañuelos, "today as in the time of the great Queen Isabella, lies in Africa, and more specifically in Morocco. All territory as far as the Great Atlas must be Spanish if we are to continue to exist in the world and to wield any influence in the concert of the nations. . . ."

And in case there might be any misunderstanding, the Valladolid professor goes on to explain:

> It is not only the entire territory of Morocco to which Spain must aspire . . . but also Orán and Algiers, with their hinterland. Spain has given generously of her blood and has fought on land and sea in this zone, a zone which should have been Spanish. It must be our aim to reconquer it as soon as possible, and we must at all times be ready to begin the attempt. . . . Our other possessions in Africa are also insignificant in comparison with their coast-lines; we must try to increase them when we can. Here lies our colonial Empire. It was ours and we stupidly and weakly let it go. We must reconquer it. When? At a favourable moment.

Another qualified Franquist, Don Luís Antonio de Vega, has written in the important weekly journal *Domingo*, of San Sebastián, an article in which the following passage occurs:

> In the Orán territory everything which is not Arabic is Spanish. All the Orán zone, which is as large as Castille, has been cultivated by our countrymen. If anywhere in the world there is land which should be claimed, it is the Orán country. There is more here to recover than mere territory, than a few bastions erected by Spain.

It goes without saying that Rome and Berlin, having cultivated in their Spain the irredentist spirit in general, zealously support each Franco claim in particular.

"In his capacity of Ambassador Extraordinary," wrote the *Popolo d'Italia* on May 2, 1939, "the old Marshal should speedily and graciously have restored France's ill-gotten gains to Spain, and should have offered to the Spanish people, by way of compensation, a part of Morocco."

"Gibraltar in foreign hands is historical nonsense," wrote another Fascist organ. "The anti-Spanish Tangiers constitutes a danger of conflict."

"Unquestionably," states the *Giornale d'Italia* in triumph, "the old Moroccan problem will soon appear over the European horizon, bringing Tangiers in its train."

The Hitler press was also jubilant:

"The Leader has taken sides in the historic conflict between the satiated and unsatisfied peoples. . . . Spain has fully-justified claims on certain territory in Morocco, which was occupied by France during the Riff War," said the *Hamburger Fremdenblatt.*

"Spain's demands for the return of Gibraltar and Tangiers now await only an opportune moment," observed the Hitler review *Zwanzigstes Jahrhundert.*

These few examples, picked at random from a whole literature in the same vein, will be sufficient to show that Mussolini and Hitler have fully achieved their ambitions. Franco's Spain is bound to the Axis not only by links of ideology and gratitude, but because the three dictators share the same dreams of grandeur, expansion, and conquest at the expense of the Western democracies.

In this hatred of the democracies the United States is not spared. Here the idea of the Empire also plays its part, and Pan-Hispanicism is presented as the future destroyer of Pan-Americanism and deliverer of the American republics from the tutelage of Washington. On the occasion of the Lima Conference the *Voz de España* of San Sebastián accused the assembly on December 9, 1938 of being "organized by Jews and atheists in order that the United States could enslave the American hemisphere." All the affiliations of the Spanish Phalanx in South and Central America are active centres for agitation against the United States. The Nazis—whose ignorance of the psychology of these countries and whose imperfect mastery of their language have been a great stumbling-block in effectively carrying out their anti-American activities —have, since Franco's victory, discovered in the Phalangist organizations an ideal vehicle for their propaganda.

This situation had been foreseen during the war by the Franco publicists. In an article published in the Phalanx review *Fé* at the beginning of 1937, Don Miguel Gran stated:

For the America of our culture, our faith, and our blood, we wish to do more than just live together in friendship. We desire unity: unity of mind, unity of economy, and unity of power. We want to put an end to "Monroeism," and to put in its place what has become our watchword: "The Spanish world for the Spanish."

And in his book *Qué es Lo Nuevo*? Señor Pemartín, one of the university authorities of Franco Spain, gives an even wider scope to the new Imperial mission:

If we leave Europe and take up a world point of view, we see that there is most certainly reserved to the seemingly weak and backward Spanish America the same noble mission of latinity as in Europe: the conversion of North America to Catholicism. To some superficial minds this will seem an impossible dream. Nevertheless it should be remembered how easily material prosperity has crumbled and the already low moral level of the United States has dropped since the Wall Street crash of November 1929. it should also be remembered that the United States is not a nation, but a huge conglomeration of peoples and races, morally depressed by the prospect of the defeat which sooner or later Japan will inflict upon them.

The intention therefore is not only to alienate the American republics from the United States, but also to shift the scene of the struggle against democratic ideas to the home of Abraham Lincoln.

On the outbreak of the present war with Germany, Franco proclaimed the neutrality of Spain. For the first few weeks the Franco press and radio adjusted their tone to the new situation. Attacks on the Western democracies suddenly ceased. War communiqués from both sides were reproduced and read without any comment. But as the German army advanced farther into Poland, the old and genuine pro-German feeling once more made itself felt. At one moment it looked as though the Russo-German Pact would create an insuperable obstacle between Burgos and Berlin. This, however, was but a passing phase. On October 6, 1939 *Arriba España* said: "For in this harmonic plan of solidarity, Germany and the

U.S.S.R. are offered two large European zones of penetration, or at least of influence, from whence they can inflict final defeat on British Imperialism."

And *Madrid* on October 5 stated: "The Reich has emerged from this amazingly rapid campaign in Poland stronger and more confident than ever in the power of her arms."

The Führer's speech in the Reichstag on October 6 was reproduced by the Franco radio almost in full. The press comments on the succeeding days made use of all the arguments of Hitler propaganda.

"The Führer-Chancellor cannot tolerate a state of affairs in which this country [Germany] lacks all essentials, while others, which he does not consider superior, are enjoying a superfluity— we refer here to raw materials, to colonies." (*Madrid,* October 7, 1939.)

"It would be useless now," wrote *Arriba España* on October 8, in a commentary on the "peace plan" of the Reich dictator, "for Europe to waste her time in a sentimental controversy" (alluding here to Poland) "when there is a peace plan on the international *tapis* which deserves the closest attention, and to which all responsible men (after having closely examined their consciences) must be favourably disposed."

"It is natural that at such a critical and decisive time as this," wrote *El Alcázar* on October 7, "the German Chancellor should put forward sufficiently wide and elastic proposals to admit of discussion. It is undeniable, however, that these proposals have a firm basis. If this is not recognized it will be because the other side persists in its intention of not considering any peace terms by which the overthrow of Hitlerism is not guaranteed."

And this attitude is adopted by the whole of the Spanish press, a press subjected to the censorship of Franco and whose opinions, therefore, have an official stamp.

It is the Germanophils of 1914 who are returning. But today it is very different, for the Spanish people are no longer allowed to speak. The interpretation and application of the officially declared Spanish neutrality is entirely in the hands of Hitler's spiritual allies. This fact is in itself serious. It would be much more serious to continue to ignore it.

POSTSCRIPTUM.   Since this chapter was written, the tone of the Spanish press has been growing daily more pro-German. It is becoming increasingly difficult for the French Information Centre to find so much as a couple of lines in the Franco newspapers once a fortnight for insertion in French journals among the comments of the "neutral" press. Over a period of a week an analysis of the attitude of twenty provincial newspapers has given the following result: 80 per cent of their news and comments are openly pro-German. The remaining 20 per cent of impartial or pro-Ally news is intentionally given as little prominence as possible. The inept attempt to turn the hatred of the Spanish people against Britain and France might have succeeded, given the animosity of the rebel Spaniards towards the British and French who had been accused by Franco's propaganda office (under Italian and German direction) of helping the "Reds" and the equally natural animosity of Republican sympathizers in Spain who consider that Britain and France betrayed the Spanish Republic, not to mention their own national interest. But Franco is not the man to crystallize Spanish opinion on this or any other issue. The prominence given to pro-German news is hardly surprising when one bears in mind that all publicity is controlled by the Germans. The comments and reports of both radio and press are scarcely ever of Spanish origin. The vast majority are translations of German material. They faithfully follow German propaganda, changing the slogans when the Germans do so. This propaganda cannot be considered apart from Franco's policy, since in Spain all publicity not only is rigorously censured, but is also subject to the orders of the Chief of Propaganda and Press. In spite of Italy's benevolent and friendly attitude to Germany, Spanish propaganda is even more pro-German than its Italian prototype.

I could quote hundreds of examples. One of the boldest headlines in the Pamplona newspaper *Arriba España* of November 23, 1939 reads: "Great Britain is making war on the interests of the entire world." Other headings from the same number are: "The blockader blockaded"; "Mines close the path to England." The editorial of *El Correo Catalán* of November 15, after accusing Great Britain and France of having pursued selfish aims in the war, states:

> George VI's reply to the offers of mediation from the Belgian and Dutch sovereigns is a rehash of the war aims expressed by Chamberlain and Winston Churchill. Only among people of muddled thinking or guilty consciences can there exist any confusion between generous peace demands and inhuman war aims. It is hardly gentlemanly to take away with one hand what one gives with the other.

The *Diario de Burgos* published on October 25 an editorial, entitled "From Napoleon to Chamberlain," which is an almost word-for-word reproduction of the arguments of German propaganda regarding the British blockade, and which ends with the words:

> The war has begun again today. As a pretext England has chosen the defence of one of those monstrosities of the Versailles Treaty. In these circumstances only one European state has persisted in following the route traced by England. And she follows this course without reason and against her own interests. Poor France!

The newspaper *Destino* published on October 21, in an article entitled "Why are the Nations Fighting?" a reproduction of Oswald Mosley's attacks on the British Government which ends with a statement of Hitler's British admirer denouncing "the vile plots of the financial interests which are provoking a World War in order to serve the aims of the Jewish bankers."

Among the British statesmen attacked by the Franco press, Mr. Winston Churchill naturally receives the hardest blows. In this, as in everything else, the Spanish newspapers, or rather the newspapers written in Spanish but directed by Dr.

Goebbels's agents in Spain, do no more than adopt one of the slogans of Nazi propaganda.

It is the Germanophils of 1914 who are governing the Spain of today. If the members of the British mission who recently went to Madrid to negotiate a commercial treaty can read any Spanish, they must realize this. And if any of my readers would like to be convinced for themselves, they need only turn on their radios to the Madrid, Saragossa, or Barcelona stations. The effect will be even greater if they do so after listening in to the *"Deutscher Reichssender."* Both speak with the same tongue.

CHAPTER XIX

Looking to the Future

IN A RADIO BROADCAST on the last day of October 1939, Señor Serrano Suñer, the President of the *Junta Política de Falange* (Political Council of the Phalanx), very courageously described the difficulties which the Franco Government was having to face in its policy of stabilization. It was an excellent speech. The fact that it was made on the very day of the formation of the new Political Council, and after a wide exchange of impressions on the part of the members of this council, makes it of even greater interest. The tone of crude realism employed by the Minister of the Interior was in complete contrast to the usual bombastic oratory of Franco propaganda, and was even reminiscent of some of the statements made by the Republican Government at the most critical period of the war.

"That we are living in difficult times," said Señor Serrano Suñer, "is so obvious that it would be absurd to deny it. Spanish economy has been ruined by the Reds' criminal prolongation of the war; there has been a drop in agricultural production (by more than twelve per cent in the case of wheat and vegetables) owing to a reduction in the cultivated regions; the transport problem caused by a forty-per-cent decrease in railway rolling-stock, and an even greater percentage in the case of motor trucks, has become acute; there have been considerable losses in the foreign market; the industrial situation is ruinous. All this is bound to have wide and far-reaching effects on the system of national supplies. Owing to the poor harvest, there is a scarcity of olive oil. The shortage of milk is such that the present production of approximately 270,000,000 gallons supplies only a quarter of our needs; in dry vegetables we have a deficit of 120,000 tons, and there are only 120,000 tons of sugar to cover a demand for 300,000 tons."

At a further point in his speech Señor Serrano Suñer touched on the political problem. "Other difficulties have been caused by the dislocation of Spanish civilian life. . . . A new régime, with a sense of strength and a desire for power, must of necessity set forces in motion which, combining with those released by the ending of the civil war, will produce a varied interplay of interests, dissatisfaction, and rebellion against discipline. The Phalanx itself is not beyond reproach. Honour demands that the Phalanx, more than any other organization, should be self-disciplined. Once this self-discipline is achieved, we can refuse to tolerate insolence in others. First and foremost we must place unity of command, reverence, and unquestioning obedience to the Leader; this is incompatible with any gesture or attitude of divergence. And no external, time-serving loyalty is enough—it must be an active quality untinged by any political flattery. . . . The Phalanx is ready to wage an unremitting war against all those who, whether in high places or low, conspire for base or treacherous motives against the régime, or who by a return to demagogic methods attempt to exploit the tragedy of Spain."

Señor Serrano Suñer's grave words, translated from the official text published in the Madrid press, show that the internal differences undermining the Franco régime have not been overcome in spite of the vigilance of the new State police, who are today, two months after Hitler's policy veered round in the direction of Moscow, still under the control of the Gestapo.

Within the army and the Phalanx itself there are growing dissension and discontent. While—by a wise political move—certain generals who had distinguished themselves in the war were given important posts in the Government and in the one existing political party, General Aranda, whose defence of Oviedo entitles him unquestionably to rank as the ablest General of them all, has been excluded from office.

In the new régime the only role of such outstanding figures of the former Monarchist party, *Renovación Española* ("Spanish Reform"), as Señor Goicoechea, Count Vallellano, and Saínz Rodríguez is to give tone and dignity to commemorative ceremonies and to contemplate an evolution which is undoubtedly very different from the one they had hoped to see. Of the other strong Right-wing party, the C.E.D.A. (*Confederación Española de Derechas Autónomas*, "Confederation of Autonomous Parties of the Right"), which formed the nucleus of opposition in the 1936 Parliament up to the time of the rebellion, and whose leader, Señor Gil Robles, was only four years ago the hope of all the enemies of the Republic, not even the memory remains. Monarchists and *Cedistas* have both been officially eliminated from the political life of the nation, although this does not prevent their working actively behind the scenes against the exclusive domination of the Phalanx.

The *Requetés*, however, command more respect. Although the "Traditionalist Party"—their political organization—is not represented in the Government—the *Requeté* Minister of Justice, Señor Bilbao, having been made a member of the Cabinet solely on personal grounds, and having been disowned by his former colleagues in consequence—these men have managed to retain the influence which their aggressive and fighting temperament had won for them. The Spanish Royal Academy has recently decided to incorporate in the

Spanish dictionary the word *Requeté,* a word invoking the long struggle against liberty waged by the most reactionary forces of Spain, from Zumalacárregui, the old Carlist guerrilla fighter, to Franco. An "etymological" article published on this occasion in *El Alcázar* on October 25, 1939 describes in colourful terms the character of the *Requetés* of today:

> It was not until the twentieth century that the word *Requeté* acquired an official standing in the country and the Traditionalist Fellowship. Between the years 1909 and 1912 the anti-religious and anti-Spanish whip of international revolution had lacerated the flesh of our country. Those were the days of the "Bloody Week," the days of Lerroux and Ferrer, of Blasco Ibañez and Soriano, of Canalejas and his "Law of the Padlock." But the demagogic wave broke against the rock of Carlist youth, organized into a civilian militia under the name of *Requetés.* Extremist bullying was met with brutal violence, and leaflets were handed out in the streets of Barcelona which read: "Requetés! Return insults with blows, blows with cudgelling, and cudgelling with rifle-shots." Thus were the concentrations of young radicals dispersed. . . . The sons of those *Requetés* of 1912 were the *Requetés* of this war, and as great-grandsons of Zumalacárregui's men, they had the good fortune to find in Franco a leader who gave to them the highest honour of victory and glory.

The brotherhood of Phalangists and *Requetés* celebrated in this Madrid article is more symbolic than real. From the very first day of victory, rivalry between both parties has given rise to incidents no less violent than those chronicled by the correspondent of *El Alcázar.* It was in the *Requetés'* favour that, with the Moors, they unquestionably formed the best shock troops of the rebel army. Their contempt for the backward heroes of the Phalanx, who throughout the war kept as far as possible from the firing-line, is as great as their dislike of the language and demagogic behaviour of the creators of the new National-Syndicalist State.

Alone among the former hierarchies, the Church obstinately continues to ally herself with the cause of Franco. I do not know how far the recent encyclical, *Summi Pontificatus,* in its denunciation of the consequences of hypertrophy and deification of the State, and of the menaces which racial ideology holds for the Catholic world, will modify the totalitarian and aggressive attitude of the highest Spanish clergy. But to judge by the fervour with which the bishops, from Cardinal Gomá downwards, defend the new régime, the solemn warning of Pius XII does not so far seem to have affected them very greatly. This is the gravest error into which the Church has fallen for many years. In Republican Spain, during the last phase of the Negrín Government, we succeeded, after tremendous efforts, in completely stemming the tide of anti-clerical feeling caused by the participation of the higher clergy in the rebellion; and we were certain that in the event of a Government victory we could have put through a religious statute from which the Catholics would have been the first to benefit. Our chief concern now is that this unreserved Catholic support for Franco will let loose a fresh current of hatred against the Church. Even from the point of view of prestige the present number of religious ceremonies is absurd. Not a day, not an hour passes without the celebration of Mass or a procession or a *Te Deum;* and in all this pomp and circumstance the Phalanx and the clergy are like two members of the same body. It is inevitable that opposition to the Phalanx will bring with it a return of hostility against the Church.

While internal dissensions between the various rebel factions are a source of continuous unrest, the hopes which the middle classes and wealthy bourgeoisie had placed in a Franco victory have been cruelly shattered. The petit bourgeois is the chief object of the repressive action which is being taken against speculators, and the death penalty has been introduced for hoarding foodstuffs and profiteering. The small shopkeeper has become the scapegoat in a completely mistaken supply policy, which relies for its success on a system of heavy fines and punishments. This has produced widespread discontent among the very classes from which the rebels originally recruited the majority of their supporters.

People who were frankly hostile to us during the war are now beginning to talk of the Republic with a greater understanding and respect. Others, who were waiting impatiently in France for a Government defeat before going back to Spain, only decided to return when the war with Germany and the prospect of air raids on Paris forced them to choose between two evils and to seek the advantages of neutrality. Many have preferred to risk visits from German airplanes rather than endure a situation so completely at variance with their tastes and feelings. Still others—and their name is legion—who are living in Spain (I am, of course, referring here only to Franco sympathizers) would give anything to escape from an arbitrary and terrorist régime, a régime of foreign origin and completely alien to the spirit and temperament of the Spanish people.

"The Spaniards won't stand for it," remarked a keen North American observer who had been in Spain from March to July 1939, and who was convinced that the situation could not last.

Political differences are aggravated by the mistaken belief that in the economic sphere slogans can be broadcast with the same impunity as in the realm of pure propaganda. While new and grandiose schemes for national reform are presented at every Cabinet meeting, thousands of Spaniards are asking themselves when the Government will make some attempt to put an end to the hunger which, eight months after the end of the war, is still ravaging the country. Señor Serrano Suñer's argument that the "Reds" are responsible for the lack of food because they did not wish—or did not know how—to cultivate loyal territory breaks down before the fact that one of the few good harvests of 1939 was the rice crop in the former "Red" territory of Valencia. It is as useless to spread this anti-Republican legend among the Spaniards who remained in Spain as it is to try to convince the citizens of

Madrid—as Franco propaganda has been trying to do—that the bombardments and destruction of the capital during the war were the work of the "Godless men."

In the matter of currency the Government is following a stupid policy of prestige—maintaining the value of the peseta artificially, instead of allowing it to readjust itself to the present financial situation and so solve many of the existing difficulties on its own account. The intelligent use of the Spanish Merchant Service in the present European conflict, if pro-German sympathies did not stand in the way, would bring in a considerable revenue, apart from all the other opportunies for overcoming the present economic crisis which the war is offering to Spain. One need only recall the prosperity which certain regions of Spain enjoyed during the last World War to appreciate the truth of this. The greater part of the gold lying in the coffers of the Bank of Spain before the Franco rebellion was acquired at that time, when in spite of the many obstacles which the indecisive and mistaken attitude of the pro-German Governments placed in the way of individual enterprise, a certain number of industrialists and shippers took advantage of the situation to profit by trade with the Allies.

Here, for the Franco régime, is the one great opportunity to escape from bankruptcy. The policy initiated by the French Government with the Jordana-Bérard agreements—culminating in the appointment of "France's first soldier," Marshal Pétain, as Ambassador in Burgos, and followed by conversations with British officials in Paris (which may perhaps lead to the granting of a considerable loan)—will possibly help the régime to overcome the difficulties of which Señor Serrano Suñer has spoken. Support for Franco is one of the aims of London and Paris. Once on the slippery slope of that mistaken attitude to Spain which has characterized their policy during the past three years, Great Britain and France had scarcely any other alternative. Historic irony has another form of "non-intervention" in store for us. While in the active period of the Spanish War, Germany and Italy played the part of Franco's supporters against the Spanish people, today the role of the totalitarian states has been usurped by the Western democracies.

In this way it is possible that Franco may remain in power longer than the natural evolution of the Spanish situation would have permitted. There is one problem, however, which the ablest diplomacy will not be able to solve. However great the assistance of Great Britain and France, these two countries cannot provide popular support for the Franco régime. Today as yesterday—today even more than yesterday—the Spanish people are bitterly opposed to those men who opened the gates of Spain to a foreign invader.

This fact is fundamental. It cannot be altered by the rancour and personal animosity of a few emigrants from loyalist Spain who, rather than use their energy in serving the cause of the Spanish people, spend their time in writing dissenting articles and in other contentious activities—thereby giving the impression that among Spanish Republicans differences and disagreements are even greater than in the Franco camp. All of them put together are not worth a single one of the refugees who, after eight months of anguish and privation in the French concentration camps, still long for the day when they can return to Spain in order to carry on the fight for freedom and their country's honour.

While in New York I received a letter from seven Spanish emigrants who had crossed the Atlantic as stowaways—keeping themselves alive during the trip on a few bars of chocolate—and who were awaiting in Ellis Island the decision of the immigration authorities. Two of them, both Socialists, had been War Commissars during my term of office as General Commissar. In their letter they neither begged for money nor asked me to take up their case with the authorities. They merely wanted to know if it was true, as reported in a Spanish Republican newspaper in New York, that a rebellion had broken out against Franco in Gerona, because—said they

—"if it is, we'll go back again as stowaways, or however we can—even if we have to manage without the chocolate." I was so touched by their letter that, with the valuable assistance of the *Sociedades Hispanas Confederadas* (Confederation of Spanish Societies), I succeeded in getting them visas for Santo Domingo, where they found work at once. It is by the words of these seven Spaniards, and not by the books and pamphlets and articles of disillusioned or embittered political leaders, that the Spanish emigrants should be judged and the faith and fighting spirit of our people assessed.

Even ten months in the French concentration camps have not been able to break the high morale of the Republican refugees. Just as Spaniards in Franco Spain date their letters: *Primer Año de la Victoria* ("First Year of Victory"), so these exiles write: *Primer Año de Espera* ("First Year of Waiting").

Every effort to support Franco from outside will meet with this strong popular opposition. A British loan and the excessive severity of the French authorities in dealing with the problem of the Republican refugees can be of invaluable assistance to Franco, and can even save him from a speedy collapse. But in the long run it is unlikely that they can counteract the widespread effects of internal disintegration. Moreover, a defeat for Nazi Germany cannot fail to have its repercussions on those totalitarian states which have not been drawn into this present conflict, however generous the policy of temporizing with them may be. And here comes into play that "solidarity of destiny" to which Chancellor Hitler was wont to refer before his judgment of the European situation had become too greatly distorted by anti-British fury and desperation. He was right when he said in his speech of January 30, 1939: "As far as National Socialist Germany is concerned, she knows the fate which is reserved for her if an international power should succeed in crushing Fascist Italy, whatever may be the motives." The overthrow of Hitler is a real menace for all those who build up a régime opposed to the national will.

Beyond the precincts in which, after this present war, the diplomats may attempt to draw up a treaty somewhat more in accordance with geography and reality than that of Versailles, it is probable that this time the peoples of the world will make themselves heard. In the last war some time elapsed before war aims began to be discussed. Today, almost before the two great opposing armies have met, these war aims are the burning question of the hour, ventilated in the correspondence columns of every British newspaper. The people want to know whither they are being led. They are not willing to leave to politicians alone the shaping of a peace on which the fate of future generations depends.

This time frontier problems will not be paramount. There is not likely to be a repetition of that entertaining scene when Clemenceau, who could not tolerate the all too intelligent Philippe Berthelot, called him to his side and said: "Berthelot —you know everything—I wonder if you can pick out this damned Vistula for us; we can't find it anywhere." To which Berthelot replied, putting on his spectacles: "Here it is, M. le Président—the *Weichsel*. The map you've got there is a German one." No; other questions—political, social, and economic—will arise to complicate the work of the new peacemakers.

From whatever angle it is viewed, the Franco State gives evidence of an instability caused by various factors prejudicial to the régime. No one can prophesy the date of its downfall, or the phases through which Spain will have to pass before regaining her freedom. The likelihood of a period of military risings in which Franco may be replaced by certain army leaders who have not submitted to Phalangist hegemony, and of the new dictator's being overthrown in his turn by another general, cannot be dismissed. In such a chaotic situation the return of the monarchy is possible, and this might put an end for the time being to the present intolerable state of continuous quarrels. But it could be no more than a second transitory stage. A Monarchist government could not assume dictatorial powers if they wanted to restore peace to the country. And from the very first moment of free discussion and normal political activity, the people would take action. In the long run the Republic is the only régime capable of reuniting the country and of smoothing out old differences among the majority of Spaniards.

The battle for Spain is not over. The democratic Spain which, with magnificent faith and courage, fought unaided against totalitarian aggression, is not dead. She will rise above her sufferings and her difficulties to become once again the Spain of the Spanish people.

Index

Abyssinia, 80, 81, 82, 90, 93, 96, 99, 247.

Adriatic, 88

Aerial warfare, 196–203

Agadir, 94

Agrarian problem, 8, 142–7

Air France, 106, 290

Air raids: on Madrid, 35; on troops, 195; casualties in, 196; moral effect of, 196, 203; general effects of, 199–203; on Cartagena, 200; on Guernica, 201; Anglo-French *démarche* on, 234; decree of Defence Ministry on, 234; on Barcelona, 280

Albania, 89, 347

Alcalá Zamora, Niceto, 11, 12, 18, 141

Alfieri, Dino, 47

Alfonso XIII, 337, 339

Algeciras, Treaty of, 352

Allard, Bertrand, quoted, 350

Alvarez del Vayo, Julio: appointed Ambassador to Moscow, 19; at outbreak of rebellion, 19–21, 210–11; at League of Nations, 41–4, 71; note of, to Non-Intervention signatories, 72; at Ebro, 134; as President of Foreign Claims Commission, 168; visits front, 173–4, 179; broadcasts casualty lists, 196; becomes Foreign Minister, 212–13; on removal of Government to Valencia, 213–14; on C. N. T., 216; leaves for Valencia, 217–18; acceptance of Non-Intervention by, 218–20; and Cabinet crisis of May 1937, 221–2; refuses ambassadorship, 223; enters second Negrín Cabinet as Foreign Minister, 226; social duties as Foreign Minister, 231–2; Memorandum of, on foreign policy and withdrawal of foreigners, 235; and French chargé d'affaires, 240; on right of asylum, 241; on Bonnet, 252; precautions of, against a Munich for Spain, 254; confers on battle of Segre, 276; in Paris to ask for arms, 278; on fall of Barcelona, 280; walks to France and back in midst of refugees, 282–3; watches army pass into France, 283–5; returns to Central Zone, 290–2; negotiates with Stevenson and Henry, 295–6; attempts to persuade Azaña to return to Spain,

i